The Journals of
BRONSON ALCOTT

The Journals of
BRONSON ALCOTT

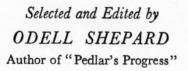

Selected and Edited by
ODELL SHEPARD
Author of "Pedlar's Progress"

BOSTON

LITTLE, BROWN AND COMPANY

1938

TO
FREDERIC WOLSEY PRATT
Great-grandson of Bronson Alcott

PREFACE

I N THESE SELECTIONS from the huge mass of Bronson Alcott's Journals I have been able to include rather less than one-twentieth of the original material. It has been my intention, however, to represent adequately all the main interests and occupations of a remarkably various life.

The task of selection, by no means an easy one, has been carried through with a strong sense of responsibility. Alcott's Journals were his chief lifework; but there is little likelihood that the entire body of them, five times as long as the Journals of Emerson, will ever be published. I have tried, therefore, to preserve the original features and proportions on a much smaller scale. When the reader finds that a comparatively large amount of space is given in these selections to such topics as religion, education, and reform, he may infer that something like the same relative emphasis is given to them in the original manuscripts. On the other hand, I have felt bound to include nearly all the references to Alcott's immediate family, to Emerson, Whitman, Hawthorne, Thoreau, Garrison, and several other famous persons. It is my own belief that I have brought together almost everything in the Journals that can have high interest or value either to the general reader or to the student of American history, thought, and literature.

Alcott's handwriting, for the most part clear, is in some places hard to read, and I may not always have succeeded in my constant effort to record his words with scrupulous fidelity. It is not probable, however, that I have misread many words, and I have not consciously substituted or added any word of my own. All omissions within the selected passages are indicated by three dots. No attempt has been made to indicate the few passages of the Journals that have been previously published.

My text has been prepared for the general reader rather than for those professional scholars whose needs can be met only by the original manuscripts themselves. Accordingly, I have not reproduced all of the occasional vagaries of Alcott's spelling. Except for such words as "Conversation," "Genius," "Mind," and "Spirit," which had for Alcott almost a religious signification, I have not preserved the original capitalizing. The paragraphing of my text is frequently not Alcott's but my own. Finally, I have brought Alcott's punctuation, correct enough according to the standards of his time, into line with modern usage. Such editorial liberties, commonly granted and taken, are entirely justifiable, I believe, when one's main purpose is to make an almost forgotten writer easily accessible to readers of one's own time. All the more are they called for when one is making ready for publication a body of writing originally intended for the writer's eye alone. Many of my alterations would have been made by Alcott himself, or by his printer, if he had ever prepared these materials for the press. Never, I think, do they change the meaning that he had in mind.

The present work was complete and in the publishers' hands before I began to write my biography of Bronson Alcott entitled *Pedlar's Progress* (Little, Brown and Company, 1937). That book would have been planned somewhat differently if I had known that it was to precede this one in order of publication. As matters stood it seemed permissible for me to give little or no space in the biography to certain persons and interests sufficiently treated by Alcott in his own words — to his work as Dean of the Concord School of Philosophy, for example, and to such acquaintances of his old age as Frank Gunsaulus, W. H. Channing, Mrs. Eddy, and the Reverend Joseph Cook. Indeed, I treated the whole last third of Alcott's career somewhat more summarily than I should have done but for the fact that his Journals grew more and more explicit concerning external events as his years went by. It will be seen, then, that these selections supplement *Pedlar's Progress* at several points; but in saying this I do not mean to imply that the two works are dependent upon each other. My brief introductions to the annual divisions of the Journals will be found, I hope, to supply all necessary information about Alcott's life. The general Introduction should meet the needs of those who bring little preliminary knowledge of Alcott to the reading of the book. The footnotes, probably too numerous for some readers and too few for others, may help still further to clarify the text.

This book owes its very existence to the generosity of Mr. Frederic Wolsey Pratt, Bronson Alcott's great-grandson, present owner of Alcott's private papers and of his library. My work upon Alcott was first suggested to me by my son, Willard Odell Shepard, to whom I am also indebted for wise counsel and for secretarial assistance. I owe a debt of thanks to Dr. Dorothy McCuskey, to Miss Sarah Bartlett of the Concord Free Public Library, and to the library staff of Trinity College. For the faithful help and companionship of my wife, who has worked beside me throughout my long task, no expression of mere thanks could be adequate.

ODELL SHEPARD

Trinity College
Hartford, Connecticut
April 11, 1938

INTRODUCTION

IN A PRIVATE LIBRARY at Concord, Massachusetts, there stand today some fifty volumes of manuscript, most of them tall, thick, heavy, and strongly bound in rusted brown and black. The paper in these volumes, though bought by a poor man at a time when good paper was expensive, is of excellent quality. On an average, there are about five hundred pages to the volume and two hundred words to the page, so that the number of words in the entire series is not far from five million. The first volume, thin and poor and tightly-packed with faded writing, is dated 1826–1827, and the last one, in every way more ample, was written fifty-six years later, in 1882. The volumes for six of the intervening years are missing, but one sees that it was the writer's habit to begin a fresh volume on the first of every January.

As a whole, the manuscript comprises a huge number of separate entries, sometimes extending to many pages but usually confined to a single page. Each entry is set down under its separate date, and few days are left unrepresented. There are many small indications that this manuscript is not, for the most part, a first-draft. A great amount of patient and persistent care has been expended upon it. Almost everywhere it shows that the man who made it took delight in order, symmetry, and proportion. Pen and pencil drawings and illustrations taken from books or photographs increase in frequency as the series proceeds. Many of the dates and a very few of the entries are written in red ink. The handwriting is curiously inconsistent, even when allowance is made for the fact that the earlier volumes were written with a goose-quill and the later ones with a steel pen. For the most part clear and even handsome, it is occasionally difficult to decipher.

Such is the physical appearance of the private Journals — or, as he often called them, the Diaries — of Bronson Alcott. In subject-matter they are bewilderingly miscellaneous. Beginning as a schoolmaster's record of daily events in the school-room and of nightly resolves and aspirations, they soon open out to include domestic, civic, and national affairs, religion and philosophy, science and art, records of travel, proposals for reform, comments upon hundreds of books and upon hosts of men and women. As compared with the Journals of Emerson and Thoreau they are not only much greater in bulk but far more extensive in range of topic. Upon first sitting down to them one feels a dismay like that of the editor in *Sartor Resartus* when he opened the "six considerable paper bags" from Weissnichtwo and saw their "miscellaneous masses of sheets . . . treating of all imaginable things under the Zodiack and above it." Traversing these acres of paper and tracing these miles of ink, one is soon lost in the maze of a bygone time. Crusades and agitations that we now look back upon as things accomplished are here discerned in their dim beginnings; persons who have been to us hardly more than unapproachable names become as it were our neighbors; and many forgotten men and women, once as vividly alive as we, return at least to a shadowy, whispering life.

Bronson Alcott often expressed his surprise, even his chagrin, at this intrusion of the outer world upon his "psychological diary." He wished his Journals to be just what Ellery Channing maliciously called them, *"une biographie universelle de soi-même."* He intended that they should contain only his "inmost thoughts, feelings, purposes, speculations, and confessions." For reasons inherent in Alcott's predominantly social nature, however, he failed to produce a true *journal intime*. Always deeply interested in the lives and minds of others, he turned to the inward soliloquy, it would seem, chiefly when his outward-going sympathies met some obstacle. Furthermore, his Yankee reticence prevented him from speaking even to himself about matters most profoundly intimate. Events that moved him most deeply are those that he records most bluntly, or does not record at all. Self-study and not self-exposure was his purpose.

The habit of journal-keeping was of course widely prevalent

a century ago, not only in America but abroad. Several of the more thoughtful persons in Alcott's circle of acquaintance practised it. His own mother kept a journal, which he began to imitate at the age of twelve. So did his wife and at least three of his daughters. As a schoolmaster he required his pupils, as soon as they could write, to keep a daily record of their "ideas," believing that this would increase their powers of reflection. But neither the prevalence of the custom nor Alcott's firm belief in its value helps us to understand its motive. Whether we regard it as a lost art or as a bad habit now fortunately overcome, journal-keeping stands in need, today, of some explanation.

Different writers, no doubt, had widely different motives. Nothing indicates that Bronson Alcott wrote his Journals, as a whole or in any part, with the expectation that they would ever be published. He did not regard them, in the way of Thoreau and Emerson, as a quarry from which future lectures and essays might be carved. He was not trying, like Montaigne, to compensate for a bad memory by making a good one of paper and ink. Neither does it appear that he was seeking the delight of creative activity for its own sake. Seldom, one would say, did he feel the pleasure that Joubert must have had, while writing his *Pensées*, in refining the expression of a thought to the tenth distillation. What, then, can have been the motive sufficient to drive his pen through more than fifty years of toil?

It is at first a perplexing thing about Alcott's Journals that, although they were composed in solitude and were reserved for solitary reading, they have by no means the tone of pure soliloquy. Again and again these words written down in lonely midnights of a century ago seem to call out, though faintly, to some friend, reader, or charitable judge. Yet if we ask to whom they were addressed there is no immediate answer. It is true that in early manhood Alcott showed three or four volumes to as many intimate friends, but he soon gave up this practice and returned to it only in old age. During most of his life he kept his Journals solely for his own eye.

But this fact is not so out of keeping with the tone of social discourse as one may at first suppose. In spite of his frequent excursions into the outer world, Alcott belongs with such journal-writers as Sénancour, Amiel, and Maurice de Guérin, whose main effort is to explore and comprehend themselves. Like them, he records the mood, thought, or event of the passing moment not for its own sake but for that future time in which, looking back over many such moments, he may perhaps catch some hint of a total tendency and character. Here we discover not only his motive but also what audience he had in mind. Alcott's Journals were addressed to his own future self.

So considered, they show his long struggle toward the integration of his experience and thought and mind. They record his patient search for the One that lies forever hidden in the Many. Believing that every life has an emblematic meaning and is an epitome of ultimate truth, he laid up these abundant materials against the time when he himself, no longer sunk and bewildered in blind activity, might hope to discern the Whole comprising all the parts. And in this effort he did not entirely fail. He made his Journals a mirror, however flawed and beclouded, not only of his times but of himself. Furthermore, his effort was prophetic. During his last five years, palsied in body but clear in mind, Alcott read over again and again the long record of all that he had seen and heard, thought and felt, said and done.

Ample as it is, this is not the only diary that Alcott wrote. Among his papers there are five large volumes of manuscript concerning his ten "Tours at the West." His minute observations of his two elder daughters in their infancy are recorded in three further volumes. Even more interesting, if it were still extant, might be the early Journal he began in boyhood and kept until the end of his peddling days. This, he says, was "destroyed by fire" at Philadelphia in 1833, leaving one to conjecture whether the destruction was deliberate or accidental.

We do not know of any accidental fire in the Alcott household at that time and place. On the other hand we do know that Alcott's thought was undergoing rapid change, in 1833, under the combined influence of his reading and of his friend William Russell. The deep effect of Coleridge's *Aids to Reflection* began to show, at about that time, not only in the topics but in the vocabulary and form of his Journal entries. One conjectures, therefore, that he destroyed his earlier Journal deliberately, having come to feel that it dealt too much with external facts and too little with ideas. There came a time when he would have been glad to have it back, and he did what he could in later years to recover the main outlines of the experiences in village life and along the roads of the South which it recorded.

Seven years before the destruction of his first Journal Alcott began the one here represented, under the influence not of Coleridge or of William Russell but of his cousin William Andrus Alcott. To this remarkable cousin — really a man of power and, in later life, of fine achievement, who himself kept a Journal — we may attribute the amusing earnestness of the first few volumes. Indeed, there is a sense in which nearly everything that Bronson Alcott wrote and did is attributable to William. Presumably because of Bronson's early abandonment of orthodox religious faith, the two drifted slowly apart, but the effects of their close association in boyhood and youth were never obliterated. One of these effects may perhaps be seen even in Bronson Alcott's prose, for William's early style was even more floridly rhetorical than his own. William it was, apparently, who first suggested that Bronson might become a teacher, who gave him his first stock of ideas about teaching, and who set him on the way toward Boston, Channing, Russell, Coleridge, and Emerson. This was doing rather well with a young man whose start toward the intellectual life had been made in a series of miserable failures as a pedlar. The fifty volumes of Bronson Alcott's Journals may reasonably be regarded as a monument to an almost forgotten man.

Very little of this huge body of writing has ever before been published, and hardly half of it has ever been carefully read except by the man from whose pen it came. Alcott showed a volume of his Journals to Miss Abigail May in 1829, thereby avoiding the embarrassment of an oral proposal of marriage. Two later volumes he lent to Emerson in 1835, when Emerson's first book, *Nature,* was on the anvil. One or two other persons, including Margaret Fuller, were similarly favored. Mrs. Alcott, whether with her husband's consent or without it, seems to have exercised for a time a rigid censorship — indicated by many excisions neatly made with scissors — over those parts of the manuscript which referred to herself. George Willis Cooke used the Journals in pre-

paring his Life of Emerson. After Alcott's death F. B. Sanborn was given freedom to use them in the preparation of his
Memoir, and this he did in the cavalier way with which students
of his work are familiar. In more recent years a few readers have
dipped here and there into the Journals for this and that special
purpose, but no one has read them patiently through — a task,
experto credite, that fills at least a month of early downsitting and
of late and weary uprising. Consequently, we have had to depend
for our estimate of Bronson Alcott largely upon the dwindling
tradition of his talk, upon the testimony of his friends, and upon
the rather trivial books that he composed in his old age.

Had it not been for the broad ægis that Emerson held over
him, the reputation of Alcott would have entirely succumbed, long
since, to an environment either hostile or indifferent. Partly by
what he did but still more by what he did not do, he left upon
most of his contemporaries the impression of a man ineffectually
good, mild, vague, and somewhat absurd. Undoubtedly, and even
obviously, he was all this; but when we ask whether he may have
been something more, the answer of bourgeois America, in his
time and in ours, is based upon inadequate knowledge and understanding. No wider gap can easily be imagined than that between
this unworldly idealist and the times in which he lived — unless,
indeed, it be the gap between him and us. Accordingly, most of
those who know anything about Alcott regard him as an amiable
and harmless drone, to be remembered with an indulgent smile
because he happened to beget a daughter who wrote good stories
for children.

But something has gone wrong here. With this view it is impossible to reconcile the opinions held of Alcott by those who knew
him best. The highly intelligent woman who was his wife for
almost fifty years never ceased, even in the occasional collapses of
an imperfectly controlled tongue and temper, to think him the best
and greatest man she had ever known. His daughters adored him.
Emerson, his closest friend during more than four decades, called
him "the most extraordinary man and the highest genius of the
time." Henry Thoreau said that Alcott was "the sanest man" he
had ever known. Hawthorne wrote of him: "There was no man

. . . whose mere presence, the language of whose look and manner, wrought such an impression." Frederick Hedge, a shrewd judge of men, remarked: "Alcott stands in my recollection as the best representative I have known of the spiritual hero." William T. Harris, a keen metaphysical thinker, asserted that "Alcott claims an eminent place among philosophers."

Most of these remarks were made, to be sure, by members of the Transcendental group, which was known in its own time as a "mutual admiration society." It is well to remember, also, that Emerson — although he was unwavering in his conviction that he had never seen Alcott's equal "as pure intellect" — had a good deal to say, first and last, in adverse criticism of his friend. Nevertheless, the testimony of Alcott's contemporaries proves that our present estimate of the man leaves out something essential. We have remembered that he lived on the bounty of others, but we have not considered why so many sensible persons were glad to contribute to his support. We have not forgotten that Emerson paid Alcott's way to England, but we have hardly asked why he thought Alcott worth sending there.

Whatever the man himself may have been, his influence was certainly wide and deep. He lived at the center of the storm that broke in our Civil War. He was the one complete representative of American Transcendentalism. More than any other man he spread the "culture" of New England in the new Middle West. And although it would be extravagant for us now to call him "Emerson's master," as his contemporaries often dared to do, he had a profound effect upon the thought of America's most influential thinker. For all of this the main evidence is to be found in his private Journals, his most considerable performance, hitherto almost unknown.

Now that there is little except his writing to represent him, one finds it hard to forgive Alcott for not writing better than he did. He misused a finer set of literary opportunities than most writers are ever granted. In the region of his birth the simpler elements of the mother-tongue had not been overlaid by book-learning. Not only did he escape the conventionalizing "rhetoric" of the schools but he had the advantages of manual toil, of extensive travel on foot, and of constant immersion in the stream of living speech. In mature years he was the friend and neighbor of three men who were writing English prose as well as anyone then alive. Moreover, he had abundant leisure, wide reading, great themes, an intelligent public, and more practice with the pen than almost any of his associates. Why, then, did he not make himself a thoroughly and consistently good writer? Why is it that those very qualities of sensory wealth and vernacular force in which he should have excelled are those in which he was most deficient?

Occasionally, to be sure, he can be simple, vivid, concrete, and clear. His verbal portraits of his contemporaries are often sparkling and vivacious. When he tries for compression, as in his much-ridiculed but little-read "Orphic Sayings," he is sometimes really powerful. Now and then he can charm the ear with a cadence that echoes on and on through the chambers of the mind. "Whereso-ever we may lodge," he says, "there is only a thin casement be-tween us and Infinity"; and Henry Thoreau himself did not often pack more beauty and meaning into so few words. But things of that sort are like angels' visits in Alcott's prose. His early style is that of a man too much aware of his audience, and from this almost mawkish formality he fell into the slovenly manner of one who despairs of ever being read at all. Early and late, the same in-decision that one sees in Alcott's thought and conduct is evident also in his writing. His characteristic rhythm suggests a hand that fumbles uncertainly here and there. Never does it make one think, as Emerson's alert and springing prose may do, of a straight lean spear driven home.

But the comparison between Emerson and Alcott is hard to make quite fairly. Why should the self-made man from Spindle Hill be expected to write as well as an acknowledged lord of language whose fine native faculty was developed in the best en-vironment and training America could offer? The one man, it should be remembered, wrote chiefly for his own pleasure, but the other, a professional man of letters, lived by and for the spoken and written word. We approach an equitable comparison, there-fore, only when we lay Alcott's Journals down beside the Journals, not the highly wrought Essays, of Emerson. Even then, of course, the superiority of Emerson's prose is still apparent, but it is seen to depend primarily upon the brilliance and force of individual sentences. In matters of continuity, ordonnance, and literary structure Alcott was the better workman.

The glaring defects of Alcott's early style are not hard to explain. He reached manhood in our American era of elegance and gentility, at a time when the ineffably refined Lydia Sigourney, also of Connecticut, was purveying the most eligible reading-matter for Sunday afternoons. Gentility and elegance were achieving wonders of refinement in American parlors and pulpits, in our libraries and newspaper offices. Such "culture" as we had was attended to chiefly by clergymen and "the ladies." In these circumstances the young Bronson Alcott would have had to tower above his generation if the simplicities of his native hills were not to seem to him, when he began to write, merely crude and vulgar. But in matters of style he was a man of his own time, so that he wrote at first in a language anxiously purged of all the downright locutions of the farm, the forge, and the mill. This is to say that his style was unsupported by the speech about him and unfed by memories of childhood. It is as though Robert Burns had written "Southron" English throughout his younger manhood, and had not learned until too late that his real strength lay in his native Doric. If anyone must be blamed let it be Dr. Samuel Johnson, in the wake of whose full-rigged style most American writers were then complacently paddling.

Alcott's fundamental error with regard to style was natural enough to a self-made man. He thought of it as something remote, difficult, involving constant strain, rather than as the free and fearless expression of one's own idiom. In a word, he set writing too far apart from speech. His contemporaries agreed that he was much more effective in speech than with the pen — an opinion in which he concurred. Writing, he thought, was a thing that Emerson could do, supremely and unapproachably. He himself could talk. And Emerson too had a high opinion of Alcott's colloquial powers. "I know no man," he wrote to Carlyle, "who speaks such good English as he, or is so inventive withal." In his long letter concerning Alcott's manuscript called "Psyche" Emerson urged his friend most earnestly to use in his writing the same language that he used in his own house. But this is what Alcott could almost never do.

Yet he did make discernible improvement. The characteristic of Emerson's style of which Alcott first became aware was what he called, significantly, its "coarseness" — referring to that admirably bold use of homely phrase and image exemplified by "the meal in the firkin, the milk in the pan." At first, no doubt, this shocked him, but he soon saw that it gave Emerson's writing a "contrast," a grounding, and a symbolic quality of utmost value to one whose thought was prevailingly idealistic. Late as it was for him to reform his own style, he did what he could to profit by the example. Little by little he began to dip his language, as Emerson did, from the stream of speech that flowed beside his door. Thoreau's "footed genius" carried on what Emerson had begun. During and after his return to the soil and his association with men who saw no antagonism between culture and hard labor, he learned to write at times rather well. Concord brought him down off his stilts, as ten years of Boston had failed to do. It put a brown substantial earth once more under his blue sky.

Alcott went to Concord to be near the man who may almost be called his other self, for Emerson and he were "carved out of the same cloud." And it is one main value of Alcott's Journals that they help us to see more clearly than we have done how much was given and how much was gained by each partner in one of the most fruitful of intellectual friendships.

In things of the mind and spirit Alcott was no man's pensioner. Of the two minds, his was the more dynamic, seminal, and male. He strode up and down in Emerson's thought, scattering seed; and naturally it was Emerson who bore the harvest. To be sure, the same intellectual forces played upon both men, and therefore one hesitates to assert that Emerson's teaching would have been essentially different if he had never known Alcott. The hints and adumbrations that came from his neighbor might well have reached him from some other source. In that case, however, they could not have meant quite the same thing.

For Alcott served Emerson best in the way of corroboration, as a living example, even as a spectacle. It was not so much what the man said as the thing he was that counted. He was a "Delegated Intellect" actually residing half a mile down the road. He did not merely teach the doctrine of the One and the Many; he lived it. He made one realize that the world of Platonic Ideas was no mere cloudland but was "as solid as Massachusetts." He had borne obloquy with cheerfulness and had made his poverty an adornment. Thus his daily life was a justification and a concrete example of many bold idealisms in which, without such support, Emerson might never have dared to indulge his pen.

A simple-minded listener at one of Emerson's lectures was horrified, not unreasonably, at the speaker's statement that Plato had no relations — or that, if he had, he "ground them into paint." Emerson acted the part of Plato to Alcott's Socrates. The mind and heart of Bronson Alcott enriched the coloring of many an essay that does not bear his name. Emerson often regarded his friend, somewhat distantly and coolly, as an object of pure contemplation. He took an æsthetic pleasure, like that of his nightly stargazing, in the singular wholeness of his friend's mind. He delighted in finding, over and over, that every link of Alcott's thought drew the whole chain with it. It was true that Alcott often contradicted his morning's dogmatic statement by an equally dogmatic utterance of the afternoon, but such minor aberrations had no effect in the astronomical progressions of a mind which brought all its wandering planets under one central law.

But is it not more than possible that Emerson overestimated the powers of his friend, even grossly? There is a revealing passage which suggests a reason for his doing so. "Alcott," says he, "is a certain fluid in which men of a certain spirit can easily expand themselves and swim at large. . . . He gives them nothing but themselves. Of course he seems to them the only wise and great man." And for this we have Thoreau's corroboration: "The feelers of his thought diverge — such is the breadth of their grasp — not converge; and in his society almost alone I can express at my leisure, with more or less success, my vaguest but most cherished fancy or thought. There are never any obstacles in the way of our meeting. He has no creed. He is not pledged to any institution. The sanest man I ever knew; the fewest crotchets, after all, has he."

So far as they go, these expressions of gratitude tell the truth, reminding one that in all his human associations Alcott tried to co-operate, mingle, and share. But are we to infer from them that he himself was no more than a magnifying mirror? Not at all necessarily. The fact seems rather to be that the individualists of Concord, steadily preoccupied as they were with the first personal pronoun in the singular number, simply could not comprehend Alcott's inclusive "We." They thrilled to the word "alone," but he to the word "together." They carried on, in another arena, the old lonely strife of the soul for a personal blessing and salvation. He was a spiritual forefather of those many who are already beginning to realize that we must be saved together if we are to be saved at all. And so, thankful as we should be for the many comments that Thoreau and Emerson made upon their strange neighbor, we must always allow for their source.

By almost any comparison, and certainly as compared with any other member of the Transcendental group, Alcott touched life at an extraordinary number of points. His Journals show him as pedlar and teacher, day-laborer and philosopher, reformer and quietist, as an omnivorous reader and as a member of many public committees, as an eager talker and as an apostle of silence, as a lover of cities and of the country, as a traveler and a gardener, as a founder of clubs and a solitary, as an indefatigable writer and a man convinced that he could write nothing, and always as a fond husband, an admirable father, and a warmly loving friend. For half a century he was one of the most familiar figures in Boston streets, and the list of his friends and associates in New England would read like a history of those times. His tours of "the West" took him into New York, Ohio, Illinois, Missouri, Michigan, Wisconsin, Iowa, and Kansas, winning friends for him wherever he went. On the whole, one may doubt whether many Americans of his century, outside of political life, were more widely acquainted than this man who strove to live ever more inwardly and who seems to have been lonely all his days.

Hardly less extensive than his human associations was Alcott's experience with books. From boyhood to old age he read insatiably. During several periods of his life he threw himself upon books with a passion amounting to monomania. He was accustomed to date the epochs of his intellectual growth from his first encounter with this and that author's work. A few books he read over almost every year. Moreover, he read widely, somewhat neglecting history and fiction but ranging rather far into other fields, such as those of natural science, which one would scarcely have expected him to enter. Like Emerson, he was fascinated but never quite converted by the writings of Swedenborg. In Jakob Boehme, the uneducated mystical shoemaker, he found a faraway brother of his own mind. Plato, Plotinus, and Proclus — always read in the highly stimulating though inaccurate paraphrases by Thomas Taylor which meant far more even to Emerson and, in his youth, to Shelley, than the originals themselves — filled his thoughts with majestic and cloudy conjectures. The little he knew of Hindu literature, and particularly of the *Bhagavad-Gita*, was easily domesticated in his hospitable mind. Apparently he was the only member of the Concord group who ever read the *Tao Tê Ching*, that profoundly Transcendental treatise which would have been so congenial to them all.

Like his intellectual associates but to a greater extent than they, Alcott showed in his reading a penchant toward the remote, mysterious, and thaumaturgic. This was due to his constant search for other minds that had seen the world as he saw it — that is, as a duplex pattern, inherently metaphorical, filled to the last atom with endless symbolisms and correspondences. This quest led him to the so-called Hermetic writers, and to the Platonizing philosophers and poets of England's seventeenth century. In fact, he was most at ease in that good season of intellectual time when modern science, young and humble and unforgetful of its limitations, still lived at peace with the ancient faiths and sanctities. He would have been entirely at home, one imagines, with Sir Thomas Browne — completely ignoring his erudition, to be sure, and scarcely observing the sudden splendors of his rhetoric, but sharing his delight in "those wingy mysteries in divinity and airy subtleties in religion which have unhinged the brains of better heads." Alcott too might have said "Methinks there be not impossibilities enough in religion," and he too resented the encroachments of reason and syllogism upon the spirit's ancient domains.

Alcott's return to the seventeenth century was as unerring as the flight of a homing pigeon. It took him back to the time of his nearest intellectual neighbors, those giants of thought whom John

Locke strove to overthrow and whom we, in our post-Newtonian complacency, have almost forgotten. Of course he was not alone in this return. We may yet come to realize that the entire Transcendental Movement was a revolt against Locke and a rediscovery of his predecessors. With the possible exception of Coleridge, however, Alcott made his backward journey with the clearest realization of where he was going and what he was going for. The Cambridge Platonists were his destination. A closer companion of his mind than any he ever found in the flesh was the strange ecstatic genius Henry More.

Margaret Fuller was right in saying that Alcott was a man of one idea, although she should not have failed to add that one idea is enough for any man if it happens to be a good one and is properly mixed with all his thinking. Alcott phrased his central idea, his single article of faith, in words that might have been written by Henry More himself: "I set out from the ground of Spirit. This *is*. All else is its manifestation." To this he joined the subsidiary doctrine of the "Lapse," ultimately from Plotinus, to explain how the many forms of nature are derived from the One and return to it again. Another subordinate doctrine, which he called "Personalism," attributed to Spirit that conscious and purposive intellect which Neoplatonists, from Plotinus to Emerson, tend to deny.

Alcott's doctrine of Personality answered to a deep need of his nature. He accepted no orthodox creed, belonged in an effective sense to no church, and was quite devoid of what is usually meant by piety, yet he was essentially a religious man. He was a Christian in the sense that he thought Jesus of Nazareth the wisest of men, that he followed his precepts and examples to a degree seldom seen in the devout; but the attribution of any special or peculiar divinity to this man he regarded as blasphemous.

The doctrine of the "Lapse" implied, on the one hand, that "visible or organic nature is to be read as the exponent and emblem of invisible, unembodied spirit." It was in this belief that Alcott studied books of natural science, convinced that they would advance his knowledge of spiritual reality. On the other hand, this doctrine suggested the bizarre notion of "Genesis," which seemed to many of his contemporaries simply insane. He believed in a sort of devolution, not unlike that taught by the ancient Gnostics, by which man is descended from pure Spirit, the lower animals from man, and insentient life from the sentient. Instead of finding the source of mind in matter he asserted, in the time of Charles Darwin and in the very presence of Louis Agassiz, that the source and cause of all matter lies in mind.

Such was the answer, unoriginal in any part, which Alcott gave to the old riddle of the One and the Many. But he did not stop, as those whom we call philosophers are wont to do, with a theoretical solution. The wise man, in Alcott's opinion, was he who saw the truth of these doctrines, but the good man was he who acted in accordance with them. To act in accordance with the truth that man descends from Spirit and longs to return to his source is to be, in some sense, a teacher — and a teacher, preferably, not of adults, blinded by their long stay in the cave of this world's darkness, but of children, who still remember their divine origin,

> And, looking back, at that short space,
> Can see a glimpse of His bright face.

First of all, then, and always, Bronson Alcott was a teacher. His teaching bound his life together as firmly as his thought was unified by a single article of faith. He held that true teaching — by which he never meant mere instruction — involves an ascent to a common spiritual level. Far more socially-minded than Emerson, who said that "we descend to meet," he believed that for all true meeting of minds we must rise above dispute and fact-peddling to the heights of Spirit on which we realize that we are one. Good teaching was therefore a sharing of mind with mind. It was a process in which all those concerned were engaged in recollecting what, in some sense, they already knew.

Hence arose Alcott's emphasis upon conversation as a pedagogical method. He taught children by it while he could, and when they were shut away he tried to approach them through their parents in the same manner. Jesus, Socrates, and Pythagoras had given him his models, he said. He used this method in the Fruitlands experiment, which was partly an educational effort, and on all his tours of the West. His superintendency of the Concord Schools showed no abatement in the enthusiasm of his teaching, no change in his theory or method, and the Concord School of Philosophy revealed once more the guiding thread of purpose which had led him through the labyrinth of his eighty years.

A strange life, this, and a strange philosophy, for a man who was a Connecticut Yankee born and bred. At first sight it is hard to recognize Bronson Alcott as American at all.

He was born, by an odd coincidence, on a farm adjacent to the birthplace of Seth Thomas, the once-famous captain of industry. Thomas was a mechanic with a talent for organization who manufactured a huge number of cheap clocks, added factory to factory, and died very rich. There, most of our less observant critics would say, was a typical American. Bronson Alcott was a good mechanic too, but he spent most of his organizing ability upon his own thoughts and impulses. He made nothing for sale, employed no one, and was not always visibly employed himself. For fifty years he went up and down the land asserting that spiritual powers and not mechanics run the world. He contributed nothing to our material wealth or physical comfort. He did not even try to found, as he might easily have done, a religious sect which would have brought him power and wealth. He lived quite cheerfully on the bounty of others. And what was there of the American in all that?

Perhaps a good deal. As compared with the Americanism of Seth Thomas and his innumerable kind, that of Alcott was far more deeply rooted in time, having behind it fully two hundred years of Puritan preoccupation with the soul and its everlasting weal or woe. And as there was more of the past in him, there may have been more of the future too. His peculiarity was not that he was an idealist, for all true Americans are that. It was, rather, that he was nothing else. He looks odd to us chiefly because he was so consistent in his idealism, and did not even attempt to serve both God and Mammon.

In other respects Alcott was American to a fault. He showed our rootless nomadic tendency, for example, in the fact that during his married life alone he lived in some thirty different houses, although he deserves credit for his American ability to make each of these bivouacs at once a home. His indomitable hopefulness, even when no more than the sunnier aspect of procrastination, is characteristic of a people always so expectant of a glorious tomorrow that it can easily ignore a disgraceful today. In his thought, conduct, and writing there is everywhere evident the American deficiency in passion. Steadily devoted and industrious he can be, but he never delivers his total force at a single blow. And although he had the versatility of the American pioneer, in most of the many fields of knowledge that he drove his plough across he cut only a shallow and winding furrow.

One thing Alcott did leave to his countrymen: a clear example of the spiritual element in our nature. He represented that other, that inward America which is often submerged and almost stifled but is never to be ignored by those who would know this land as she is entire. "Come again in a hundred years," Emerson wrote in his Journal in 1836, "and then compare Alcott and his little critics." The time has passed, and perhaps we may need another century more; but yet it is surprising how swiftly the fashions in men can sometimes change, like the kinds of trees in the forest.

The wood-choppers of New England, when they are clearing the evergreens from a hillside, ordinarily leave one old "jack pine" to stand alone. Then the weeds come and the briars, and the little chattering aspens and birches crowd up the hill, so that the great dark pine is hardly visible, unless in winter, and seems to be intruding more than they. But year by year the small brown seeds of the pine drift down the wind, and young pines spring in the old tree's shadow. Year by year they crowd out and overcome the birches, the aspens, the briars, and the weeds. Come back in a hundred years and you may find them once more possessing all the land.

Bronson Alcott grew like such a tree on some rocky New England hilltop — a tree that takes no thought for symmetry and yet achieves it by the law of its own nature. If the winter is hard, it is stronger; if the tempest tears off a bough, it is only the more stately in its poise against the sky; and no force nor flattery of the elements can dissuade it from being completely a pine. So this man lived. He was odd, even absurd, and often unfortunate, but in the face of all difficulty he got his work done and remained incorruptibly himself. Nearly all that he gave his strength to was somehow broken and defeated, yet his whole career was one steadily mounting triumph. He was a man by no means great, brilliant, learned, or worldly-wise who did nevertheless keep the holy faith of those who live in the Spirit. "That is failure," he once said, "when a man's idea ruins him, when he is dwarfed and killed by it; but when he is ever growing by it, ever true to it, and does not lose it by any partial or immediate failure, that is success, however it seems to the world."

CHRONOLOGICAL TABLE

1799.　　　Bronson Alcott born at Wolcott, Connecticut, November 29.

1817–1823.　Peddling trips to Virginia and the Carolinas.

1825–1828.　Taught school in Cheshire and Bristol, Connecticut.

1826.　　　Began Journals.

1828–1830.　Taught schools in Boston.

1830.　　　Married to Miss Abigail May.

1830–1834.　In Germantown and Philadelphia, teaching, reading, and thinking.

1832.　　　Birth of Louisa, November 29.

1834–1837.　Teaching at Temple School, Boston.

1835.　　　First met Emerson. *Record of a School.*

1836–1837.　*Conversations with Children on the Gospels* — two volumes.

1838–1839.　Taught school at home in Beach Street, Boston.

1840.　　　Removal to Hosmer Cottage, Concord.

1842.　　　Trip to England, May–October.

1843.　　　Arrested for refusal to pay poll tax. "Fruitlands," June–December.

1844.　　　Lost Journals and letters of the "Fruitlands" period.

1844–1848.　In Concord at "The Hillside," later known as Hawthorne's "Wayside."

1848–1855.　In Boston. Increasing use of "Conversations."

1855–1857.　At Walpole, New Hampshire.

1855–1882.　Conversational "Tours at the West."

1857.　　　Purchase of "Orchard House," Concord.

1859–1865.　Superintendent of Concord Public Schools.

1863.　　　Death of Alcott's mother.

1868.　　　*Tablets.*

1872.   *Concord Days.*

1877.   *Table Talk.* Removal to the "Thoreau House." Death of Mrs. Alcott.

1879–1888. The Concord School of Philosophy.

1881.   *New Connecticut.*

1882.   *Sonnets and Canzonets.* In October, incapacitated by a stroke. Journals end.

1888.   Died in Louisburg Square, Boston, March 4.

ILLUSTRATIONS

The Journals of
BRONSON ALCOTT

The Journals of

BRONSON ALCOTT

⚜{1826-1827}⚜

*W*HEN ALCOTT *began the first volume of his Journals,
July 3, 1826, he was teaching the Centre District School at
Cheshire, Connecticut, and was boarding with his uncle, Dr. Til-
lotson Bronson, Principal of the Cheshire Academy. This was
Alcott's third school. His debts, due to failures in peddling,
amounted to six hundred dollars. His wages were eighteen dollars
a month "and found." At his own expense he transformed the
schoolroom, providing a separate desk for each pupil, and bought
many books for the use of pupils and parents. The most influential
books read by him were Pestalozzi's* Hints to Parents, Robert
Owen's New View of Society, *and the Bible. Close study of the
Gospels caused him to abandon all belief in the doctrine of Original Sin, in the Holy Trinity, and in the Divinity of Jesus; but it
also convinced him that Jesus, as man and teacher, must be a chief
model for his own teaching and life. He read William Russell's*
Journal of Education, *then beginning, and wrote for it, in June,
1827, an outline of his work at Cheshire. In the same month he*

*closed his school because of opposition to his methods and ideals,
and returned to Spindle Hill. There he reread John Locke, stud-
ied Paley's theological writings, continued his meditations upon
the New Testament, and corresponded with the philanthropist
William Maclure, then at New Harmony, Indiana, concerning
Pestalozzi. At this time he visited many Connecticut schools. In
August, at Brooklyn, Connecticut, he first met Samuel J. May, the
Unitarian minister and reformer, and his sister, Abigail May, later
Mrs. Alcott. By them his thoughts were turned toward Boston;
but in November he took a contract to teach the West Street Dis-
trict School at Bristol, Connecticut, at twenty-three dollars a month
and board.*

*The journal entries for these years are chiefly concerned with
Alcott's work as a teacher, in which his whole attention is absorbed.
As his theological beliefs are loosened, the intensity of his religious
devotion to the task of teaching is increased. Opposition has already thrust him back upon himself, awakening a strong sense of
independence and of personal dignity. The tone of extreme solem-
nity is deepened by his custom, possibly derived from newspapers,
of referring to himself in the third person or in the editorial
plural.*

1826

September 22   *Cheshire, Connecticut*

Those who in modern times attempt in education anything different from the old established modes are by many regarded as
publick innovators on the peace and order of society, as persons
desirous of destroying the structure which secures present happiness, and of substituting in its place anarchy and confusion. They
are regarded by some as dangerous and by others as ignorant and
imbecile members of society — as visionary projectors against
intelligence and wisdom, as persons beside themselves. By their
friends in particular are they regarded with feelings of distant
coldness, as those who, by their arrogance and presumption, are

obstinate in bringing shame and disgrace upon their own heads. Like the friends of the Great Reformer, they lay hold on a person of this character, saying:

"*Certainly he is beside himself.* He presumes to dictate to the intelligence and wisdom of men in high office, to men possessed of every means for obtaining accurate knowledge of the subjects in investigation, to men of liberal views and expanded minds through whose intelligence and efforts our fair and comparatively perfect fabrick of publick instruction and government has been raised, which distributes so much happiness and enjoyment among every rank of civilized life. He sets all this wisdom and skill at defiance, attempts to demolish the whole structure, and plunge mankind into anarchy and confusion and bring chaos again. At one blow he is striking at the very root of wisdom. He is levelling the foundations of virtue and happiness, and doing his best to establish the reign of vice, infidelity, and misery. *He hath Beelzebub, and by the prince of the devils casteth he out devils.* Though to appearance his theory of Reformation may be fair and comely, as it opposes the wisdom of wise and good men who have hitherto lived and adorned the doctrines which they professed, it must in essence be deformed and poisonous. — How knoweth this man more than others? *How knoweth he letters, having never learned?* Who is he? What is his parentage? *Learn and look, for out of Galilee cometh no Prophet.* Hath he ever been the inmate of a University? Hath he ever sat in the Council of the Nations? Hath he ever taught in our privileged seminaries or Churches? *Where then hath he these things?*"

The answer is ready: He has studied the Scriptures. He has separated their spirit from the shackles of form, of mode, and ceremony by which they have been so long restrained. He has studied Man, Human Nature. He has traced effects to their causes. He has studied Man as he is from the hand of his Creator, and not as he is made by the errors of the world. He has drunk at the Fountain, and not at the distant streams. He has listened to the instructions of *Him who spake as never man spake,* who saw as man never before saw, who did as man never before did. — And, making due allowances for the imperfections of human nature, *he is going to do likewise.*

November 11

Of all employments, that of an instructor opens the most full and spacious channels of enjoyment. From our fellow beings are we indebted for a greater proportion of our happiness; and in instruction the very subject of our attention is a fellow being, the very object of our labour is the means of obtaining and imparting that happiness. Hence on this subject everything is favorable to the indulgence of those feelings which carry complacency and joy and rapture to the heart.

November 25

What moral attainments are those of which our instructor is not in want? Of what injury may the want of a single one prove to the individuals under his care, to the community in which he dwells, to the world of intelligent minds? How does it become him to husband well his passing moments in the study of morality, and to illustrate it in practical clearness before his imitating charges, to take care that his feet depart not from the path of wisdom, that his lips speak no guile! Let him remember that error is contagious, and especially from him, when exhibited before those who look toward him with confidence as an example to them in all things. Let him see that his practice be an unwavering comment upon his principles, that the correspondence be visible and connected, to the apprehension of his disciples.

December 6

It is not from books entirely that instruction is to be drawn. They should only be subservient to our main purpose. They should lie by us for occasional instruction only. When doubts and uncertainties arise, they may sometimes explain the difficulty and point to the truth. Frequently, however, they lead us astray. They are imperfect. Adherence to them has been the cause, and still continues to be, of perpetuating error among men, and that to an alarming extent. Ideas, when vended in a book, carry with them a kind of dignity and certainty which awe many into implicit belief. They often impose the most irrational and absurd conclusions on the fearful understanding. It dare not doubt. Fear keeps it ignorant.

Authority lifts her head and commands instant belief. Reason, thus hushed into slumber, sleeps in secure repose. To dare to think, to think for oneself, is denominated pride and arrogance. And millions of human minds are in this state of slavery and tyranny.

How shall they escape?

Rebel! Think for themselves! Let others grumble; dare to be singular. Let others direct; follow Reason. Let others dwell in the Land of Enchantments; be Men. Let others prattle; practise. Let others profess; do good. Let others define goodness; act. Let others sleep; whatever thy hand findeth to do, that do with all thy might, and let a gainsaying calumniating world speculate on your proceedings.[1]

1827

June 7

"The number of those who advocate any particular theory is thought by many to be a fine test of its truth."

This sentiment is thought to be erroneous. Men, as they have been trained, are averse to thought; the labour attending mental action is opposed to enquiry; and opinions are implicitly embraced without reflection, to save the labour of thought. Hence a few original thinkers have given laws to the world. Others have blindly followed. We come then to this true principle: The number and age of those who advocate any particular doctrine is no test of its truth, but, on the contrary, it is an indication of its incorrectness.

[1] When Alcott wrote this ringing call to "self-reliance" he had not yet so much as heard the names of Emerson and Carlyle, with whom the opinions expressed are now chiefly associated.

*P*UBLIC OPPOSITION *to the methods used by Alcott in his school at Bristol was met by him with manly vigor. His engagement was not renewed. In April he went for the first time to Boston, and, after a journey to New York and Philadelphia for study of educational systems, he opened, in June, the Salem Street Infant School, with seventeen children, mostly foreigners. Two months later there were sixty, "and all happy." During the summer his acquaintance with Abigail May grew rapidly into a mutual love. He heard many preachers, including the young Ralph Waldo Emerson, met Dr. Channing and Elizabeth Palmer Peabody, roomed with Josiah Holbrook and helped him to found the American Lyceum, served as Superintendent of the Chauncy Place Sunday School, and decided that "Unitarianism looks now a little pale and puny." He wrote several articles for the* Journal of Education *and saw much of its brilliant editor, William Russell. In October he opened a school for boys in Tremont Street, which prospered at once and was widely discussed as one of the important influences in the reforms of the day.*

The Journal for this year shows the young man from Connecticut delighted and somewhat surprised at the success of his first months in the capital of New England. Happy in his love and in his first professional success, his naturally social disposition expands in an environment which seems, at first, wholly congenial. His reading is for the time neglected, and a lifetime of talk begins.

1828

February 17　　　　　　　　　　　　　*Bristol, Connecticut*

Our moral opinions are subjects of discussion among those who are bound to the faith of antiquity,[1] determined to support it at all events. The clergyman here, in a recent discourse, alluded to our opinions, attempting to controvert them and establish what he called the truth. We are unable to bring these men to discuss the points in question. They seem unwilling or afraid to bring them forward except among their own party. We are not desirous of discussing them, though we think those opinions which we entertain will not suffer from discussion, but their truth become more apparent.

If we can succeed in identifying Christianity with the discipline of the family and the school, as the only system of practice, we conceive that a very important point will be gained — a point which is of more importance in our estimation than is usually supposed. For until the Christian system is brought directly into the details of family and school government, as the rule of practice, the world, we fear, must blunder along as it has in all preceding ages.

June 1　　　　　　　　　　　　　　　　　　*Boston*

In the afternoon, visited Miss May[2] in relation to the Infant School, for which she has applied as assistant teacher. We are unwilling she should engage in this school with hopes of continuing in it when we leave, for we are very desirous — and are becoming every day more interested in her — that she should assist in the more desirable situation which we propose for ourselves in a school of higher order. And we have reason to think that she herself is more interested in the latter situation than in the former, and would assist us with pleasure.

But perhaps we are indulging a pleasing hope which we can never realize. Let us pay regard to the sage lessons that have been

---

[1] Calvinistic theology, which Alcott had never accepted, although it was nearly universal in Western Connecticut during his youth.
[2] Alcott's future wife.

taught us by our eventful life, and prepare for every disappointment. In this changing world, let us prepare for every change.
With high hopes and pleasing expectations at present, let us check
our imagination, and in all the schemes which we now have con-
certed let us prepare for the possibility of defeat. Our life is to
be devoted to the teaching of Infant Schools, and female assistance,
if the right kind, is our chief hope. In the acquisition of this lady
to assist us we think we should obtain that kind of help which
is indispensable.

June 14

Our life is to be devoted to the amelioration of our fellow
beings, in attempts to establish the reign of truth and reason and
arrange society — our systems of education — in accordance with
the laws of our nature as we find it in its incipient state. We are
aware that the projects which we contemplate are opposed to the
ruling opinions and prejudices of the age, and that we shall render
ourselves unpopular and be deemed visionary and an enthusiast.
We care little about these things. Our opinions have not been
formed prematurely. They are the result of experience with mankind, of deliberate conviction, the dictates of common sense exerted upon the common affairs of life.

June 16

The opinions which we have been led, step by step, to form
upon moral subjects, from our course of reading, observation, and
thought, for the last five years — at which time we began to think
for ourselves — are, we find, of a character too liberal and charitable, to use a common significant phrase, for the general mass of
thinkers even among the rational and liberal class here, with whom
we have become acquainted. Our sentiments are not decidedly
Unitarian. They do not embrace all the minute particulars of that
class of opinions. They are not so decidedly Christian as theirs; or,
in other words, they do not attach that particular divinity to the
person of Christ and the system which he gave us, that this de-
nomination do. At present we are disposed to consider the author
of the Christian system as a great and good and original man, and
the system itself as one of superior merit.

July 15

We are too much affected by the influences of physical causes, are too vacillating in our feelings and character to secure the full confidence of those with whom we associate.[3] Melancholy, the habit which we have been compelled to imbibe in the scenery through which we have passed, lays her leaden hand at times upon our mind and feelings. Our thoughts and prospects are then tinged with the pale and tintless coloring of her pencil. We are now raised by the prospects of hope and now depressed by the dark influence of doubt. Our imagination is active in looking forward to the future, now with the prospect of enjoying the fond anticipations of domestic and civil happiness, now it calls forth the most gloomy and afflicting scenes — which are soon doomed to pass.

What a peculiar temperament is ours! — And the subjects about which we are interested, on which our mind is active, are peculiarly fitted to increase the perhaps unhealthy excitement. The cultivation of the mathematical sciences might perhaps tend to bring us down from the region of conjecture and enthusiasm to that of reality and fact. We are perhaps becoming intemperate in our moral and mental habits. We are perhaps indulging hopes and expectations of human perfection which are essentially erroneous. We may find hereafter that we are in the common error of the inexperienced and young. We may have mistaken arrogance for independence, imagination for reality. Let us examine ourselves. Let us be careful. Let us attend to the things about us, living in the world and among our fellow beings.

August 2

At the dwelling of Mr. May [4] we became acquainted with his sister, a young lady apparently near our age — an interesting woman we had often portrayed in our imagination. In her we

---

[3] The reference is chiefly to Miss May, and the present passage of self-criticism was probably inspired by her. It contrasts strangely with passages of her own later journals in which she is shown to have become extremely "vacillating" in mood at a time when her husband had attained an unchanging serenity.

[4] In August, 1827, Alcott had visited the Reverend Samuel J. May at Brooklyn, Connecticut. Interested even thus early in every sort of reform, May had been attracted to Alcott by his growing reputation as a teacher with novel theories and methods.

thought we saw its reality. There was nothing of artifice, of affectation of manners; all was openness, simplicity, nature herself. There was intelligence, sympathy, piety, exemplified in the tenderness of the eye, in the beauty of moral countenance, in the joyousness of domestic performance. In refined and elevated conversation with a lady thus estimated by our reason and thus offering herself to our imagination, we could not but be pleased, interested, captivated. How could we but be in love with them — with their possessor? We conversed on a variety of subjects. She had thought for herself. She had thought liberally. Her views compared with ours. Her sentiments were also ours. Her purposes were like ours — the instruction of the young. Everything seemed to favor the commencement of an acquaintance of a pure and sentimental kind. The results of this interview are to be determined by time.

September 2

Our friend "A" returned from Hingham. Had a most interesting interview. I do love this good woman, and I love her because she is good. I love her because she loves me.

September 21

The province of the instructor should be simple, awakening, invigorating, directing, rather than the forcing of the child's faculties upon prescribed and exclusive courses of thought. He should look to the child to see what is to be done, rather than to his book or his system. The Child is the Book. The operations of his mind are the true system. Let him study these carefully and his success is sure. Let him follow out the impulses, the thoughts, the volitions, of the child's mind and heart, in their own principles and rational order of expression, and his training will be what God designed it to be — an aid to prepare the child to aid himself.

September 28

Attended the exercises at the Chauncy Place Sunday-School; the number of scholars near seventy — prospects on the whole encouraging. Heard a sermon from Rev. Mr. Emerson on the Universality of the Notion of the Deity — a very respectable effort.[5]

[5] Alcott's first reference to Ralph Waldo Emerson, whom he did not come to know until seven years later.

October 5

I am dissatisfied with the general preaching of any sect of men, and with the individuals of any sect. The general style of preaching, as regards thought and manner, among the Unitarians approaches nearer my views of correct preaching than that of any other class, but even this, it seems to me, is very objectionable. There is too much merely doctrinal, too little of practical thought. Hearers are returned home little better prepared, in too many instances, for the intelligent performance of their duties. Religion, after all, is not made a sufficiently rational, spontaneous, and social affair. Duty is too much involved in beliefs, in theory, in form, rather than in practice, in intelligent feeling and action. The morality of the pulpit is not sufficiently adapted to that of everyday life. Preaching is too much an affair of another life — to teach men how to *die* rather than how to live, to present the felicities of another life as objects of attainment rather than those of the present. It takes the thoughts of men too far from themselves — to heaven, rather than to the concerns of earth given us by our Great Employer.

October 26

Dined with "A" at her eccentric Aunt Scott's.[6] The old lady is known as the wife of Gov. Hancock, and still considers herself invested with the honors of Revolutionary respect. She is fond of society at the advanced period of life to which she is now arrived, and, to enjoy it, is constantly admitting persons of her acquaintance to see her, being too much absorbed in her own Madamism to call on others. These persons she receives to her august presence as she sits in her chair. Their happiness appears to consist in their attendance at her hour, and in the entertainment which she then offers them — herself, her table, her aims, her association with Gov. Hancock, whom she speaks of by the familiar name of "*my* Mr. Hancock," still retaining her primary idea of possession.

She seems to be a lady of very little force of mind, depending upon the idea of her connexion with Mr. Hancock as the basis of her fancied greatness. Her manners are very abrupt, though apparently very sincere, and the sincerity and amiableness of her

[6] Perhaps the original of "Aunt March" in Louisa M. Alcott's *Little Women*.

disposition makes her, even in her foibles, somewhat interesting. As a specimen of character she furnishes a good subject for the moral philosophers, showing the influence of station upon weak and ignorant minds, how much circumstances give tone and quality to untaught natures, and how deep and strong are the impressions and associations of early years.

The servant did not come at her call. She exclaimed, in all the peevishness of pampered age: "Servants! Why are ye so long in bringing the dinner?" The dinner was brought. We sat down — Madame, "A," and myself. The old lady would have the pudding first. She would have the old fashion, "for it was best." She helped me most bountifully. Two large pieces of her "fine apple pudding" were entrusted to my disposition. "A" gave me some of her "fine cider-sauce" for it. If —— was only there, how he would love some of it! She should like to compare some of her sauce with A's mother's, and see which was the best. "A" did not put enough of it on her pudding. I must have some more. She would help me herself, and give me enough. She requested "A" to reach her the bowl of sauce. "A" offered to help me, without complying with her wish as expeditiously as she desired. The peevishness again came over her. "Give me the sauce!" she exclaimed in a tone of heightened impatience. "He shall have enough, I say." The sauce was handed. She dealt out the sauce by spoonfuls. The roast beef was placed upon the table. She would carve for herself. Gov. Hancock's wrist was lame. She learned to carve when living with him. She had not forgotten how, only her loss of strength made her less powerful than she wished; but she would carve, and would carve in the old-fashioned style. The knife was dull. She had sent it to be sharpened, but it was duller than ever. The old-fashioned way of carving — "altogether the best" — was to cut sidewise of the piece. Crosswise was an innovation of later times. She did not "approve the improvement."

The old lady commenced with some difficulty. She succeeded in furnishing me with a piece of her "fine roast beef." "Was it tender? Was it done enough?" I assured her it was "very good," for indeed it was according to my education of taste. She eat no meat herself — the broth only, with bread or potato. I dispatched her two first pieces of roast beef. The knife was indeed too dull to carve with. "Where was the file?" It was procured. "Would I sharpen the knife?" I drew it across the file a few times, and offered to help myself to a piece of her fine roast. No; she would do it herself.

Mention was made by "A" of my engagement at the Sunday School at a quarter past one o'clock. She would not go, she said, and lose her dinner. "The children might all go to Old Nick first." I helped myself to another piece of her roast, and at the ringing of the church bell, the time for the exercises at the school to commence, arose to leave the table. "Was I going? I must come again, come and take tea with her, come when I could eat without being in a hurry."

I left for the Sunday School.

October 26

There is a city in our world upon which the light of the sun of righteousness has risen. There is a sun which beams in its full meridian splendour upon it. Its influences are quickening and invigorating the souls which dwell within it. It is the same from which every pure stream of thought and purpose and performance emanates. It is the city that is set on high. "It cannot be hid." It is Boston.

The morality of Boston is more pure than that of any other city in America. Channing is its moral teacher. His system of instruction is that of Christ. It is the system of Redemption, of Improvement, of Happiness. Its course is not terminated by the duration of the earth; it enters that of another kind of being. It is an introductory course to immortality — a discipline of the powers of the soul for its future employments.

November 29

The incident of most interest and importance in the retrospect of this year[7] yet remains to be penned. It is my connexion with Miss May.

This good woman came to Boston soon after my arrival. I saw her occasionally, and our correspondence was continued both by conversation and note. The hopes which I had indulged were

[7] Alcott is writing on his twenty-ninth birthday.

alternating between doubt and certainty for a time. She was not to assist me in the Infant School. I could not see her exclusively. I dared not the thought which I was indulging, for she knew too little of me. It would be premature advance. I must, it seemed to me, wait for favorable circumstances to disclose the truth which I so much desired to reveal, and ascertain its acceptance. This seemed the only resource within my means. I wished its approach, but saw no way by which I could produce a disclosure so important in the history of my happiness. After some thought, I handed my friend my Journal, in which from time to time I had written my opinions and feelings regarding her. This I thought would lead to a disclosure. It had the very effect which I hoped. It led to the connexion in which I now so much rejoice, and from which I have already enjoyed much, and anticipate the fullest felicities of this existence.

December 4

When I look back upon the scenes of my very early days, upon childhood and youth, upon the entrance into manhood, what a varied eventful life is presented to my view! In childhood confined to the narrow range of thought which the observation of the few objects and incidents in a small isolated town could furnish, thrown into the society of ignorance and selfishness, and removed from the means of moral and intellectual improvement. A mind ardent in the pursuit of knowledge and a heart seeking for happiness in the sterile soil of my native town and its cold and frozen climate, without books, without friends to which I could apply for instruction and happiness, an independent spirit sensible of its degradation, a curiosity to see beyond the limits of my paternal home and become acquainted with the great world.

At 15 years of age planning schemes for future employment and acquisition, moralizing upon the follies and vices of my townsmen, discussing points of thought and action with my father, usually differing from him in opinion and asserting my own independence yet submissive and obedient to his wishes and enjoying his confidence and affection — the pride of my mother, her favorite, the servant of my younger brother, the object of ridicule among the forward and impetuous of my companions, with one congenial spirit [8] beside my mother to whom I could speak my whole soul, diffident in action, independent in purpose, looking always forward for the end of achieving something worthy their hope.

At 18 leaving home alone, unacquainted with the world, its follies and vices, confiding, open, sincere, and going to a distance of 600 miles to explore the scene of things about me, engaging in business, neglecting it for intellectual pleasures, speculating upon conduct, mind, manners. Spending my time in this manner till the age of 23, imbibing some of the follies of society, avoiding its vices, learning much of its character the more to despise it, involving myself in debt through confidence in its integrity and openness of conduct in myself, returning to my native town at 23, ill, desponding, disgusted, the pity of ignorance, the recipient of disgrace for having been honest and confiding. At 24 regaining my health, invigorating my purposes, determining to prove my claim to reputation, commencing school, disciplining mind, summoning and elevating my principles of action and proceeding in my purposes through the period of 3 years in the instruction of district schools. At 27 encouraged in every form, mind awake to the moral movements of the world, engaged in thought upon its moral condition and the means of melioration, leaving my native place, coming to Boston encouraged in my purpose, forming acquaintances, a connexion for life, happy in prospects and active in the present, attempting the knowledge of myself and others, teaching an infant school for support, poor in purse but rich in contentment, blessed with the opportunity of good society and the means of intellectual and moral improvement, enjoying the confidence and love of a congenial spirit, drinking largely at the fountains of happiness and rejoicing in the goodness of God.

[8] His cousin, William Andrus Alcott.

*D*URING THIS *year Alcott's reputation as a teacher rapidly increased, and his school, often favorably noticed in the Boston newspapers, was visited by many prominent persons. In particular, he secured the support and enjoyed the friendship of the great Dr. Channing, for whom at this time he had the utmost respect. In April his father died at Spindle Hill, aged fifty-seven. He wrote articles on Pestalozzi and other educational topics for Russell's* Journal of Education, *and read, besides the works of Jeremy Taylor and Sampson Reed's* Growth of the Mind, *certain unsigned articles in the* Edinburgh Review *by Thomas Carlyle. At this time, too, he read William Godwin's* Political Justice *with great enthusiasm, so that when Frances Wright — a freethinking coadjutor of Robert Owen — came to Boston he called upon her and was undismayed by her novel notions of the marriage relation. "Fearless free-thinking and brisk correspondence with Abigail May" filled much of his time, and he was more than once a visitor at the home of the Mays in Brooklyn, Connecticut.*

Alcott's attention is much occupied at this time with matters of public preaching, still the most interesting entertainment that Boston had to offer. The deep respect for clergymen with which he came to Boston, inherited from two centuries of New England history, gradually gives way to an attitude shrewdly if not harshly critical. In this respect his thought is following the same lines as that of the young minister Ralph Waldo Emerson, whom he has already heard make "a very respectable effort" in the pulpit but does not yet personally know.

1829

February 15

Amongst the list of divines here of the liberal character, Dr. Channing ranks pre-eminent, both in originality of thought and felicity of expression.

His mind is a remarkable one. It soars high. It leaves the region of material vision and seeks affinity with the objects and essences of spiritual forms. It looks far into futurity, and assembles the realities of its scenes. It casts a penetrating and extensive look over the whole range of the moral kingdom, and defines in the happiest outlines the relations and dependencies of every scene. It throws upon the principles of Christianity a light which dissipates the darkness in which it has so long been enclosed, and reveals to the plainest understanding its beauty, its accordance with the wants of our nature, its power in elevating that nature to the heights of virtue and happiness, and its influence upon the mind in the investigation of truth as the great end of its action.

With Channing are associated other lights which beam with less radiance but which, like him, receive theirs from the same source and reflect it in different degrees upon the great truths of Christianity. Of these lesser glories of the moral world are Gannett and Greenwood, Ripley, Pierpont, Lowell, Frothingham, Young, Palfrey, Tuckerman, Motte, Emerson,[1] &c.

To be favored with the acquaintance of such men as these is a privilege which I am desirous to obtain and secure. My pursuits are closely connected with theirs. The same principles are the basis of our efforts. The same objects are before our view.

[1] Alcott's second mention of Ralph Waldo Emerson.

May 3

Heard Mr. Gannett [2] in the forenoon on the effects of the Lord's Supper upon communicants. With my views on this subject, the effects which he mentioned could not be produced. I do not regard the participation in this ordinance as the best profession of religion.[3] Profession, it seems to me, consists in practice. It *is* practice itself. A true follower of Truth is best known by avoiding everything like a connexion with or profession in any peculiar form in which that truth has been presented. He bows to the authority of no man. . . . He would not stop the progress of his own mind by narrowing its observation to the doctrines of a sect and creating a prejudice against others.

May 17

I have perused the *New Harmony Gazette*[4] for 1827–8 within the last month, and am pleased with many articles which its pages contain. Am unwilling to assent to many sentiments believed by its editors. With Mr. Owen's views of society in general I am pleased. With those of Mr. Owen and Miss Wright concerning marriage I am likewise pleased. There are many fine sentiments expressed in the columns of this periodical. The objection which I have to it is chiefly in reference to its open attack upon the Christian religion, or rather to the disrespect which its editors pay to religious opinions generally. I fear they are not fully imbued with the spirit of liberality, that spirit which induces its possessors to treat the opinions of all with respect and to acknowledge frankly the truth contained in all. With all their impudence of expression, however, their work will do good.

[2] Ezra Stiles Gannett, who had been since 1824 Channing's colleague at the Federal Street Church.

[3] A similar opinion was at least the ostensible reason for Emerson's withdrawal, some three years after this passage was written, from the Unitarian ministry.

[4] The organ of the socialistic community at New Harmony, Indiana, of which the leader at this time was Robert Owen, the Welsh reformer. The substantial agreement between Owen's teachings and Alcott's early thought renders the more remarkable the latter's prompt refusal, on religious grounds, to join the Welshman's American followers. See, below, the entry for December 22, 1829.

June 7

There is no sentiment which excites the indignant emotions of my nature and calls my powers of self-command into more vigorous action, lest I should utter something unworthy the character of a Christian, than the one that attributes to human nature entire depravity.[5] I feel all the nobler powers of my soul vilified by this expression. I feel the religion of Jesus to be abused, and the wisdom and justice and goodness of God a mere name. Those elevated and generous views of his character and purposes, those manifestations of his love in the moral and intellectual creation of man, become dimmed and lost in the shadows of such a picture.

November 2

There mingles in my reflections a peculiar feeling of desire to accomplish something worthy the purposes of my existence — a feeling of conscious power with the weakness of ignorance, a suffering from the comparison of my own mind with those distinguished for their commanding talents and philanthropy. The early neglect to which I was subjected, by which a train of habits were generated still opposing my progress in self-discipline and the acquisition of knowledge, follows this first impression and sometimes damps all the ardour which the former had awakened. The idea that half my life is gone and so little is accomplished worthy a mind and heart destined for such noble activities and acquisitions, overpowers me. But I soon rise and again plod on my way, hoping and regretting.

December 22

Passed the evening with Dr. Winship, who is anxious that I should engage as an instructor of the children of the Free Inquirers of Boston, who are determined to have some one willing to leave disputed points out of his system of teaching and inculcate nothing but what can be demonstrated to the senses and perceptions of the children. Such an individual they will amply reward by a salary of 1000 or 1200 dollars per annum.

[5] This passage was written after hearing a sermon on depravity, argued from the opposition of children to the commands of their parents.

But there are several reasons which render it not only inexpedient but absolutely wrong for me to engage in this way. I have very little confidence in the character and intentions of this Society. They do not love virtue nor truth. They oppose religion not because they deem it injurious to the interests of man but from that love of independence which always results when numbers are concerned. They are indifferent to everything truly good — a low party in religion, pretending to the same relation to "truth as it is in Jesus" that the political parties of the day do to the true interests of civil government. Mrs. Wright, whose cause they nominally represent, may be, and *is*, right in many of her views, but their party are not wise enough to understand her, or good enough to apply her precepts. I shall have nothing to do with them.[6]

[6] Compare the entry for May 17, 1829.

It should be remembered in reading the present passage that Alcott's annual income at this time was about five hundred dollars, and that he wished to marry as soon as possible.

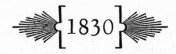

*I*N THIS YEAR *of Alcott's marriage his Journal, though not
neglected, falls off in interest. It was for him a year of external
activity. A gift of two thousand dollars, presumably from Mrs. Alcott's father, Colonel Joseph May, enabled Alcott to pay off his
peddling debts, and also to print, at his own expense, one thousand
copies of his essay on Infant Instruction. During this year he read
Epictetus and the* Politics *and* Ethics *of Aristotle. His newly
formed acquaintance with William Lloyd Garrison began to draw
him toward phases of reform other than the educational. At the
end of the year he was invited to form a school, in conjunction with
William Russell, at Germantown, Pennsylvania, and in November
he closed his school in Boston.*

1830

January 21

Looked over Hume's Essays. How much the thoughts of this
writer are abused. Had he lived at this day, would he not have
been one of the most enlightened and pure?

January 24

Heard a good sermon from Mr. Emerson [1] on *Conscience* as a
fundamental principle in morals and human nature.

[1] A penciled note in Alcott's handwriting and of later date shows that the
reference is to R. W. Emerson, whom Alcott did not yet know. He had first heard
Emerson preach on September 28, 1828.

April 8

I am not pleased with the style of thought and expression into which I fall in epistolary writing. It is not easy and familiar, is not enlivened by the detail of common incidents and feelings which constitutes the chief beauty of a good epistolary composition. The thoughts in mine are in themselves too abstract, too general in their application, and too metaphysical in their character, to diffuse themselves through the light medium of common expression; and fall therefore into a more sententious, laboured method of communication. They are entirely destitute of wit and humour, embody little but moral relations and truths; and, perhaps, bring forward much too prominently the theories and views of the writer. Improvements in these respects would be very gratifying to me; for, of all the letters which I have heretofore penned, I have never been satisfied with any. All have too much the marks of labour and care. They seem not the happy expressions of a mind writing from the fullness of thought and feeling, without premeditation and foresight.[2]

April 13

My acquaintance in Boston has not extended to many individuals since my residence here. I have not sought the acquaintance of many, and my manners and habits are not such as to predispose those whom I have seen in my favour. Popular manners, the chief requisite to success, I do not possess, and my appearance in public assumes so much of the rustic awkwardness and simplicity of natural life that I am often offending the more cultivated tastes of those with whom I sometimes come in contact. The character of gentleman is now so much expressed by artificial mannerisms and conventional rules of etiquette that good sense and folly are alike able to assume it, and the latter is frequently quite as successful as the former. The union of good sense with its natural and simple expression, though in violation of some of the refinements

[2] Just before he composed this true and clear-sighted criticism of his own prose style Alcott had been writing to Miss Abby May, whose style was much more racy and idiomatic than his. In later life Alcott came to think, with some reason, that he had done his best writing in his private letters.

of art, is after all the main charm with all truly pure and cultivated minds, and mannerism is only essential with the superficial and the servile. Good sense can hardly be otherwise than polite; but what is deemed good manners may often be but the varnishing of folly and ignorance.

Sunday, May 23

Agreeably to preceding expectation, I was this day married by Rev! Mr. Greenwood, at King's Chapel. Passed the evening at Col. May's,[3] and came to Mrs. Newell's, my place of board, with my friend, Miss May, after the civilities of the evening.

October 15

Heard Mr. Garrison,[4] whose efforts in the abolition of slavery have been made known to the public through "The Genius of Emancipation," at the Julien Hall, on this interesting subject. His lecture was full of truth and power. He proposes to give three lectures at the same place. I sent a communication to the *Daily Advertiser* on

October 16

This, I trust, will aid his purposes and the cause of truth and humanity.[5] Heard Mr. Garrison again this evening. This lecture consisted chiefly in a statement of facts concerning the cruelty with which many slave-holders had treated their slaves at the South. Mr. G. lectures very well. There is sometimes a want of discrimination, perhaps, between the slave-holder who keeps his slaves from motives of expediency and the one whose principles are in favor of slavery.

[3] Colonel Joseph May, father of the bride.

This entry shows the humorless "gentility" of Alcott's early writing at its absurd extreme.

[4] Alcott's first mention of William Lloyd Garrison, with whom he was soon to establish a lifelong friendship. The three lectures here mentioned were the beginning of Garrison's antislavery work in Boston.

[5] A penciled note by Alcott states that this communication was "not received by Editor." More probably, it was received but silently ignored by him, for at this time nearly all of Boston was strongly opposed to Garrison. He spoke at Julien Hall only because he had failed to find any Boston church that would allow him to use its pulpit for his condemnation of slavery.

November 8

Evening: Attended a meeting of a few individuals friendly to the abolition of slavery to concert measures for the foundation of an Anti-slavery Society in this city.[6] Mr. May, Rev. Mr. Collier, Mr. Blanchard, and Mr. Sewall were the persons present. Arrangements were made to have another meeting on Monday, 22nd. ult.,[7] and, in the meanwhile, persons who might be thought friendly to the cause made acquainted with the purpose of the meeting. The cause is a good one, and will, I trust, succeed.

[6] Thus was founded what Alcott called the "Preliminary Anti-Slavery Society," out of which grew, two years later, the New England Anti-Slavery Society. For a full list of the charter members, the names of Garrison and Alcott must of course be added.

Alcott's own thought and feeling with regard to slavery were much more moderate than Garrison's when the two men met in 1830, partly because Alcott had seen a good deal of slavery in its most favorable aspects during his peddling trips through Virginia and the Carolinas.

[7] I.e., *instant.*

THE OPENING of this year found Alcott in Philadelphia, making acquaintance with many persons. In March the birth of a daughter, Anna, distracted his attention for a time from all other matters, but two months later he opened a school at Germantown with six pupils. Here he was closely associated with William Russell, who, with his better-trained and far more logical mind, began at this time to exert an influence upon Alcott's thought never sufficiently acknowledged. During this year Alcott extended his knowledge of Francis Bacon and read Cousin, Herschel, Aristotle's Metaphysics, and Shelley — who interested him, it would seem, chiefly because of his association with Godwin.

1831

March 16   *Pennsylvania*

11 o'clock — evening. At this hour a child[1] was born to us. This is a new and interesting event in the history of our lives. How delightful were the emotions produced by the first sounds of the infant's cry, making it seem that I was, indeed, a father! Joy, gratitude, hope, and affection, were all mingled in our feeling.

[1] Anna.

"Unto us a child is given." Be it our ambition and delight, to train it up by the maxims of Him of whom the prophets of old spoke the same words. As agents of the Supreme Parent, may we guide it in the paths of truth, duty, and happiness. May the divine blessing rest upon it. May its mind be the depository of everything pure, beautiful, and good — its heart of all sweet and tender affections.

March 25

Commenced "an Historical account of the Development of the Intellect and Moral Conduct of my little girl, from birth, to be continued as her mind and heart make progress." Had often thought of this previous to my becoming a father, and to my seeing a paper in *Nicholson's Journal* on this subject. The article is interesting, but the observations and conclusions are, I think, imaginative and unsound. I shall try to avoid them, in mine.

About June 18

The history of one human mind, commenced in infancy and faithfully narrated by the parent until the child should be able to assume the work himself, and carried onward through all the vicissitudes of life to its close, would be a treasure of inconceivably more value to the world than all the systems which philosophers have built concerning the mind up to this day. It would be the history of human nature — a history which has never yet been written, a revelation of human character for which we look in vain amid the vices and crimes, the virtues and sacrifices, of those pages which now bear that name. . . .

June 24

. . . The progress of my little girl is deeply interesting to me. I have kept a record of her progressive development which has already extended to more than 40 pages in manuscript, and, if continued, will make matter for a volume by the end of the first year of her existence. She is now four months old.

Should this continue to prove interesting to me, and seem, at the end of the year, worthy of presenting to mothers, I shall be inclined to publish it.

July 1

Among the regrets which at times somewhat oppress me are those which arise from the defects of my early education — from the want of a knowledge of ancient languages and the more popular modern tongues, especially French and German. Translations of the works of the ancient Greek and Latin authors may, it is true, supply this inability in part, but those who desire to find truth at the fountain, pure and running from it, are unwilling to drink at the distant streams which, however pure may be the channels through which they flow, must become more or less adulterated.

July 31

I must teach in some form — at present, and perhaps hereafter, the young. Infancy seems to me the period when most good can be done for the improvement of the character, and this the period of life upon which I am inclined to spend my direct personal labours. I am unwilling to waste my efforts upon those whose habits are fixed, and whose natures are too often sophisticated beyond the hope of reform — who are beyond the reach of human exertion.

. . . The minister has long preached, and what has he accomplished? Ask our penitentiaries, our prisons, our jails, our almshouses, our domestic firesides; look into our civil and political codes and institutions, our periodical publications of a religious nature, our schoolrooms, our churches; count the number of various societies whose object is the suppression of some mighty vice which is preying on the heart of society — our societies for the suppression of intemperance, of war, of slavery, of oppressive governments; look into the individual life and behold the shifts of trade, of avarice, of petty prejudice, bickerings, quarrels, spites; view the low and debased forms of character which live both in high and in humble life, the little regard which the precepts of Christianity seem to exert upon the lives of men. And when this mighty catalogue has been filled out, then is the answer at hand of what the minister, with all his boasted authority, has done. He has done little because he has not known how. He has preached; but there have been causes operating against him more powerful than all his teachings, and he has failed. Early education is the enduring power.

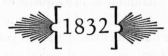

THIS YEAR was memorable in Alcott's career because of two events: his first reading of Coleridge's Aids to Reflection, *which meant to him an intellectual rebirth, and the birth of his daughter Louisa. Still living at Germantown and conducting his very small school there, he continued his studies under the guidance of William Russell, wrote a number of articles for various educational societies and reviews, and made careful day-to-day observations upon the development of his two children.*

1832

June (undated)

There is no city in this country in which there is more mental and philanthropic activity than in Boston. The better mind and conscience of this continent are there. Philosophy and literature, if not adequately cherished and cultivated, receive more attention than in other cities. There is a purer moral atmosphere — more unity and order in details as well as in general sentiment and arrangement, than exists where man is less studied and respected. It is the place, I think, for all generous efforts to improve humanity to be located. But even there, notwithstanding all the light which exists, objects are yet seen in distorted and exclusive forms. It would be difficult to succeed in a generous experiment on man, either in the way of mental, moral, or spiritual improvement. The splendid genius of Channing is inadequate to break through the remaining clouds of prejudice and intolerance which linger in its horizon. The day of human emancipation is yet distant. A generation yet to come will see the blessed vision. At present, faith must rest in the things not seen, which are to come.

October (undated)

. . . Commenced a correspondence with E.W.L.,[1] a little girl living with me, on general topics for her benefit. She is endowed with wonderful intuitive and reflective powers, and is able to discuss with much ability subjects connected with the nature and duties of man. Her mind is essentially metaphysical and ethical. Her letters abound in thoughts much beyond her years, and are curious specimens of psychological attainment. I have never known a little girl to possess equal power at her age. She is now nine years of age.

October (undated)

The frequent perusal of poetry seems necessary to the vigour, vivacity, and freshness of the mind. Milton, Byron, and Coleridge abound in much that produces this effect. The same is true of Wordsworth. These I regard as the first poets in the language. In Coleridge in particular there are passages of surpassing beauty and deep wisdom. He seems to have studied man more thoroughly, and to understand him better, than any previous poetic writer, unless it be Wordsworth. And his prose writings are full of splendid ideas clothed in the most awful and imposing imagery. There is in this man's soul a deep well of wisdom, and it is a wisdom not of earth. No writer ever benefited me more than he has done. The perusal of *Aids to Reflection* and *The Friend* forms a new era in my mental and psychological life.[2]

[1] Elizabeth W. Lewis, daughter of Mordecai Lewis of Philadelphia.

[2] This is an exact statement of the fact, for it was chiefly the reading of Coleridge's *Aids to Reflection*, as edited with very ample notes by Dr. James Marsh of the University of Vermont, that led Alcott to abandon the philosophy of John Locke and made him a Transcendentalist. This change in his thought was completed before he knew Emerson. His discovery of Coleridge and Wordsworth was probably due to Dr. Channing, who knew both men personally and did much to extend their influence in America.

WILLIAM ANDRUS ALCOTT

WILLIAM RUSSELL

November (undated)

. . . A daughter [3] born on the 29. ult.[4] — my birth day, being 33 years of age. This is a most interesting event. From the great experience of domestic life which has been mine, I have derived much enjoyment, finding in the ties thus originated the necessary connexions with sympathetic existence from which my abstract habits incline me too strongly, perhaps, to escape. A family, while it turns the mind toward the tangible and practical, supplies at the same time fresh stimulus for the social and spiritual principle; it brings around the soul those elements from whose presence and influence it is fitted to advance its onward progress, and opens within the sweetest affection and purest purposes. The human being isolates itself from the supplies of Providence for the happiness and renovation of its life, unless those ties which connect it with others are formed. The wants of the Soul become morbid, and all its truth and primal affections are dimmed and perverted. Nature becomes encrusted over with earth and surrounded by monotony and ennui. Few can be happy shut out from the Nursery of the Soul.

[3] Louisa.
[4] Alcott often wrote "ult." for *instant*, as Emerson also sometimes did.

HAVING BEEN awakened by Coleridge's Aids to Reflection, Alcott made in this year a rapid and continuous intellectual advance. This year, in fact, was the seedtime of his mind. Before closing his Germantown school in March he had read Coleridge's Biographia Literaria, a treatise on Aristotle, and a little of Swedenborg. In the spring, leaving his family at Germantown, he opened another school in Philadelphia and gained access to the Loganian Library. During the early summer he lived alone in an attic on Library Street, reading with the avidity of a man who has just discovered his true intellectual society. Here he first encountered the Dialogues of Plato, in the translation by Thomas Taylor, and he read them with a sense of coming at last to his own. Here too he read Berkeley, Shaftesbury's Characteristics, Goethe's Wilhelm Meister, and all that he could find of Carlyle in the British magazines. Frequent association with Dr. Channing, who was then a visitor in the city, must have deepened the effect of this reading. In September, after a vacation at Spindle Hill and Hartford and Boston, he returned to his school in Philadelphia and to his attic, and there before the end of the year he read Cary's translation of Dante, Taylor's translations of Proclus and Plotinus, Wordsworth's Excursion, Okely's life of Jakob Boehme, and an abstract of Kant's philosophy. With the help of this eager and adventurous reading, which seems to have kept his mind in a state of steady excitement, he worked entirely free from the influence of Calvin and John Locke, who still dominated the thought of New England, and faced in the direction of Transcendentalism.

1833

February (undated)

The observation and record of results in the experience of my two children, though extremely crude and unsatisfactory, occupied a place in my attention.[1] The stream of thought which had begun to flow in one direction and to absorb all the other rivulets as contributions to itself, hastened onward gradually toward the ocean of universality and infinitude, the primal fountain of inexhaustible energy. Additional life and light seemed added to the acquisitions of the past. The leading idea which dawned upon my mind was this:

The human soul has had a primordial experience in the infinite Spirit. The infinite is embodied in the finite, to be developed and returned again to the source of infinite energy from whence it sprang. This is spiritual and earthly experience, and all the phenomena of humanity arise from the union and evolution of these elements. The finite is but the return of the soul on the path of the infinite — the wheeling orb attracted toward, and yet preserved in the cycle of, the central sphere.

February (undated)

My plan with reference to Philadelphia is limited in its scope, and embraces but a part of my ultimate endeavours. I have but limited faith in the moral intelligence of the Philadelphians as efficient patrons of early education. Psychological and ethical science is comparatively little cultivated by the most intellectual

[1] Alcott is here reviewing the observations, reading, and thought of the preceding month. The passage suggests that his central doctrine of the "Lapse," loosely stated in the second paragraph, may not have been originally derived from Plato or Plotinus, whom he had not yet read, but from his daily psychological "observations" upon his infant daughters, Anna and Louisa.

men of the city. The general mind is chiefly absorbed in physiological and natural science. Man's spiritual and celestial nature, as treated in psychology and theology, is merged into investigations which lead only to views partaking largely of materialism, or of pseudo-religio-philosophy. Anthropology, in its wide, free, celestial spirit, is not a popular subject of investigation. Thought is much broken into sectarian fragments, and the general inquirer and practical experimenter in the ideal world stands but little chance of being understood and sustained.

May (undated)

Plato I had long wished to read, but could never before find a translation. It had long been my impression that there were in his writings great and profound ideas which the light of existing thought and science had not been bright enough to attain. This impression I find confirmed on perusal of the few fragments of his writings translated by Taylor.[2]

Modern philosophy has widely departed from the genius of the ancient school. The living spirit has departed from it, and left it but a dead and corrupt mass of material elements. *That* had intercommunion with the invisible and the infinite; *this* is limited to the consideration of the finite and the visible, and is incompetent to the investigation of primary causes and ultimate laws. It stops at secondary causes and can penetrate no deeper. It limits and circumscribes the infinite by the frail and powerless energies of the finite. It shuts God from the universe, and, carried to its legitimate issues, results in Pantheism — building up on an inconceivable basis the whole fabrick of religion, which it must assume as independent of man and nature. It makes of exterior nature a self-existent substance, and sees not in the laws and vicissitudes of things the movement of Spirit.

These illusions, which never had much influence over my own mind, have all been swept away by the Platonic theory, and I see clearly what before was obscured by the gloss of exterior matter: Spirit all in all — matter its form and shadow.

[2] The *Cratylus, Phaedo, Parmenides*, and *Timaeus*, which, at this time, Alcott supposed were the only "fragments" of Plato that Thomas Taylor had translated.

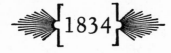

1834

*D*URING THE *first six months of this year Alcott kept his school in Philadelphia, but with a growing conviction that he would never thrive as a teacher in that city. Leaving his family in Germantown in order that his children might have the advantage of country air, he continued to live in the attic on Library Street and to read there with an insatiable avidity. Carlyle's* Sartor Resartus, *then appearing in* Fraser's Magazine, *led him into German literature, from which he gained a sense of sudden enlightenment. Before the summer came he had made some acquaintance, always by means of translations, with Goethe, Richter, Herder, Lessing, and Schiller. Carlyle's life of Schiller and Schlegel's History of Literature interested him deeply. At about the same time he read Burton's* Anatomy of Melancholy *and Spenser's* Faerie Queene.

Realizing how late in life his intellectual awakening had come, Alcott would have been glad to spend all of his time in reading and in thought, but the problems of livelihood were ever more pressing. His friends W. H. Furness, William Russell, and W. E. Channing, bestirred themselves during the early summer to secure a school for him in Boston. Miss Elizabeth Peabody, at Channing's suggestion, gathered an enrollment of thirty children and agreed to serve as Alcott's assistant. Handsome rooms were secured at the Masonic Temple and were fitted up to Alcott's specifications, at a cost to him of over three hundred dollars. He brought his family

*from Connecticut to Boston in September and, late in the same
month, opened the "Temple School." This was by far the most
famous, and for a time the most successful, of his schools for children. His pupils came mostly from the upper social class of the
city, and from the homes of Calvinists, Unitarians, Baptists,
Swedenborgians, Episcopalians, Methodists, Universalists, and
Free Enquirers. Alcott's hope to add a Catholic and a Quaker child
was not realized.*

*During the first months of the year Alcott wrote little in his
Journal, being busied with the preparation of certain books for
children, which were never published. In midsummer, when he
was occupied with the move to Boston and the arrangements for
his new school, he wrote nothing whatever. As a whole, however,
the Journal of the year is unusually thoughtful, showing the effect
of recent reading and a swift progress toward pure idealism and
the Transcendental philosophy.*

1834

April 22

The endeavour to nurse my mind on the literature of England
has been a great drawback to my spiritual and intellectual growth.
Ignorant until quite lately of the treasures which lie in Germany, and, from the want of scholastic education but little acquainted with the lore of the ancients, I have been from infancy
plodding my way onward to life and light, shrouded in the darkened atmosphere of self-ignorance and feeding my yearning spirit
with the godless nutriment of a literature spawned from the
heart of moral disease. I have fed, over-fed, and at last found
that the food cannot fill; it cannot supply the deeper wants of
my nature; it is but children's pap — for the animal, not for
the spiritual sustenance; for body, not for the soul.[1]

---

[1] The first expression of a strong dislike of England and things English —
possibly caused by recollections of the War of 1812 — which Alcott did not
overcome for many years. Compare the entries for June 6–July 4, 1842.

Of this truth I am conscious from the perusal of Goethe, Schiller, Richter, and whatever comes from the higher order of mind in Germany. All that I have read teems with the spirit of a new life; it comes from the heart; it does justice to the spirit of man. Far removed is it from the dust of the earth, from the plodding business of sublunary life; or if it descend to these it throws around them its own divine light. . . . Imagination and Reason blend in one whole, and the human spirit is led onward by their mutual aid.

How long has it taken me to make this discovery! Thrown into the world and left to seek my intellectual pittance for myself, how have I been vainly striving to feed on husks! In current literature, in surrounding life, in art, how little have I found that could satisfy! . . . In youth I was preserved, being left to seek my own sustenance, and, finding literature wanting, I lived on Nature, who, unconscious to myself, kept me unspoiled. At a later stage a generous heart saved my head from famine; and though it fed me scantily, the food was pure and my desire was unhurt. With varied tastes corresponding to the scenes around me, at last came the era of meditation, and emancipated me from the thraldom of sense into which I had been enticed by the morbid food of English literature. Coleridge assisted me in the beginning, Wordsworth too exerted a genial influence, and by these and my own innate tendency to pure ideality and a life of intellectual pursuits, I was led to the full view of things. Herder, Schiller, Richter, Goethe — and even Bulwer and Carlyle, though Englishmen yet German in education and in spirit — were understood and believed. Before this, however, Channing had spoken intelligently to me, and I had sympathized with the spirit of Plato, perused Plotinus, and found the depths of Aristotle, Bacon, Locke, and Kant. With these last I was dissatisfied. They narrowed the range of the human faculties, retarded the progress of discovery by insisting on the supremacy of the senses, and shut the soul up in the cave of the Understanding. While Nature was always in act, and sent her spirit before to apprize the soul of her coming progresses, they tardily waited for the act, that they might — as they quaintly termed it — "catch her in the fact." And then they deemed themselves philosophers, because they could tell *what they had seen!*

But philosophy is of a prophetic as well as historic spirit. Before facts emerge from the deep womb of Nature she knows and foretells their appearance. Her realm is that of faith, and she sheds her light over the dim domain of sense, even the very light by which phenomena are rendered apparent to the material age. It is her agency that sharpens the outward vision. On the darkened screen of Theory she paints all her pictures, and experiment but brings them more distinctly and in detail to the apprehension of the understanding.

Theory points the way, and urges toward the world of fact. Without her guidance all would be inexplicable . . . the Divinity would never emerge from the courts of pure intellectuality to display his presence in the distant confines of space and in the flitting moments of time. In Eternity and on the unseen spaces of ideal form, absorbed in his own being, rayless, and remote from human ken, would He dwell — occasional shadows but transiently telling of his existence, and these too evanescent and dubious to be identified and seen.

April 22

My ideas, at present, are better than my style, and for many ideas, distinct and vivid in my own mind, I have no sign. This, more than anything else, is, I believe, the cause of my failure, and of the complaint not infrequently made that I am mystical. My ideas are, I believe, clear. There is no confusion of thought on intellectual subjects. The obscurity lies in the language which I employ and which, in my present state, is too scanty for my purpose.

April 24

To us [2] the past *is* of value. Not, however, in the way of example; for the parallel is wanting, the analogy is dim. Circumstances are widely different. Man is operating on vastly different external relations. We are spread over a wider space; we have freer air; Nature spreads itself around us on a wider scale; our situation is wholly new. Nor are *men* the same. Physical differences have moulded us in accordance with their spirit. Our physical and intellectual make are national; and, despite the foreign asso-

[2] Americans.

ciations of our ancestral education, Nature has assumed her rightful influence and has shaped us in her moulds. Living on the accumulated treasures of the past in a new theatre of action, we have monopolized the best of time and space, and stand on a vantage ground to which no people have ever ascended before.

April 27

I have so long lived an inward, reflective life that the relations of external things to my temporal prosperity have been almost lost sight of. I am not perhaps sufficiently inclined to yield to the dictates of earthly prudence. I cling too closely to the ideal to take necessary advantage of the practical, and my wife and children suffer from this neglect. I may not sympathize with a true spirit in the deprivations to which this course subjects them. Disinclined from making much of outward success, I may seem unkind, indifferent, improvident.

But this course seems to me the only one that I can pursue in justice to all relations and purposes in life. I have set out in an attempt to find the truths of my own nature, to explain and embody them in life, in education. Sacrifices must be made to the spirit of the age. With a new purpose, I must expect difficulties which are not thrown in the way of those who pass on unopposingly in the current stream of things. In proportion to the value of the ends which I aim at must be the sacrifices that I make, the obstacles to encounter, and the distance of the day when success will crown my efforts.

April 28

Here I am, removed from the third to the fourth story — blessed at last with my one little window fronting the City Library and the Athenæum, with a bed, a trunk for my clothes, a wash-stand, two chairs, and my books. On these I am to feed and content myself during the summer.

Well, it matters little, after all, what surrounds us, how few are the things in which we feel a property and to which we attach ourselves, if the mind have wherewith to feed and the heart to comfort itself. Man can live on his own faith, if his faith be fastened on Love and Wisdom. 'Tis not necessary that external goods should enter largely into the supply. Wiser is he who, in the absence of these, retreats into his own spirit and, in the abstractions of contemplation and the practice of theories, lives out the delights of the inner life, triumphing over space and time by the activity of his own thought!

April 28

At school today I was informed by one of my pupils that at the end of the present quarter both himself and brother would leave me. . . . This intelligence I had expected, but it is peculiarly unfortunate in this instance as regards the welfare of the children. . . . No pupils more require the moral influences which it is my purpose to impart, and this for various reasons. The elder [3] is a boy of strong impulses which have been little restrained or directed by moral culture. He has been placed under circumstances which have called these forth and given them strength and dominion. His imagination, fed by tales of romance and adventure, has got the mastery of his intellect, and thus wrong-headed impulse sweeps all before it. Of moral truth and beauty I have tried in vain to give him an insight. He cannot understand them.

He had been placed at a school where cunning, as is almost always the case in our institutions of education, was made the usual motive of action. Forbearance, kindness unmixed with selfishness, he laughed at as weak, undignified. He had all the false notions of the world, and resisted every attempt to supplant them by purer ideas. . . .

Such were the circumstances under which the boy was received. Of course little could be expected, but the best influences and happiest adaptation at school. . . . He will now be removed, and placed under circumstances less conducive to the formation of his character. His impulses will find free scope and he will doubtless fall a victim to misdirected measures. Temptations will come in his way and he will yield. The good convictions of his mind will die away.

[3] This was Charles Godfrey Leland (1824–1903), the future author of *Hans Breitmann's Ballads* and many other books, but now chiefly remembered for his studies in gipsy folklore. In his *Memoirs* Leland speaks of his old teacher as "the most eccentric man who ever took on himself to train and form the youthful mind."

May 9

I have been deemed by some, and perhaps by the larger portion of those who know me, to be theoretic, enthusiastic, visionary. It has been said of my views that, however just they may be in the abstract, they can never be reduced to practice, that the spirit of the time will never sustain me in the course upon which I have set out, and that it is vain and a waste of effort to persevere in a work which, sooner or later, must terminate in defeat.

Now these are misapprehensions of the whole spirit and scope of my views. That I have not as yet been able to reduce my theories to successful practice has not been owing to the impracticability of my schemes, nor to the want of interest on the part of those who have attempted to sustain me, but to the profundity and universality of the theory upon which my practice has been founded. . . . I am not only theoretic but practical, in the highest sense of the word, and if I am not so regarded it is because of the difficulty of the ends which I am endeavouring to secure, not to the impossibility of securing them. He who effects all that he attempts cannot, in the present state of society, attempt much, for the very fact of his full success is a proof of the adaptation of his plan to the perverted minds of those to whom it is addressed. . . .

Theory, say what we will, is after all the very life of Truth. It is Truth freed from the mists of sense. It is Truth unveiled in her very features to human eyes. . . . Theory is a prevision of the future. It is the ark in which are safely placed the precious lives of those truths that are to float unhurt over the destructive deluge of past errors, and destined to repeople the renovated earth with pure forms and free institutions.

May 13

Our literature is remarkably barren in all that relates to pure morality or deep metaphysical analysis. I seldom find a work on these subjects that interests me. Commonplace sentiment, superficial philosophy, are abundant. The French and Germans, particularly the latter, excel us and even the English on these subjects. But there is little reaches us from these quarters. It is better to recur to the great works of genius for life and vividness.

The poets, not less than the philosophers, are the most effectual teachers of morality. Both should be read in order to do justice to the imagination and reason. The novelists also should be added. I find my mind more and more disposed to replenish itself from the stores of fiction. Facts are too sterile unless connected by the invisible bond of cause and effect, or clad in the vivid hues of the fancy. Like the leafless trees in winter, they are the mere memorials of the summer blossom and autumnal fruit.

June 12

And the name of that chamber was "Peace."
PILGRIM'S PROGRESS.

This sentence keeps chiming in my ears as I sit at my desk this morning in my chamber, the window of which opens to the sun-rising, and before me are the trees clad in the rich foliage of the season — the morning breeze scarcely stirring their leaves, and the sunlight settling in no unquiet repose on the sloping roof-tops of the houses around me. The aspect of nature at this hour is that of peace and refreshing quiet. The mind, invigorated by the visitations of the night, is returned with transparent vision to the objects of earth and breathes in the spirit of the scene. Peace and quietness are impressed upon it from without; it drinks in the natural scenery and finds growing up, in the ideal landscape within, fresher and fairer objects — waving trees, clad in green, calmer sunlight. The chamber within is tenanted by the glad spirit of "Peace."

June 18

May we not believe that thought gives life and meaning to external nature, that what we see, hear, feel, taste, and experience around us acquires these properties by the self-investing power of our spirits? Is not the living Spirit of all things in our spirits, and do they not, through the vivid action, the picturing, life-starting agency of this same Spirit, rise up, tinted and shaped, before us, even as in starting from the bed of rest the external world becomes visible to us with the opening of our eyes — not so much to let in the light as to let out our spirits upon the scene which they color and animate with beauty and life?

The reality is in the mind. Sense but gives us an outward type of it, an outward shaping to reduce it to the cognizance of the understanding, and in space and time to substantiate the indwelling forms of our spirits. We throw ourselves outward upon nature that we may the better look upon ourselves, and this process is rendered more conscious to us in the act of waking than in any other.[4]

June 20

There is a world of true and lasting felicity into which my spirit sometimes strays, and catches glimpses of its soul-enkindling scenery. But there it stays not long. It is beckoned back again by some one of the thousand toils of the present and visible, to resume the little tasks of yesterday and complete what the present calls for. Would that it could remain longer where it so loves to dwell! Would that its toils might be *in* and *for* the relations of this sphere! Light might then be its pervading element, a clear and untroubled vision its constant privilege!

October 18								*Boston*

How apt am I to ascend and lose sight of the things of sense, to climb the ladder to the topmost round and there reel with the giddy prospect stretching off into indistinctness and bewilderment. Am I caught in the net of a wildly-roving fancy, or do I rise on the wings of a celestial imagination whose shapes find no correspondence and refuse to stay pinioned to earth, but ascend to seek their realization in the infinite? Verily, an Ideal glitters in my spirit, and why should I tarnish its celestial lustre by trailing it through the slime of earth? . . .

There is in man a star of whose rising he retains a dim remembrance, having seen it emerge from the horizon of a celestial country; and ever and anon during his terrestrial sojournings across the country of earth it gleams upon his memory to enlighten his dark way and comfort him with assurance that he

---

[4] This early example of Alcott's "idealistic" thinking shows how far he had already progressed, before his meeting with Emerson, away from the prevailing philosophy of John Locke and toward Transcendentalism. One should not forget in reading such passages that while Emerson was writing his first book, *Nature*, he had in hand Alcott's Journals for 1834 and 1835.

has not wandered away from his native home. It rises not in the horizon of sense, the opaque orb distant from his former dwelling-place, but in the land of light; and its setting shall not be seen with other eyes than those of the spirit as it passes over the mountains of time and shines no longer to illumine the vales of space. Ideal, primal, original, is its shining, illumining the firmament of creation.

October 20

Never let me cease to worship the bright Symbol of the Infinite! Oh, deliver me from the thraldom of sense, of custom, of this world's dark and devious entanglements! Preserve me from the temptations of this terrestrial life, from the loss of my early possession — a faith in thy power. As I spread my being over space and extend it in time, keep thou me from dissipating thy richness on the poverties of things! Let thy spirit uphold me in the coming trials and experiences of life; and when time and space shall have waked from my being the lovely and beautiful spirits which thou didst there nurture and commune with, and these are become the familiar companions and friends of *my* spirit, then, with them, in gentle repose and tranquil hope, may I recede from the bounded and mutable, no longer a fit residence for my redeemed nature, into the limitless and unchangeable where thou art the Light and the Spirit of Life! [5]

October 26

My companion and the little ones lie before me, for I am now in the chamber where they repose. Sunk in material sleep, their spirits are, I trust, feeding in no unquiet mood on spiritual nurture and gaining that energy of life which shall fit them for the terrestrial toils of tomorrow.

Today I have been more than usually observant of their conduct at home while under the supervision of their mother. Some habits, I regret to say, have been permitted to attain a strength and fixity that will require no small degree of skill, delicacy, and yet force of discipline to remove — more than the mother will be

[5] One of several passages in the Journals that were evidently intended as prayers. Compare the last entry for 1837.

able to put forth in the fondness and timidity of her heart. I
ought, I believe, to assume this responsibility and relieve her
from the delicate and yet necessary work. I have this evening
concluded to do so, and enter upon the task tomorrow.

. . . I have left the mother to shape her methods for herself; but I find that without something more than this theoretical
influence my duties as a father will be imperfectly discharged, and
my relations as a husband be feebly met. It is my duty to act, and
act in the way of example. My speculations, however true, must
be actualized to the observation in practical methods under the
eye of the mother, or a part of their value will be lost, or mis-
understood by her — to say nothing of the consequences that must
result to the children. I must no longer delay so important a
work.[6]

November 5

Louisa is yet too young for the formation of just views of her
character. She manifests uncommon activity and force of mind at
present, and is much in advance of her sister when at the same
age. Example has done much to call forth her nature. She is more
active and practical than Anna, a different form of character essentially. Anna is ideal, sentimental. Louisa is practical, energetic.
The first imagines much more than she can realize; the second, by
force of will and practical talent, realizes all that she conceives,
but conceives less. Understanding rather than imagination, the
gift of the sister, seems to be her prominent faculty. She finds no
difficulty in devising ways and means to attain her purposes, while
her sister — aiming at much, imagining ideal forms of good and
shaping them out so vividly in her mind that they become present
enjoyments — fails when she attempts to realize them in nature.
She has been dwelling on the higher and more speculative relations of things, and the practical skill is not opened out for their
attainment.

[6] Alcott's record of his dealings with his two eldest children shows that this
resolve led on to a certain amount of physical chastisement, particularly of
Louisa.

*T*HIS WAS *the year of Alcott's greatest professional prosperity, and it was also one of the happiest years of his life.
The Temple School flourished. In June Alcott's third child, Elizabeth Sewall, was born. In July Miss Peabody's* Record of a School,
*an admiring account of Alcott's teaching from day to day as ob-
served by her, was published. In the same month Alcott and Emerson first met, at Alcott's rooms in Boston, and three months later
Alcott paid his first visit to Emerson in Concord. It was in this
year that Alcott gave up, for the rest of his life, all use of animal
food. In October he began the series of conversations with children
on the Gospels which were soon to bring him and his school into
serious disfavor with all conservative minds. At about the same
time he formed the plan for conversations with groups of adults
which was to constitute a main interest and activity of his later
years.*

*The Journal of this year is the record of a rapid and many-
sided growth. Perhaps more clearly than any other it shows the
results of Alcott's readings, at Philadelphia and Germantown, in
the Transcendental philosophers. A peculiar interest attaches to it
because Emerson had it in hand while at work on his first book,*
Nature, *between which and the Journal there are several interesting
similarities and even identities of thought. Writing in his own
Journal on the fifth of June, 1836, Emerson says: "I have read*

*with interest Mr. Alcott's Journal in MS. for 1835. He has at-
tained at least to a perfectly simple and elegant utterance. There is
no inflation and no cramp in his writing. I complained that there
did not seem to be quite that facility of association which we expect
in the man of genius and which is to interlace his work with all
nature by its radiating upon all. But the sincerity of his speculation
is a better merit. This is no theory of a month's standing; no peg
to hang fine things on; no sham enthusiasm, no cant; but his
hearty faith and study by night and by day. He writes it in the
book, he discourses it in the parlor, he instructs it in the school. And
whatever defects as fine writers such men may have, it is because
colossal foundations are not for summer-houses, but for temples
and cities."*

1835

January (undated)

In the varied universe wherein man holdeth his individual being, is there aught more worthy of interest or study than himself,
a member of this same wondrous Fabrick? We investigate the
qualities or apprehend the laws of this universe to little purpose
if the relations which they hold to our being are not made the
primary objects of observation and thought. The true and the
devout inquirer takes an humble stand in the grounds of his own
being, and from this he goes forth to the survey of Nature and
of Providence, being guided and illuminated by a faith that per-
ceiveth in all things and in all beings the same sustaining, upholding Life that quickeneth and filleth his own conscious being.
To him the universe is significant because of the self-conscious
Life that actuateth his own individual spirit.

Hence it is that the spirit which is ever striving to find in the
manifestations of Nature illustrations of its own being, its functions and laws, doth ever receive the ready and satisfactory answer.
Nature willingly vouchsafes to such an one a reply. Docility,
meekness, confiding trust, are rewarded. By seeking communion
and fellowship with Nature, by proving constant to her require-

ments, such an one endoweth himself with her powers; and taketh all her meanings into himself, setting a value and a name upon her operations and subordinating these to his own spiritual activity. In the mighty Self within him he beholds energies whose ceaseless play shall overcome the kingdoms of Time and Space and establish an eternal dominion, making the universe the instrument of its power.

January 2

After a day of great interest in the duties of the school, I passed the evening with Dr. Channing. The conversation turned chiefly on the uses of history.

Dr. C., from the deficiency of his own knowledge on this subject and a still lingering tinge of that scholastic discipline by which his mind was formed, sets a much higher value on mere historical knowledge than belongs of right to it in a scale of human acquirement. He says that he is daily reminded of his own deficiencies and is compelled to recur to authorities, when, as I feel, he should have the facts in his own mind. History, he thinks, is one of the most effectual revelations of human nature — the facts of the past are the manifestations of the capacities of the human race. He thinks we cannot conceive of the dignity and destiny of man without the lights of history.

Now, while I would not take from his view of the importance of this knowledge, yet I think much knowledge of our nature can be derived from the study of individual life. History is rather the exhibition of the power of the individual than of the people. Enter into the subtle mechanism of the life of a great man, penetrate the secret by which he vivified and shaped the conceptions that thrill through the life of a people and spread themselves out in their institutions, and you have studied the true elements of history, you have viewed things in their universality, in their origin. All without, all that shapes itself in this external life, is contained in this individual life, and is but its product in time and space. Here is the mighty energy that awakened and saved, deadened or wrecked, a people. Biography is the only true historical record of human nature, for this is the history of spiritual causes, of which physical changes — all the vicissitudes of external life —

are but the consequences. Events in the external world are so complex, so infracted as it were by the interventions of Providence, so far removed from the simple powers on which they depend, that they become perplexing and of dubious meaning unless seen in the light of a spiritual sense, and then they are of small value because they are seen in their insignificance.

In biography we are presented with life in its spirituality; we behold humanity, and we see it not in the soiled glory of its original prerogatives but in its native dignity. For an individual becomes known and remembered because he retains his innate excellence, and, amid a world of contaminated spirits, shines forth as by contrast in all his brightness to their wondering, admiring eyes. The record of wickedness ceases to be interesting when we have penetrated its motives, and we feel that our common nature — so far from being represented in its true light — is deformed and dimmed; it is libelled, and we are indignant at the injustice. It is the sentiment of excellence that lifts our nature into the light of true perception, so that we can behold all its lineaments and penetrate our own individual being.

When God would reveal himself to a people he entrusts the sacred truth not to that people in their aggregate capacity but to a gifted spirit among them, who transfuses it from himself into them.

January 4

He who kindles the fire of genius on the altar of the young heart unites his own prayers for humanity with every ascending flame that is emitted from it through succeeding time. He prays with the Universal Heart, and his prayers bring down blessings on all the race below. — But here come my two children to spend an hour with me in the study, and I resign my thoughts to their spirits whence, if I do my part, shall soon shoot forth branches to heal and bless the people. For genius is the endowment of every spirit, and parents are its supervisors while on its terrestrial mission. May I fulfil my divine behest!

I have conversed with the little ones, whose imagings appear on the paper above — fit emblems of the essayings of an inapt skill on terrestrial things.[1] These marks — who knoweth their meaning? Who shall divine the ideas that sought linear expression in these shapings? Within was a heavenly spirit, and it attempted to picture forth itself, even as the terrestrial father had been shaping forth the images of his own spirit on the same page. Look at the beginnings! Behold the imitative strokes! These were *letters*, the Spirit's letters. They were types of ideas; and doubtless the mind had within it, while delineating them, a glad sense of fellow-feeling, a temporary equality, a self-complacent skillfulness in the divine art of shaping forth the soul in emblems.

And the spiritual instinct was here also, for these marks were made while the father was absent. The pen was seized when no eye save the Spirit's beheld it; and suddenly was it dropped when the parental eye surprised it, the eye that visioneth to the little one the ideal of responsibility. And here had been no permission to write!

January 6

There is indeed but one way of exhibiting spiritual truths in their unity and symmetry, and that is in their connections with and operations through the events to which they give external life and shaping. These events are indeed the exhibition, the expression, the form, of the truths and principles that flow into and fill them with meaning. . . . What is Revelation but the manifestation of the Spirit in and through Matter — an enacting on the arena of the external world of the Spirit's internal energies? Life is a perpetual Revelation of the Infinite, Invisible One. The undying Life is ever throbbing in the soul of Man, and investing him with the immortality which is its essential being. Man lives and is from God. He is, as it were, the fast-flitting pulse of the Divinity. Say, rather, that in his fleshly heart the Universal Spirit throbbeth; and his life is summed up and numbered by the pulsations that stir within this central member.

[1] The childish scrawls that interlace with the manuscript of the preceding paragraph have a meaning only to the eye of faith, but there is no difficulty in distinguishing the graceful curves drawn by the elder daughter, Anna, from the energetic and crabbed backhand of Louisa, who was at this time two years and two months old. Probably the page represents Louisa's first attempt at writing. If so, she chose a remarkably appropriate context for her maiden effort.

And here, in this corporeal vesture, doth the Spirit first incarnate itself and display its subtle plyings. From this, as from a fount, doth the Infinite gush forth into the light of Life. Behold the first shaping in the maternal womb, where the humanity of the soul is assumed and the flesh made the heir of immortality by a spiritual affection. Go, ye who would have faith in the soul of man; go and study the miracle of conception and birth, even as thou beholdest it in thine own species — for there thou hast its most perfect type!

January 13

After an interesting day in my school and a period of meditation yesterday, devoted to the inner life, I walked with Miss P[eabody] to Cambridgeport to see Mr. Allston the artist, a man whom I had long wished to see. We reached his house at an early hour, after dark, and remained with him till past 12 o'clock. Interesting subjects were discussed: art, conception and execution, Canova (whom he conceived to be a man of talent, not of genius), Coleridge, Wordsworth — and, as collateral topics, Hazlitt, Lamb, Northcote, Mrs. Siddons, Miss Kemble, Matthews, Disraeli, etc.

I was particularly impressed with the uncommon artlessness and modesty of this man of genius — a man of higher endowments and skill in the art of painting than, perhaps, any other individual in our country. I felt myself in the presence of a superior spirit — an external shaping of the higher traits of the human soul. The power of genius was there.

Mr. Allston was an intimate friend of Coleridge.[2] He saw much of him while he resided in London, and travelled with him on the Continent. They passed six months together in Rome. Mr. A's conception of Coleridge's character and genius is of the most exalted nature. He speaks of him as being versed in all things and as wanting nothing in original endowments. If there was any absence of power in any one faculty of his spirit, it was in that of humour — deep, broad humour, the usual property of the Eng-

[2] This conversation took place when Coleridge had been dead less than six months. It was of utmost interest and value to Alcott because Washington Allston was the only man he ever knew who had been closely associated with the chief of his own modern masters.

lish mind. In this there might be a slight defect; but he had, he said, "more wit, genuine wit, than any other ten men in England."

One fact concerning Coleridge was to me deeply interesting, and the phenomenon might have been looked for from a spirit like that of Coleridge. It was this: he said that there could not be conceived a greater difference in the appearance of the countenance of Coleridge than during the times of conversation and of thought. When absorbed in meditation "the outward man," to use his expression, "seemed to be a corpse. The eyes were inverted, as it were, and turned inward; the under lip fell, and the general expression of the countenance was that of idiocy, so entirely was the soul withdrawn from the external world and the animal functions. But the appearance of a friend, a stranger, a human being, seemed to awake him from this exterior sleep; the eyes radiated supernatural splendor, the mouth was full of meaning, and the whole countenance was, perhaps, more purely angelic than that of any modern living man. He gave us the idea of a seraph more fully than had been given in others."

Mr. Allston gave us several interesting anecdotes of Coleridge — imitated his manner of reciting his own poetry, as also that of Wordsworth, gave us an account of his Lectures on the English Poets, and entertained us highly by the intellectual character of his remarks.

January 21

I am more interested in the domestic and parental relations than I have been at any former period. Life is fuller of serene joy and steady purpose. I am happier, have more of the faith that reposes on Providence and the love that binds me to human nature, more of the assurance of progression, than I have been wont to enjoy. There is more unity in my life. Theory and practice are more harmoniously blended. The internal and external life constitute a whole to which thought, sentiment, and action form the parts.

My children are objects of great delight. They are both in health. Nature has given them good constitutions of body, fine endowments of mind, and the influences to which they have been subjected and the discipline pursued with them in their moral and spiritual culture has brought out their characters in interesting forms. They are indeed the charm of my domestic life. They keep alive and vivid the sentiment of humanity, and are living manifestations of the theories of my intellect; for they are the models of our common nature from whence these theories are in no small degree framed and delineated. So long as they move before me in the majestic dignity of human nature, unspoiled by dalliance with things, shall I have a strong bond to unite me to them, and in this union to find the tie that binds man to his race as well as to his Author. They are elements in the study of self — elements in the study of our nature — elements in the investigation of the Divinity that dwells within this nature. I know not how much the more spiritual I am from the parental relation, how much I have been indebted to them for the light that hath dawned upon my own mind from the radiance of their simple spirits. Certain it is that the more I associate with them in the simple ways that they love, the more do I see to revere, the profounder are my conceptions of our nature, the more glorious and solemn become the purposes and ends of its common destiny and the better do I appreciate the sentiment of Jesus, "of such is the Kingdom of Heaven."

Verily, had I not been called to associate with children . . . I should never have found the tranquil repose, the steady faith, the vivid hope, that now shed a glory and a dignity around the humble path of my life. Childhood hath saved me. Once did I wander a little way from the Kingdom of Heaven, but childhood's sweet and holy voice hath recalled me, and now I am one with them in this same Kingdom, a child redeemed.

January 29

I have become acquainted with but few persons since my return to this city. I have not sought acquaintance. From the character of my tastes and pursuits, I am necessarily denied extensive sympathy either in thought or purpose with the individuals whose acquaintance I might desire to obtain. . . . Yet society is nevertheless important as a means of quickening my own spirit. This influence I shall find with the few, and these I have seen already. . . . I have had interesting interviews with the following persons: Dr. Channing, Mr. Allston, Mr. Walker, Mr. Tuckerman, Waterston, Miss Peabody. I wish to know Mr. R. Emerson and Mr. Hedge.

February 5

This evening I heard Rev. Mr. Emerson give a lecture at the Temple on "The Character of M. Angelo." This is the second lecture of a course embracing biographical sketches of eminent men, before the S[ociety] for the Diffusion of Useful Knowledge. I did not hear the first lecture. Miss P. informs me that it was a beautiful one. The speaker took a general view of the theory of life and of the means to be used in order to realize it. Few men among us take nobler views of the mission, powers, and destinies of man than Mr. E. I hope the people of this city will go and learn of him the conditions of virtue and vision, by what self-denial, what exertion these are to be sought and won. The lives of the great and good are examples of this strife of the soul.

May 3

Spring now opens upon the eye. With its germinating life would I awake to thought. For a time I have been swallowed up in the outward and actual. Now I must revive the In-dwelling Life to find the fruition and repose suited to the ends of energetic and deep meditation, the philosophic life. In the new relations that now prospectively open upon me shall I find occasion and stimuli for the renewal of my essential being. Sensibility will, I trust, be quickened, faith revived, thought fructified, by the appearance of the young celestial whom I am soon to know — not as now prefigured by types of flesh but in its outward individual shaping.[3] If the Divinity wills, I shall soon behold the little one, a semblance and reduplication of myself and an image of the Infinite and Unshadowed One. Then do I hope to look on and see the on-going of the In-dwelling Life that ceaselessly enacteth itself in the spirit of the newly incarnated one, if perchance some

---

[3] Alcott is expecting the birth of his third child.

light may gleam upon my own spirit, not wholly rayless, and I may seize some apprehensions of the essential and co-ordinating powers of the soul.

June 24

At sunset this day a daughter [4] was born to us. She seems a very healthy child, is well formed. The mother is comfortable. . . . I shall now commence the Record of this newcomer, in connection with the lives of her sisters. I shall endeavour to give some representation to the inner life as it is enacted in the spirit of childhood. Such facts, phenomena, laws of the spiritual Kingdom, are the essential data of the spirit's history and the only materials of spiritual philosophy. . . .

Nothing can show itself in the exterior that has not a prior being and shaping within. We do not apprehend the spiritual kingdom by mere observation of external facts. We must enter within and find of what spiritual laws these phenomena are the exponents and signs. Infancy and childhood, yea, the life of every individual spirit, is the outraying of the inner life that first arrayeth its absolute will in the kingdom within. Except an adult be converted from the outward and his vision be turned inward to the life of the Spirit as it reveals itself in the consciousness of the little child yet in Spirit, he cannot apprehend the true life of humanity.

I would seek to become full of this consciousness. I would commune with God in the hearts of infancy and children — my own children, my pupils, the divine and unsoiled Child, even Jesus Christ, who ever remained in the Kingdom and Life of his Father, a beloved Son!

July (undated)

A few days since Mrs. Morrison came in town, bringing me letters from Mr. R[ussell]. She is still with us. Last evening she saw several of our friends — persons with whom we wished her to be made acquainted. Among these were the following: Mr. Waldo Emerson, Charles Emerson, Mr. and Mrs. Child, Mr.

[4] Elizabeth.

May, Miss Elizabeth and Mary Peabody, Mrs. Bliss, Miss M. Emerson, Miss E. Hoar, and others.[5]

July 29

Waiting is repose, that night of the soul without which it doth no miracles. For repose is faith perfected from watching, and all the spirit acts in this state.

Hence I go to the country. Hence do I seek the scenes of my early life, my birthplace, the imagery that gave form to my mind, the beings that first warmed my heart into love, the outward on which my young spirit first plied its powers and essayed to know itself. The air of my native hills will revive me. The fare that was wont to sustain me will send a quickening flow of life through my frame. Young life will come up in my memory. The emblem of myself in my little ones will aid me in self-interpretation. . . . I shall grow, and be able to measure their growth. They need my tendance. They suffer for the heart's fare — love, kindness, sympathy, air, water, nature's greenness, and the patience that never tireth.

July 31

I passed this morning looking at pictures. I visited the Athenæum, the American Gallery, the Diorama. It does one good to go into the presence of even the representations of life, whether material or human, as shadowed in the arts. To commune with beauty is the essential want of human nature. The child and the aged alike seek for its forms. . . .

At the Athenæum was nothing that called forth the deep and pure sentiments of the soul. Some portraits of men eminent among us for political talent, some landscapes by Fisher and Doughty, two or three paintings by the old masters, of common subjects,

[5] The date of this entry may have been the twelfth but was more probably the fifth of July. In later years Alcott referred to this "party" — held at his own rooms, 3 Somerset Court — as the occasion of his first meeting with Emerson. Mrs. Morrison was a friend from Philadelphia. Miss Elizabeth Hoar was at this time betrothed to Emerson's brother Charles, whose early death prevented their marriage. Mary Peabody was later the wife of Horace Mann, and Mrs. Bliss was to marry George Bancroft. Miss Mary Moody Emerson was the poet's famous and eccentric aunt. Lydia Maria Child was already well known as a novelist.

were all that attracted me particularly. At the Gallery there is nothing attractive, although the collection was purely the fruit of American genius and exhibited for the benefit of the artists.

How, indeed, is it possible for the arts to assume their place among a people all whose ideas serve to check and keep under the sense of the beautiful as an element of our nature, whose manifestation "profiteth nothing"? Between beauty and utility there is a close affinity, and both serve their purpose in the great ends of human culture; but we have denied this affiance, and cut ourselves off from the goods that the contemplation of beauty hath in store for us. We acknowledge one God, even the God of Utility, and ask, as the grand test of all our efforts, "of what use is it?" — confining the term "use" to the outward interests of life instead of lifting it to its true place in the soul. As well might we inquire of what use is the soul, for in truth we find no use for it in the practical theories of the time. The soul is in our way. . . .

Divest the outward scene of beauty, cease to represent this in the arts, call it not forth in the social and actual relations of human life, and of what use is this life? How doth the charm and the glory of life fade away! How doth man degrade himself to a drudge — a thing among things!

August 1

In the afternoon I attended a meeting at Julien Hall for the purpose of celebrating the emancipation of slaves throughout the English colonies, as this is the day when the act of the British Parliament giving freedom to the slaves goes into effect.

There were present Rev. Mr. May, D. L. Child, Esquire, and George Thompson,[6] as speakers. The audience was respectful, though somewhat limited in number, the hall not being filled. Several slave-holders were present, and indicated signs of violence. . . . After the dismissal of the meeting they were found standing at the passage to get a nearer glance at Mr. Thompson as he passed, perhaps to intimidate him and others. I took my stand near the door to watch their movements. Mr. May came down and passed by them. On seeing them standing in this sus-

[6] An English reformer and lecturer against slavery who was soon to be driven out of Boston by threats of violence.

picious manner, he, however, returned and passed by them, ascending the stairs. Meanwhile Mr. T.'s carriage had come to another passage-way, and Mr. T., having entered it, was driven off, leaving these disaffected men to go home without causing disturbance.

Before they left the door, however, one of them said to the by-standers: "We will give five hundred dollars for him in any one of the slave-holding States." I said "And what would you do with him?" "Do with him!" said he, with a look of mingled malignity and scorn, uttering at the same time an oath, "we would hang him!" "Sir," said another, "if we had him at Vicksburg we would bring Lynch's Law to bear upon him at once." With that they departed.

August 4

I wish I could write as I feel and think — as I sometimes converse even. Not that I have ever, in any one instance, practically realized my conception of expression in any one of these forms, but approached more nearly in these than with my pen. I do not practise writing enough to give readiness, ease, grace, clearness, strength, to my style. I live too much in the ideal, and commune so little with varied forms and images of things that I lack illustration. My thoughts take the forms of general propositions, maxims, ideal principles, so that when I come to arouse these and set them forth on paper, and look about for the common imagery and means of illustrating them, I have forgotten the facts and circumstances that suggested these ideas and cannot at once, or in a natural and simple manner, let these principles down to the details of fact, circumstance, common relations, in which they are intended to work and to which they are practically adapted. . . .

My thoughts do not easily flow out in popular terms. Intent on the inner life, seeking to represent it to myself mainly, having little communication with the popular mind whose associations and thoughts differ materially from my own, I come to the work of composition under great embarrassment. I have written heretofore for my own benefit. I have had myself mainly in view. That other presence, the public, has not come before me. I have lived in myself . . . so that I am unfitted for the general mind, intent as this is upon the outward and phenomenal rather than the inward and permanent. But I do not despair. Time will make me intelligible, and I shall not wholly misrepresent myself.

I have not lived long. I began late to live; and since I began to live I have lived fast. Thought and purpose have crowded upon me in swift and rapid succession. I have been engaged in the practical relations of life. Little leisure has been given me for continuous deep thought. The elements that have floated into my being from all quarters of the intellectual and spiritual kingdom have not as yet found their appropriate and fit place in my thoughts. The field of survey has been wide, and over some departments of it I have not as yet cast more than transient glances.

August 7

"Awaken!" — the sound lingers in my ear, and even as I write it comes back to me from the sounding bell that now announces the hour of twelve. Midnight! 'Tis a time fit to commune with such spirits as this, and this midnight bell is the fit tongue for such sublime and godlike strains.[7]

Let me rise and look forth upon the scene. The clouds that poured forth their burden all day long have passed away. A serene sky spreads its immeasurable azure over the earth. Before my vision rises the spire of the church, and down upon the housetops and the face of things falls a peaceful light. Quiet broods over the face of nature. All things lie as if in the arms of the protecting Spirit who sheds a serene and mildly radiating lustre upon her sleeping child from the face of the moon. Her nursling, the toiling, troublous world, is asleep. To the sons of sense the scenes of their toil and strife, of pleasure and gain, are closed; in the still life of unconsciousness are they lost, and for a brief and unmeasured moment they are ushered perchance into the presence of Divinity, in the imagery of dreams, those furloughs from the senses. . . . Sleep on, ye care-taking, pains-taking, body-and-

---

[7] Alcott has just been reading in Coleridge's *Essay on Method* a passage ending with the word "awaken." The following paragraphs, more or less affected by Coleridge's poem "Frost at Midnight," record a sort of communion with the spirit of the dead philosopher and poet.

thing-taking ones, and get all ye can from the life of the Ideal ere ye return to this scene of outward reality and show! Sleep; and bring with you, when ye come, some remembrance of what ye saw while in the absolute life of the Spirit.

But as I dwell here there comes from the distant scene a gleaming light, the beacon of the mariner, that lingers around our shores. In the dim distance I see its twinklings, and readily does it shape itself into the Ideal of my own hopes. For here in this confinement, looking forth upon the night, do I stand, and from the high casement image to myself the beacons of that haven where soon shall my spirit find repose from the storms of the sensible, visible scene. I sleep not. I image not, as others, my heart's life in dreams. The city, the harbor, are the images that lie before me, and over these doth my spirit go forth in the swift vision of the senses and find types of its hopes, its purposes, its ends.

Nor need I sleep to commune with the Ideal. All Nature is my Ideal. Life is an Ideal. Man, Providence, God, these live in my spirit, and they come to me during my waking moments and image fit life within my heart of hearts. When these die out let me die also. Nay, I have already died to the world and the flesh, and this is life to the spirit. . . . The glory of these shall never depart.

August 11

I dined with Dr. Channing and passed the afternoon with him.[8] The conversation turned on the following topics: Retribution, Government, Art, Education. On the principles of these we agreed. There was some slight difference as regards points of application in detail. Dr. Channing has less faith in education than I have, distrusts direct influences more than I do, and has much less confidence in the young mind than I have. His views on all these points grow out of his want of practical knowledge, however. Theoretically, he is full of faith. As a theologian and moralist his views are sound, beautiful, exalted. He wants a more thorough acquaintance with man, with children particularly, to perceive all their bearings and find that reliance on means by which

[8] At Channing's summer home in Newport, Rhode Island.

these are to be applied and diffused. I converse with him with great pleasure. His sincerity, his trust in human nature, his deep humility, are touching proofs of his wisdom. He lives too much alone to apprehend the practical operation of truth on humanity. . . . I derive faith, however, from his speculative views, in the improvement of man, and find confirmation in him of what I am purposing to effect. He encourages me.

August 28

I look back upon these pages whereon I have imaged some dim and imperfect signs of my spiritual and intellectual life, some emblematic hints of what I have been doing and designing, some notes that indicate where in the realm of space and time I lived and felt and thought and acted. As I read the written words the past comes up before me and I commune with my past self, my former states of thought. I trace the history of ideas from their embryon forms to their maturer shaping in my ideal and their consequent enaction in the outward circles of being. I live over myself. I resolve myself back into original elements. The great analysis, of which my outward being is the living image, is made known to me, and self-understanding is the fruit.

September 18

I am purposing to hold conversations with some of the thinking spirits of the time at my own rooms, on subjects connected with the nature and destiny of man. There are a few persons in this city . . . who have thought themselves free from the errors of tradition and education and who are ready to listen to views of human nature worthy its divine lineage and home. . . . An evening now and then spent in this way would serve to discipline my own mind in the art of expression. It would fit me for that dialectic use of my mind so important to the dispenser of moral truth. Socrates and Plato were fit representatives of this divine art. Jesus followed in their steps; or rather, the three, left to the simple promptings and intuitions of the Spirit, obeyed the instinct, and conversation — the simplest, the natural out-speaking of the soul — was the favorite medium of instruction to their docile disciples. The works of Plato are a splendid specimen of ideal Conversations, while those of Jesus in the Gospels are inimitable expressions of the real, familiar communion of the spirit of man with man. In such way is it that humanity is reached, and in this way will every philosophic teacher address his disciples. Other forms may be useful, but the living man in the presence of the living man, uttering the very thoughts and feelings of his inmost heart, bodying forth in his own acts and words the ideal within him, being in himself the truth that he announces — this is the form of address that can worthily give power and efficacy to truth. Speak truth rather than write it — or, if written, give it the life of the spoken, living word.[9]

September 19

The young heart pines and dies, or lingers out a morbid existence, when bereft of its needed sympathy. This sympathy my own children have not found to their full satisfaction. They are very susceptible, and need the more interest to be taken in their hearts' wants and aspirings. They require a deep and apprehending love, or their natures cannot flourish as will many children of a more hardy make. Their mother's health has excluded from them much of that earnest and deep-felt attention, that timely sympathy in their wants, upon which the tranquillity and temper of childhood depend. Morbid affections have gathered around their hearts. The ideal after which they have so long striven has not been attained to their hearts' content, and the struggle of the affections with obstacles has become a fixed association in their hearts, difficult to be erased. They want that tranquillity which springs from a nature in harmony with itself. Life is a sense of want, and the faith in the attainment of the satisfactions of these wants is dimmed; doubt has usurped the place of faith, and the spirit is thus left to mourn over its loss or to combat with imaginary as well as real evils, thus engendered by its loss of tranquillity.

I shall be able, I think, to relieve them and the mother by personal supervision. . . . To what nobler object can I devote myself than the restoration of my own flesh and spirit, in the lives of my little ones, to its pristine integrity, peace, and glory?

[9] This is the first clear statement in the Journals of that method of adult education to which Alcott gave the best years of his life.

September 20

Wouldst thou be a student of human nature? Place but a feeble faith in the records of the learned, in the volumes of the uninspired, but go into the kingdom of thine own heart. There is the library that never misinterpreteth. There is truth in its heavenly purity, set forth in thine own mother tongue, even in the sense of thine own veins. . . . All other volumes are valuable as thou readest this aright; for by this dost thou interpret all — even the Sacred Volume itself.

September 21

Every visible, conscious thing is a revelation of the invisible, spiritual Creator. Matter is a revelation of Mind, the flesh of the Spirit, the world of God. All growth, production, progress, are but stages of the spiritual Being. They denote the Spirit struggling to represent, reveal, shadow forth itself to the sense and reason of man. They are tests of his faith in the infinite, invisible, spiritual life that flows through and quickens all things and beings.

The various kingdoms of matter, with all their array of forms and stages of growth, maturity, decay, are but so many modifications of the spiritual kingdom, whose laws they obey and by whose unseen yet ever-sustaining energy they are kept in their individual condition and attain to their absolute consummation and place. They are emblems and significant types of the Divine Spirit in whom alone is absolute Being and Life, Growth, and Vitality. They reveal the Latent One.[10]

September 25

Mr. H. Tuckerman [11] gave me today the privilege of reading at the Athenæum, a privilege that I have sought since my return to Boston but sought hitherto in vain. I shall now have access to their extensive collection of works — to the periodicals domestic and foreign, to the many volumes over which I shall delight to turn

[10] Although it may have had an independent origin in Alcott's mind, the thought of this passage is closely related to the Swedenborgian — and age-old — doctrine of "Correspondences." Compare Emerson's *Nature*, Chapter IV.

[11] Henry T. Tuckerman (1813–1871), in later life an industrious author, who was at this time one of Alcott's closer acquaintances.

my eyes as leisure or interest may prompt. I shall be able to find what has been done in some departments of thought, although, as regards my own favorite topic, the authors are few and not all to be found in this collection. Indeed, the libraries of this country are shamefully deficient in metaphysical works. The Philadelphia Library, including the Loganian, has but a few of the standard works in this branch of human investigation. Now and then we find a volume has been given to these institutions of a profound nature, or has happened to come into the collection by accident almost. I doubt if there be a complete edition of the works of Plato in three-fourths of our college libraries. There is none in Philadelphia. The Boston Athenæum contains Taylor's translation, which I own. I have not seen the Cambridge Library.

September 26

All principle, truth, exists primarily in the abstract, the universal, the infinite, without limit, particularity, definiteness. To incarnate this truth, to bring it within the cognizance of the senses, to connect it with the flesh and blood, to find its shadow in the finite and particular, this is the purpose of life. Our original life is a spiritual, abstract, indefinite consciousness. The life of the senses, the sentiments, and the ideas, represents, re-shadows, revives, this same primal life in the concrete.

September 27

Coleridge's *Essays* [*sic*] *on Method* [12] are profound disquisitions based on the ground of the spiritual philosophy, of which he is the greatest and indeed almost the only representative among modern metaphysical thinkers. . . . They remind me of some of my earlier attempts to set forth the principles of human culture. . . . I was then a disciple of Experience, trying to bring my theories within the Baconian method of induction, and took the philosophy of Aristotle as the exponent of humanity while my heart was even then lingering around the theories of Plato without being conscious of it. A follower of Aristotle was I in theory, yet a true

---

[12] Coleridge's "Essay on the Science of Method," written for the *Encyclopædia Metropolitana*, was printed, not published, in 1818. The copy read by Alcott probably reached him through Dr. Channing.

Platonist in practice. Christianity had not found its philosophical interpretation at that time in my heart. Its spirit was striving for forms agreeable to the understanding. The heart's problems were seeking solution from the skill of the head. I was looking outward for the origin of the human powers, making more of phenomena than I ought, studying the concrete without a sense of the grounds to which this was indebted for its forms and continuance. It was Coleridge that lifted me out of this difficulty. The perusal of the *Aids to Reflection,* the *Friend,* the *Biographia Literaria,* at this time gave my mind a turn toward the spiritual. I was led deeper, to seek the ground even of experience, and found the elements of human consciousness not in the impressions of external nature but in the spontaneous life of Spirit itself, independent of experience in space and time. Thus was I released from the Philosophy of Sense. Since that time I have been steadily pursuing the light then let in upon me, and striving to apprehend, represent, and embody it not only in theory but practice. The lights of Aristotle, Plato, Bacon, bright and glorious as they are, have all been lost in the transcendent radiance of the Gospel of Jesus, who is the exponent of human nature and whose theory of Life and Being is a sublime synthesis of Infinite and Absolute.

September 30

I arise in the morning and one of the first sounds that meet my ear is that of my little one murmuring the spirit's melodies as she reposes on her mother's arm, with opened eyes and loving heart surveying the things of the outward scene and investing them in the glories of her inner life. Happy being! Ineffable Life! The heart's holiday, the time of serene untroubled joy when the spirit is in harmony with itself, with the infinite Life that flows through all its functions and conforms the outward world to its own perfection. Subtle, mysterious existence, the type and reality at once of the celestial, the unity of Being of which God is the living identity — a oneness with the Divinity, the pure spiritual life!

Verily, the Divine Life is alive in the infant's heart. All the manifestations are of a celestial type. They have no objects in the terrestrial. They are taken from the Spirit's land. They are apprehensions of its own infinitude through material instruments.

Wouldst thou behold beauty that comes not to thy sense amid the varied scenes of the outward world, purity that is not in the living forms of those with whom thou transacteth the business of life's busy scene, truth that no sophistry nor outward beguilement can perplex? Go thou and look into an infant's face, and say if thou hast that yet within thee which there beholdest. . . .

Look not into the world, oh parent, for the image of the Father. There it is dimmed, disfigured. But look into the radiant face of childhood ere earth hath left its traces upon it, and be blessed — nay, saved!

October 4

Let no one call Plato unintelligible. Let him not throw him aside as a vain and worthless dreamer; but let him look into his own soul, his own life, for the dimness of vision of which he complains in Plato. To the pure and truth-loving, to the universal genius, Plato is simple. A simple heart, a pure life, is the qualification necessary to read Plato, as well as a profound acquaintance with the human soul from the life of experience.

October 17

"In the Beginning was the Word (Revelation) and the word was with God (of the same nature) and the word was God" etc. — (It shows the very nature of God, or absolute Spirit, to reveal Himself perpetually.)

— I go to Concord this afternoon to see Rev. Mr. Emerson, one of the purest spiritualists of the day — *himself a revelation of the Divine Spirit,* an *"uttering Word."*

October 20

On Saturday afternoon I came to Concord with Mr. Bradford.[13] We reached the residence of Mr. Emerson after a ride of three hours. The evening was passed in very interesting conversation. On Sunday various interesting topics of an intellectual and spiritual character were resumed. On most subjects there was striking conformity of taste and opinion. We have much talk on the charac-

[13] George Partridge Bradford, 1807–1890, a Transcendentalist of high attainments and blameless life who was one of Emerson's most valued friends.

ter and life of Christ. On this there was some diversity of idea — more the effect, as I deem, of difference of association than of thought. Mr. E's fine literary taste is sometimes in the way of the clear and hearty acceptance of the spiritual. Carlyle is his ideal. His portrait I saw for the first time. I have not found a man in whose whole mind I felt more sympathy than in his. With Mrs. E. I was also much pleased. These two persons have and represent a new idea of life.

I have been quite interested in this visit. I have found a man who, with all his tastes for Grecian literature and philosophy, can apprehend something spiritual in Christianity. To him it is "not altogether foolishness," for he has the sense of the human, and the love and faith for the pure and the perfect in universal Man.

With his brother, Mr. C. Emerson, I had some interesting conversation. He has much of his brother's spirit. They are both scholarlike in their views and tastes, and yet the man is not lost in the scholar. I shall like to renew my acquaintance with them on fit occasions. To have a few such friends is the joy and content of life. In communion with such the spirit finds itself, and for the brief time of their presence forgets its independent life, being lost in the common being of humanity.

October 21

An abolition meeting is held in Washington street, a riot ensues, and William Lloyd Garrison is conveyed to prison by the city authorities to prevent his being injured.[14]

On returning from Concord I visit the gaol with my wife and see Garrison.

November 28

This morning my pupils celebrated my birthday at the school-room. As they had made the arrangements and were deeply interested in the festival, I sought to please them. — They assembled at the usual hour. At ten o'clock they crowned me with laurels — and Louisa, my little girl, being three years old. An address was then given in the name of the school by one of the pupils, at the

[14] Newspaper clipping.

end of which they presented me with a fine edition of *Paradise Lost*. I then gave them a short account of my life. Ending this, an Ode was pronounced by one of the little girls, and we then partook of some refreshment.

The whole gave much pleasure, and was significant of good will and wishes, as well as gratitude to me for my instruction.

December 2

On Saturday, Nov. 28, after the celebration of my birthday, I rode to Concord to see Mr. Emerson. Last evening I returned, having had a very pleasant time with him and his friends. I shall seek his face and favor as a precious delight of life.

While at Concord I saw Rev. Mr. Hedge [15] also. With him and Mr. E. I had some very interesting conversation. These men are the most earnest spiritualists [16] of the time. I found much in their ideas and purposes of like character with my own. — Time shall unfold what we may do for the good of humanity.

I was pleased to find so ready and sincere an apprehension of some of my own favorite theories from persons whom I could respect and who were without guile — persons whose culture places them on the Mount of Clear Vision and who know what they see. Rev. Mr. Goodwin of Concord and Dr. Ripley spoke encouragingly to me also. Mr. G., in his confidence in the theories of the "Record," has adopted some things in the discipline of his family. This is encouraging.

December 11

The act of arranging schemes of thought and action, both for myself and others, is just so much discipline and preparation for the great purposes of my being. To me a thought or an act becomes doubly significant and interesting when represented in a scheme and presented to my outward sense. A diagram, a scale, a synthetic

[15] Frederick Henry Hedge, 1805–1890. A poet, scholar, and Unitarian preacher — at this time settled in Bangor — he was one of the two or three prime movers in the Transcendental Movement.

[16] The word is here used in the most general sense. For the "Spiritualism" that sprang up in America about the year 1848 Alcott had no respect, seeing that its real tendency was materialistic.

view, in which parts are subordinated and stand in the relative
dependence to the whole, in which one's inner will is shown in
its outward act on the drama of time and space — this is like a new
phase of self.[17]

December 18

This afternoon I run my eye over the pages of Basil Mon-
tague's edition of the Works of Bacon. Splendid conceptions truly
are there — magnificent sentences emblematic of truth; yet all
is dry, without the greenness and life that one asks for in a philosopher of his pretensions, of his vast reputation. Why it is I cannot
tell, yet I do distrust Bacon. His method is taking, his genius commanding, yet neither gains my full faith. There seems to be something wanting. He reminds me of magnificent frameworks, but
there is wanting the life to animate, quicken, and illume. He never
touches the heart. He dots down truth on his immense map, but
you must animate the form and give her views. I should call him
a splendid topographer of knowledge, scarce a philosopher. He
methodizes life and spirit all away.[18]

December 20

Church-going: this enters not, as a necessary element, into my
plan of life. Neither is it an episode in my life's drama. I am not
conscious of growth from attendance on the preached Word.
Other minds do not affect my views of the spiritual truths of the
Bible. I find greater enjoyment in my own interpretations. Add
to this the little uninterrupted leisure that my profession leaves
me for self-retiring thought and meditative insight; and I feel
that I owe my own mind the duty of yielding up to its inner movements one day in seven. Why should I put it under the direction
of another? Why turn myself out-of-doors in order to let in
strangers? Why distrust myself so constantly as to give myself

[17] Alcott drew many of these diagrams, which he usually called "scales of
Being," in his Journals. The suggestion of them seems to have come from William Russell.

[18] Alcott was reluctant to abandon his early enthusiasm for Lord Bacon.
While still at Cheshire, in 1828, he had striven to interpret Bacon as a thinker
of idealistic tendency who had studied nature merely as the emblem of spirit.
The present note suggests that this effort had failed.

up to another — and that, too, on subjects upon which my own mind yearns for time to dwell in the quiet of self-seclusion? Why go to church to think — or rather, to have my thoughts put out of their natural sequence and growth, according to the wonted associations of my spirit?

Example. This is not to be set aside, truly. The worldly-minded may misapprehend the course of such a mind. They may pervert the intent of this home-study, this spirit-worship in the retirement of one's own mind. So will they all that the spiritual may do — even church-going itself. For this they explain according to their own intents — going for example's sake, for effect, rather than for personal improvement. Formality is to be avoided as well as indifference.

Besides, I have a service at my schoolroom. This takes out my morning hour, and to go regularly from this to church would indeed be, unless I mistake my soul's good greatly, a wanton waste of holy time. I should not spend my day as I ought. Conscience would not be satisfied. I should not be as well fitted for my duties as I am by a day of calm, serene, quiet self-retirement — communion with my own spirit as it is spontaneously led into itself by the force of the week's action and observation. . . . Truth alone warms me — original truth growing before me out of the spiritual stock. This is what I yearn after. Mere novelty of illustration, grace of delivery, eloquence of sentiment, unless the spontaneous outburst and embodiment of truth, are lost upon me. I feel myself despoiled of my time, tricked by show, glitter, by the sound and apeing of the oracle, without the Heaven-descended Word. I am not to away with such imposture, well meant as it is, and as good as the market affords.

It is not my duty, I cannot so regard it, to attend the churches. My own spirit preaches sounder doctrine than I there hear, and I must listen to its divine teachings. Not in contumelious distrust of the good results of the preached Word on society will I refrain from the temples, but in the deep conviction that the Lord appeareth to me more visibly in other courts, and that there am I to seek and find Him, worshipping in the holy temple of Self.

December 21

I set out from the wide ground of Spirit. This is; all else is its manifestation. Body is Spirit at its circumference. It denotes its confines to the external sense; it individualizes, defines Spirit, breaks the Unity into Multiplicity and places under the vision of man parts of the great Whole which, standing thus separate, can be taken in by the mind — too feeble to apprehend the whole at once and requiring all save an individual thing to be excluded at a single view. — Infinitude is too wide for man to take in. He is therefore permitted to take in portions and spread his vision over the wide circumference by little and little; and in these portions doth the Infinite shadow forth itself, God in all and all in God.[19]

[19] This is one of the clearest and most compact statements that Alcott ever made in writing of his main metaphysical idea.

DURING THE early months of this year Alcott was hard at work upon two abstruse manuscripts called "Breath of Childhood" and "Psyche," both based upon his observations of his own children. These became so involved in thought and expression that Emerson finally advised him not to publish them. Under the influence of Sylvester Graham, a physiologist then lecturing in Boston, Alcott continued his desultory reading of scientific books, primarily for the hints and symbols of metaphysical truth he expected to find in them. The success of his school began to wane. Miss Elizabeth Peabody, his assistant, left him, apparently because she had heard the talk of the town about his educational methods and ideas. Yet he published at his own expense the very "Conversations on the Gospels" that were the main cause of his declining prosperity. On September 19 the first meeting of the "Symposium," later known as the "Transcendental Club," was held at the home of George Ripley. Two weeks later it met at the home of Alcott, in Front Street.

1836

January (undated)

It does one good to see a man stand forth and declare the whole truth without reserve or compromise — and that, too, with an elegance worthy of the truth. Mr. Emerson is a man of a sincerer and purer, a holier and kindlier faith than most among us. He speaks worthily of human nature and despairs not, but hopes everything from its development. There is nothing narrow or sectarian about him. These lectures must do good. In them have been given elegant views of the Spiritual Philosophy. These are admirable heralds of Carlyle, who comes to visit us in the autumn.

February (*undated*)

I do not expect great light from any source, as I believe no revelation can be made to the consciousness of an individual through that of another. The intuition must come from the direct vision of the subject, without other intervention. Suggestions from other minds may, and often do, aid indirectly in the clear unfolding of truth, and he lacks docility and a wide comprehension who shall shut out these human facts, by any act of his will, from the vision of his mind. Every man's ideas, sentiments, senses, are individual revelations of the Infinite and Spiritual. United, these are the Revealed Will and Truth of God. But then, each sees only that which his own being displays to him, and shutteth his eye to the rest.

February (*undated*)

Rev. Mr. Emerson made me a pleasant visit on Monday evening and took with him, for criticizing, the Ms. copy of "Breath of Childhood," as I am desirous of obtaining the opinion of one so well qualified to judge of the merits of English composition. His opinion, frankly given, will be of great service to me. There is not among us a scholar of a richer taste.

March 5

Mr. Emerson returned my Ms. copy of the "Breath of Childhood" with suitable criticism on the style both of the thought and of expression. This I had asked him to do, and he has not disappointed me. He has given me some very valuable suggestions, by which I shall profit. He has pointed out some of my chief faults. He has spoken kindly and encouragingly of my thoughts and purposes, of my MSS.

I have found none before to aid me in this respect — have been left to find my own manner, to find my own style, to work unassisted by the voice of advice or of encouragement. It is pleasant to find that I have not wholly failed of success. My errors I feel to be within the grasp of my thought and purpose. I shall ultimately master them. Indeed, I seem to have mastered them already, by the consciousness of their existence and a clear apprehension of the direction in which they lie. As yet, I have written little or nothing with reference to the eyes of others or with a view to methodical statement. I have chiefly given myself full freedom of thought and imagery, striving only at the impulse of the moment, not reaching any presumed result or train of procedure. I have written to the mood of the time, inserting the various shades of thought, as they appeared to me from time to time, in all their variety of feature and connexion. I have never sat down to deliberate thought, to a considerate composition of a work. Of course what I have written has but a general unity, knit loosely together by the subtle threads of association felt only by myself. Hence the "mannerism" of which Mr. E. spoke. Hence the laconic phrases of the time. Hence the fitful glimmerings of an idea which is scarce matured, but dwelt upon to diffuseness.

March 11

I am now finding an interest in the phenomena of the external world. I have a desire to apprehend the laws of which these phenomena are the pledge and appearance. This embraces the science of physiology.[1] I have a dim yet assured instinct that these laws, when viewed from their true point in the vision of Spirit, will appear much more than has generally been supposed. Yes, I fancy that the hour is coming when all that moved in the mind of Jesus and prompted those sublime ideas on the soul's origin and immortality — that exposed nature and mastered its synthesis, that knew men and prescribed the healing of the human body as well as the soul — that all this shall come out as an actual distinct idea in the mind. I imagine that it will be possible, yea, certain, that the miracles, so called, wrought out by this faith in the spiritual and

[1] Alcott was following with keen interest, at this time, the lectures in Boston of the physiologist and dietician Sylvester Graham.

apprehension of the material, shall be made as common facts, the necessary and natural results of spiritual laws. The study of organs and functions will, I apprehend, become but another view of the Spirit's activity in body. Physiology is none other than the study of Spirit incarnate. We must wed the science of physiology and psychology, and from these shall spring the Divine Idea which, originally one in the mind of God, He saw fit to separate and spread throughout his twofold creation.

March 12

Spirit is the sublime architect of Nature, and man is the *chef d'œuvre* of its art. Spirit buildeth all things. Renovation is its working, and time is its work-day. Matter is the element upon which it works and with which, by an undetected skill, it forms to itself the Ideal which it hath preconceived. Yet the material is mortal. The arch giveth way, and man cannot cross the bridge of time. So Spirit restoreth and continually rebuildeth the bridge, that the terrestrial travellers may find footway over the stream on their way to the Country of Immortality. So Renovation repaireth the ravages of Decay and maketh the frail to be strong by her upholding, unfailing agency.

May 22

The universal Spirit floweth through every form of humanity, never losing its own essential life, yet assuming, to the external sense, every variety of manifestation without marring or fracturing the divine unity. The flesh continueth the same Blessed Spirit. Only in the forms there lieth our peculiar individuality. Family is but the name for a larger synthesis of spirits united by one common tie of the flesh — like the leaves and blossoms, the buds and flowers, that shoot forth from the same stem.

August 2

Mr. Waldo Emerson called upon me this morning, inviting me to accompany him to his residence in Concord. — I had a most interesting visit, returning on Wednesday. The character of Mr. E. rises as I view it narrowly. He is one of the few men, of whom his time is not worthy; yet by his genius may he make it more worthy of himself. He is now writing a book of a high intellectual character which he calls *Nature*. In beauty and finish of style he is unrivalled among American writers. There is also more philosophic depth than in any other writer. He is superior to Channing. I left with him "Psyche"[2] for criticism.

September 11

I have just finished reading *Nature*, by R. W. Emerson. It is a beautiful work. Mr. E. attempts to show the meaning of Nature to the minds of men. It is the production of a spiritualist, subordinating the visible and outward to the inward and invisible. Nature becomes a transparent emblem of the soul. Psyche animates and fills the earth and external things.

The book is small, scarce running to 100 pages, 12mo., but it is a gem throughout. I deem it the harbinger of an order of works given to the elucidation and establishment of the Spiritual. Mr. E. adverts, indirectly, to my "Psyche," now in his hands, in the work.[3]

September 19

This evening met our Symposeum[4] at Rev. Mr. Ripley's. Present were: Emerson, Hedge, Ripley, Brownson, Francis, Clarke, and myself. After discussing various topics connected with the opening of our purpose, we invited Dr. Channing, Dr.

[2] An elaborate and highly mystical composition of Alcott's which, partly because of Emerson's unfavorable opinion, was never published, although rewritten several times.

[3] This corroborates the assertion, often made and as often denied, that Alcott was the "Orphic Poet" mentioned in the fifth paragraph from the end of *Nature*. The existing manuscript of "Psyche" has no passages exactly corresponding to those which Emerson attributes to this "poet," although the thought and style of the paragraphs so attributed are Alcottian throughout. Emerson first saw "Psyche" only some five weeks before his book appeared, but he had seen an earlier version of it, called "Breath of Childhood," in the preceding February. What is perhaps more important, we know from his Journal entry of June 5, 1836, that he had just been reading Alcott's highly important Journal for 1835, in which the ideas of *Nature* are either expressed or clearly implied. Probably, however, Alcott's contribution to Emerson's first book was made not so much by any manuscript as by means of conversation.

[4] Alcott's regular spelling of the name of the loose organization later known as "The Transcendental Club."

Monday, September, 19

This evening met our Symposium, at
Rev. Mr. Ripley's. Present were, Emerson, Hedge,
Ripley, Brownson, Francis, Clarke and myself.
After discussing various topics connected with the
opening of our purpose, we invited D. Channing,
D. Walker, Mr. J. Phillips, Mr. Channing, Dr.
Frothingham, Mr. Dwight, and Bartol, to *join*
meet with us. and decided to meet *next* at my house,
on Monday Oct. 3.

Thus has our "Symposium" opened, and
we hope to see each other not seldom. During
the ensuing winter we may meet frequently.
What good may come to us, and to our people,
time must unfold.

Walker, Mr. J. Phillips, Mr. Channing, Dr. Frothingham, Mr. Dwight, and Bartol to join with us, and decided to meet next at my house on Monday, Oct. 3.

Thus has our "Symposeum" opened, and we hope to see each other not seldom. During the ensuing winter we may meet frequently. What good may come to us and to our people time must unfold.

October 3

This afternoon being the time for the meeting of our Symposeum, several gentlemen met at my house. Emerson, Ripley, Brownson, Francis, Hedge, Clarke, and Bartol were present. The topic for consideration was "American Genius — the Causes which Hinder its Growth and Give Us no First-Rate Productions." The discussion was lively, well sustained, and interesting. Emerson gave us many good things, as usual.

Our next meeting is to be at Mr. Brownson's on Tuesday 18th. ult., in afternoon. Other gentlemen are then expected to join with us in the conversation — our subject, "Education of Humanity."

November 17

Mr. Emerson passed the afternoon and evening with me. We discussed various important topics. I read him my Preface and Introduction to the "Conversations," [5] in which he expressed pleasure, advising me to print the Introduction separate as a worthy view of my principles and views of education. He thought it would be useful as a document to pass to a friend who might be inquiring concerning the doctrines and principles of my School. I may print a few sheets for this purpose.

[5] *Conversations with Children on the Gospels.* The first volume was published early in 1837 and the second late in the same year.

{ 1837 }

A YEAR of calamity bravely borne. Under the attacks of various Boston newspapers, which did not stop short of personal abuse, the Temple School melted away. Alcott continued his Conversations on the Gospels with his few remaining pupils, and even published a second volume of them, based upon notes taken by Margaret Fuller. The public opinion of these Conversations, however, seems to have agreed with the view said to have been expressed by a Harvard professor, that one third of them was nonsense, one third was blasphemous, and the rest was obscene — the "obscenity" consisting of a few lines in which Alcott spoke with a beautifully simple reverence about the physiology of birth.

Popular feeling ran for a time so high that Alcott was hooted by the children in the streets and expected daily the sort of violence from the Boston mob to which his friend Garrison had recently been subjected. In April he moved into a cheaper house and sold both the furniture of his school and his private library. Emerson, Margaret Fuller, James Freeman Clarke, William Henry Furness of Philadelphia, and many others wrote in his defense, but could not save him from public obloquy or from a deep sense of at least temporary defeat. He felt that his best gift to the world, his power as a teacher of children, had been returned with revilings. In the midst of these troubles his friend George Ripley informed him that the preachers of the city regarded him as an interloper and that the teachers bore him no good will. One is not surprised, therefore, that Alcott was taken seriously ill, so that he wrote no word in his Journal for over two months.

But Alcott recovered his health at the seashore and at Emerson's house in Concord. He opened a new school, with six pupils, in the basement of the Masonic Temple. He received from J. P. Greaves, an English Transcendentalist, a most encouraging letter which showed that his influence was at work in England. At the end of the year some unknown friend sent him a purse of one hundred dollars.

In March of the following year Alcott wrote: "On looking over my Journals written during the last ten years, I find this of 1837 to contain more of my inner life than those of prior date." The reason is clear: adversity had once more thrust him back upon himself.

1837

January, Week III

The lecture of Mr. Emerson on Thursday evening of this week was on Religion. . . . The speaker always kindles a sublime sentiment when, in those deep and oracular undertones which he knows when and how to use, he speaks of the divine entities of all being. A solemn and supernatural awe creeps over one as the serene pathos of his manner and the unaffected earnestness of his bearing come upon the senses. Here, I think, lies Emerson's power. At long intervals of remark bordering almost on coarseness — now the tones that he weaves into his diction and the pictures of vulgar life that he draws with a Shakespearean boldness of delineation depicting farmers, tradesmen, beasts, vermin, the rabid mob, the courtesan, the under as well as the upper vulgar, and now sliding into all that is beautiful, refined, elegant, both in thought, speech, action, and vocation — he bursts upon the hearers in strains of thought and charm and diction that affect the soul by their bewildering loftiness and grandeur. The burlesque is, in a twinkling, transformed into the serious. The bold and sketchy outline becomes a deep and sublime idea. This is the poet's, not the logician's, power. His ideas are clothed in bold, sharp, natural images. He states, pictures, sketches, but does not reason. His appeal is through the imagination and the senses to the mind. He leaves things in the place in which Nature put them, never deranging that order for a special logical analysis. All his ideas come orbed and winged. Footed and creeping things stand in contrast to give them effect; nor do slime and puddles become insignificant or unworthy in his creation. They occupy their place, as in great nature, serving as types and contrasts to the clean and solid ground of ideas. Nature shines serenely through the calm depths of his soul, and leaves upon its unruffled surface the images of all her works. . . .

The day shall come when this man's genius shall shine beyond the circle of his own city and nation. He shall flash across the wide water and receive the homage of other peoples. Emerson is destined to be the high literary name of this age. Other men we have who chaffer in the nooks and corners of this wide sea, and whose wares are peddled in this place and that; but this man's genius is cosmopolitan, and shall be in demand wherever man has risen above the mere mechanics and utilities of life. A race of more worthy artists shall take the place of our present vulgar artisans, and clean and tasteful products shall spring from their labours. Our hawkers of letters and writers by brain-force shall yield to regal and honorable booksellers, and these shall be served by artists who know the spirit that is given them, and will not trade it in the market or profane it by vulgar toil.

And much do we need this purification of the temple of literature. Emerson's whip of small cords — delicate and subtle of speech, eloquent with truth — shall do somewhat to drive the buyers and sellers of slang and profanity from the sacred place, and the nation reap fruits of his honorable daring in a regenerate and tasteful literature, free from sordid interests, sectarian cant, and the shallowness of a godless philosophy.

Honorable-notion and sham-image killer is he! Up-turner of all time-worn and vulgar associations thickly strewn over the soil of our land, now all exposed to the light of day by his shining and driving share. Drive on thy team, young and hopeful artist, till not ever a stone or sod shall not have been presented in a new aspect and new relation to the radiant orb of day! Break up the old and effete ground, and sow lavishly the seeds of new and refreshing nature, that thus, in due time, a rich spiritual harvest may be gathered and garnered! [1]

January, Week IV

He that seeks not to affix things external to the soul, to subordinate the shows of nature to the Ideas of the Spirit, doeth nought. His life is a waste. "He liveth in a vain show and disquieteth himself in vain." To the soul are space and time given not as adding aught to its indwelling treasures, for it is richer and fuller than these phenomena, but to serve and honor it. Space is the soul's workshop, and Time is its work-day while incarnate and plying organic instruments. The soul humbles itself, takes upon itself the frail and finite flesh with all its infirmities; it descendeth from its high throne to lift matter into the light of its presence. . . .

Man is God conditioned, God subdivided from himself in order to look backward upon himself. He that doth not believe himself a God hath lost all sense, all remembrance of his Father. He is an outcast from the paternal mansion, an orphan and forlorn. He is not, as was the tender and loving Jesus, identified with the Father, and hath no consciousness of his immortal relation. He dieth, in his thought, when his body deserts him. He maketh the body, indeed, himself. He liveth in matter. He is matter, for the idea of the Spirit hath quite died out of him — and when that which his mind knoweth vanisheth, what has he to hold his nature?

In this idolatrous state are most men of our time. The man shall be stoned even now that shall utter what Jesus of Nazareth uttered two millenniums ago — who shall declare in full faith that "I and my Father are one," who "maketh himself equal with God." Verily, life is yet a mystery to the many. The divine words

---

[1] Written before Emerson's fame began, this passage shows the same prophetic insight that one finds in Alcott's early portraits of Thoreau and Whitman. Alcott wrote the first thoughtful estimates of each of these three men, and in each instance he anticipated the main conclusions of later criticism.

of Jesus are yet sealed words; and he that interprets them in their true spirit is a blasphemer, and men would stone him with obloquy.

February, Week VIII

A great good is always done to a man when he shall be led to distrust the truth of the opinions and the fitness of the age in which he lives. Men should fight against their own age, inasmuch as the work which they have to do is always in it, and whatever of honorable name they shall obtain, of lasting good which they shall effect for their race, is to be achieved by overcoming the evils of their time. A man's work is always in the present, and whether he shall live thereafter and become a part of all time depends on the fact of his knowing his age and marrying all that is best and worthy in it with all other time — and this he cannot do save by reforming the evils peculiar to it, and thus revealing the eternal truths and principles which these overlie and obscure.

February, Week VIII

Sadly did I hear of the distrust with which Dr. Channing regarded my Friday Evening Conversations.[2] Is it not unworthy of him? Whence this pusillanimity of mind in one whom the nations deem the brave and bold defender of sacred truth? Truly might I pause, were I not assured by an instinct more authentic than another's, however wise, that my doctrine is from heaven; and that, with my friend and brother, even Jesus, I am a meek and simple follower of the Divine Word within, which I must announce and interpret in the face of all obstacles. I must and shall speak as I feel. I shall preach the Gospel as it is revealed to my own soul. By so doing I but exert the right of my nature. If this Gospel be at variance with popular views, mine be the glory of braving that all-dominating force, and of showing other and worthier doctrines to the sense of my kind.

[2] These first regularly held conversations of Alcott's were conducted by him at the Temple, in Boston, during the winter of 1837, at first for the teachers of the Chauncy Street Church Sunday School but later for parents and for all who cared to attend.

February, Week IX

Dr. Channing's efforts have been put forth to good purpose on many occasions — always, however, by way of quieting and allaying. He never makes an Idea; but, after these have begun to work and have put the public mind into action, then does he give his assent to them — usually, however, with so much compromise and timid modification, lest he should stir up the fears and passions of conservatives, that much of their good effect is lost. Dr. Channing always has the last word to say, never the first. Hence he gets the credit of wisdom which belongs of right to those who have set this wisdom afloat in a community, and opened the eyes of men.

March, Week X

After an absence of a long time, I called on Dr. Channing. I spent Monday evening of this week with him. But not satisfactorily. He does not touch on the highest subjects. He plays about them. I want to come at principles. I want to get his view on the creative nature of things. Yet he puts me off with common-places. Does he rate my intellect at so low a measure as to fear that he shall overpower it if he touches on these? Or does he fear to differ, and thinks the time better spent in small-talk? Or does he so mistake my genius as to fall on those subjects most alien to it? I think the latter. We scarce ever find each other. He sets up a man of straw and fights against it.

March, Week XII

I spent Tuesday evening of this week with Dr. Channing. We conversed mostly on the connexion of the Divine and Human Nature. I attempted to show the identity of the human soul, in its diviner action, with God. At this he expressed great dislike, even horror. He felt that doctrines of this character undermined the very foundations of virtue, confounded the nature of good and evil, destroyed human responsibility, and demolished free will. Singular perceptions this man has. He seems unable to take the views of another; and, though professedly free and declaring the doctrines of freedom, he binds himself to an imperfect creed and denies to others the assumption of views contrary to his own.

Least of all does he comprehend the scope and amplitude of my views. He does not know me. He distrusts me. He may — I think he does — appreciate my aims; he respects my intentions, approves my purpose; but he does not do me justice as regards intellectual endowments. . . . He is a disciple of the understanding, despite his professed reverence for the reason and spirit. He is not disenthralled from the slavery of sense and the visible. He asks demonstrations, where self-affirmation declares the truth to a nature in harmony with itself. He came too early to be the clear and lucid seer of the spiritual domain. . . . He cautions me as if I were a rash and sense-driven youth, liable to dash my brains against the dogmas and formulas I encounter. He fears for me.

I told him this evening that a good purpose, sustained by purity of life, always supplied the wisdom and the skill to carry its purposes through every conflict with the powers that be. Virtue endows the intellect with wisdom, and wisdom is valorous. It heeds not dogmas or conventions. It drives over their ruins to its own divine end.

March, Week XII

A notice of the *Conversations on the Gospels* appeared in the *Daily Advertiser* from the pen of the editor this week. . . . It is quite as favorable as I anticipated. It is the mere echo of the gossiping tribe among us. — As regards the book, I have nothing to say. The criticism is well enough. But the editor has stepped out of his way to comment on my school, of which the Conversations give but an imperfect sketch, and from which no fair inference can be drawn as to the results of culture aimed at by its exercises. . . .

Emerson wrote me a letter at the close of the week in which he speaks of the notice of my enterprise in the *Advertiser*. He says:

I have written him today, and enclosed a plain paragraph such as I thought he could and would print on Monday; but I do not know.[3] I hate

---

[3] Nathan Hale, the editor of the *Daily Advertiser*, did, in fact, refuse to print Emerson's mild letter of expostulation against the treatment Alcott's book had received.

to have all the little dogs barking at you, for you have something better to do than to attend to them. But every beast must do after its kind, and why not these? And you will hold by yourself and perfectly forget them. Whatever you do at school, pray let not the pen halt, for that must be your last and longest lever to lift the world withal. You are so deeply grounded in God that I shall not fear for any loss of faith in your ends by opposition; but I do not want these people to hurt the school for the moment. But you will bide your time, and, with views so large and secular, can better afford to wait than other men.

— the first sympathy that has stolen on my ear from the desolate and doubting present. Only Emerson, of this age, knows me, of all that I have found. Well; one man, *one very man through and through!* Many are they who live and die alone, known only to their survivors of an after-century.

April, Week XV

Amidst the clamor and misapprehension that rings round me, sounding forth even from the children in the streets, it is gratifying to receive from one friend words and sentiments of approval and confidence. Emerson, in a note accompanying the preceding sheets of this record,[4] says:

> Very soon after writing these acknowledgements of confidence and hope, your faith and patience have been exercised. I never regretted more than in this case my own helplessness in all practical contingencies. For a knowing and efficient friend can do a man with a mob a better service than he himself. But I was created a seeing eye and not a useful hand. When the hard times have passed away, presently, people will not be so sour and peevish, and reason will be justified of all her children.

It is much to have the vision of the seeing eye. Did most men possess this, the useful hand would be empowered with new dexterity also. Emerson sees me, knows me, and, more than all others, helps me — not by noisy praise, not by vain appeals to interest and passion, but by turning the eyes of others to my stand in reason and things.

[4] That is, of the Journal for 1837.

April, Week XV

This has been a week of few incidents, but of sober reflection. An unusual degree of excitement has pervaded this metropolis regarding my book. I have been severely censured. I have come by friends to my enterprize who respect my character for the publication of this work. At one time the excitement threatened a mob. The plan was to make the assault at one of my Friday evening Conversations. But no such outrage was attempted, and the minds of the disaffected are now settling into quietude.

Such a state of feeling calls for serious reflection. I have, of course, been much exercised in this way. What my future movements shall be, time must decide. At present, I see not my way. The only course which, as a man of honor and dignity, I can pursue is to preserve unbroken silence on this subject, inasmuch as I have committed no offence nor stepped from the line of my duty.

April, Week XVI

Though my mind has been deeply and earnestly intent on the aspects of the time during this week, I have committed but few thoughts or accounts of circumstances to this paper. This is not the hour to record the permanent and real, while the sense looks forth on little save the apparent and tangible. Forms are now, instead of substance. Things overlie and shut out ideas. The popular soul is an idolater. I would not prostrate myself in this worship of the outward, but retire reverently within, and commune in quietude and silence with the divine forces of the common Being whereof all men are emanations.

April, Week XVII

Doth a man desire to be alone in this wide domain of the terrestrial? Doth he wish to shut himself from the approaches of his kind, and bear a solitary nature on the earth? Then shall he do this on one condition: let him reflect! Let him commune with his own Soul! So shall he outstrip and outlive the race of his contemporaries, and find companionship with the great and wise of bygone centuries as the reward of his toil. Thought severs a man from his age. It beggars him of sympathy, to enrich him with the friendship of all prior intellects. It unfits him for falling in with the notions of his time. It lifts him from the dust and smoke of the present action and interests into the clear and untroubled vision of the future.

April, Week XVII

On Tuesday evening of this week I heard Mr. Emerson repeat his lecture on "Manners," at the Warren Street Chapel. I had a few words with him after the lecture. He thinks that my medium of success to the public must be made through the pen rather than by practical action. He values my professional labours somewhat lower than most of my friends. Herein, I think, he errs; while as a writer he over-estimates my ability. Yet I find more sympathy with him than with other of my contemporaries. His apprehension of my genius and labours is more just and generous, and his friendship springs from worthier qualities of my nature and has more heartiness in it.

May, Week XVIII

I took a short walk with Mr. Ripley [5] during this week. I am pleased to find him so cordial. He seems to enter the movements of the time with not a little of interest and intelligence. Of the ministers of this city he is, perhaps, the most in favor of fair and free discussion. He tells me that his brethren have been considering the subject of freedom of discussion at their weekly meetings during their last two sittings, and that they have been led to it by the manner in which my book has been spoken of, and my enterprise, in the public prints. From him I learn that these gentlemen, with a few exceptions, regard me as an interloper into the theological field, and deem this a fit occasion to make their sentiments known. They do not countenance my speculations, nor look with friendly eyes on my enterprise. Besides this, the teachers of public schools in this city, owing to the freedom of remarks in which I indulge or to the present state of education among us, owe me no good will, and here a favorable moment has come for a movement

[5] The Reverend George Ripley, a prominent member of the Transcendental Club and founder of the Brook Farm Community.

against me. There is already a strong sentiment unfriendly to me and my purpose. But amidst this are most worthy and wise advocates of my principles and course. Neither the ministers nor the teachers, with their allies, can, I fancy, defeat my plans.

May, Week XIX

Among other things, in his letter of this week Emerson has the following:

In the few moments' broken conversation I had with you a fortnight ago, it seems to me you did not acquiesce at all in what is always my golden view for you, as for all men to whom God has given the "vision and faculty divine"; namely, that one day you would leave the impracticable world to wag on its own way, and sit apart and write your oracles for its behoof. Write! Let them hear or let them forbear; the written word abides, until slowly and unexpectedly and in widely sundered places it has created its own church. And my love and confidence in that silent Muse is such that, in circumstances in which I can easily conceive myself placed, I should prefer some manual or quite mechanical labour as a means of living that should leave me a few sacred hours in the twenty-four, to any attempts to realize my idea in any existing forms called intellectual or spiritual, where, by defying every settled usage of society, I should be sure to sour my own temper.

My friend sympathizes more intensely in my speculative than in my practical genius.[6] I would fain give my powers fit exercise in each of these modes of action. I would realize and embody my idea as fully as my time shall suffer. Still it may be that the speculative more than the practical element preponderates in me, and that it were wiser to obey my friend. Time shall decide for me.

May, Week XX

I spent a few days with Mr. Emerson at his own house in Concord. . . . Little difference of opinion seemed to exist between us. The means and method of communication with the age were the chief points of difference. Emerson, true to his genius, favors written works. He holds men and things at a distance, pleases

---

[6] Alcott usually means little more by this word than *individuality* or *idiosyncrasy*. He believed and said that all persons have "genius" of some sort, at least in childhood.

himself with using them for his own benefit and as means of gathering materials for his works. He does not believe in the actual. His sympathies are all intellectual. He persuades me to leave the actual, devote myself to the speculative, and embody my thoughts in written works. . . .

Emerson idealizes all things. This idealized picture is the true and real one to him. All else is nought. Even persons are thus idealized, and his interest in them and their influence over him exists no longer than this conformity appears in his imagination. Beauty, beauty — this it is that charms him. But beauty has pure and delicate tastes, and hence all that mars or displeases this sense, with however much of truth or of interest it may be associated, is of no interest to his mind. Emerson seeks the beauty of truth: it is not so much a quest of truth in itself as the beauty thereof; not so much the desire of being holy and true as of setting forth in fit and graceful terms the beauty of truth and holiness. With him, all men and things have a beauty; but this is the result of his point of vision, and often falls wide of the actual truth. To give pleasure more than to impart truth is his mission. What is beautiful in man, nature, or art — this he apprehends, and with the poet's power sets forth.

His genius is high and commanding. He will do honour to his age. As a man, however, this visit has somewhat modified my former notions of him. He seems not to be fully in earnest. He writes and speaks for effect. Fame stands before him as a dazzling award, and he holds himself somewhat too proudly, nor seeks the humble and sincere regard of his race. His life has been one of opportunity, and he has sought to realize in it more of the accomplished scholar than the perfect man. — A great intellect, refined by elegant study, rather than a divine life radiant with the beauty of truth and holiness. He is an eye more than a heart, an intellect more than a soul.

May, Week XXI

I wrote a letter to Emerson, apprising him of the proposed meeting of like minds,[7] on Monday next, at Rev. Mr. Ripley's.

[7] The group known, at first, as "The Symposium," and later as "The Transcendental Club."

These meetings, given to conversation on topics of high moment, were deemed quite profitable as well as interesting when last held, during the summer and autumn of 1836. We purpose to renew them. The following gentlemen are expected to attend:

1.	Rev. Mr. Ripley	8.	Rev. Mr. Dwight
2.	" " Hedge	9.	" " Bartol
3.	" " Emerson	10.	" " Robbins
4.	" " Brownson	11.	" " Stetson
5.	" " Francis	12.	" " Parker
6.	" " Furness	13.	" " Putnam
7.	" " Clarke	14.	(he [8] never came)

These gentlemen are all intent on advancing the honor and interests of humanity. They comprise the few among us that take higher and diviner views of the soul than men have been wont to take in past times. They incline to the spiritual doctrines, each taking his own view of subjects. We propose to meet and disclose to each other our views and purposes — to receive and impart light, if light we have among us to confer. I value this opportunity as one of benefit to myself. It puts me in possession of the current genius of the time, acquaints me with its cherished purposes and means of action, and thus brings my own mind in communion with its co-mates.

October, Week XXXIX

Quiddle, quiddle, on half-dozen souls, at No. 3, Temple.[9] To this am I doomed. And how soon the wise, in plenitude of wisdom, shall shine favor on outcast, time shall show, as ever. Perchance these shall grow suddenly generous, forgiving as venial the errors of its ill-fated child. Yet meanwhile here he is, in tub, with corn, rain, sunshine, lampshine, and fireshine. But how long these shall be vouchsafed oracle saith not. But instead omens of ill do appear. Tub saith: "Thou yieldest no rent, and standest in

[8] Probably Dr. Channing.

[9] The small and comparatively undesirable schoolroom to which Alcott had been reduced by the misfortunes of the preceding year. This passage is one of several in the Journal of 1837 that show the effects of a reading of *Sartor Resartus* — recently published in America by Emerson, two years before the first English edition in book form.

danger of ejectment, with all thy tublings." Cistern-cock saith: "Thou shalt not quench thirst, unworthy, for thou dost not pay for thy tank." Corn cleaves to hand of clutching seller, and crieth: "Not for thee, nor thine! Thou art a shirk, and showest no hard hand." Sun threatens to withhold his face, and saith: "I will honour thee with peep at barred window sometime soon." Fire smouldereth: "Thou art lazy, and dost not ply thy saw, or return aught to the woodman." While Lamp sayeth, flickeringly: "Shall I shine for thee, when thou fuelest me not? Destitute! thou hast naught available about thee." And so only Moonshine remains. And he taketh this as fit emblem, so sayeth the age, of his weak and leaden shine, and feedeth on so-called moonbeams.

October, Week XLI

W. L. Garrison

This gentleman spent an evening at my house during this week. I find, on more intimate acquaintance, a soul free, devout, intent on the melioration of human woes and eradication of human evils. He is not by any means narrowed in his views by any popular interest. He sees slavery in its true bearings. More than any other man among us he has exposed its evils and brought the subject before the mind of the nation. But he sees other great national evils, and would do somewhat for their removal. His soul needs wider scope than this now popular topic yields. He is too great and free a spirit for his party. They cannot apprehend the sweep of his spirit, and would cast him off. His political and theological views have already exposed him to the obloquy of politicians and priests. . . .

The day is not far distant when minds of creative genius, true lovers of humanity, shall associate for its regeneration. To this every sign of the times now points. Men intent on separate evils shall at last be led to the parent principle, which is to kill every abuse and usage and establish truth in the common mind.

October, Week XLII

Deepest wisdom is nearest. Not in the midst of the ages alone, but in the midst of every soul. Wouldst be wise, O man? Look then into thy soul, and thou shalt find wisdom — yea, more than did Plato or Jesus. For thus they waxed wise. So thou. Bring the ages into thy day. Behold eternity in it. Summon thy soul into thy presence. Is not a greater than Plato or Jesus before thee? Thou mayest know this: those thou can'st but fancy. Let thy instinct save thee.

November, Week XLIV

I call that man no wise Christian who belies the divinity of his nature by denying the identity of his soul with God. I deem his creed false to the spirit of his master's teachings. He ever declared the union of his own soul with God, and, as constantly, denied all superiority of nature above others. I pronounce the man that sees not this intimate and divine union yet destitute of the spirit of his master, and a vilifier of his holy religion. For this debases the eternity of the soul and the dignity of man's nature. I say that the Christian world is anti-Christ.

November, Week XLV

Thus, day by day, amidst this hour of small profit in the actual, do I live. Circumstances, age, do not favor such work as I have to do. Only, or chiefly, do I live in Idea. I order my life before mine own eyes and those of my household, but the age will not employ me. I am an Idea without hands. I find no body for my thought amidst the materials of this age. It denies me timber. What shall I do but content myself with my lot, and await in patience the hour when the age shall give work for my faculties and honor my art, supplying materials therefor — when souls shall be proffered instead of bodies, and I shall practice my art on these, moulding them into figures of beauty by wise discipline?

Complain not then, my genius. Thou shalt know thyself in fit time, and do thy deed before the ages. Ply well thy faculties. Thou mayest fit thyself by wise self-insight, by study of the time, for future toil when the age shall have reason to see thy purpose. This shall one day approach thee, now at a distance. Wait thou, and watch its tardy steps. Study its signs. Question it. Chide it.

Shame it. Preach to it. Prophecy against it. Call it by its true name. Sit in judgment on it. Note its usages, abuses, evils. Cry out against its institutions. Cast its destiny. Foretell its downfall. And open upon it the future time.

November, Week XLV

Let a thorough scholar — a man whose nature has not been stolen away by precedent of books, but who sees man ever above and of more value than the speech he employs — let such a man leave the conventional city, wherein nature, having profaned herself, is ashamed to acknowledge her misdeeds but sinks these out of hearing in speech, and visit a rural retreat of simple people. Let him mark their speech, observe their manners. Shall he not find himself again in the presence of his proper nature, of which the city had well-nigh bereft him?

These people put themselves into their speech. They do not hide their souls. Words are things with them. Their souls slide over their tongues. They are not hutched within and hidden from sight. And in this simple, free state of being their language is more true to nature. They speak it in greater purity than the artificial citizen or closeted bookworm. It is nearer to the soul, and the vocabulary of speech is wider at the same time that it is more faithful to the soul. I never hear a countryman speak without being reminded of the dignity of our common nature and the richness of our common tongue. He reminds me of Shakespeare. He has retained his epithets. Language appears in its simpler, worthier forms. He deals with its staples. Its great words slip from his tongue. The needs of the soul shine in his speech. His vocabulary is not shorn of woods, winds, waters, sky, toil, humanity. It hath a soul in it. Its images are of God's shaping. It deals in the product of nature, and shames art — save when she, like him, is faithful to the uses and ends of nature. I would rather study simple countryman amidst the scenes of nature, as dictionary of my native tongue, than commune with citizen amidst his conventions, or read with professor in college or hall, the tomes of a library. There is life and meaning in it. It is devoid of pretense. It is mother-tongue.

November, Week XLVII

Now I am visibly idle. My hand is without service. The age hath no work for me. I stand with folded arms, desirous of doing some service for soul; but the age hath nothing of that sort on hand. . . . Unheeded, I gaze on labourers around me. All hands, how busy! What noise of instruments! What roar of elements!

"Fool!" saith all the age, "didst thou think the soul, of which thou talkest and for which wouldst fain labour even unto death, hath aught like this? Thou speakest, mystically, of instincts, faculties, whose needs these arts shall never supply. Behold, all Nature labours and lends her stores to supply all needs."

And so I look; and, verily, the human soul doth herein belie itself. It hath spread out all its faculties into a brawny arm.

November, Week XLVII

This year has been one of trial.[10] It has been rich in discipline, and has done me good. I have been thrown upon my own resources, and have found these. My faculties have been sharpened for work. I have had much of self-insight, have learned the dignity of standing alone before my age. Experience thus precious I have cause to regard with thankfulness. Doubtless the year upon which I now enter shall be equally rich in means of self-discipline, and my faculties strengthened by the events through which it shall conduct me.

Save me, O ye destinies, from idleness, from tame and servile engagements, from compliance with the vulgar aims and pursuits of my age! Lift me above its low maxims, and make me a light shining amidst darkness!

So shall my year be one of blessing and reward.

[10] Alcott is writing on his birthday.

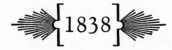

*H*AVING ONLY *three pupils remaining, Alcott closed his
Temple School in June; and although he opened another in
October, at his own house in Beach Street, he never again gave his
full strength to teaching. Emerson at this juncture proposed that
he should try to live by writing, but when Emerson himself decided that Alcott's most highly valued manuscript was unpublishable, "action" of some sort seemed the wiser course. To Alcott,
"action" meant reform, of the associational kind that Emerson did
not favor. The year is marked by an increasing interest not only
in such practical reformers as Garrison and Ripley but also in public conventions and committees. To eke out his meager income
Alcott began to depend upon the "Conversations" which he had
instituted some years before and was to continue for more than
forty years. The "Symposium" or "Transcendental Club" continued to be an important resource, and in October he was again
cheered by letters from England showing that the* Record of a
School *and the* Conversations on the Gospels *were preparing for
him there the audience he was denied in Boston. The storm of
public and official obloquy that broke over Emerson after the delivery, on July 15, of his Divinity School Address tended to bring
the two friends more closely together.*

1838

January, Week I

Emerson's doctrines I like in the main. . . . I think his view of the social relations faulty in this respect: men are too purely ideas with him. He makes affection an idea, and despoils it of its life. Men are uses, with him. Like Bacon, he slurs the affections. He loves his Ideals, and, because these have not actual life, contemns the men who live around him as unworthy.

This is the vice of his theory, but not of the generous, friendly theorist. He plays the seer alone in his theories, and will have no need of heart, while in life the fair and noble affections thereof belie his philosophy. The *man* will, by and by, find full acknowledgement in this.

January, Week II

No man lives more recluse than myself. Seldom do I spend an hour with a friend. Not often do I read a book. I am self-subsistent, yet not from choice. How often do I sigh for society, how do I yearn for sympathy, and have neither!

I suppose there is no possibility of such delights at present. My studies lead me aside from the thoroughfares of ordinary thought. My sympathies cluster around the ideal and withdraw me from the actual wherein most hearts beat and in which the thoughts of each are absorbed. Thus am I sundered from the society and sympathy of my kind, and am an exile, dwelling in the distant yet fairy lands of thought; and therein do I find but now and then a brother-exile to whom I can unbosom my soul without profanation and in simple faith. To most, my speech is unintelligible, and hath terms that have small currency in the markets and shops of the actual. . . .

In such predicament I hold society with my own thoughts. To refresh these, now and then I read some wise book, but have limited access to such. Valued authors, whose works served to cheer my solitude and quicken my faculties, I was compelled to dispose of last spring to meet demands of creditors. Then did I lose society of Plato, ever in company with Socrates and the wise Stagyrite; then did Taylor (Jeremy) turn his face from me, and other souls familiar with beings of faery, Spenser among the rest. — And living friends? Alas, of these how few! Emerson, single contemporary with me who seeth the same visions, haunteth the same tracts of faery, goeth and returneth, knoweth the passway to the Island of Beauty!

January, Week III

Emerson's faith in me is most grateful. The faith of the faithful is noblest testimony to the simple soul. His confidence in my purpose serves to confirm me in it the more. It is the testimony of one instinct as active in two souls, and establishes its verity. "I know of no man," said he to me, as we threaded the street that led to his lodging, "of diviner faith in the soul, or who, amidst every hindrance, stands as firmly by it as yourself. Abide by yourself and the world shall come round to you at last."

"Self-trust! Self-abiding!" — are not these the mighty fires that in all ages have overcome the world? Self-trust is, indeed, faith in the Mightiest. Self-abiding is obedience to the Perfect. Whoso trusts and abides shall mould all things to his will. This spirit is the pledge of the largest and fullest success. It is the genius of the reformer.

February, Week IX

Reading at the Athenæum, Emerson came in, and I had an agreeable interview with him in one of the upper rooms. He told me that the success of Carlyle's *French Revolution*, 800 copies of which are already sold (it was published at his risk, in friendship for the author) gave him liberty to publish in like manner my MS. volume.[1] I engaged to prepare it for the press and then submit it to his inspection, trusting to his judgment corrections which he may deem needful, and also the manner of bringing it before the public. He wishes to publish it at his own risk, dealing for me with the bookseller.

[1] "Psyche."

March, Week X

I considered some of the possibilities of my lot during this week. What was it possible for me to do, should I discontinue my school as I may find myself driven to do ere long?

Among others, the following was entertained as most feasible: retire with my family to some country town and receive a few children into my household as boarders and pupils. Concord seemed a desirable residence, as being near to Boston, healthful, and affording the society of my friend Mr. Emerson.

Such an arrangement, by placing the subjects of my instruction under my sole direction and discipline, while it would provide the means for my support — and this, too, under the most agreeable circumstances — would also enable me to demonstrate more fully than I can do by means of a day-school the doctrine of culture, which I would settle to the acceptance of the community. I should have the genial influences of rural life as coadjutors. My family would be placed under more agreeable relations, and the influence on my own mind would be improving, as also upon my health. I should have leisure for thought and writing, and the society of Mr. E. would be no small favour. I shall dwell on this plan, and see what days will make of it.

March, Week XIII

I feel a deeper interest in the doctrines of physiology as I become more familiar with them, and am assured that nothing is more needful to me, in illustration of my doctrines of soul, than the facts of physical science, wherein and whereby — as organ and function — this great all-pervading life manifests its wondrous laws. Physiology is the science of the soul working in its organs, and constitutes the language needful to denote the subtler facts of the science of psychology. I need knowledge of physics as means of setting forth the doctrines of the soul.

Nature concretes Soul. God publishes himself in facts, whether of the corporeal or spiritual world. These are his words. He composes his Gospel in facts. He reveals himself in faculties and organs, and the one is but instrument of the other. What is physical science but an illustration of the order, and statement of the laws, of spiritual science? What but the cypher in which soul is denoted in the forms of matter? What but a language by which soul is made palpable and obvious to the human senses? And hence the need of arming the intellect with such facts, as instruments of scientific demonstration. The poet, seer, philosopher, saint — each perceive the significance of such facts, and each, according to his faculty of insight, presents it to the same faculty in others of his race.

April, Week XVI

I had an interview with Rev. Geo. Ripley, editor of the *Philosophical Miscellanies*.[2] We have much talk on theology. He asked me for an explanation of my theory of God. This I gave as clearly as I could. In reply to my views he said that, so far as he could apprehend their character, they classed with the doctrines of atheism. They virtually denied the being of God. They abolished all else but the human soul. Nature, Providence, God, were nonentities. The soul was all. Yet he admitted that occasional statements of mine implied a belief in a superior Nature which found no place in my philosophical theory. The same was true, he said, of the views of Emerson as given forth in his lectures on Human Culture.

June, Week XXII

I spent three days with Emerson this week. We discussed various matters — among others my book,[3] parts of which I read to him and left the sheets for him to overlook and decide on their fitness for publication.

His theory of life is noble. He resides in the pleasant village of Concord. He gives his days to observation of nature — walking much, and recording his thought, when suggested, in his Commonplace, ready to use in his lectures. There he also sees his friends, and whatsoever of life or light shall chance come from interview with these supplies matter, also, for the Diary. Hence the freshness of all his discourses, taken as these are from life and nature.

[2] George Ripley had just brought out the first two of the fourteen volumes in his *Specimens of Foreign Standard Literature*. These two, consisting of his own translations from Cousin, Jouffroy, and Benjamin Constant, had the special title here given.

[3] "Psyche."

June, Week XXVI

Emerson returns my MS., with his criticisms thereon.[4] He points out the defect of the book, and seems disposed to have me withhold it from publication. I judge the counsel wise, and feel inclined at present to lay it aside, giving myself the rather to action, whereby I shall chance to ripen my faculties and enrich my genius for worthier composition at some future day. Why should I court the public but to stagger its faith and belie my own ideas? I deem silence, living, deeds, a fairer style of publication. And my ministry will, I hope, favor such purpose.

For the present, then, I will withhold these papers. I will act, and let thinking spring more directly from deeds.

I insert, in this place, the receipts of my school for the four years under consideration.

Receipts of	1834–5	$1794.00
"	1835–6	1649.00
"	1836–7	1395.00
"	1837–8	549.00
Receipts for 4 years		$5387.00

But my expenditures have exceeded by $5000 the receipts of this period, including the support of my family and the publishing of the *Conversations on the Gospels.*

September, Week XXXVIII

In the evening, I met at Lexington a large circle of persons for Conversation. The evening was given, chiefly, to the consideration of the subject of "Free-Will." Mr. Dwight, with a few others, joined in the Conversation. All present seemed interested in the discussion. I was invited to visit them again. This I purpose

[4] Emerson had seen at least two earlier manuscripts of "Psyche" (see entries for February, 1836 [undated] and for August 2, 1836), had offered to publish the work at his own expense, and had repeatedly urged Alcott to turn from teaching to authorship. The discovery that the manuscript was unpublishable must, therefore, have caused him some embarrassment. His comment dealt not with the faults of Alcott's thought but with those of his style, concerning which he said "Tis all stir and no go."

to do. I intend to hold courses of Conversations in several of the
adjacent towns during the coming autumn and winter, on the
"Theory and Practice of Self-Culture." This I can do, I fancy, to
advantage both to myself, and those who may patronize such purpose. Whatsoever shall be my employment in the city during the
day, I can meet evening circles in the villages and discuss with
them the doctrines of culture. Parents, teachers, youth would
enjoy such meetings. I deem this as the most direct and ready
means of quickening the mind of the people. I should gather all
the best minds in the village, and guide their thoughts to the
worthiest topics. This is to be my way, I think, of publishing
myself.

October, Week XL

Emerson passed an evening with me this week. He tells me that
he intends to resume his lectures, early in December, at the
Temple, giving ten or a dozen discourses, as usual, on his favorite
topics, thus disposing of the materials which he has gathered during
the spring and summer at his rural abode in the town of Concord.
Fresh and fair as the seasons which grew these idyls in the soul of
the poet must be their influence on those who shall hear them
delivered. Pieces of nature must they be. I shall watch with interest the favor these meet with from the people of this metropolis. If they draw an audience at all, it must be a choice one. Not
a little of moral courage will be needful in order to attend them,
so strong is the sentiment of the town against him. His Cambridge
address [5] has staggered the slender faith of many. Fashion has
declared against him. He has already paid the penalty of his
former popularity. His lectures will, of course, be honored by the
absence of coxcombs. Bigots will hold him as a profane person.
Only true souls who honor integrity and independence, who have
insight into principles, seeing through the shallowness of tradition's usages, will make show in his lecture room. His word will
try men. It will reveal the true from the false; the real from the
apparent. I doubt not that he will be sustained. All fair, noble,
free souls will appear. The age is not without such.

The enjoyment of his visit was somewhat marred by the in-

[5] The Divinity School Address, delivered July 15, 1838.

trusion of French magnetism and English phrenology. These came in during the evening, and must of course be entertained. And while he left at nine, these tarried until twelve o'clock. Any other evening rather than this. But patience! patience! I shall spend next Sunday with him, and then we will hold all such at bay, and this with all due civility.

October, Week XLI

I received during this time a communication with valuable books and pamphlets from Mr. Greaves [6] of London. He writes that he needs twelve copies of the *Conversations on the Gospels*, of which he speaks as "an invaluable work," and desires me to send him a dozen copies of Vol. III, deeming this already published according to advertisement in Vol. II. He also sends for a few copies of the *Record of a School*, 2nd Edition, and closes his letter by inviting "any instructions, admonitions, or divine sympathies that shall further the universal good." He delegates a gentleman by the name of Wm. Oldham to write in his behalf. There must be a circle of persons in London of free opinions with which one would like to become acquainted.

October, Week XLII

My theory of Conversation as the natural organ of communicating, mind with mind, appears more and more beautiful to me. It is the method of human culture. By it I come nearer the hearts of those whom I shall address than by any other means. I reach the facts of the case. I am placed thereby in the simplest relations. There is nothing arbitrary, nothing presuming. Conversation must be my organ of address to the public mind. . . .

Those works which have made the deepest impression on the human mind have been composed, in part at least, in this form. Socrates, in Plato, communicates his wisdom by means of dialogues. . . . The Gospels also confirm the same. Jesus was perfect master of the art of conversing. It was his chosen organ of communication with men. How perfect the specimens recorded by his biographers — especially by John!

[6] James Pierrepont Greaves, 1777–1842, founder of a Transcendental school in Surrey later known as Alcott House.

I would revive this lost art, and prove its primary place among the means of culture.

LIVING MEN

How rare are such men! I will write the names of every such man in our midst on this very sheet — yea, on this very page:

I. Emerson, Alcott, Brownson, [Bancroft],[7] Ripley, Hedge, Francis, Furness, Clarke, [Stetson], Dwight, Parker, Osgood, W. Channing,[8] [Robbins].

II. W. E. Channing, Dewey, Follen, Garrison, Walker.

These I deem the free men and the brave, by whom great principles are to be honoured amongst us. Class I are philosophical, and therefore more potent. Class II are practical, and therefore less efficient. The first apprehend things in their principles; the second, in details.

The men who are to give currency to new ideas that shall create a new literature for us, worthy of the soul, have yet scarce appeared. These are but the heralds of such master-minds. Emerson is the only man of the number who possesses creative genius, and in him more than any other are my hopes centered. His influence is already greater than that of any other man — or, if not wider, is deeper, and commands the best faculties amongst us. The young and growing minds are turned towards him. He is shaping their course in the fields of literature and philosophy, and the ideas which inspire his own soul shall waken theirs. He acts on the minds amongst us who are to do the thing. . . .

As to my share in this grand revision of thought and its expression in literature, time must show. I would write my word in and from the souls of the people, through the medium of Conversation, thus drawing truth from the facts of common experience rather than from the history of opinions as set forth in the systems of philosophers or creeds of theologians.

[7] The names of Bancroft, Stetson, and Robbins are crossed out in the manuscript.

[8] William Henry Channing (1810–1884), nephew of Dr. William Ellery Channing (1780–1842), who is named below.

October, Week XLII

An attempt is now making to foist upon us the superficial philosophy of France as the only authentic creed of the soul. Eclecticism is claimed to be its last, best word. The works of Cousin are studied as the modern gospel that is to illuminate the soul of our nation, breathing the breath of life into our literature, philosophy, theology, to revise all our institutions.

I deem this attempt unworthy of us. French thinking is not American thinking. Eclecticism is not deep enough for us. We ask a philosophy of life. We demand something more than a philosophy of criticism. We need an eye to read the facts of the present moment and in the light of our own life, not in the dim haze of opinions of those who have gone before us.

We too have eyes. To us the world and the soul and God are bared. We, as were the ancients, are in their presence. We too experience their life. We live in them. Not alone in the memory but in the life that we now live are these revealed to us. And we demand the right of seeing these face to face for ourselves, having put aside the spectacles of the past. We are not blind. Traditions, creeds, systems, are to us but as waymarks, footprints, that indicate the career of the soul in its past sojournings to the beatific land of Truth; as inns and havens wherein we are not to tarry save for a day and a night, not our goal.

History is useful to me no farther than I am conscious of the same facts in my own experience. It is in the light of these that I apprehend the facts of history. I am the highest, and therefore the only authentic, fact, that can legitimate the facts of all the Past. Erudition is not insight. It is not what I take upon my memory that sheds light into my soul, but what I see by self-intuition, that makes me wise. . . . All history is contemporaneous with my present life. It is a commentary on my experience. My light illuminates the darkness that antiquity may cast over it. I pierce this darkness, and see the same old eternal verities that once charmed the ancient world. I become a contemporary of truth, not of men. I am beyond the range of history. I antedate its records, which can only testify to the facts of which my own soul bore prior testimony.

November, Week XLV

I walked to Boston from Lexington on Sunday morning. It is quite refreshing to think on foot. The brisk circulation that walking promotes, and the vision of nature which presents fitting images for the thought as it rises in the soul, make the exercise vastly conducive to the highest ends of culture. The Peripatetic philosophers had facts in their favor. Body and soul were by this means quickened and envigorated to the fulfilment of the great ends of living and thinking. Amidst the scenes of nature, under the wide cope of heaven, treading erect the plane of earth, man finds all his faculties addressed. Thought at once seizes its images and reflects its face upon the soul. Study is perfect only when aided by the presence of nature. Without this the mind labours through the memory, and can do nothing more than evoke the ghosts of departed thoughts into its vision.

December, Week XLIX

EMERSON'S INTRODUCTORY LECTURE

This was a grand and inspiring statement of the primal facts of the soul.

The audience was choice. The truly worthy of the metropolis were present. Fashion was not there. Timid conservatism was not there. Bigotry did not show her face. Young men and women, yet rich in promise and hope, were there. The free, the bold, the seeking, docile, were there. Reverent faculties came to find devout exercise, and found such indeed.

I recognized every hopeful devout person of my acquaintance, whether youthful or of matured age, present at the lecture. It was a hopeful fact, in the history of thought amongst us, that so many were assembled on such an occasion. It was full of meaning.

December, Week L

I received a letter on Monday of this week from Jones Very of Salem, formerly Tutor in Greek at Harvard College — which institution he left, a few weeks since, being deemed insane by the Faculty. A few weeks ago he visited me. . . . He is a remarkable man. His influence at Cambridge on the best young men was very fine. His talents are of a high order. Some disquisitions of his on the genius and works of Shakespeare I am soon to read. They are said to be compositions of a pure and noble genius.

Is he insane? If so, there yet linger glimpses of wisdom in his memory. He is insane with God — diswitted in the contemplation of the holiness of Divinity. He distrusts intellect. He would have living in the concrete without the interposition of the meddling, analytic head. Curiosity he deems impious. He would have no one stop to account to himself for what he has done, deeming this hiatus of doing a suicidal act of the profane mind. Intellect, as intellect, he deems the author of all error. Living, not thinking, he regards as the worship meet for the soul. This is mysticism in its highest form. He is more of this spirit than my English correspondents, Greaves and Oldham.

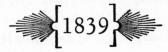

{1839}

*A*N ACTIVE *if not a busy year. Near Boston and at Scituate,*
where the summer was spent with Samuel J. May, Alcott
gave many Conversations. A plan to combine peddling with con-
versing was abandoned because the family thought it beneath his
dignity. Alcott saw much of Theodore Parker, whose future em-
inence he foretold, of Emerson, and of Margaret Fuller, with
whom he exchanged diaries. At a meeting of the Transcendental
Club in September he suggested the name of the future Dial, *using*
the title he sometimes gave to his own Journals. Many letters came
to him from England, and in November he was flatteringly re-
viewed in the London Monthly Magazine, *which attributed to him*
Emerson's Nature. *Following his recent determination to "act,"*
he attended the meetings of many reform societies and was prom-
inently present at the Chardon Street Chapel convention of the
Non-Resistants.

Beginning now the custom of rereading books already well
known to him, Alcott went through Coleridge for the third or
fourth time, read Goethe's Faust *and Carlyle's* Miscellanies,
Landor, Jakob Boehme, and the Gospels. He turned for the first
time to the Orient, and read Confucius. He meditated much on the
personality of Jesus, and gave a series of Conversations on Christi-
anity.

For once, Alcott was tired of teaching. The school did not prosper. In June the parents of several children asked him to dismiss a Negro child from his school; and this he refused to do. A few days later he found that he was teaching only five children: his own three daughters, the son of his friend William Russell, and the Negro child.

This year was another seedtime in Alcott's thought. His failure in teaching continued to thrust him inward. He spent much time on the Common, partly in order to think and partly to satisfy a renewed longing for nature. In March, when his external fortunes were at a low ebb, he wrote a long and admirable letter to his mother, calling himself "ever a Hoper." Most important was the rapid and extreme development of his focal idea that "Nature is the efflux of soul." After a month of hard thinking on this theme he visited Emerson, late in April, not for new ideas but for clarification. He was disappointed by the results, but refused to be drawn out of his own orbit — that of the intuitive and prophetic mind. He turned again to natural science for the clarification of spiritual law. This whole ferment of thought culminated in the firm self-dedication of June the ninth, and it produced, also, one of the more interesting of the Journals.

1839

January 5

The book for children which I would write kept haunting my thought all the while, during the morning, as I was engaged with my pupils.[1] Really the child has no primer. The young Soul has, heretofore, in all ages of the past, entered the mystic domain of literature through stripes and tears. The facts of his experience have, as yet, found no expression in literature; they have existed in the young bosom alone, and none save the child have been

[1] The book he was dreaming of was to be written by the most famous of his pupils — Louisa May Alcott.

privy to them. Youth has had but partial representation; maturity and age are the periods of the Soul which alone have been drawn out into some fullness, and portrayed with some accuracy.

January 8

The *Pilgrim's Progress* is a work of pure genius. Reading this evening a passage from it, my early childhood was revived in my memory with a freshness and reality that no ordinary mind could have caused. This book is one of the few that gave me to myself. It is associated with reality. It unites me with childhood, and seems to chronicle my Identity. How I was rapt in it! How gladly did I seat myself, after the day's labours on the farm, in the chimney niche, with the tallow candle in my hand, and pore over its enchanting pages until late in the night! That book was incorporated into the very substance of my youthful being. I thought and spoke through it. It was my most efficient teacher.

Walking one day, I remember, with a cousin of mine some five or six years older than myself, he carelessly slipped into a puddle of water in the way. So full of Bunyan's images was my fancy, that I said to him, calling him by name, "there you have fallen into the 'Sloth of Despond.'" I had read the book as without words; things and images had been before my mind's eye; *Sloth* was a word with whose meaning I was acquainted, *Slough* I had never heard, and had no dictionary, no person of my acquaintance to aid me; so I inferred the meanings from the connexion of the words in sentences. The book was, indeed, my dictionary. By it I learned the English tongue. The dialect in which it was written was quite analogous to that of the simple people of my native town.

I read this book many times during my early childhood. It is the first book, almost, that I remember having read. I did not possess a copy; but a cousin, living at a distance of four miles, had a splendid edition, with fine engravings . . . and often did I get it, and keep it long. And besides this, a neighbor had a copy of "Emblems," written by Bunyan,[2] which I often borrowed.

[2] Probably, *A Book for Boys and Girls: or Country Rhymes for Children*, 1686, in later editions entitled *Divine Emblems*.

January 13

. . . Last evening, just before going to bed, I happened to run over Emerson's critiques on my "Psyche"; and the effect was to make me despair, almost, of writing aught worthy of myself. It lamed me; it made me blind and dumb. I had music in my soul, but no voice. — Tonight, I feel quite encouraged. I shall sing one day. The influence of my own thoughts as they lived in me, at an earlier and possibly fresher period of my life, inspired me. I feel that I am not, at this time, in the relations most favorable to the exercise and growth of the best within me.

January 24

I collected Emerson's printed works for binding in one volume. I added to the collection some criticisms on them, which appeared in the public prints; with a paper of Robbins' also. These are the following.

1 — *Nature.* — 1836
2 — P.B.K. Oration at Cambridge, Aug. 1837
3 — Wm. Channing's Review of Address, Jan. 1838
4 — Address at Divinity College, July 1838
5 — Brownson's Review of Address, Oct. 1838
6 — Dartmouth Address, July 1838
7 — Brownson's Review of Address, 1839
8 — Robbins' Thoughts on Unity, Progress, and Government, April 1838 [3]

These I deem first fruits of a new literature. They are indigenous. Like a plant uprooted from its native soil, the earth yet cleaves to the roots. Nature and the Soul are conjoined. The images are American. The portrait is set in a frame of western oak.

January 27

. . . God is in procession, not progress. Man alone progresses. His life is efflux of God through his faculties.

The other evening I tried to state this sublime doctrine of the procession of the Godhead through the Soul, to some min-

---

[3] In a penciled footnote Alcott says that he has sent the above-named writings "to Mr. Greaves of London."

isters of the Gospel (so called) — the one a settled preacher, the other a student of theology. They made atheism of it! God was perfect, said they. "You make him imperfect, as man is. It is atheism. You have no God!"

These theologues knew of no other God save of tradition. They were not versed in the divine life of the Soul. They had read theology in books, not in men. — It is vain to make such apprehend the mystery of the Godhead.

I have lived in God, during the day. I cannot write out the insight of the hours.

January 29

The Conversation at Lynn, this evening, was well attended. Very was there. We had a splendid talk on Instinct. It was seen that on all the great occasions of life the Soul acted from instinct, and various instances from the corporeal, mental, and spiritual life, were enumerated, in illustration. We had deep insight into the Soul. Robbins, Very, and Brown had each fine statements to make.

I had much conversation with Very, both before and after the general talk. He passed the night at Robbins' with me. He is a remarkable phenomenon. He affects me as a spectre. His looks, tones, words, are all sepulchral. He is a voice from the tombs. He speaks as having once lived in the world amidst men and things, but of being now in the Spirit: time and space are not, save in memory. This idea modifies all his thoughts and expressions, and the thoughts and expressions of others also. It is difficult for those who do not apprehend the state of his Soul to converse with him. I find it quite possible, by translating his thoughts into my own vocabulary, mentally, and then, in turn, translating mine into his. By so doing, we talk with ease, and understand each other. His speech is Oriental. By putting modern life into Eastern images, speech becomes quite possible with him.

. . . We slept in the same apartment, and had much conversation after we retired to our chamber.

I think he will decease soon. He dies by slowly retreating from the senses, yet existing in them by memory, when men or things are obtruded upon his thought. Nature to him is as a charnel house, and the voices of men, echoes of the dead who haunt its dark chambers.[4]

January 30

. . . Emerson's lecture this evening was on Comedy. He stated the law of this fact. Halfness of utterance was its condition, which he illustrated by many apt instances.

This lecture again revealed his limits. It was instinct with wit but was destitute of humour. Both are necessary to comic effect. Wit is the contribution of the intellect, humour of the heart, to the production of the comic effect. Emerson has the first. The theory and the instances were perfect examples of its pure action, but the heart found no statement in the theory or instances. It was the sparkle of wit, cold and intellectual, without the genial quickening of effective humour. Men laughed most heartily, but there was no reverent, kindly feeling in the emotion.

February 2

My little circle was docile, gentle, diligent all the morning. They seemed to have begun anew, some mysterious force acting in their wills. I asked them, one by one, as they entered the room at nine, whether they had made resolutions to be faithful to conscience. With one exception (and that the child who refused to smite my hand yesterday) they answered in the affirmative.

This afternoon I gave to settling some bills, looking at books in the bookstores (a thing which I am apt to do), and writing Journal. — In the evening I read my Journal for the week to my wife. She thought some passages, particularly such as had reference to herself, were caricatures, and must come under the ban of her scissors some day.[5] I said that I wrote from my convictions,

---

[4] Jones Very did not, in fact, "decease" until 1880. The present vivid passage — so much more successful than any of Emerson's attempts to solve the enigma of Very's mind — has been published by F. B. Sanborn in his *Memoir* of Alcott, and, in part, by George Willis Cooke in his Introduction to the reprint of *The Dial*.

[5] This passage suggests a probable explanation of the fact that hundreds of pages have been cut — apparently with scissors — from the journals of this period. No reference to Mrs. Alcott, except the present one, is to be found in the journal for this week, but after the passage of February 5th, concerning the unfortunate experience at the butcher's, ten pages of manuscript have been torn out.

and what seemed to me plain fact. As she was party in the same life, I spoke of her in the simplest way whenever occasion seemed to require it. I hoped that I had done her no injustice. She was one of the facts to be noted in the history of my domestic life.

February 5

The butcher again took advantage of my simplicity this morning, at market. I asked for what I did not want, not speaking the dialect, nor having the air of the market. He, well knowing what I wanted, took me literally, saying, "You see what it is; this must be the piece you want, and here I will cut for you." So he cut me my flesh. Instinctively I felt that he was cheating me. But who can chaffer with Blood? He knew what I wanted well enough; but any revision of the carnal code of practice was above his morality. The piece was sent home, and forthwith I was sent for, from the schoolroom, to survey the strange flitch as it lay on the kitchen table. I knew this marketing to be a fool's errand for me, and could only plead guilty of not knowing one piece of flesh from another. And so by that I might not be used in this service more.

What have I to do with butchers? [6] Am I to go smelling about markets? Both are an offence to me. Death yawns at me as I walk up and down in this abode of skulls. Murder and blood are written on its stalls. Cruelty stares at me from the butcher's face. I tread amidst carcasses. I am in the presence of the slain. The death-set eyes of beasts peer at me and accuse me of belonging to the race of murderers. Quartered, disembowelled creatures on suspended hooks plead with me. I feel myself dispossessed of the divinity. I am a replenisher of grave yards. I prowl, amidst other unclean spirits and voracious demons, for my prey.

February 6

. . . I met a number of persons, chiefly strangers to me, at Mrs. S's in Chestnut St., after the lecture. How cheap a true and simple soul feels amidst fashionists! Such assemblies are an excellent provocative of self-complacency. I came home feeling strangely wise. The contrast exaggerated the fact. Excellent,

[6] From the year 1835 to the end of his life Alcott was strictly vegetarian in diet. He did not, however, as is often said, forbid the use of meat to his family.

sensible people were there; yet all seemed to pay a heartless worship to the God of Usage. I worshipped not as a true devotee. Emerson seemed to feel the embarrassment of the show; and after the claims of civility to the company were answered, took me aside, and we had conversation for an hour on our favorite topics, relieving the inanity of the scene.

I went with him to Mr. Adams, where he stops when in the city, and we had further conversation, chiefly on the Theory of Fable. I reached home before midnight — full of life and hope.

February 26

A single day's life in the Ideal makes this actual, when we come into it again, seem quite old and strange. Sunday I was in God. Descending to earth and entering again into the routine of daily toils, how old and alien they are! Last evening I walked out, for the first time since Saturday. Boston seemed as ancient as Herculaneum, and I walked its streets, familiar to me on Saturday, as if I had been absent from them a century or two, and innumerable events had transpired since I was last in them. So eventful are thoughts, and so timeless.

March 2

K——, a dapperling who treads 'Change and once lent me a round thousand during my days of prosperity in the Temple, besides sending me his children, came into the bookstore where I was reading this afternoon.

"How d'ye do?" said he, with an air of infinite good will.

"Quite well," said I, retaining the book in my hand.

"And how is your school?"

"I have none."

"But you have a few children, have you not?" inquired he, with apparent concern.

"Yes, a few children come daily to my house, but that does not give me a school."

"You will have more by and by. It takes time to get a-going."

"No; less before more. I must have parents before I can have children. My teaching is to them."

He began to look blank. "A man," I continued, "who swims

with the stream, shall, indeed, do well; but if, for conscience' sake, he turn and breast it, implying that it sets the wrong way, he is deemed 'foolhardy.' And if he ducks under and disappears it is 'just retribution' and 'best of all means of amendment.' Yet, see! he rises again, in his time, a lord of the wave, whose current he has turned in his own direction."

He had something to say to the bookseller, and I resumed my reading without selling my thought to the Mammon-King.

On such terms can you alone treat with those whose Gospel is of Profit and Loss, whose treasures are at the mercy of the winds and waves of popular feeling, and whose pilot is Custom.

March 13

I need the influences of Nature. The city does not whet my appetites and faculties. Life is got at too great an expenditure of labour. I know not how much I lose by this artificial style of living. This morning, at Lynn, I walked out before breakfasting and had a vivid experience of the bald ugliness of life in cities when thus contrasted with the fresh grace of existence amidst the scenes of nature. I felt guilty before the fair sun, genial earth, and envigorating air, and confessed to them. The light, blithe season of my boyhood and youth revived in my mind, and I seemed breathing the air of my native hills once more, treading their summits at morning's dawn, and looking again into the dignified manhood of my being, enjoying the foretaste of noble thoughts and magnanimous deeds.

March 17

The fore-face of my Janus is most vivid — as this letter implies:

Boston, March 17, 1839

Dear Mother:

It seemed good to behold your painstaking handwriting once more, and read that you and those about you were well and prosperous. It had been a long time since I had heard a word from you. I wrote you some time in October, I think, while you were with your children at the West, and Abba wrote you also, I believe. I wish I could come and sit with you in the "South Room" where so many studious hours have glided by me, and tell you what I have to say; but this cannot be now. Yet I fancy you sitting there in your easy-chair, decked in your cleanest, whitest Sunday cap, with spectacles well-polished, reading — or, more likely, talking about your children with P——, declaring that never mother had children so kind and good as yours, and wondering that it should be so. (For this good reason: that they have been loved and cherished by the kindest and best of mothers. This is clearest reason, and leaves no cause of wonder.) I hope you will come and prove us. In the midst of our destitution — and this can never be greater than when you were last with us — we will show the reality of our love; and this is all, to you. I should love dearly to have you with us again, and the children's pleasure would be unfeigned. In May or June our summer plans will be laid, and then we will let you know all about them.

I have a few children as pupils at present, but how long I shall have them is uncertain. They come daily to my house, and are with me from 9 till 12 and from 3 till 5. But I am living rather by talking than by my school, and shall be able by and by, I trust, to live by this entirely. I meet circles of thirty, forty, or more persons for ten or twelve evenings and hold Conversations on vital subjects with them. These circles I have in Boston and also in the neighboring towns. I think you would enjoy these meetings greatly, for you love talk as well as I do, and all of the Bronsons. Only think of your bashful silent boy, who could hardly look any one in the face, getting bold all at once and going about to talk and make talk! Is it not strange? — and as strange to me as to you, I dare say. But we know not what we are growing up for, and often do just the contrary from what we thought we should.

I am full of hope, as usual. The future looks bright and encouraging. As to money, I take no second thoughts about it. I have many friends, and am making more daily. It only needs for me to be faithful to my principles, to reap not bread nor shelter nor raiment alone but, what is better, a useful name and peace of mind. In a few years I shall reap what I have sown, and be above want. And this experience of penury, meanwhile, will have ministered to the productiveness of my harvest, will sweeten my bread, and be seen as a good, not an evil.

So you see I am still the same Hoper that I have always been. Hope crowned me while at the plow-tail, as I turned the furrows across the field-plots of my native hills; and Hope will irradiate my brow through the tombs. I fancy that I was quickened and born in hope; that Hope, in the kind and serene form of Mother, nursed me, rocked my cradle, and fed my youthful aspiration while seeking light and joy amidst the scenes of my native home. Those visits to the libraries of my townsmen; those mystic scribblings on the floor or barn-side or snow or sand-beach; those hours given to reading at night or noon or rainy day; and even those solitary wanderings over Southern lands and meagre jottings by roadside, were this same Hope, seeking to realize its objects in things of sense. My grandfather, too, was a Hoper. My mother inherited the same old sentiment, and my father fell a martyr to it — witness that same homestead which you speak of selling. I have a double portion of the sentiment, and bless God for the choice inheritance. — All right and title to the little farm I quit. Sell it if you can. Put the money in your pocket, and take the good of it while you need it. And one day you shall come and live with me.

But here I am near the end of my sheet. Dr. Alcott takes this. I seldom see him now. He is one of the busy bees, always making honey, and cannot endure such a drone as I am. I hope he will fill the hive with other than wasps' hoardings, upon which the world has been feeding for ages, but to sting. Success to this honey-making buzz of his! But by and by the young bees will swarm, I fancy, and seek hives and make honey in their own fashion, in spite of all this din of pans and kettles.

Love to all.

Your grateful Son,

A. BRONSON ALCOTT.

Abba has told you, I suppose — if not, she will — that a young Hoper is on his way into the midst of us, and before I write again will be a cradled Babe with a name. His sisters will jump for joy. I have the promise of a Boy. Yet strange, that grief should bear him to me, is it not?

A.B.A.

(— But my thrill of Hope proved a pang of grief — a true son of its mother — a Joy in a Winding Sheet.[7]

August, 1841)

March 18

AFTER TOOTHACHE

What a strange and alien nature is this so-called Pain! The Soul feels him to be an intruder into her realms, and is restless until she banish him thence. Pain gives a man a singular sense of that apparent duality bred by sin, and makes him for the time a

---

[7] This note, added many months later, is apparently the only written reference that Alcott ever made to one of the great sorrows of his life. A male child who lived only a few hours was born to the Alcotts on April 7th, 1839.

believer in its positive being; but when gone into its kingdom of phantoms, how unreal it is! Pain is Old Sin in a new mask of terms, reappearing to the Soul in the bones and marrow and nerves.

March 23

I closed the winter term of my school today. I hesitated about relinquishing it entirely, but at last concluded to meet my pupils yet another quarter and see what this time shall bring to pass. I shall give a week's vacation soon. I begin to feel somewhat jaded by the toils and confinements of the season. I have been very busy since I came to reside in Beach Street, and particularly since the opening of the current year. Besides the cares of the school, in which I spend five hours daily, and household chores, I have talked three or four evenings of each week, and have written the preceding pages. I need a short respite, at least, from the recurrence of these labours. To this end, I purpose spending a few days with Emerson at Concord. The airs, imagery, and society thus obtained will serve to recreate my being.

We have much, I fancy, to say on the present aspects and tendencies of the times. A day of controversy is coming over our heads. Renovating ideas are at work in the very heart of society. Old forms are soon to be cast off. The Soul is shedding its slough and renewing itself. The timid, the bigoted, are looking on with fear. Views with which our names are associated are to be assailed as the prolific cause of this overturn of things. We are to be made the butt of sectarian scandal. Persecutions most fierce and unrelenting are to be waged against us. Our tempers are to be tried. I shall like to learn the mood of this my brother as he looks out upon the scene of action from the seclusion of his rural retreat.

"Brother" — that is a kindling name! I feel the sentiment of kindred quicken within me as I write it. He is a brother of mine, and an only one. All other men seem strange to me when I think of him; for no other knows me so well, and I value none so dearly. I may confide in him. I know his temper. It is noble. Bravest amongst my contemporaries, he walks the earth magnanimously, and I behold his port and despair not of men. A spirit, like his, shall not be cowed. An insight like his shall gain its meed of honour. My brother, we shall do and dare! God is on our side. We believe in the Real, and shall come off victorious in our warfare against the Seeming.

March 31

Man, while in the body, is in a state of suspended animation. Death awakes him from his torpor, and he breaks the bonds of those substances in which he was incarcerated in time. This is the resurrection.

Man is older than nature. The synthesis of his being is broader. Nature is included within it. Matter, both organic and inorganic, are consequent and sequels of his birth. He is older than either, and survives all their changes. Nature is the Soul's cast-off wardrobe. Behold the traces of his build and habits in it.

The Soul builds its own temple and institutes its own rites of worship.

My Body in an engine of marvellous analytic powers, subjecting substances to its test from the whole domain of nature. I say "Body" including, of course, the action of the indwelling and analytic works of this engine. The Soul climbs out of itself, weaving its net of cellular tissue and incarnating members even as the spider darts from his center sustained by the web he spins.

Fluids form solids. Mettle[8] is the Godhead proceeding into the matrix of Nature to organize Man. Behold the creative jet! And hear the morning stars sing for joy at the sacred generation of the Gods!

A true man globes, or heads, or gives circularity to his thought. Poetry does this. Philosophy skulls it. It "murders to dissect." Piety and poetry must preside over all investigations, or the murderous and bloody knife of impious analysis will probe the very heart of Truth.

April 3

Speaking of the influence of Associations the other evening, I said that "wherever two persons had conference with each

[8] Sperm.

other an invisible, though implied, Person was ever prior to the concert, and to this third Person deference was always had as to a common arbiter."

This is a remarkable fact. Each man's Ideal holds him in check or prompts him forward, and the two Ideals become one Person to whose decision each refers his conduct, while the actual men may be at the same time heaven-wide of each other in their purpose and word. Thus wherever two persons meet together a third meets with them. An angel or a demon accompanies the Soul into the presence of its fellows.

April 5

Most men are on the ebb; but now and then a man comes riding down sublimely, in high hope, from God, on the flood-tide of the Soul as it sets into the coasts of Time, submerging old landmarks and laying waste the doings of centuries. A new man wears channels broad and deep into the banks of the Ages. He floods away ancient boundaries and sets afloat institutions, creeds, usages which clog the overflowing current of life, stranding these on the shores of the past.

April 10

Instinct presides over the duplex life of the Soul. It underlies all the phenomena both of matter and mind. Instinct builds organizations. It is primal, initial, spontaneous life. It organizes, replenishes, analyzes, comprehends, decomposes, and wastes every structure of nature, which it constructs and consumes. Every function of Instinct, through all the tribes and orders of nature, symbolizes the transcendent glory of the Soul, and indicates its supremacy over organizations, which it constructs, preserves, and razes. It is the architect of nature.

Love and gravitation are a two-fold action of one Life. The one is the conservative instinct in man, the other, of nature; and each preserves the various elements of its distinctive kingdom in harmony with the immutable and eternal Law of Spirit.[9]

[9] In this meditation, as in much other thought of the period, Alcott is apparently following the lead of the physiologist Sylvester Graham, whose relation to Transcendentalism has never been sufficiently considered.

April 13

What fact in the Soul do vultures, hawks, herons, eagles, kites, etc., cover? The same of beasts of prey? Is man, by nature, a beast of prey? — Read Audubon's *Biographical History of Birds* [*sic*] and Cuvier's *Natural History*. Also *History of Man*. But this last is not written.[10]

April 13

Vox Populi is not *Vox Dei*, save where interest or passion are silent. It is the still small voice of the private soul that is authentic. Multitudes always lie. The single man's oracle is alone authentic.

My neighbour Brownson will christen me "Political Atheist" for writing this sentiment. But his name is "Legion." I know not how many devils he hath.

Holiness, like the gastric fluid, dissolves all evils. The Devil is ever afflicted with dyspepsia. His gastric juices are depraved by intemperance.

April 14

We want a pathology and diagnosis of sin as well as of physical disease. Physiology and psychology are one — polar effects of the Soul. And each has its therapeutics.

Health: Holiness — Disease: Sin. One fact, out there in Organization or in here in Faculty. A wise man reads the cause in the consequence, the Disease in the Sin, the Health in the Holiness.

I too would be a physician, apprehending this Body as well as this Soul — or rather, this Soul's Body. Can I attend a course of anatomical and physiological lectures and witness dissections? *Cui bono?* Little — or the schools and professors are. Yet I might see, in spite of their endeavours to blind me. Nature and God would be there in spite of them. But rather God defunct — his corpse merely. So let me study life in the Vital God's, and read the sayings of the wise who have communed with facts face to face. Nature and God are always here. I have little time for the

[10] Essentially the same arresting thought is expressed by Thoreau in his journal entry for October 26, 1857.

dissecting room. Physics and physiology I shall master in my own way, being my own professor and pupil. I attend the School of the Soul, and this hath ever its subjects near by. It employs no resurrectionists. It frequents cradles rather than tombs.

April 17

Solidarity is an illusion of the senses. There is nothing solid. The nature of the Soul renders such a fact impossible. Modern chemistry demonstrates that nine tenths of the human body is fluid, and so of the elements of nature in smaller proportions. Matter is in constant flux — ebb and flow. Nothing abides. It is a mote floating in the beams of Spirit, and casts its shadow on the screen of Time.

April 20

In the evening I read a few numbers of *Nicholas Nickleby,* by Dickens. There is genius and wit in the book. It is written in the manner of Smollett and Fielding. I cannot vouch for the verisimilitude of the characters, but the power of delineation is considerable — I should perhaps say, great. The book is intended as a satire on English manners, society, institutions, and he takes his subjects from all classes and places. His characters are drawn with life, and make a distinct impression on the imagination. The caricature is broad and the moral fine. Could the same thing be done for us, it would correct many great evils and usages now current. — It is a good while since I looked into a work of this character.

April 22

Parker [11] asked me today, on my saying that men must have behaved well in order to have such fine sunshine, what I would do with the Mosaic account, which gives the priority of creation to the elements. I said that was the historical, not genetic, account of the matter. It was the story told in the order of the senses. The man and nature are. The senses begin in the concrete, and analyze from the surface to the center. But this is not the order of generation. The Soul is prior to the elements of nature. It was

[11] Theodore Parker.

the Soul which said " 'Let there be light,' and there was light."
Light is generated from the Soul, and is the base of matter.

April 23

I go forth from the city in faith. My wife distrusts this measure. She sees not whence shall come the bread for herself and
little ones. Neither do I see with eyes of sense; but I know that
a purpose like mine must yield bread for the hungry and clothe
the naked, and I wait not for the arithmetic of this matter.

April 27

I bestow a benison on Nature whenever I walk forth in hope
and joy and breathe forth my Soul into her atmosphere. I give
more than I take. So if I slug in bed during the morning hour when
Nature needs me, and I in turn need her, I suffer the penalty of
lassitude, morbid doubts, and Nature is the less invigorating to
all who breathe her airs. Were all the citizens to rise at dawn and
honour Nature by appearing in her presence, breathing her airs
and making these instinct with life and joy — of course there
must have been no evening's debauch — how salutary would be
the atmosphere of the city!

You breathe not to renovate your own body merely, but the
common body of Nature; and the healing, salutary influence that
you shall exert upon Nature depends upon your own virtue.
Your atmosphere is narrow or broader according to your spiritual
health.

The common atmosphere of the earth is said to be more than
forty miles in altitude. Let all souls be pure, and this would be
sweet and envigorating, void of miasmas and pestilences. For what
is the atmosphere but the reflex current of all the living souls on
the planet, returning on its ebb to be renewed and impelled with
vital force in sustaining floods over the world, expired and inspired by the all-renewing Soul? Let all men see to it that they
sweeten the airs of God by vitalized deeds, and not live on the
lungs of their neighbours. Disease comes riding on every gale to
such. Holiness neutralizes miasmas, and renovates the atmospheric
tides; so a sweet soul circulates around the globe, and sends health
to panting, yawning, languishing invalids on every breath that

it launches into the common current. Like ocean, it tumbles round the world, and stirs the whole mass of fluid air.

April 28

My thought, I perceive, is quick with the doctrine of Nature. A cosmogony is growing in me. A few days with my friend will be quite opportune. His tastes are sylvan. He haunts the groves, delights in the freedom of the fields and the song of birds. He is a true son of Old Pan. I shall learn, perchance, of him the secret by which the wood-god veils the features of Psyche from the profaning gaze of mortals.

April 29　　　　　　　　　　　　　　　　　　　(Concord)

This morning I rode to Concord. Dwight stepped into the stage at Lexington. We had miscellaneous talk during the forenoon at Emerson's, and attended a wedding at the village inn. The rite, as performed by Emerson, was quite simple. There was no formality in it. He spoke from the soul, and honoured it.[12]

I think I could sit under the ministry of Emerson; but he is the only man of whom I could say the same. He seems to apprehend the sacred facts of life and do them reverence. He speaks from the vital present, not the dead past.

We had some conversation after dinner on high themes: the genesis of Nature, the dependence of the elements of the corporeal and physical world on the Soul, etc. Afterward, a walk to E's favorite haunts.

Dwight left towards evening. After tea we conversed on style, my Conversations, the future. I looked over E's commonplace books. These are full of elegant sketches of life and nature. They are the materials from which the lectures are compiled. He does not record the history of his facts, but idealizes whatsoever he observes and writes his thought in this general form. He works like an artist from his sketches and models.

April 30

The day was rainy. Morning was given to talk on high matters. In the afternoon we rode to Waltham and supped with Mrs. Ripley. Eclecticism, Culture, were the topics discussed.

[12] Compare Alcott's journal-entry for June 9, 1875.

In the evening we had a general consideration of the age, men, means, etc. Channing, Brownson, Ripley, Furness, Hedge, Francis, Clarke, W. Channing, Dwight, Parker, Miss Fuller, Miss Peabody, Mrs. Ripley, were severally spoken of. Also the relative fitness of preaching, lecturing, conversation, writing, to the quickening of the Soul.

May 1

We conversed a while this morning on Space and Time. Called on some friends in the village. Afternoon, a walk, with miscellaneous colloquy.

Evening: Emerson read his lecture on Comedy before the Lyceum, after which we had agreeable conversation at his house, with some of the villagers, on Conversation.

May 2

More conversation. Walking. Evening, a concert of vocal and instrumental music. Conversation on Music.

May 3

Walking, conversing, during the day. Evening — met a circle of persons at Mrs. Thorow's [18] for Conversation. Topic, *Futurity*. Various points of sight were taken. Knowledge, Memory, Hope, Pre-existence, Faith, Elements of the Soul, Incarnation, Miracles, were spoken of in illustration of the future life.

Emerson was far from being satisfied with this Conversation. He said the people were stupid, and that I did not meet them wisely.

May 13   (*Boston*)

I find myself seeking the Common to meditate. It is plain that I am not at this moment in my true relations to the time. I am solitary. No one enters into my purpose. None perceives my true position. None can advise or help me. I must be self-subsistent and take counsel of my own heart alone.

[18] Phonetic spelling for *Thoreau*, giving unmistakable evidence of the local pronunciation at the time. When next he encounters the name, Alcott spells it "Thoro," and more than once in his later Journals it becomes "Thorough."

My week's intercourse with Emerson has done me good. It has classified me. I apprehend my genius the more clearly. I define my theatre of action the better by comparison with his. He is a scholar. He lives to see and write. He looks abroad on Nature and life and sketches their features with his pen. He sits in the theatre of Nature and draws the players and scenes. He is an observer, an eye, an ear, a pen. Creation is a spectacle to him, and he sets himself to criticise her order and denote her qualities in the form of speech. He is a literary artist and detaches his thoughts from Nature and life and represents them in elegant images to the eye.

But I am no scholar. My might is not in my pen. This is feeble. I do no justice to myself in literary composition. My organ is action [14] and voice, rather. I am an actor and a sayer, rather than a writer. I do not detach my thoughts from my life. I am concrete. Thought manifests itself in deeds and spoken words.

I act rather than observe; foresee, rather than live in memory. I do not live in the present so much as in the future. My eye is fixed on the distant more than the near. Hope is my sight. I am of the race of prophets; and I should put out my eyes and damp my enthusiasm by seeking to play the philosopher or the critic. I analyze life and nature not by speculation but action. I am of a temper too earnest and intense to rest in contemplation, to observe, describe, merely. I must think, and set my thought in the drapery of action and living speech. I cannot sit and seize the warm life-thought as it runs through my vitals; but am one with my thought — and this runs in my blood and irradiates all my features. My genius is epic.

I must not suffer myself to be drawn aside from the true ends of my nature by any false notions of my gifts. I am not to be perverted to the literary man merely. I have more than the scholar in me. I am rather a study for scholars. I will let them analyze and write; let me hold inviolate the unity of my intuitions, nor seek to dissolve the divine synthesis of my being. — The words of the prophet shall give law to the canons of speech; the scholar

---

[14] Writing in his Journal on about the twenty-first of March, 1842, Emerson says of Alcott: "It must be conceded that it is speculation which he loves, and not action."

shall correct his own diction by such utterances, and the philosopher find in him new facts for broader generalizations.

May 20

The philosophers apply their knowledge according to rule, and carry it so far that at last one cannot discriminate between talent and genius. Talent strikes conviction, but genius does not convince. To whom it is imparted it gives forebodings of the immeasurable and infinite, while talent sets certain limits, and so, because it is understood, is also maintained.

June 9

. . . I am the better fitted for this mission that my character has been formed wide of books and schools. It is, of course, more natural and human, and my thought and speech more simple and vernacular. This gives me nearer access to the minds of the people. I am free, unfettered by the conventions of thought, usage, habit, and shall come directly to my point, as a less simple person encumbered by much learning could not do. I cannot but think that my action will make an era in the history of man. I shall found a new school in theology, and any revision of this will work a change in every department of thought and action: in philosophy, science, art, literature. My style or method is simpler than that of my predecessors. I do not except even the prophet of Nazareth. I keep closer to Nature. I take the childlike soul as the ideal. And no man contemporary with me, not even Pestalozzi, has spent more time with children. I begin my career at the age of forty.

June 11

JESUS

This, of all lives, is the most refreshing. It quickens hope and faith. What a noble fact this man is! He is the grandest hero of all history. He is the epic genius, developed in all its magnanimity and grandeur. I read of Jesus with the deepest delight. He demonstrates my most exalted ideal of true heroism. He is the bravest of men.

His grandeur is in his meek self-trust, his constancy to the

Soul. How vital his faith in it! How noble his reliance upon it, under all the varied circumstances of his grand life! He carried his principles into practice. He tested them on every occasion. His life was an experiment of the omnipotence of the Soul; and his death was divine!

Alas, how few apprehend the depth and grandeur of this man's character! Christendom has made its lofty epic beauty of no effect by its vulgar traditions. I will yet divest it of these, and reveal its glory.

June 14

Very dined with me today. He was on his way to Concord to spend a few days with Emerson. He seemed much better both in body and soul than when I saw him last. His interest in man and nature is reviving in him, and he may yet regain his human position and walk about among men as one of them, and not, as heretofore, a spectre. I had a good deal of conversation with him, and feel encouraged about him.[15]

Brownson called in while he was here. What wide polarity between these two men! They sat opposite each other at the table, but were sundered by spaces immeasurable. It was comic to behold them. They tried to speak, but Very was unintelligible to the proud Philistine.

June 18

As the time for making my summer arrangements draws near, I find myself busied in the question of ways and means. All manner of fancies come into my head. I write few of them in these pages. The morrow's thought corrects most of them, and throws me back upon my favorite doctrine of waiting for God to act. Today, I had a dream of walking through the villages as a pedlar, holding communication with the people to whom I should thus gain access on the vital interests of life. I saw, for the time, fine features in this plan. On mentioning it to my wife and my friend Russell in the evening, I found them rather disposed to mock at such a notion. They seemed to shrink from the popular preju-

---

[15] The encouragement was justified, for Emerson was able to report before long that Jones Very had become "lamentably sane."

dice which such a step would provoke. I should not hesitate to take any course sanctioned by my sense of duty, that should advance my great purpose. I see in the occupation of peddling many facilities for speaking that I could not enjoy in other relations. My epic would have a thread around which I could spin whatever of heroic action and utterance occasion should favour. It would be an *Excursion* [16] realized in life. My purpose would dignify my pursuit, and ennoble me in the eyes of the simple and true. I can conceive of being induced to engage in such an occupation, and of making it an instrument of the most exalted purpose.

———

Yet the best of my life I shall never be equal to the work of writing. It eludes my pen. If written at all, it must be by another. I am too feeble an artist to work miracles with my pen. The miracle is in my thought and deeds. Let another write.

June 22

I closed my school today.[17] It is quite obvious that labours like mine cannot take root in this community, and more especially in this city, until parents and adults are better instructed in the principles and methods of human culture. My labours are not appreciated. I have a mission to parents, and must enter upon it. When their eyes shall be opened to the wants of the Soul, then shall I be permitted to minister to the needs of childhood. Meanwhile, I must address myself to adults in the spirit of the words of Jesus: "Except ye be converted, and become as little children, ye shall not apprehend the doctrines and disciplines of the Kingdom of the Soul."

June 23

Jesus used the word "I" as identical with the Soul. He and the Soul were one. The life was identical; and therefore he used no circumlocution but said "I" as the shortest and most scientific statement of the fact.

[16] The reference is, undoubtedly, to Wordsworth's *Excursion*, which Alcott first read while living at Philadelphia in 1833, and again while crossing the ocean in 1842.

[17] The school held at his own house in Beach Street, Boston.

So every true and devout soul should say "I," and plead for its divinity and oneness with the Godhead of the Soul.[18]

June 28

I began making an alphabetical index of contents in this Diary today. This I find a work of some magnitude. The topics touched upon in these pages are various, and innumerable relations are implied, yet not stated, in every paragraph, to the passing times and moods of my thoughts and actions. There is so little objectivity in my records that I find all is left in vagueness, even after the analysis which an index presents to the eye is completed.

But with this old defect I have grown familiar, and am better pleased with this registry of my life than with my former attempts. It is more full, draws more direct from the facts of my being, and is more successful in the quality of objectivity. I have never written out so fully my inmost thoughts, feelings, purposes, speculations, and confessions. This volume, which embraces the period of but six months, contains much more than I have written during the course of any former years. It includes hints of my inmost doings and endeavorings, and is a psychological Diary for the time which it embraces. No important thought, emotion, or purpose has transpired within me that has not been noted therein. I have spoken of myself as of a second party. I have unveiled myself without the least attempt at concealment. This book has been my confessional, and I have enjoyed the times when I approached its pages.

July 9

I am weary of the pedantry of Christians, obtruded everywhere — at church, in civic and domestic life, in forms, usages, and so-called Christian courtesies. These disciples of the Nazarene disgrace their master, who spake simply and disliked quotations. But now these modern followers of his do nothing but quote, and that profanely. They constantly interpolate their own scripture with Oriental texts whose meaning they misapprehend, and

[18] A passage to be remembered in extenuation of Alcott's own pervading yet usually modest egoism.

speak in a foreign instead of a vernacular tongue. Would that I could hear a simple man speak simply of the great facts of the Soul, in the language of his own time!

July 15

Conversation, dialogue, is the most difficult of all composition. Few have been successful in it. Of the highest philosophical dialogue, Plato is the most remarkable writer. I think St. John quite his equal. Both Socrates and Jesus were remarkable talkers. Few are the instances in history in which this style of communicating with the ages has been chosen by the wise. The method derives high authority from the illustrious persons who have practised it. It seems to be the chosen instrument of severest, sublimest wisdom.

July 24

My children are so much more interested in the Book of Nature, whose pages are ever fresh and fair and teeming with new meanings, that they care little about the mere literature of the same. They are unwilling to pass their time within doors, or fix their thoughts on formal lessons. I spend an hour or more in the morning daily with them, but to small profit. Their thoughts are on the distant hill, the winding river, the orchard, meadow, or grove; and so I let them have the benefit of these. I would have them fill their fancy with moral images, and their hearts with high associations.

The country is much to every young soul. How much it was to me I can never sufficiently feel. I am under the deepest obligation to it. It kept me pure. It soothed and refined my disposition. It was discipline and culture to me. I dwelt amidst the hills. I looked out upon rural images. I was enshrined in Nature. God spoke to me while I walked the fields. I read not the Gospel of Wisdom from books written by man, but from the page inscribed by the finger of God. The breath of that mountain air, that blue and uncontained horizon, not less than my mother's gentle teachings — not by words, but smiles of kindly approval — were my teachers. Nature was my parent, and from her, in the still communings of my solitudes, I learned divine wisdom, even when a child.

August 3

I rode to Jamaica Plain this morning to see Miss L. M. Fuller.[19] Finding her absent, I walked to Spring Street and spent the afternoon with T. Parker. We discoursed on theological subjects chiefly. Parker is a student of German theology and sympathizes with the new views. He has made translations of several German works, which he intends to publish. He will be found on the side of freedom when the hour comes that shall try men's faith. I deem him one of the true men of the Age.[20]

August 5

I had an agreeable walk amidst Emerson's sylvan haunts this morning, discoursing with him on the great questions of the time. We agree, save in measures. He, faithful to his own Genius, asserts the supremacy of the scholar's pen. I plead the omnipotence of the prophet's spoken over the written word, and the sovereignty of epic action over both.

August 9

I looked over a life of J. Calvin. His biographer describes him as "a hard, dry, passionate man with a bilious temperament." In this description we have the elements of his theology. Purity, placability, and mercy were alien to his experience. They entered not into his plan of redemption. Lamentable is the influence of this man's mind over the faith of Christendom. Calvinism is now preached instead of Christianity. His genius has superseded that of Jesus. Paul and Calvin divide the modern church. They have usurped the throne of Christ and won disciples from his school. But neither apprehended the spirit of their professed master. They imposed elements of their own into his pure and exalted morality.

[19] The first name of Margaret Fuller was, in reality, Sarah.
[20] Theodore Parker was at this time only twenty-nine years old and was not yet widely known. This passage is one of the many in which Alcott shows a prophetic insight into persons of his acquaintance.

September 18

Our circle [21] met this afternoon at Bartol's, Chestnut St. We discussed the subject of a Journal designed as the organ of views more in accordance with the Soul. Present were:

Francis	Parker
Alcott	Bartlett
Hedge	Russell
Wm. Channing	Robbins
Dwight	Morrison
Ripley	Shattuck
Miss Fuller	

Russell read Marston's letter, which met with great favor and led to earnest inquiries concerning him and his friends across the water. A good deal was said about our Journal, but no definite action was taken upon it. Its idea and plan are not defined.

October 13

I should like to read a Diary of the Prophet of Nazareth, written by his own hand, and detailing his hindrances, hopes, purposes — a faithful portrait of his own heart. Such a document, now brought to light, would reveal as nothing else the injustice of time concerning this noble man. Christendom would read it with dismay. Church and State would be riven asunder by it. Few, if any, of our institutions would stand in the light of its sublime ethics. Something like the finding of such a record is needful to a republication of his doctrines.

October 18

Individual is the basis of general improvement. The democrats talk of improving the masses, but take small interest in individual reform. They seem to fancy that two or more men together become invested with powers not their own when apart

[21] The Transcendental Club. This was one of the few meetings that Emerson did not attend. It was apparently at this meeting that Alcott suggested for the journal of American Transcendentalism the title which was later adopted — *The Dial.*

— have somewhat superadded; and so speak of the might and majesty of masses, not of individuals. I never hear them descant with enthusiasm on man, but on men. A rabble is respectable, God-inspired! A man is base, influenced by Beelzebub! Men possess the Godhead in their collective capacity, but apart are demons, whom the State must watch lest they rend it asunder, and the Church disown.

I read men quite otherwise. I look for the Prince of the Devils in the midst of the mob; for God, in the seclusion of a single soul. Beelzebub rules the masses, God individuals. The Kingdom of Truth is within, not out there in Church or State. *Vox populi, vox diaboli.*

November 2

Miss Fuller called and sat an hour with me today. We discoursed on her Conversations which she begins on Wednesday next; on Heraud and his Journal.[22] I gave her the number, received yesterday, and my English epistles, for perusal. We had some talk also on my Conversations. I suffered her to take my "Diary" from January to July to read. I have done this before, finding her one of the most intelligent of my contemporaries, having more insight into character than most.

December 5

Emerson passed the afternoon with me. We had desultory conversation on Swedenbourg [*sic*], Bruno, Behmen, and others of this sublime school. I proposed that some measures should be taken to put English readers in possession of the works of these great minds. Confucius, Zoroaster, Paracelsus, Galen, Plato, Bruno, Behmen, Plotinus, More,[23] Swedenbourg, etc., should be in the

---

[22] John A. Heraud, an English journalist and verse-writer of Transcendental leanings, editor at this time of *The Monthly Magazine*, in which he had reviewed Emerson's *Nature*, ascribing it to Alcott.

[23] Undoubtedly Henry More, the Cambridge Platonist, whom Alcott had read in Philadelphia and returned to frequently in later years. The inclusion of Confucius and Zoroaster in this list indicates a comparatively recent literary interest. "Behmen" is, of course, Jakob Boehme.

Alcott's plan for a "Bible of the Nations" was discussed by the two friends for many years.

hands of every earnest student of the Soul. Had I the means, I should like to collect these works and set scholars upon translating them into our tongue. It would be a noble enterprise, worth living to execute. We should have access to the fountains of truth through the purest channels.

December 19

I was invited to dine with Emerson, N. Frothingham, and Miss Fuller at Geo. Bancroft's, but declined. Is it a meet place for me at the tables of the fashionable, the voluptuous, the opulent? Am I not rather at present living in rebuke to all such? Above the temptations, what have I to do amongst the Sadducees? . . . I seek the dwellings of the publicans, the workshops of the artisan, rather, and make my appeal to them with more of hope.[24]

[24] "Nor willingly will he give his hand to a merchant, though he be never so rich," says Emerson of Alcott in his Journal for March, 1842.

1840-1846

*I*N AUGUST, 1844, Alcott lost at Albany his Journals for the three preceding years. He was never able to recover or to reproduce them. The Journals for the remainder of 1844 and for 1845 are also missing.

This unfortunate gap can be partially filled in. Selections from the Journal of 1841, not represented here, are to be found in The Dial for April of the following year; passages from Alcott's English Journal, copied by him and sent to his wife in letters, are still extant; and, finally, we have Mrs. Alcott's Journal for the period of her husband's absence abroad and for the months at Fruitlands. Considering that Alcott incorporated this portion of his wife's Journal with his own, the present use of her interesting record seems justified.

In April, 1840, the Alcotts moved from Boston to the "Hosmer Cottage" in Concord, where three months later their fourth daughter, Abby May, was born. Alcott turned eagerly to the farm-labor and gardening of which he had long been deprived, but found time to amuse the Boston press by writing fifty "Orphic Sayings" for the first number of The Dial, which appeared in July. In August he walked — with Ripley, J. F. Clarke, and Parker — to the famous "Come-Outer" convention at Groton, the first of several such gatherings of reformers in which he was a prominent figure. He helped to lay the plans that developed into Brook Farm, but finally drew free from them as not sufficiently "ideal."

During the winters of his early residence in Concord Alcott labored with his axe in his neighbor's woodlots and "conversed" wherever he was invited. These congenial but ill-paid tasks did not, however, prevent the frequent recurrence of "family straits." In January, 1841, Emerson invited the Alcott family to live with him, but wiser counsels prevailed. In March Mrs. Alcott's father died, leaving her $3100, which was finally invested in her name. At this time Alcott's debts amounted to $7000. Household expenses were increased by the frequent and long visits of reformers of many sorts, which caused Alcott to call his home a "Come-Outers' Haunt."

In February of 1842 Emerson offered to pay Alcott's way to England, and on the eighth of May Alcott sailed. Landing at Dover on the fifth of June, he went almost at once to Alcott House, near Richmond, which, a few years before, had been named in his honor. There and at London he remained throughout his stay, except for a brief visit to Derby and a trip through the western and southern shires. In these months Alcott enjoyed that "pure success" which Emerson had thought he needed, but the contrast between the homage he was receiving at Alcott House and the obscurity in which he had recently lived at home was too extreme. He moved almost entirely among reformers. His opinion of England, never admiring, was not improved by what he saw and heard.

Arriving in Boston on October 20, 1842, Alcott set out at once to find a suitable site for his "Eden." The Englishman, Charles Lane, whom he had brought home with him, began to institute certain reforms in the Alcott family to which Mrs. Alcott had some difficulty in adjusting herself. Alcott did most of the family cooking at this time and during the Fruitlands period, while Charles Lane taught the children. In January Alcott was arrested for refusal to pay his poll-tax, but was denied the privilege of going to jail. On May 20 Lane bought the Wyman Farm in the town of Harvard, Massachusetts, for $1800 — acting against the advice of Alcott, who did not like the land. On the fourteenth of June the

Lanes — father and son — and the Alcott family moved to this farm and called it "Fruitlands."

The story of the gallant and harebrained "Fruitlands Endeavor" has been too often told to need rehearsing. Most of the more palpably absurd tales that have been told about it are due either to later mythologizing or else to the fanaticism of Charles Lane, the former editor of the London Price Current, *rather than to Alcott, who knew something about running a New England farm. It lasted, after all, for only seven months, and even during that time both Alcott and Lane were frequently absent on reforming missions. The chief importance of the experiment was that it brought Alcott to the turning-point of his career. When failure was seen to be inevitable he felt despair for the first and last time in his life. According to his own later statement, he took to his bed, refused to eat for day after day, and hoped that he might die. It was the thought of his family that brought him back for forty-five more years in the land of the living. But he came back a different man — no longer a zealot though still zealous, no longer a reformer in the ordinary sense though still a teacher. He had put forth all his strength and found that it was not enough; but he had also found that "underneath are the everlasting arms."*

Leaving Fruitlands on January 16, 1844, the Alcotts spent the rest of the winter in a neighboring farmhouse and then moved to the village of Still River, near at hand. They returned to Concord in November, and two months later bought the house then known as the Cogswell Place or "Hillside," which Nathaniel Hawthorne was to rename "The Wayside."

The following spring and summer were entirely devoted by Alcott to the gardening and carpentry that he loved and that the new home needed. In August Charles Lane arrived to spend two months, and in September Alcott visited his brother Junius at their boyhood home on Spindle Hill. October brought Robert Owen to lecture in the village and to visit at "Hillside," — but Alcott had seen almost enough of professional reformers.

In 1846, having found at last a settled abode, Alcott established

himself in a definite routine of living. The winter he gave to read-
ing and to such Conversations as were called for. The summer was
spent largely out of doors, though not in the way of Thoreau, Em-
erson, and Ellery Channing but in that of the gardener and hus-
bandman. Alcott's reading for this year carried him through most
of Carlyle, much of Coleridge and Goethe, Swedenborg, and
Boehme, all of which he had known well for years, and it included
also his first reading of the Bhagavad-Gita. *He began at this time*
the custom of reading Spenser's Faerie Queene *to his daughters.*
His acquaintance with Thoreau ripened into friendship during
many long evening talks in the hut at Walden Pond. With Emer-
son he regularly spent his Sundays.

The Journal for 1846 is a first-draft, very crudely and often
almost indecipherably written.

Selections from Mrs. Alcott's Journal, extending from April,
1842, to July, 1844, are given first and continuously. Her hus-
band's records covering the same period are then resumed.

1842

April 1

Engaged for the last few weeks in . . . preparing my husband's wardrobe for his voyage. The time draws near for our
separation. I am summoning all the important and agreeable
reasons for this absence, and amongst the most weighty is the
belief that these trans-Atlantic worthies will be more to him, in
this period of doubt, than anything or anybody can be to him
here.

Wife, children, and friends are less to him than the great
ideas he is seeking to realize. How naturally man's sphere seems
to be in the region of the head, and woman's in the heart and
affections!

May 6

Mr. Alcott leaves us this day for Boston, expecting to sail tomorrow or Sunday for England, in the ship *Rosalind*, furnished by his friend Emerson with all the means to accomplish his voyage and visit to England. Noble friend!

May 7

Rose early, feeling sick and sad. The morning bright, but cold. . . . I put on my hood and walked away a few minutes. I uttered one audible fervent desire to an almighty Providence: "Increase my faith!" . . .

Must we be robbed of our treasure to know its real value?

May 9

I will hope all things, believe all things.

May 10

I can think now with more composure of Mr. Alcott's absence. My thoughts begin to dwell on the fact of his arriving safely, and the desire for letters. Is not sorrow, all sorrow, selfish?

May 11

Some flowers give out little or no odour until crushed.

May 20

Spent in preparing my children's summer frocks and thinking much of my dear husband. . . . Dearest, best of men, I ought to know that you will live here in the confidence and reverence of your age, as well as in the remembrance and eternal honor of posterity. . . . Few know you now; but there are those coming up to the true perception of all that is divine and sublime in your principles and life. Patience, yearning soul!

Sunday, May 22

Twelve years today since I pledged my life, in the presence of the world, to my dear husband. My love was plighted two years before. These have been great years for my soul. Wise discipline, circumstances the most diversified, have conspired to bring great energies into action. I have not been always wise, or prudent; I have looked too much to consequences, not enough to principles and motives; but I feel encouraged. Defeat has given me strength.

May 29

Three weeks today since Mr. Alcott sailed. . . . I am trying to get accustomed to the thought that I can do without him. I think I can as easily learn to live without breath.

June 20

Junius returns from the post-office with a letter dated "June 1st, two miles from London," from my husband. Welcome! Welcome! Now can I think of him as greeted by friends and co-adjutors, surrounded by elements of kindness and love — no longer as exposed to the tempests of wind and water.

July 8

Passed the morning with Elizabeth Hoar at Dr. Ripley's old mansion house, sweetly fitted up for the reception of Mr. Hawthorne. A charmed spot. The sweetest arrangement of the simplest articles of purest taste: Etruscan vases, antique flower-stands of old roots of trees exquisitely surmounted by baskets or boxes for flowers.

I left this scene of enchantment for once dissatisfied with my home. I have ever felt that, with Mr. Alcott's ideas of beauty, we have suffered for want of room. We have always been too crowded up. We have no room to enjoy that celestial privacy which gives a charm to connubial and domestic intimacy. I have suffered in my tastes, and encroached on the rights of my husband and children by this intense proximity.

I am enjoying this separation from my husband. It is giving me his soul and heart in the full melody of his rich words, even more fully than in the grand diapason of his sweet voice and the rich deep harmony of serene looks. I feel lonely at times, my solitude seems insupportable, but his letters fortify me to bear the latter cheerfully and meet the demands of my family with swift duty.

. . . I know that God is near to me, in as much as He is extending such a prodigal beneficence over this dear partner of my holier joys, my deepest treasury. May he not love us the less for having found those who deserve to be loved more. — Am I not his wholly? Am I not alone his? I would possess none other. . . .

His last letters, dated 18th of June, reached me the 6th of July. A sweet drawing of his residence at the Alcott House, Ham Common, Surrey. He found Mr. Greaves not living. This was a sad disappointment. He says of him: "It was as we had supposed. Mr. Greaves *was* the soul of the circle here. A prophet of whom the world heard nothing, but who has quickened much of the thought now current in the most intellectual circles of the kingdom. He was acquainted with every man of deep character in England, and many both in Germany and Switzerland. Strauss, the author of the Life of Christ which has shaken the faith of the Old World and is now exerting alarm in the New, was a pupil of Mr. Greaves at the time he held conversations in one of the colleges of Germany after leaving Pestalozzi. He was truly a remarkable man. Nobody remained the same after meeting him. He was the prophet of the deepest affirmative truths, and no man ever sounded his depths. And our dear Charles Lane, a man of the deepest sharpest intellect I ever met with, was converted from infidelity by him. . . . His influence was not unlike that of Jesus, and his friends cherish his memory with a like affection. . . . I was not permitted to see him with these eyes, but am not bereft by his departure of his presence and society. . . . He was buried from Alcott House in March, breathing his last at the very hour when the Divinity moved me to visit this charmed spot."

July 21

Letters from A.B.A. today per *Acadia*. He does not forget his home, though surrounded by those spiritual affinities which he has so long desired to enjoy. No, dearest; in the midst of joy you do not forget those who have so deeply participated in your sorrows. It is your defeat which has nerved me up to do and to bear. It is your life has been more to me than your doctrine or theories. I love your fidelity to the pursuit of truth, your careless notice of principalities and powers, and vigilant concern for those who, like yourself, have toiled for the light of truth.

July 26

We have had a fine day at the Cliffs. Uncle Junius took us all — being Abba's birthday, July 26 — into his little boat *Undine* (or "Water Spirit") and rowed up there. We enjoyed it highly. . . . I seldom omit these occasions for showing my children the joy I feel in their birth and continuance with me on earth. I wish them to feel that we must live for each other. My life thus far has been devoted to them, and I know that they will find happiness hereafter in living for their mother. I place on the opposite page a few lines my husband addressed to me just before my Louisa was born. I was suffering under one of those periods of mental depression which women are subject to during pregnancy, and I had been unusually so with Louisa — which accounts to me for many of her peculiarities and moods of mind, rather uncommon for a child of her age. United to great firmness of purpose and resolution, there is at times the greatest volatility and wretchedness of spirit — no hope, no heart for anything, sad, solemn, and desponding. Fine generous feelings, no selfishness, great good will to all, and strong attachment to a few.[1]

August 22

The children have been decorating their father's miniature with all sorts of everlasting flowers, from the amaranthus to the field-chrysanthemums. Thus would they emblem the enduring nature of their love for this dear absent father — just now, perhaps, the sport of the winds and waves. No! Not just so. A divine soul must be the care of a Divine Providence. The sparrow falls not without cognizance of a supreme love. How much more shall he be cared for whose meat and drink is to do his Father's will!

Dear children . . . may each garland around his head prove a bond about your hearts!

My letter of yesterday, per *Britannic*. This will probably be

---

[1] Louisa was at this time ten years of age.

my last, as Mr. A. had then gone to London to make his arrangements for sailing. I was relieved that his friends Mr. Wright and Lane were not to accompany him. It seemed premature, more particularly as we are not favorably situated here for any experiments of diet — having little or no fruit on the place, no house-room, and surrounded by those whose prejudices are intolerable.[2]

Mr. Emerson was greatly apprehensive that Mr. Alcott had dipped his pencil in Rembrandt's pot of gay coloring, and that his friends would find themselves in a barren field with no sun to cheer them. . . . He says: "Mr. A. lives in such a region of high hope that he does not feel the atmosphere of less elevated humanity, who are perishing in the chills of a cold and selfish world, or who are lulled into extreme forgetfulness of others by their exclusive interest in themselves." All this may be true, but the resources of the great Ruler of the Universe are not so scanty or so stern as to deny men the privilege of free-will. All of us can carve out our own way, and God can make our very contradictions harmonize with his solemn ends. — It surely has been even thus with ourselves, having chosen the pioneer whose faith beheld the rising star, and whose fearless tread has led us onward to the Gate of Delivery. . . .

With what trust has my husband felt that this great idea, which has filled his mind and at times occupied his whole being, would be actualized! Is it not about to be realized? In his Journal of '38 he says: "I know that some mission awaits my faculties, and the days shall bring this to light. What have I to do but wait and watch? My hour shall come."

September 4

Letters from my husband per *Caledonia*. I rather expected himself, but he did wisely to stay longer if by so doing he can secure more friends to his purpose. He speaks of several as manifesting an interest in their movements. He says "now is the winter of my discontent past." May he find the spring and summer of his future bearing a rich harvest of life and love for him. He has

---

[2] The implication is clear that the more extreme dietetic experiments at Fruitlands were due not to Alcott but to Charles Lane. See Mrs. Alcott's entry for November 29, 1842.

long been solitary. May this union bring with it the desired peace and joy which he has yearned to realize! A new scene seems opening before me. May I keep my mind and judgment unbiassed!

September 8

Been to see the Hosmer place at Stowe in reference to its capabilities for our united scheme of life. Find the house on many accounts agreeable, though not well arranged for chamber-room to accommodate so large a family. Should think a place nearer Boston, and yet more remote from neighbours, more agreeable for such a plan of life.[3]

September 16

Visited the Codman farm in Lincoln. Found it admirably calculated for a large family associated on terms of good fellowship. Very fine house, 260 acres of land, 50 acres woodlot, quite retired from the world but accessible from the great road leading to Boston, and near the contemplated railroad. But I dare not dwell long on any place till I have seen the persons. Let me see them safely across the ocean, and I shall be content with anything.

Whether my capabilities for such an association are at all equal to the demand I know not. My powers of adaptation to circumstances have usually been found sufficient to sustain me comfortably to myself and agreeably to others. My children, I am sure, must be benefited. If *they* are, surely then am I not injured, for they are the threads wrought into the texture of my life — the vesture with which I am covered.

September 18

Been preparing my cottage for the reception of my husband and his friends. I would have him find his home swept and garnished. The lord of our house and life shall find that his servants and lovers have not slept or idled during his absence from the field of labour. We have toiled, and shall reap the harvest of his "Well

[3] Mrs. Alcott's initial attitude toward the plan that eventuated at Fruitlands is shown by the fact that she began to seek a suitable home for the "Community" even before her husband's return from England.

done, good and faithful!" This is all I could wish, all he can give, to fill me with joy and content.

October 21

Good news for Cottagers! Happy days, these! Husband returned, accompanied by the dear English-men, the good and true. Welcome to these shores, this home, to my bosom!

October 23

After despatching the duties of the morning, walked with friends and children. — I was deeply impressed by Louisa's ebullition of feeling: "Mother, what makes me so happy?" Mr. Lane relieved me from replying, for a big prayer had just then filled my breast and stifled utterance. I wished to breathe out my soul in one long utterance of hope that the causes which were conspiring just then to fill us with such pure joy might never pass away — the presence of my dear husband, the gentle sympathy of kind friends, and the inspiring and exhilarating influence of Nature, who so lovingly embraces us the moment we approach her. . . . We have planted and watered in our natural life. May we reap and garner in a divine love!

November 29

Mr. Alcott's and Louisa's birthday, passed, as usual, in the interchange of little gifts.

Circumstances most cruelly drive me from the enjoyment of my domestic life. I am prone to indulge in occasional hilarity, but I seem frowned down into stiff quiet and peace-less order. I am almost suffocated in this atmosphere of restriction and form. Perhaps I feel it more after this five months of liberty and option. My diet, too, is obviously not enough diversified, having been almost exclusively coarse bread and water — the apples we have had not being mellow and my teeth very bad, my disrelish of cooking so great that I would not consume that which cost me so much misery to prepare. All these causes have combined to make me somewhat irritable, or morbidly sensitive to every detail of life. A desire to stop short and rest, recognizing no care but of myself, seems to be my duty; and yet without money we can do nothing. I urge myself on from the consideration that this seems but a state of transition, and that instead of rest I only need a different mode of action. And so I wait, or rather plod along, rather doggishly.

I hope the experiment will not bereave me of my mind. The enduring powers of the body have been well tried. The mind yields, falters, and fails. This is more discouraging to me than all else. It unfits me for the society of my friends, my husband, and my children.

They all [4] seem most stupidly obtuse on the causes of this occasional prostration of my judgment and faculties. I hope the solution of the problem will not be revealed to them too late for my recovery or their atonement of this invasion of my rights as a woman and a mother. Give me one day of practical philosophy. It is worth a century of speculation and discussion.

December 24

Left Concord to try the influence of a short absence from home. My duties for the past three months have been arduous and involved.

1843

January 1

Returned last evening from Boston, glad to resume the quiet duties of home and love. How little satisfaction to a heart and mind constituted like mine is all the circumstance and show of society! How little is the social compact understood, or felt! Is it not one tissue of selfishness, fraud, and corruption?

I left home toil-worn and depressed. I returned feeling quickened by a new spirit of confidence and love. I received a note

[4] These words cannot have been pleasant reading to Alcott and Louisa when they came upon them after Mrs. Alcott's death. Over the whole passage Louisa has written "Poor dear woman!!" Bronson Alcott crossed out the word "all" and wrote "friends" instead, to suggest that the fault lay chiefly with the English guests, Wright and Lane. What Mrs. Alcott wrote is certain, although her husband probably best knew what she meant. His own influence upon her and the household was never of the sort here described. One suspects that Charles Lane was the chief "suffocator."

from my husband during my absence — one thought I will preserve here as another illustration of his perfect trust in God and
goodness. He says: "I sincerely believe that you are in the arms
of a benignant Providence, who shall do for yourself and us more
than we can conceive or ask. Let Him guide. Relinquish all self-
willfulness. Be willing to be used as He shall direct. I am in the
hands of a holy Destiny that shall make me be, and do, better
and wiser than I can do for myself."

January 4

I am quite absorbed in my mental condition — felt since my
return from Boston an unusual quietude — less tenacious of my
rights or opinions. I do believe that the miracle is about being
wrought. To be truly quickened into spiritual life one must die
a carnal death.

January 8

After the usual Sabbath exercises of music, reading, and appropriate conversation, we dined — discussing fully our duty to
our neighbour, Mr. Adams. Sent him an eighth of our meal as
his portion.

January 15

Established today a household post-office. — I thought it
would afford a daily opportunity for the children, indeed all of
us, to interchange thought and sentiment. Had any unhappiness
occurred, it would be a pleasant way of healing all differences and
discontents. It is to be opened every evening after supper, and
the letters, notes, or parcels to be distributed to the respective
owners. A budget-basket hung in the entry is the receptacle for
all communications. No child or person is to open the budget
during the day, but the post-master is to do so and distribute in the
evening, each child taking turns to be post-master.

January 17

A day of some excitement, as Mr. Alcott had refused to pay
his town tax and they had gone through the form of taking him to
jail. After waiting some time to be committed, he was told it was

paid by a friend. Thus we were spared the affliction of his absence and he the triumph of suffering for his principles.[5]

Sunday, January 22

Mr. Edmund Hosmer and six of his children came to pass the morning with us. Our little service was quite interesting. After singing, we listened to some of Krummacher's Parables, which led to conversation, and then partook of a simple dinner which Mr. Alcott had neatly prepared in the morning: an oatmeal pudding, apples, bread, and nuts. The children then retired to the school room and played school while the gentlemen discussed the overthrow of state government and the errors of all human government.

January 23

Mr. Alcott and Lane go to Boston. Anna commences her visit to Mrs. Hawthorne.

Established a little plan for the children — to give them every evening during their father's absence . . . a ticket with "Bon" or "Mauvais" upon it, as an expression of my approbation or dissatisfaction of their conduct through the day.

The domestic post-office has worked well. It has been the means of inducing the children to interchange kind notes of reconciliation and reëstablishing friendships or slight disaffections among them.

Wrote to Mother and Junius.

Am greatly beset by men to whom we are owing small sums of money. Mr. Alcott feels that nothing can just now be done but let them wait. I wish I could be more comfortable under this state of things. I have expressed my mind very explicitly, and yet I have not said all I feel, for I do not know how to do it advisedly. The subject of the House and Farm is adverted to and

[5] Here Bronson Alcott adds the note: "A mistaken kindness in that friend." The "friend" was Judge Hoar.

It is to be observed that Alcott's arrest for refusal to pay his town tax preceded that of Thoreau by two years and a half. Indeed, it seems likely that Thoreau's whole theory and practice of "civil disobedience" was corroborated if not suggested by the example and the argument of his elder friend. See the entry, below, for July 25, 1846.

discussed. There is not that unanimity of opinion which it seems to me ought to prevail before consistency of action. . . . Mr. Alcott has been learning to prepare our meals, and has succeeded admirably in simplifying the arrangements throughout. Mr. Lane gives us all two lessons in music, and the children are learning to dance of evenings. Our days pass very agreeably in the interchange of light labors and serene enjoyments.

March 6

Went to Lexington to pass the day with Brother Sam,[6] in the hope that he would suggest some means of paying up our little debts before leaving for our new establishment.[7] He seems quite at a loss himself, and feels dissatisfied that Mr. A. finds no means of supporting his family independent of his friends. — They have to labor. Why should not he? — It is a difficult question to answer. I leave it for time to settle. His unwillingness to be employed in the usual way produces great doubt in the minds of his friends as to the righteousness of his life, because he partakes of the wages of others occupied in this same way. It is certainly not right to incur debt and be indifferent or inactive in the payment of the same.

Sam is much embarrassed how to proceed, with no means to help us himself and no confidence in the disposition of others to do so.

June 1   *Fruitlands, Harvard, Massachusetts*

This day we left our little cottage home at Concord after a residence of three eventful years. During that period my May was born, my father died, Mr. Alcott went to England, returned with his friends Lane and Wright.

Mr. Lane, with my brother, purchases this estate, which I hope will prove a happy home. If we can collect about us true men and women, I know not why we may not live the true life, putting away the evil customs of society and leading quiet exemplary lives. Our labour for the present must be arduous, but

[6] Samuel J. May was Principal of the State Normal School at Lexington from September, 1842, to September, 1844.

[7] These "little debts," owed in Concord and by no means all that Alcott owed at the time, were paid in full by Charles Lane just before the removal to Fruitlands. They amounted to $175.

there is much to strengthen our hearts and hands in the reflection that our pursuits are innocent and true, that no selfish purpose actuates us, that we are living for the good of others, and that though we may fail it will be some consolation that we have ventured what none others have dared.

June 4

Walked over our little territory of woodland, vale, meadow, and pasture. Hill, grove, forest — all beautiful, the hills commanding one of the most expansive prospects in the country. The Escutney, Wachusett, Monadnock, all visible from the same eminence. One is transported from his littleness and the soul expands in such a region of sights and sounds. Between us and this vast expanse we may hold our hand and stand alone, an isolated being occupying but a foot of earth and living but for ourselves; or we may look again, and a feeling of diffusive illimitable benevolence possesses us as we take in this vast region of hill and plain.

I gathered an apron of chips while the children collected flowers. Like provident Mother Earth I gathered for use, they for beauty. Both gave pleasure. It was very characteristic in me, and most natural in them.

Sunday, July 2

Readings as usual from 10 to 12 o'clock.

Mr. Alcott most beautifully and forcibly illustrated on the black board the sacrifices and utter subjection of the body to the Soul, showing the ✝ on which the lusts of the flesh are to be sacrificed.

Renunciation is the law; devotion to God's will the Gospel. The latter makes the former easy, sometimes delightful.

July 18

Sam and family pass the day at Fruitlands.

July 24

I did not think so much curiosity could have existed among our friends to see our new home. Amongst the first who came here were:

Wood Abraham
Mr. Larned from Providence
Mr. Hecker from New York
William Russell — Andover
Waldo Emerson — Concord
Ellery Channing —   "
Mr. Hill — Harvard
Mr. Willard — "
Shakers —   "
S. J. May, Wife, and Children — Lexington
Mr. Bower — Andover
Mr. Orris — Oberlin College
Samuel Greele — Cambridge
Mrs. Gaskins — North Carolina
Mr. and Mrs. Ripley — West Roxbury
Mrs. Hay and Son — Philadelphia
Mr. Palmer and Son — Fitchburg
Miss Page
Mr. Merriam
Mrs. Bassett — Lynn.

August (undated)

A busy toilsome month, somewhat relieved by the aid and presence of Miss Page, an amiable active woman whose kind word and gentle care-taking deed is very grateful to me.

Mr. Alcott and Lane visit Boston. Mr. A. returns quite ill. Continues quite feeble. Children have regular instruction from Mr. Lane, Miss Page, and their father when able, with sewing exercise with me.

August 26

Visited the Shakers.[8] I gain but little from their domestic or internal arrangements. There is servitude somewhere, I have no doubt. There is a fat sleek comfortable look about the men, and among the women there is a stiff awkward reserve that belongs to neither sublime resignation nor divine hope.

Wherever I turn I see the yoke on woman in some form or

[8] A small community of Shakers had been established for many years near Fruitlands.

other. On some it sits easy, for they are but beasts of burden. On others, pride hushes them to silence; no complaint is made, for they scorn pity or sympathy. On some it galls and chafes; they feel assured by every instinct of their nature that they were designed for a higher, nobler calling than to "drag life's lengthening chain along."

A woman may perform the most disinterested duties. She may "die daily" in the cause of truth and righteousness. She lives neglected, dies forgotten. But a man who never performed in his whole life one self-denying act, but who has accidental gifts of genius, is celebrated by his contemporaries, while his name and his works live on from age to age. He is crowned with laurel, while scarce a stone may tell where she lies.

Miss Page made a good remark, and true as good, that a woman may live a whole life of sacrifice, and at her death meekly says "I die a woman." A man passes a few years in experiments in self-denial and simple life, and he says "Behold a God."

There certainly is more true humility in woman, more substantial greatness in woman, more essential goodness, than in man. Woman lives her thought; man speculates about it. Woman's love is enduring, changeless. Man is fitful in his attachments. His love is convenient, not of necessity. Woman is happy in her plain lawn. Man is better content in the royal purple.[9]

December (undated)

Our situation here quite uncomfortable. Mr. Lane moody and enigmatical. We shall probably leave here as soon as we can see our way clear where and how to go.

December 25

Christmas. Interchanged little gifts with children. Had a little merry-making in the evening with the neighbour's children.

Weather severe. Constant succession of snow-storms. My eyes have become quite troublesome. I have humoured the weakness by not using them much of evenings. Play with the children. Sing, and try to cheer the scene within to render the cheerlessness

---

[9] The opinions or feeling expressed in this paragraph, and in the entire diatribe, were quite as much those of Bronson Alcott as of his wife.

without more tolerable. We are completely blocked up. Our neighbour Lovejoy has twice broken a path for us, so that we are able to get the mail.

1844

January 1

Mr. Alcott just returned from the Convention. Concluded to go to Mr. Lovejoy's until Spring, having dissolved all connection with Fruitlands.

January 6

Mr. Lane leaves with William [10] for the Shakers at Harvard. We send a load of goods to Mr. L's.

January 7

Take catalogue of books and pack them to await the first favorable opportunity for completing our removal.

The arrangements here have never suited me, and I am impatient to leave all behind and work out my way in some more simple mode of life. My duties have been arduous, but my satisfaction small. The family [11] since our residence here has been variable and uninteresting. The care of Mr. Lane and William has been at times exceedingly arduous. My children have been too much bereft of their mother, and she has murmured at a lot which should deprive her of their society.

January 16

Removed this week from Fruitlands to our neighbour Lovejoy's, taking three rooms and use of kitchen for fifty cents per week. We find ourselves quite comfortable for winter quarters.

'Received this week from brother S. J. M. ten dollars. Also Mrs. Whiting paid me twelve for cloak, and Cousin M. D. M. sent ten for silver slice, which I regret parting with as it was a

[10] Lane's son.

[11] The Fruitlands community, numbering at one time some sixteen persons.

gift from my dear Miss Robie, but several calls for money without any visible means to answer them impelled me to part with it. I am sure she would not think hardly of me for it.

I have been driven to many of these straits during these last few years, but I hope we shall be settled soon to some mode of life which shall either be more independent of the aid of others or less irksome to ourselves.

Mr. Alcott cannot bring himself to work for gain; but we have not yet learned to live without money or means.

January 28

Visited Boston this week with Mr. and Mrs. Lovejoy. . . . Intend visiting soon Hopedale and Northampton Communities. Quite uncertain what course to pursue in relation to our future subsistence. Wait in hope till something be revealed. Should like to see my husband a little more interested in this matter of support. I love his faith and quiet reliance on Divine Providence, but a little more activity and industry would place us beyond most of these disagreeable dependencies on friends. — For though they aid, they censure. And though they give cheerfully of their abundance, yet they feel that we should earn something ourselves. . . . Mr. Alcott is right in not working for hire, if thereby he violates his conscience; but working for bread does not necessarily imply unworthy gain.

February 3

Returned from visiting Communities, quite convinced that there is nothing there for us, no sphere in which we could act without an unwarrantable alienation from our children. At Northampton the life is quite elementary and aimless, except to pay off the debt. At Hopedale I could find nothing higher than living quiet inoffensive lives and aiding in all the moral reforms by going into the world and lecturing. — There was some "sackcloth and ashes" there. Brook Farm — there was more neatness, order, beauty, and life than in either of the other places. Still I could find no advance on the old world. Education at Brook Farm is of a higher and more elaborate kind, but no better than our schools afford, and I see but little gained in the association in labour.

March 22

It has been a day of soul-sickness to me. I scarcely know where to begin to bring about a more joyous condition; and yet it is wrong to indulge whilst my children are in no wise participators of my anxiety, neither can they alleviate my suffering by their sympathy.

March 31

Mr. Alcott returns, feeling, just as I did, that the Communities are not yet ready for us as now arranged — or we are not adapted to them as now constituted. We must then take up the family cross and work on, isolated and poor, a while longer. We will economize still further, and reduce our wants to the lowest possible scale. I will hire a small tenement.

April 24

Removed to Still River village, a quiet little nook in God's creation where, with his blessing, we will try to vegetate and bring forth abundantly of spiritual as well as material food. Our home is humble, but we have much comfort and few responsibilities — Mr. Alcott labouring unremittedly in his garden, producing rapid and beautiful changes. What a few days since was stone and stubble, a rude rough chaos, is now squared into neat regular beds and borders, verdure presenting itself and food promising for us.

What a holy calling is the husbandman's! How intimately he relates himself to God!

May 23

Fourteenth anniversary of our wedding day. Whom confidence and love have wedded, let not doubt or distrust put asunder.

July 14

Have been engaged for a few days in preparing Mr. A. and Anna for a journey to the West to visit his brothers [12] and, if possible, find a field of action free from the corruptions of society and trade as now instituted.

[12] Junius and Chatfield, who lived, with their mother, near Oriskany Falls, New York.

I wish him success. He has long been a seeker, but I can only exclaim with the poet of old: "Where is wisdom to be found, and where is the place of understanding?"

1842

[Bronson Alcott's Journal is here resumed.]

May 8 *Ship Rosalind, at Sea*

Embarked at 11 A.M. and left the wharf immediately. In two or three hours the land faded from sight. Before night I betook myself to my berth and looked over my letters of introduction. . . . Propitious gales till

May 15

Off Banks of Newfoundland, becalmed. A stately iceberg, from Labrador probably, passed near us. — Reading Wordsworth's *Excursion*. This, with the Essay of Epitaphs and the Ode on Childhood are favorites of mine. Some of the characters in the *Excursion* have much in common with experiences of mine. The likeness is closer than I was aware, and the sentiments of the Wanderer seemed but repetitions of my own.

May 17

Had a spirited conversation on deck after tea on Reform. My doctrines were at first taken as pleasing fables, but grounds of fact were yielded me little by little, and before we closed I succeeded in taking firm and vigorous root in the solid *terra firma* of reality. Mackintosh [13] seems quite a frank and tolerant Scot, yet an advocate of property and of the established order. I like him very well. We have pleasant talks now and then. He knows several persons in whom I am interested, and his wife is a good-natured and social woman. [14]

[13] Son of Sir James Mackintosh, the philosopher and historian.
[14] She was a daughter of Nathan Appleton, the wealthy Boston merchant, and sister of Mrs. Henry Wadsworth Longfellow.

May 27

Reading Emerson's Essays. Divine poems these, having the exalting effect of poesy on the mind. 'Tis like the fragrance of woods and fields, so sylvan, so balmy. Delicious, these improvisations on Love and Friendship, reviving all my ties at Concordia. Again am I a youth, and, after long wanderings in the solitary wilds of thought, I am a denizen of the realms of affection, a dweller in the courts of humanity.

May 28

. . . As yonder needle at my ship's helm inclines, so doth the heart of a friend, in all the latitudes of life's drifting interests, incline with constancy to the heart it loves.

May 30

We are in the English Channel. A waterman with provisions comes on board. Several others in sight. It seemed like meeting neighbors to see these bluff hearty persons and hear them speak in their rude brogues. . . . Made land. I took my bunk late, but sleep forsook me. Troops of gentlest, fairest, sublimest thoughts usurped my brain all night.

June 5   *London*

Took passage in a small boat from Deal for Dover, the winds adverse to our ascending the Thames. . . . Took lodgings at the King's Head, where we slept.

June 6

We reached London Bridge, in the very heart of the city, at 5 P.M. . . . The cabman drove us at once to the London Coffee House, Ludgate Street, near St. Paul's. After taking some refreshment, I walked around St. Paul's and then down through Temple Bar, Charing Cross and the Strand, and back to my lodgings to bed. St. Paul's is a commanding structure, overwrought with ornament and built by Sir Christopher Wren. But I found myself transmuting the material into the spiritual architecture instantly, and St. Paul, with the other Apostles, seemed to me to emblem the fortunes which their doctrines have had in the world. There they stand above the din and smoke of the town, their voices spent ere they reach the multitude below, their sublime inspirations all hardened into dogma and ritual, their prophet a mystery even to the few who tread the aisles within. Effigies and echoes of the Everlasting Word — its Christ a ghost, and its priests ossified at the heart.

London seems a rare union of the costly, elegant, magnificent, with the useful, convenient and plain. Everything I see implies great resource and is executed in a finished style. All is solid, substantial, for comfort and use. But all is for the Body.

June 17

I am sure that I shall not remain longer than I can help in London. The din and huddle about me pain and confuse my senses. Everybody looks leonine. The voice, build, gait, manners of the men and women I meet, their opinions, sentiments, institutions, betray the race I am seeing. Every Englishman is a fortification. Organized of blood, he finds necessities for spilling it. Warlike in his temper, his dispositions reappear in the genius and cast of the British institutions. A peaceman he is not, whatever he may pretend to be. He lacks repose, tenderness, poise. Strife, unrest, antagonism, declares its presence everywhere.

This I say of the metropolis. The country may report better of itself and tenants when I visit it.

June 25

Ride to Chelsea and spend an hour with Carlyle. Ah, me! Saul amongst the prophets. 'Twas a dark hour with him, impatient as he was of any interruption, and faithless in all social reforms. His wit was sombre as it was pitiless; his merriment had madness in it; his humor tragical even to tears. There lay smouldering in him a French Revolution, a seething Cromwellian Rebellion [15]; nor could the deep mellowness of his tones, resonant in his broad northern accent, hide the restless melancholy, the memory-fed genius, the lapse of prophecy into the graves of history whereinto,

---

[15] Carlyle was at work upon his *Letters and Speeches of Oliver Cromwell.*

with his hero whom he was disinterring, himself was descending — the miming giant overmastered by the ghosts he evoked from their slumbers, the dead dealing with the dead dolefully enough.

I said: "The living breathe with the living, nor go prowling about the sepulchres by the sweet light of day — intent on the charities and humanities for dispelling the darkness and driving afar the spectres."

His conversation was cynical, trivial, and gave no pleasure. He needs rest; must get this book off his brain to find his better self and speak sanely to his contemporaries. I know his trouble; also his cure. Emerson will sadden when you tell him what I write, but 'tis another instance, and a sad one, of the suicide of pen, in which literature so abounds. But this of Carlyle is the most melancholy of these times, and 'tis doubtful if he come out of it soon, if ever.

I purpose calling again, wishing he may be in better mood.

July 4

Visited Westminster Abbey. Prayers were being chanted, with responses from the choir, as I entered. The service is imposing, but derives its interest from historical associations, altogether. It is a spectacle merely. There is no worship in it. A pantomimic ritual. A masked show.

Here are the tombs of the English kings, of Mary and Elizabeth and Henry VII. Their effigies repose on the mausoleums which enclose their relics, the dead aping the dead. Here, too, is the Poets' Corner, and Shakespeare, Milton, Goldsmith, and Ben Jonson have their tablets of fine marble workmanship, with other names known to fame. But all seemed ignoble to me, and the Abbey, with its Gothic architecture, its cloisters and tombs, its chapels and aisles, but an eulogium on the desecrated genius of man, a monument of his fallen greatness.

From the Abbey I went to the Royal Academy, but saw portraits only of horned sanguinary Britons, of the pride and folly of England. The statuary was best, but the subjects were chiefly busts of royalty, of the nobility and gentry, and held no attraction for me. My eye is pained, my thought revolts, at portraits and originals, and I sigh to be given back to the land of my birth.

July 5

Saw George Thompson at a meeting of delegates from all parts of the realm to discuss the Corn Laws and devise measures for the relief of the people. Statements were made of the distresses of the working classes, most appalling to hear, and a petition was drawn for asking Parliament's instant attention and relief. But the delegates have little or no hope of finding favor, and have extreme measures, I believe, in reserve. Blood is to be spilled, and not on questions of policy but of life. The growling, hungering multitude will bear their wrongs no longer.

I passed the night at Carlyle's, but we sped no better than at first. "Work! Work!" is with him both motto and creed; but 'tis all toil of the brain, a draught on the memory, a sacrifice of the living to the dead, instead of devotion to living humanity and a taste of her ennobling hopes. Ah, woe is me! My brothers all are sold to the dark spirit of Time. No man hopes aught of himself or of another. The golden chain of love is snapped asunder, and each sits now sullenly apart, weaving a chaplet for his own brow, or else rushes madly into the embraces of another, a refugee from himself.[16]

July 6

I returned to Alcott House, where I met some of the freest men in the Kingdom. The conversation was lively and impressive. Reform in all its aspects — social, political, moral, individual — was discussed. . . .

This visit of mine now promises a harvest of good to us all. I shall glean valuable information to serve us; *The Dial* will be made known and more widely circulated here; possibly a new journal created, supported by contributors from both countries; the *Healthian* [17] circulated in New England, valuable books col-

[16] On August 2 Alcott wrote to his wife: "I have . . . seen Carlyle again, *but we quarrelled outright*, and I shall see him not again. Greatness abides not here. Her home is in the clouds, save when she descends on the meadows or treads the groves of Concord. I will take the hand of the Deity with a warmer love, a nobler hope, on my return from this sad sojourn amidst the satyrs and sorcerers."

[17] A small and short-lived magazine published by the members of Alcott House.

lected; definite and friendly relations instituted between disciples of the "Newness" on both sides of the water; and I hope to import living minds into New England to plant there the new state of things.

July 12

I left Emerson's letter to Miss Martineau with a friend of hers in Regent's Park and then visited St. Paul's Cathedral. This is a grand structure — a monument to the artist, Sir Christopher Wren, and the age in which he lived. It is a triumph of human genius over the material elements. Here are statues of Howard and Dr. Johnson, with numerous effigies of sanguinary warriors in whose prowess and fame England so delights, desecrating her noblest cathedral by making it the receptacle of these blood-stained priests of Moloch. The view from the top of the great dome commands all London, its suburbs and the surrounding country for many miles. A huge den this, truly, wherein Beelzebub whelps, the roar of whose voice reverberates throughout the whole civilized world. But the reign of the Beast is near its end; and London with its gaudy glories, its cruelties and enormities, its thrones and hierarchies lording it over the souls and bodies of men, shall become the foot-stool of a nobler race of kings.

July 19   (*Alcott House, Ham County, Surrey, England*)

Had much conversation with Mr. Wright[18] on our union in New England. He inclines to return with me. Evening: we walked to Wandsworth (6 miles) and had a lively conversation there on Education, and engaged to resume our discourse on Tuesday evening next.

July 20   (*London*)

Dined with Fox and met Harwood, Dr. Elliotson, Mr. Lalor, and others. The conversation was prolonged till late in the evening, and ran on various topics: Pythagorean diet, Taxes, Gov-

---

[18] Henry G. Wright, the teacher at Alcott House, who did in fact accompany Alcott to America but finally refused to join the Fruitlands community because he thought the regimen too severe. Against the later mention of his name Alcott has written in pencil: "Apostate too, Aug., 1843."

ernment, Magnetism, Poetry, *Dial*, Emerson, etc. It gave me little satisfaction. There was much argument, protestation, and but little insight from the heart. Our Club in its dotage, even, was wiser, far. I seemed to have fallen on Dr. Channing and the Unitarian Association.

July 21

Called on J. M. Morgan [19] and saw his painting of a Design for a Self-Supporting Institution, at his rooms in Holborn. He descanted long, and with great good will, on his plans for relieving the needy and distressed; but relies on the Church for support and seeks to redeem his own name from disgrace by denying his former intimacy with Mr. Owen. He is another sad instance of apostacy from the principles so livingly affirmed by Mr. Greaves. I recognized but little of the wise humanity that pervades his *Hampden in the Nineteenth Century.* Morgan, Biber, Heraud, Oldham, Smith, Marston — these are all fallen, and there remains but Lane and Wright in whom the divine fire still burns.

I saw George Thompson again, and heard O'Connell, Jos. Hume, M.P., Jos. Sturge, and Sidney Smith at the Anti-Corn-Law Conference at the King's Arms, Westminster. The meeting reminded me of our Abolition and Non-Resistance Conventions, and the speakers of Garrison and Wright and Phillips. Fierce denunciations, discontent, sedition, desperation, rang throughout the hall; but neither people, delegates, nor leaders seemed at all aware of the remedy for the social evils under which they are now writhing in sorrow, disappointment, hunger. It is not bread nor wages, and so I told Thompson, but property, gain, and the lust of gain — that these are the parents of the ills they suffer. But Thompson is too busy to hear, and the people too hungry to believe.

Had a short interview with Robert Owen at his rooms in Pall Mall. He read me a letter which he had just written, addressed to Sir Robert Peel, proposing his remedy for the distress of the nation; but he seemed little wiser than the Premier, Parliament, and reformers. Property, property still, and the people still enslaved to their lusts and passions. He asked me to break-

[19] John Minturn Morgan, an English philanthropist who was at this time interested in the communistic theories of Fourier.

fast with him at my convenience, which I promised to do, but scarce know why. 'Tis a base errand, this, of eating and drinking with lions, and I am getting heartily ashamed of it. Surely I am made for better things.[20]

Evening at Heraud's. Barham, Marston, Wright, and others were there. We discussed printing a new Journal to be supported by contributors from the old world and the new, and issued quarterly. A good deal was said. Heraud and Barham deem Carlyle's interest essential to its success with the public. I put the work on its own merits, quite independent of names, and Wright agreed with me. I gave my theory of the new journal, the hopes it must meet, the audience it must create, the contributors it must secure. I proposed that it should answer to something like this: "The Janus, an Ephemeris of the Permanent in Religion, Philosophy, Science, Art, and Letters." My idea was obviously too broad and daring for them, and so we separated.

Two letters from my wife at the close of this stormful day. I read them and found peace in the gardens of Concordia.

July 22

Returned to Alcott House. Read and reread those epistles from my wife and children, and meditated on my work present and prospective. The world shall accept, has ever accepted, the false before the true. It takes the superficial before it finds the central, worships the idol before the idea. The puppets now prophesy falsely, the priests divine for gain, the people hunger for bread; but humanity cannot feed long on the husks of doctrine, nor breathe freely these murky airs of theory. It will find the living kernel, and feed thereon to fulness; for the day of false things draws to a close.

July 23, Sunday

Many persons at Alcott House. We discoursed on the New Ideas and the New Time. Assuredly these hopes are forerunners

[20] In October, 1845, Robert Owen visited Alcott for several days in Concord, and lectured there. The fact is barely mentioned in the Journals. Indeed, Alcott seems never to have realized, and certainly he never acknowledged, the extent of his debt to this highly important reformer.

of their own fulfilment. A new Eden is ere long to be planted, and this visit to Britain is to hasten the hour of the fruit and the harvest.

July 24

Went to London. Attended a meeting of Chartists at the New Hall, Holborn. Lovet, Vincent, Hetherington, Fox, and others addressed the meeting. They were fierce in their denunciations of the Clergy and the Government, recommended education as the hope of the people, and were averse to all physical force. This party corresponds with our Non-Resistants, though less imbued with the spirit of meekness and charity. Garrison and Wright would have been heard gladly. I was tempted to speak, but desisted. England's air is too dense for the freest speech.

July 25

Visited the Tower, and the Thames Tunnel, each having its interest and the latter bespeaking an improvement in British genius on the side of humanity. A most melancholy place, that Tower — a Golgotha, the Bastile of freedom. Great pity that the late fire did not raze it to the ground — armed knights, spears, catchpoles, thumbscrews, guillotine, mortars, axes, moat, drawbridge, crown jewels, and all together. Here have been enacted some of the bloodiest scenes in English history, and Bunyan must have drawn largely upon it for his Doubting Castle and Giant Despair. It is a relic of human barbarity, and could have been designed and executed by the sanguinary Britons alone. It is a choice bit of rhetoric for H. C. Wright,[21] and worth his transportation to England. Evening: discussed education again at Wandsworth with Mr. Wright.

July 26

With Wright and Lane at Alcott House, having further conversation on our future plans. Mr. Wright decides on going with me to New England. Mr. Lane will remain till Spring, perhaps

---

[21] Henry Clarke Wright, 1797–1870, an American reformer and friend of Garrison, not to be confused with Henry G. Wright, the young English Transcendentalist.

longer. I begin to think of returning, having attained the end for which I came.

August 2

I submitted myself to Mr. Casci, a cast-taker in Drury Lane, Mr. Lane desiring a cast to correspond with one of Mr. Greaves. I dislike this moulding of the external features mechanically; but this was quite successful, and the sensation of being sealed up in plaster for ten minutes worth all the pain of looking at your effigy afterward. It is a conscious death and entombment, and deserves well the trial of every supernaturalist.

August 4

Had a meeting at Alcott House for discussing social evils and their remedy. Many persons were present and we had a lively time — Goodwin Barmby, A. Campbell, and others. Barmby interests me. He is the priest of the beautiful, and is seeking to realize his idea in a "Communitorium" of his own. He is an Oriental, and tends to the East.

August 5

Prepared a number of *The Healthian* for September for the press. Received an invitation to act as chairman at a temperance meeting in London on Monday next — which I declined, of course.

August 6–7

Collected some valuable books in London, and saw Heraud again; but he gives me no pleasure, the poor self-worshipper gaping all the while at his own ghostly image in his books.

August 8

Goodwin Barmby writes in a note received today: "I have a prophetic hope in my heart that better days for society and myself are at hand. The swallow-heart tells of the advent of summer, and I hear a voice call 'Home! Home!' May the Cincinnatus spirit in you evolve other Cincinnati! Good agrarian, temple, sanctify the field. Why do you say that the way to the East is by the West?

The family is good, the neighbourhood is better, the Communitorium is best. You are an older man than I am. When you want
blood I will let a vein. Take it; for in blood there is redemption."

August 10

Copied many passages from the MSS. of Mr. Greaves.[22] His
sayings are immanent with a deep wisdom and remind one of
Pythagoras and Jesus. I shall make a collection for *The Dial* or
my own "Janus," which I hope to issue on my return to the United
States. An organ I must have — an instrument wherein my thought
shall not be lost amid the confusing discords and witlessnesses of
popular letters.

August 11

Mr. Birch, a gentleman from Derbyshire and friend of Mr.
Greaves and who has done much for Alcott House, called on us
again today. He is deeply interested in the New Ideas; is curious
about Emerson, reads everything of his; and does all he can to
promote a better state of things. The *Conversations on the Gospels,
Record of a School, The Dial,* he admires. On leaving, he tempted
me to visit him, and put into my hands a £10 note; so I shall go
into Derbyshire soon. He is an opulent lawyer, and resides at
Derby. I await letters from home to pass a day or two with him.[23]

[22] James Pierrepont Greaves, 1777–1842. An English merchant ruined by
the French Revolution, he spent several years in Switzerland as an associate of
Pestalozzi and, in later life, became the leader of the group of Transcendental
reformers whose center of operations was at Alcott House. Two articles about him,
written by Charles Lane and containing extracts from his own writing, appeared
in *The Dial* for October, 1842, and January, 1843.

[23] Alcott remained with Mr. Birch, in fact, for more than a week, leaving
London on August 15th and returning through Gloucester, Stroud, Cheltenham,
Cirencester, and Windsor.

[*Here ends the Journal kept by Bronson Alcott in England,
as preserved, primarily, in letters sent to his wife. His Journals
for 1843, 1844, and 1845 are missing.*]

1846

January 3   (*Hillside, Concord*)

There is a martyrdom of the mind no less than of the body.

———

The chaos about thee is but the confusion within thee.

———

Who are the teachers of this time?

(Native)   (Foreign)
Emerson   Carlyle
Garrison
[Alcott],[24] no
    for me the time is not quite ready.

January 3

My little circle were earnestly interested in a tale, conceived yesterday, at the moment, for them; and they caught the moral of my fable quite greedily. A little Orphic fancy it was, of the Gentle Tamer who dwelt on the skirts of the forest, and whose chambers were roughly invaded from day to day by the wild beasts from the woods, but who tamed them into gentleness by his soft manners and kind disciplines and behaviors — but their forms also, transforming them through the bodies of lambs and doves into children, and from children into angels and inhabitants of the starry spheres.

My animals left for their homes applying the moral to themselves, their fancy quick with images and calling each other by characteristic names.

Time was when these fancies spontaneously pictured themselves in my mind, and the presence of a circle of children tempted them from off the lip. It was a great pleasure to weave the visible world of persons and things into some story, and go masquerading with these mimes through the invisible world.

Symbolical is all that meets the sense,
One mighty Alphabet for Infant Minds;

[24] Alcott writes his own name and then crosses it out.

And we, in this low world, placed with our backs
To bright Reality, that we may know
With young unbounded ken, the substance
From the shadow.

January 8

Very pleasant, this school of little children now. I take courage
of myself on finding this faculty of touch still lively, and the response of these subjects so visible. Even the hope of practice one
day has risen again. In God's own time, let this happiness come!
There will be some relation between me and my time; and so,
occupation for myself, and my contemporaries also.

January (undated)

All that I have written seems quite worthy of the flames. What
with the loss of my papers at Albany and these I have burned
today, I feel somewhat relieved. When Nature is not unseemly,
why mar and distort her countenance? Art is then art only when
it beautifies and ennobles its objects. I regret a little the loss of
many Letters from various esteemed persons, and my MS "Prometheus of Creation"; but if leisure is permitted in days to come, I
hope for clearer views of Being, and the gift of luminous utterance.

January (undated)

You can never hurry mankind, goad them never so fiercely.
Expect brute resistance. No measures will avail that have their
sources in the mere animal will. . . . Organic changes are wrought
by spiritual powers.

January (undated)

Professor Faraday, I read, is about presenting some discoveries of his to the Royal Society on the relation of Electricity and
Magnetism to Light. I venture the conjecture that the three are
states of One Substance, and that this, by whatsoever name it shall
be designated, is the *immediate* Breath of Life, the nexus of Spirit
and matter.

Forests are magnets, conveying electricity from the Heavens to the Earth. Plants are alike conductors of magnetism, and the nerves of all animals. The hair on the human head is an electric pile, and in lesser measure the skin itself. The like of all animals. The magnetic current circulates through the pores, and rushes from the atoms of all bodies. Nature is charged with the quickening fluid, and from the chaos of matter creation springs at the incoming of the organic Light.

January (undated)

A man's unfitness for public life is a proof, often, of his elevation and integrity.

January (undated)

Emerson is constitutionally a pantheistic sophist. The idealism of his mind, debasing the primitive ascendency of the moral sentiment, leaves him without basis for upholding the verity of Being. He is unable to escape wholly his taint of unbelief, in which he was bred, and his fine powers carry this mark into all his designs.

No; 1874 [25].

January (undated)

Had I intimated nothing deemed hostile to human institutions, the ban of exile, or of exclusion from all places of public usefulness, would not have borne against me. But now I am looked upon with distrust, and while there is little hope of aiding forward mankind save by forming the young, I am prohibited from communication with these. How am I to work?

March 16

Why hast thou mourned so long, and for the last five or six years folded thy hands in sadness, or put them wildly forth to do what thou wouldst not, or what thou didst deem thyself desperate to undertake? Ah! was it that the world was not heaven, and none would join thee to make it such?

---

[25] Written by Alcott in red pencil and in the year named, to show that he no longer believed what he had written above.

Tragedy is life without grief — as there can be no spar without the dripping of the water in caves. Grief is the stalactites formed in the cave of the heart, whence the light of joy is shut out and where the tears are congealed.

———

Count thyself divinely tasked if in thy self or thy family thou hast a devil or two to plague and try thy prowess and give thee occasion for celebrating thy victories by ringing all the bells of joy within thee.

Two devils, as yet, I am not quite divine enough to vanquish — the mother fiend and her daughter.[26]

March (undated)

Remember me the Dismal Swamp, with its hurricane and lightning flashes — conducting my way 'neath falling cypresses through the darkness — the muddy pools through which I waded — and came at last, near midnight, to the friendly cottages, and found shelter.[27] . . .

Sounding, creaking forest. The timber dashed athwart my path by the roaring tempest. Myself darting through the falling trees, discerning my way by lightning flashes.

March (undated)

I once thought all minds in childhood much the same, and that in education lay the power of calling these forth into something of a common accomplishment. But now I see that character is more of a nature than of acquirement, and that the most you can do by culture is to adorn and give external polish to natural gifts — by no means create or develope what is not inborn. A fine

[26] By the words "devil" and "fiend" Alcott often referred, quite unmaliciously, to persons who seemed to exist primarily for the discipline of the virtuous. In Mrs. Alcott and Louisa — quick-tempered, sharp-tongued, and of dark complexion — he thought that he saw diabolic traits. In later years, however, he was glad to be able to attribute his wife's peculiarities not to the "Adversary" but to a no less fanciful "Portuguese" descent.

[27] Alcott recalls this incident of his peddling days in Virginia, evidently, because he feels that it was symbolic of his later life and of his present situation.

brain is a gift of God. Only from the head of Jove springs the Minerva.[28]

March (undated)

I fancied that of this earth a heaven could be fashioned, and set in good earnest to mould it to my ideal. My youth and early manhood was given to a strenuous and ardent toil for this end, and not till later manhood did I acquire the fruits of this endeavour — a serene and hopeful resignation to build my heaven in the mind. And, lo! as this thought was born was my heaven itself born also.

April 5

Rise at 5 — Light fires — Bathe (Shower bath) — Call children, assist in their bathing and dressing — Shave and dress — Breakfast at 6. Reading of a hymn, with Conversation. Music — Prepare wood — 7, Read, Study, write till 10. Instruct the children — 12, Dinner. Labour till 3 in Garden — Readings with mother and children. 5, Bathe and help children's bathing. 6, Supper. Music and Conversation. 7 till 9, Reading and writing. 9, Bed.

April 7

Emerson passed the evening with me, and invited me to pass Sunday evening next with him.

If the freshness of this intimacy could be renewed, as in its early youth-time!

We discoursed of the state of literature in our country. I told him of the interest and value of these Germans — Goethe, Schiller, Richter — to me, and of my debt to them and Carlyle during these winter days.

April (undated)

Rose refreshed with the night's sleep, yet feeling the inadequacy of the day's tasks to call into masterly activity all my powers. I suppose I do not yet command the domestic facts of my daily life from the high summit of faith, and so these humble duties droil and drug me a little. Well, I will nevertheless work, drudg-

---

[28] This radical change of belief, involving Alcott's whole theory of education, is attributable chiefly to the influence upon him of his English correspondent, James Pierrepont Greaves.

ingly though it be, and the clear sky will some day open upon me. I shall climb the hill and behold the blessed country even here.

April (undated)

Anna wrote a little poem in her Journal and Elizabeth studied the points and capital letters. I corrected their Journals which they wrote very faithfully. Louisa was unfaithful, and took her dinner alone. Abba [29] did not come into school for lessons in reading and spelling, so I had her read from her slate at table before she eat her dinner. The little heart was very sensitive, and felt this gentle reproof of her unfaithfulness.

April (undated)

Forests were first dwellings for mankind, and unwillingly we abide even in the tilled field. A simpler and yet more healthful poesy is emblemed in the wood than the garden; yet both are typical of human affections, having their roots and blossoms in the heart and head of humanity. When I was seeking a family haunt, the woods about this village had a great attraction, and unwillingly I yielded to the necessity of settling near the roadside and the shorn beauty of the field. — The sylvan nature claims the presence of Pan.

April 16

I encouraged my children to think out the thoughts and doings of the day, while I went to pass the evening with a circle of my friends at Miss Hoar's.

The Conversation ran mostly on the significance of Christ as the genius of modern culture. Elizabeth Hoar agreed with me in declaring the friendly influence he was, standing in this particular in a more tender and intimate nearness to the heart of mankind than any character in life or literature. The Conversation was suggested by my asking Miss H. who were the teachers of the Nations at this time; and she mentioned Jesus, with Goethe, Carlyle, and Emerson.

Henry Thorough [*sic*] thought we asserted this claim for the fair Hebrew in exaggeration; and declared against our estimate

[29] Abba May, Alcott's youngest daughter, later called May.

with some vehemence. I asserted his claim as a poet — the poet of the moral instinct — yet as the mythological personage now to Christendom, who had no clear perception of his ideas and actions. Miss Emerson [30] phrased, as usual, her somewhat fanciful superstitions about him.

There were some pleasing passages in the Conversation. As I walked home with Elizabeth Bartlett, she said she had profited by the talk.

April (undated)

I set out six apple trees near the semi-circular walk which I have just cut opposite my house in the garden. They were Hubbard Stone, Nonesuch, Bell Flower, and Hood's Early Sweeting. My wife's hands assisted me in transplanting. The little ones came down to see us. Already the little plot seems dearer for this work of hope and promise.

I know not that I am not serving mankind as greatly in these humble services — in setting trees and teaching my children, these human shoots — as in the noisier and seemingly more widely useful sphere of public activity.

In the afternoon, I set my currants by the fence-side in front of my garden; and then made a neat path up the hill-side from the kitchen-door back of the house.

April (undated)

The girls took a walk with me over the hill behind the house, to the piny dells and spruce groves spreading northward of us down to the Concord River. I observed several very handsome trees for transplanting to my yard and door-plot opposite. It is a cheap and refreshing pleasure, this of ornamenting the retreats of daily toils. I would draw some lines on the landscape, restoring what men have taken from it, and completing, in some simple style, what God designed.

April 22

I come daily to the bath, just before supper, with the greatest pleasure. It is strange that the use of the bath is so little known

[30] Mary Moody Emerson.

with us. None could dispense with it after having proved its virtues. It is highly restorative, and after the fatigue of toil I am fitted for an evening's study by its efficiency. The mental effect is surprising.

"And Jesus, when he was baptised, went straightway out of the water, and the Heavens were opened unto him, and he saw the spirit of God descending in a bodily shape like a dove, and lighting upon him; and there came a voice from Heaven, saying 'Thou art my beloved Son, in whom I am well pleased.' "

April 25

I need a more adorned sphere as the show and implement of my being. The indigence of the mundane world about me affords no imagery of my thoughts and aspirations. One cannot people a world of ideas with clowns and brutes, nor create an apartment in the ideal mansion of road-dust and locust thorns.

The petty traffic of my townspeople passes by my door; and I have not as yet been able to plant a screen of pines, larches, and spruces, to protect my eyes from the market dust, the tramp of beeves, and the roll of anxious wheels.

Shall I dwell alway at the inns, and open my lips to clowns, satyrs, and the apes and mules of civilization?

I am scarcely in human relations with any one of my townsmen. The coarse tie of appetite brings us sometime together in the field, road, and farm house.

April (undated)

The Pegasus of the multitude is a mule.

April 30

Sodding is the tug of the sinews with ideals — the wrestle of the mind with earthly mould.

> I deem sodding
> A sternest Godding,
> Bone and muscle
> In mundane tussle.

May 1

Mother and children all very active in preparing to celebrate May Morning at Mr. Emerson's — Miss Ford having prepared a May-pole, dressing it gaily with evergreens.

Brought a load of trees from the woods — spruce, larch, and pines. Conveyed the children, consisting of several from the neighbourhood, with May-pole and Miss Ford, to the Emerson's. The waggon was neatly trimmed with running pines, and a wreath of the same on our bonnets and hat, and as we passed along the road we sang, "Merrily we go." At Emerson's several joined us, with the mothers and other company, and then the children danced around the May-pole.

May 3

Emerson called, and I walked with him to the haunts near Walden Water, and he led me by the wood-paths to the summit of the ledge on which he purposes to build himself a lodge for study and writing. The prospect was commanding for our champion country — Monadnock on the North, Wachusett and the spires of Groton and Sudbury on the West and South West, and near was the Concord River, and close by on the opposite side was Thoreau's cot. It was a fit spot for a poet's lodge. We descended by a hatchet-path to the dell near the railroad, to a spring of water near the railroad, some distance from the hilltop. Here he hopes to ensure retirement and uninterrupted seclusion for writing.

We conversed on many topics. I find intercourse with E. more grateful than with most of my contemporaries. What a distance between the company of such as he and the labourers with whom I am now brought into closest communication in my daily callings!

In the evening I had an hour's quiet reading of the oriental wisdom in the Chapters of the *Bhagvat Geeta*,[31] on "Works" and the "Performing of Works."

[31] This appears to be the first recorded instance of Alcott's reading in the literature of India, which meant more and more to him in later life. The passage is followed by several pages of "Extracts" from the *Bhagavad-Gita*.

Alcott may have borrowed the book from Emerson — who, however, had made only one earlier reference to it in his Journal, and who made few later ones. Thoreau's single reference to the *Gita* was made six years after Alcott's.

May 4

TAX-PAYING

Staples,[32] the town collector, called to assure me that he should next week advertize my land to pay for the tax, unless it was paid before that time. Land for land, man for man. I would, were it possible, know nothing of this economy called "the State," but it will force itself upon the freedom of the free-born and the wisest bearing is to over-bear it, let it have its own way, the private person never going out of his way to meet it. It shall put its hand into a person's pocket if it will, but I shall not put mine there on its behalf.

Free-born persons are citizens of a State where the law of force is unknown.

May 6

I read a lecture in the *Bhagvat Geeta* on "The Principles of Nature and the Vital Spirit."

The whole of this Lecture I would transcribe, if I had the time, into my Journal. Have a strong desire to copy the whole of Book XVIII entire — 135 Quarto pages.

May 7

Ever the feminine passes swift into mystery, and is undistinguished amidst the powers of Nature, working with earnest force in darkness. The masculine cometh with impiety ever to the light, and blossometh forth to the senses, revealing all things to the sun.

May 8

Evening. Emerson came in to consult me on the lodge he intends building on the peak of his woodlot, near Walden Water. He showed me H. Thoreau's design, to which I added another story, as a lookout.

He tells me of Carlyle's sending him his daguerreotype, and of his returning the like to Carlyle.

[32] Sam Staples, a famous man in Concord history who was at this time Alcott's neighbor. He had already arrested Alcott for refusal to pay his poll-tax, and was soon to arrest Thoreau for the same reason.

We talked about the *Bhagvat Geta*,[33] and of printing the "Bible of Mankind."

Emerson, Miss Fuller, Thoreau, and myself, are the only persons who treat things in the new spirit, each working distinct veins of the same mine of Being.

May 10

I read at the breakfast table the stilling of the tempest, and one of the Hymns on Meekness.

Louisa seemed quite pleased with the Hymn, and applied some of the sentences to her own state.[34] She copied it also into her Journal.

Elizabeth took great pains with hers, and wrote much and very neatly.

I read more of the *Bhagvat Geeta* and felt how surpassingly fine were the sentiments. These, or selections from the book, should be included in a Bible for Mankind. I think them superior to any of the other Oriental scriptures, the best of all reading for wise men.

Best of books — containing a wisdom blander and far more sane than that of the Hebrews, whether in the mind of Moses or of Him of Nazareth. Were I a preacher, I would venture sometimes to take from its texts the mottos and moral of my discourse. It would be healthful and invigorating to breathe some of this mountain air into the lungs of Christendom.

May 11

Replenished our stores from the grocery in the village. Maple sugar, flour, cheese, &c. We endeavour to use no articles of foreign or slave production in our diet. In apparel we cannot as yet dispense well with cotton and leather, the first a product of slaves and the last an invasion of the rights of animals.

Brought from the Walden Wood some more trees — pine, hemlock, and a few maples and birches — and set them in my yard.

[33] Alcott's spelling of the title of this favorite book varies widely.
[34] Her "state," in her father's opinion, was almost chronically tempestuous.

May 17

Arranged the interior of the house for summer. Removed the stove from my study, and disposed pictures and furniture more to my convenience and taste.

Intended to read a little in *Bahgvat Geeta,* but various little chores used up all my day.

Evening: I saw Emerson and had full discourse, mostly on the *Geeta* and the genius of the Oriental faith. I know of no literature more purely intellectual. Its philosophy and poesy seem to me superior to, if not transcending greatly, all others.

Almost all moral teaching has been oppressive, but I think this sweetly pure, and spiritually sane.

E. gave me a letter from G. Waldo, in which he speaks of negotiating with the King of the Sandwich Islands for land for me, if I will have it. But I have now more than I can treat well, and am cured, I think, of seeking contentment in foreign parts.

This labour and these domestic toils are good medicine for such as I.

June 5

Emerson called and talked an hour in the garden. I told him it seemed good for me to be using the rake on this little spot — as good, or better, than attempting broader reforms in a popular, or in any manner. I seemed to be as worthily employed as any of my contemporaries. No voice came to me of potency to summon me away into other spheres of society.

June 8

My long-stretching bean-rows, trim as an air-line, the peas binding the central wall and extending from the front gate to the brook, have a very pretty effect. I see not how one can abide in the emblematic world without eyes. Nature! The outlines of all things and designs are drawn in Nature, and it is the sweet privilege of Man to divine and fill out these sketches, completing in Art what is begun in Nature. I think I garden more to the eye than to the appetites.

June 28 AT EMERSON'S

Read some passages from Paul, Krummacher, and Henry More on Charity, with many colloquial elucidations. The company were quite attentive, and the conversation on the readings sensible. The children gave very good answers, and maintained the liveliness and reason of our meeting. I think all felt the hours well passed.

Walked again with Emerson to Walden Water. We talked a good deal on our common topics, an account of which would fill many pages, even had I the genius of transmitting it to paper. The best passages of life come often in conversation, and elude the catch of the pen.

Among other things, I spoke of the service which the head was now giving to the hands, as partaking a little too deeply of drudgery and beginning to tire me a little, and that I was sometimes inclined to appeal to the discernment of my wisest friend for some position of relief, and one that should yield me the pleasure of profit to intellectual being — and bread also to myself and family. There are needs of men, my fellows, which I might satisfy if suffered to use my genius in its natural ways.

I hinted, too, of the service which my friend, holding as he now does the most cultivated ears, might render me by a worthily spoken word to the best audiences he shall gather in the N. England cities, and proposed to him to try his hand next winter in some half-dozen portraits of his contemporaries.

Now he is busy in preparing his volume of his poems for the press. Of these he read me two or three — The "Monadnock" and one on the Freedom of the Earth called "Concord." [35] I guess the best philosophy will forthcome clearest in the poems. He is the first truly western poet, Occidental as our forests and hills.

Returning along our little green lane, I felt more vividly than before the rare privilege I enjoy of passing at once from the busy and painstaking toil of the week into the presence, and being admitted to the first thoughts, of this our first great poet — and a friend of mine, too. It seemed to compensate for my rugged lot — the best, doubtless, which the benign yet equitable Disposer can yield me in justice to the imperfect use which I make of the talents

---

[35] This title was later changed to "Hamatreya."

and opportunities bestowed. Thanks for the one as for the other!

July 4

FOURTH OF JULY

Discoursed with the spirit of my time over the rake and barrow, dressing the alleys of the garden and winding my peas and beans.

I cast my silent vote for the emancipation of the human soul, amidst the plants I love. The aroma of the buckwheat, eloquently humming with the winged freemen of the hives, disturbed now and then by the gunner's crack aiming death to the joyous songsters of the air and groves. They ventured not, these monstrous boys, into my coppice of protecting boughs, nor into my peaceful glebes. Ah me! War rages near me, and the fields of this my Concord are beleaguered round with armed ruffians. Happy for myself if I am as yet a freeman, and a soul at peace.

It is at any rate a delightful fancy to cherish the dream of self-emancipation, and on this anniversary of political independence to feel an inward conviction of freedom which no civil chains have yet bound. Alone in my benefice, why should I not rejoice in that freeness that cheapens all conventions, and makes me, in thought if not in deed, independent of the States and times, an honest and upright man in the midst of my age?

There is no audience for me save the attentive Nature in which I abide and toil.

July 25

THOREAU IN JAIL

Had an earnest talk with Emerson dealing with civil powers and institutions, arising from Thoreau's going to jail for refusing to pay his tax.

E. thought it mean and skulking, and in bad taste.[36] I de-

---

[36] Emerson's own comment upon this famous episode (Centenary Edition, VII, 219–223) is indeed wholly unfavorable, but not for the reasons Alcott suggests. Alcott had himself been arrested, three years before this, for refusal to pay his Town Tax, and on that occasion Thoreau, writing to Emerson (Letters, Jan. 24, 1843), had been amused. Alcott's Journals show that his theory of "civil disobedience," with which Emerson never fully agreed, was formed long before he knew Thoreau, who, in this instance, would seem to have followed his lead.

fended it on the grounds of a dignified non-compliance with the injunction of civil powers.

July 26

Read Landor's Conversations between Petrarch and Boccaccio concerning Dante. I cannot but think this one of the most delicate pieces of criticism modern times has afforded. Landor is a distinguished mind, and I think him more likely to survive than any modern writer, unless it be Carlyle.

I am almost tempted to place them thus in vigor and depth of discernment: Landor, Carlyle, Emerson.

Looked over Carlyle's "Supplement to Cromwell's Letters," and find it characterized by the same masterly dealing with historic facts.

Landor is the most finished writer of the three.

Thoreau spent an hour or two, conversing mostly on his late imprisonment in jail.

August 23

Emerson came and passed an hour in my study. We had a happy talk on poetry and the methods of poetry.

My tongue was loosed at last, and served my thoughts, particularly in some flights on human destiny and the destiny of the worlds.

September 13

Emerson called after dinner and we discussed in the summer house. Happy he who, seeking confines, is not himself confined therein. Worthy place, the arbour, for the reception of the poet as my guest. Happiest of men, to receive so happy a nature as this poet under a canopy made by my own hands.

When I became an osier, and supple to the hands of creation, then I wrought me an osier tent [37] and was happy under it in a spiritual day.

[37] Alcott's summer house was made of willow-wands or "osiers" cut from the willows in the meadow near his house.

September 18

> Sweet is the toil and swift the hours glide by
> While I my grounds delight to beautify.

Henry Thoreau came to see me. He was pleased with my summer-house and I took him to the hill top and showed him the site of my purposed "Lookout." He climbed a tree and measured the wide horizon with his eye. An ascent of 20 feet will give a wide prospect.

December 9

Read *Typee*, by Melville — a charming volume, as attractive even as *Robinson Crusoe*. I almost found myself embarked to spend the rest of my days with those simple islanders of the South Seas.

*THIS WAS one of Alcott's quietest years. During January
and February he passed every Sunday evening at Walden
Pond with Thoreau. A fugitive slave lived for a week in his house
at this time, eating at the table with the family. In the spring Alcott gave most of his time to gardening and the general improvement of his grounds, which even to-day bear the marks of his
labor. During the summer and autumn he devoted himself entirely to the task which he seems to have enjoyed more than any
other that he ever undertook — the building of a summer house
for Emerson.*

*The influence of Thoreau upon Alcott's thought and writing
grows more and more apparent.*

*Like that for 1846, this Journal is a first draft. Much of it is
written in the hand of a man engaged in severe manual labor.*

1847

January (undated)

Man, well-natured, is a denizen of Nature. Scholar, forester,
farmer, courtier, he craves possession of this, his patrimony, this
all of Nature, its usufruct and culture, or else pines and dies. For
he lives in Nature, and takes Nature into his mind. Nor is he

born till he has harvested her fields and is harvested in turn by
her. It is the fortune of genius to harvest the mind, and not
the stubble of literature.

> As dolphins quaff the liquid tide,
> So Nature's humours through his Spirit slide.
> To all on Earth he is allied.

January (undated)

The tongues are oftener hindrances than helps to the Mind.
Genius is the Hermes of Intellect, and dispenses quite easily with
the dialects of times. I thought today, as I inscribed my thought
by the woodside on a fly-leaf, of Orpheus, whose dialect I spake
not nor could read — that to all divinities the babblements of men
were nought, since the Spirit spake one tongue, nor could the
faintest of its voices fall meaningless on their ears, in what tract
of place or time soever.

January (undated)

Nature is the armory of genius. Cities do little for it; books
and colleges less. It craves the bolder intimations of ocean, mountain and lake, forest and plain, the entire view of the horizon
and the firmament, an actual conflict with the elements, a famili-
arity with the phases of the seasons, to give that athletic and vigorous use of the intellect which are the power and charm of culture.

January (undated)

Snatch colour from the sunrise. Dawn kindles the live coals
and tints our thoughts with its glow. Colour is the humour of
the Spirit, the flashing tides of Mind flowing forth to the surface.

January (undated)

The reporter of the laws of the cosmos and scribe of ideas
must be much afoot, in close communion with men, things as
these stand in Nature, overseeing and criticizing, from this uprightness and sweep of vision, citizen and society. Here, in this
true theatre of thought, the mind commands the broad horizon of

existence, and speaks veritably to mankind. The standing man thus discovers the right and true thought, by this rectitude of port, and recovers from the obliquity of sight which the prone positions at the desk are wont to create and confirm.

A countryman and naturalist also, the mind becomes effeminate as well as urbane and venal when impressed into the citizen and merchant, who deal not with Nature and persons at first but second hand. I for my part seem always puny and insignificant, a meanness and pretence, when caught in towns, and lose that command of my powers that Nature finds for me whenever I court her presence. The town robs me of myself, while I never return from Nature without spoils that ennoble and fill me. For this reason my best rhetoric is from the naturalist and poet, who speak from a close handling of that of which they report and sing. For Nature, the ever-present theme of the mind, supplies facts and diction, with the method of treatment always, if we will use our faculties aright.

February 2

The hunters are astir these sunny days, and from this my espial I hear every now and then the bolt dealt sure from the fowler's gun. Man is harried by his propensities. Everywhere in Nature I find the old felon, Murder, dogging Mercy. I cannot step upon my hill-top or plunge into the pine woods behind my house without encountering this huntsman. I am upon his track, he on mine — I in quest of my game, he of his. One cannot escape these Nimrods anywhere.

And now, as if to domesticate this wolf in my fancy, there arrives from the Maryland plantations a fugitive [1] to sit at my table and fireside, whom yet another Nimrod will seize and hurry swiftly into bondage or death if he can.

February 7

I had a Possessed One sitting by my side all winter; and it was remarkable to see what sway was exerted by the eye, the dialect of the moral sense, over the fancy of the damsel. She was as

---

[1] Alcott's house, like many another in Concord, was a "station" on the "Underground Railroad."

facile in my eye as a bride in the arms of her lover. It was pathetic to see how inexorably her will was bound in chains, and that never, by indirection and with extreme repugnance, never by her passions, but only by the service of others, could she put forth hand or foot or a faculty to serve herself, so completely had the devils bound her in chains which of herself she could not break.[2]

February (*undated*)

The State springs from man's inability to supply individually his animal wants, and rises into form with the rise of traffic between individuals to this end. Hence merchants at all times have played the games of State — kings, politicians, craftsmen, and husbandmen being their counters. Only poets and philosophers maintain life and independence of mind and character.

————

Why should I need a State to maintain me and protect my rights? The Man is all. Let him husband himself. He needs no other servant. Self-helping is the best economy. That is a great age when the State is nothing and Men are all. He who founds himself in freedom and maintains his uprightness therein founds an empire.

————

The State is man's pantry, at best, and filled at an immense cost — a spoliation of the human commonwealth. Let it go. Heroes will live on nuts, and freemen sun themselves under the clefts of the rocks, sooner than sell their liberty for the pottage of slavery. We few honest neighbours can help each other; and if the State desires any favours of us we will take the matter into consideration and, at a proper time, give them a respectful answer.

————

Individuality of character is always taken by the multitude as a proclamation of war against their usages and institutions; and rightly enough, because, established in the immortality of ideas, it threatens the overthrow of those mortal concerns which have

————

[2] Many minute indications make it highly probable that this "possessed" damsel was Alcott's daughter Louisa.

no deeper root than in the caprices of the vacillating and unsettled crowd.

February (undated)

The subject of cotton, coffee, wool, wine, ice, iron, tobacco, spice, women, beeves, and slaves, finds it not easy to dispense with his creditor, the State.

Could a man be thrown fully upon his own resources for a year, he might happen to see, and in no way short of this can he come to feel, the partnership in iniquities of which society is formed — and the people, silent partners, are themselves upholding, to their own impoverishment and shame.

February 9

Our friend the fugitive, who has shared now a week's hospitalities with us, sawing and piling my wood, feels this new taste of freedom yet unsafe here in New England, and so has left us for Canada. We supplied him with the means of journeying, and bade him a good god-speed to a freer land.

> Him pangs of freedom filled with strange surprise,
> And with wild rapture lights his eyes.

He is scarce thirty years of age, athletic, dextrous, sagacious, and self-relying. He has many of the elements of the hero. His stay with us has given image and a name to the dire entity of slavery, and was an impressive lesson to my children, bringing before them the wrongs of the black man and his tale of woes.

February (undated)

The aged Cephales in the Republic says that "as the pleasures respecting the body languish, the desire and pleasure of conversation increase."

So vivid was my sense of escape from the senses while conversing with Henry [3] today that the men, times, and occupations

[3] Thoreau.

of coming years gave me a weary wish to be released from this scene and to pass into a state of noble companions and immortal labours.

February (undated)

When St. James, nothing seemed more just than denunciation, and covetousness the sin of sins. So my chapter on rich men was conceived and written in a like spirit. But when I became St. John, though covetousness was esteemed of all sins most deserving of an angel's ire, yet I felt inclined rather to pity than denounce. Renunciation of denunciation is virtue's virtue for the soul of charity. A man must have been Christ, and then all the twelve disciples, to understand and practice Christianity.

February (undated)

It is much to have a platform as free as the minds of the freest of the time; and this service Garrison has done for us moderns. But Garrison himself, I now discern, is far from catholicism and the comprehension of the whole truth. He does not see it. The most intolerant of men, as trenchant as an Ajax, he has not yet won those self-victories which lead to the discovery of the unconquered territory of the enemy, and so of the superior powers of those who have won themselves and are the willing subjects of self-rule.

He snuffs the prey like a vulture, nor will he rest till his beak and talons are fast in the eagle's breast and the lion has seen him torn in pieces. He has perfect skill in the use of his own weapons, nor has he ever lost a battle. He cannot give quarter even, and is as unrelenting to friends as enemies. Mercy is no attribute of his justice. He knows all the manners of the snake, and, were he self-freed, might crush his head; but, as it is, will only scotch the hydra and play with his tail.

February (undated)

While our country affords the finest scope for the display of talent and genius, we have no culture worthy of the name. Neither the imagination nor the reason are addressed by grandeur of intellect or character, or — what exerts an influence even more potent, perhaps — the occupations and amusements of a period. . . .

What substitutes have we, for instance, for the falconry, chivalry, hunting, archery, of earlier and what we esteem barbarous times? And yet these, the toils of leisure as well as of business, were heroic, and gave a fine culture to body and mind. Even war had its advantages. And the wrestling and quoit-throwing, once the sports of youth and grave men, but now passed away. The plays and games of Greece were the schools of genius and valour, and the people were refined by the refinements of the best — at a less cost, too, perhaps, than with all our modern notions of decorum.

March (undated)

EMERSON, THOREAU

I was conversing last evening with Thoreau, and it appeared to us that, save Emerson, we had no masters of pure thought and composition on our side of the Atlantic in these days. Nor were Emerson's merits of the highest order. Continuity and flow were wanting, as we find them in some of the older poets. . . .

One other thing I miss in these my friends is the want of stateliness and vastness. I do not mean by this sustained flight merely — as in Bacon or Burke, whose qualities are rhetorical chiefly — but a breadth and sweep which conveys boldly to the eye the mind's circuits, and the rhythm of whose wings falls distinctly on the ear as from a vast distance.

His swallow's flight is an emblem of some moods of genius, but of repose rather than of active energy. And this is perhaps an apt type of Emerson's Muse — as in the *Hermione*, where he sings the Indian song:

> On the mound the Arab lay
> And sung his sweet regrets
> And told his amulets;
>   The summer bird
>   His sorrow heard,
> And when he heaved the sigh profound
> In sympathetic sorrow swept the ground.

BRONSON ALCOTT
From a photograph taken about the year 1875

Yet his Muse takes bolder flight sometimes, and skirts with vigorous wing along the horizon's rim; as when, from Monadnock, he surveys the globe:

> — the treacherous kite
> Farm-furrowed, town-encrusted sphere,
> Thoughtless of its anxious freight,
> Plunges on forever[4]

where the imagination grasps the image and bounds, while it sweeps impetuous along its circuit of winged ideas.

I am often reminded of Sir Thomas Browne as well as of Quarles when reading Emerson, and this not because of any very striking resemblance of thought or diction but chiefly, I believe, from like tendency. Quarles is livelier though less lofty, with an eye as sure and a wing as tireless. Browne would please me the better were his flights always longer sustained and the promise of his genius made good in its performance. His swift ascents and precipitate fallings disappoint. Yet there is not, perhaps, among moderns, an instance of a like audacity of thought with the same sure-footedness. He soars high, yet comes always safely to his feet again, and his descents are as perilous as his flights. This is no Phaëton's territory. . . .

If Emerson have sometimes Sir Thomas Browne's temerity, of whom he reminds me, and of Quarles, and a more graceful sweep, he yet falls short of both in reach and vigour. Sure of their quarry, these falcons always bring down their game. But there is not the beaked intellect and brave gluttony of their genius. It is a graceful yet feebler bird, of finer plumage and easier digestion; and there is no stately whetting of bills on the crags, no far-fetching eye, nor dire scenting of the prey from afar.

Thoreau's is a walking Muse, winged at the anklets and rhyming her steps. The ruddiest and nimblest genius that has trodden our woods, he comes amidst mists and exhalations, his locks dripping with moisture, in the sonorous rains of an ever-lyric day. His genius insinuates itself at every pore of us, and eliminates us into the old elements again. A wood-nymph, he abides on the

---

[4] The two passages of verse are inexactly quoted.

earth, and is a sylvan soul. If he could but clap wings to his shoulders or brow and spring forthright into the cope above sometimes, instead of beating the bush and measuring his tread along the marsh-sides and the river's sedge and sand, and taking us to some Maine or Indian wilderness, and peopling the woods with the Sileni and all the dryads!

But this fits him all the better for his special task of delineating these yet unspoiled American things, and of inspiring us with a sense of their homelier beauties — opening to us the riches of a nation scarcely yet discovered by her own population.

In this respect the contrast is striking between him and Emerson, whose Natures — caught, it is true, from our own woods — are never American, nor New English, which were better, but some fancied realm, some Atlantides of this Columbia, very clearly discernible to him but not by us; and our pleasure comes laden with the spoils this princely genius brings home, of the shores and climates of his far-off Indies, for our solace and refreshment — spices and gems, and the airs of Araby the Blessed.

If I were asked to name the chief dissatisfaction I have in these two fine townsmen of mine, I should say it is that neither my East nor my West Indian has a sky to his world. They are earth-birds, and so keep near their element . . . and it is swallow-circuiting, partridge-drumming, and the wading of water-fowl. They venture so timidly into the towns and society — unlike Carlyle, whose genius is no denizen of Nature but a cormorant of cities glutting himself on his game — unlike Goethe, amidst dove-cotes and pheasant-houses. . . .

Yet I am not unmindful of this best gift of the gods, seldom granted to one mortal — the enjoyment of such contemporaries as these: having Thoreau if I will betake me to Walden; at the Road Forks [5] may have Saadi, Confucius, and Zoroaster; and without stirring abroad have Belus, Minos, Memnon, and the Sphynx.

Emerson took refuge in the intellect while a demonic man, and his poetry lay as a robe of light on the merchant-genius he still was.

Thoreau took his position in Nature, where he was in deed and in spirit — a genius of the natural world, a savage mind amidst savage faculties, yet adorned with the graces of a civiliza-

[5] At Emerson's house.

tion which he disowned, but celebrating thereby Nature still. Both were forcible protests against the preternatural life of preceding times, and both sought the firm lands of the Nature they had and filled.

But I, for my part, asked for that denizenship in Life from which the hypernatural might be displayed in intellect — humanity and Nature alike in a complete Genius.

March (undated)

The Teachers' Institute, under the supervision of Horace Mann, held their session of ten days at the Court House in our village, and gave me an opportunity to see what the State is doing for the rising generation. A hundred or more teachers of the common schools were in attendance from day to day. Mr. Mann gave the instruction mostly, and I was gratified to find him recommending better methods of teaching.

But I learned little from teachers, or the teachers' teachers, on education. The time was passed in exhibition of methods, with the least reference to the principles of the mind or the philosophy of culture; and the hope of improving the state of mankind by these tardy and circuitous means seemed visionary. Such aims were scarcely worth the efforts they cost, nor could they issue in the creation of men for private or public business on a grand scale.

The Secretary of Education deemed it unsafe to introduce me to the teachers, and, on pressing my desire to give them the benefit of my experience as an educator, I was informed that my political opinions were esteemed hostile to the existence of the State, and that I could not aid the cause of popular culture. . . . Yet many of the teachers expressed a wish to know something of the principles and methods upon which my enterprizes in education had been conducted, and of which they had but vague notions.

The reform in this, as in all things else, must begin in individuals.

March (undated)

I read the story of Antigone to Miss Lord this evening, with my notes on it, which led us to speak of Emerson's *Ode to Chan-*

ning, in which the poet has not, as I think, justified the moral sentiment of man from the demonic agencies. In a poem for modern men, and especially in these days of slave advocacy, the possibility of emancipation should have been made indubitable. . . .

I don't like to have merchants and politicians find refuge from their own duplicity under his broad shield. Let him send them swift, with glaring eyes, to the horns of the altar of justice, to expiate the offended gods, nor let them have covert or quarter from his omniscience, but start from out every cotton-bale, every compromise with slavery, as from an avenger. . . .

It is only the heroic Muse, chanting her epopee, who brings

"Astonished thousands at her side."

July 14

Went with Emerson and Thoreau to Walden and cut some hemlock for columns to the Summer House, and brought them to the spot in Emerson's field. Dressed the cucumbers in the conservatory.

August 12

Began Emerson's arbour. Provided timbers for the platform and laid some of the planks. H. Thoreau assisted me.

August 13

Laid the planks to the platform and set the nine upright joists, to form the corners for the nine Muses to this poet's bower. Set a few uprights to see the effect.

October 5

Emerson sailed today from Boston in the packet-ship *Washington.*

October 18

I call this my style of building the "Sylvan." One merit is its simplicity. The curved rafters to the gables and the depending brackets under the cornice are original with me. The edifice seems

to be upheld by the broad cornice, the rafters aspiring in handsome curves to their apex and uniting at the ridge-pole, with
broad weather-boards and the bending brackets depending therefrom as if to find the ground and take root therein. It occurred to
me today, as I set my sweeping brackets, serving both as braces
to the building and as supporters of the heavy cornice, that I had
seen the same style in pictures of the Egyptian architectures. Such
things must originate in the one idea of the Infinite Beauty and fitness of the curve over the straight line in building. The highest
art will employ the curve always. The serpentine is ever mystic.

I seldom reach home from my work at Emerson's till quite
dark; and, after a supper of cream, honey, and wheaten cakes,
with apples and peaches, find myself pursuing my charming occupation to bed and all through the night long, in happy dreams.
And when the morning comes it is with an urgency to resume my
toil again as soon as the needful family chores are done, and I
am at E.'s field with my hammer and saw again.

November (undated)

My townspeople come every day to examine my work. It
would be quite amusing to report the remarks they make upon it,
applying many strange epithets to this strange production of art.
"It is odd," "The strangest thing I ever saw," "A log cabin," "A
whirligig," etc. etc., are a few.

It impresses all as something very curious, and belongs to a
department of handicraft with which they are but vaguely familiar.

The finest work of M. Angelo, set in the market place, would
doubtless provoke as many and as alien remarks.

It needs acquaintance with the state of mind from which a
work of art is produced, on the part of the observer, in order to
appreciate it and criticise it.

{1848}

DURING THIS uneventful year Alcott "journalized largely." He had the time for so doing. Emerson, who had left for Europe in the preceding October, did not return until July. Thoreau was kept busy in the management of Emerson's household and affairs. Anna was living at Walpole, New Hampshire. In April Mrs. Alcott and Abby left home to spend the summer in Maine. There was left Ellery Channing, with whom Alcott at this time became better acquainted. He began, however, to feel the need of more association, and in November the family took a house in Dedham Street, Boston. Alcott also rented rooms at #12 West Street, next door to Elizabeth Peabody's famous "atom of a bookshop." There, on December 9, he gave the first of a series of Conversations "On Man."

1848

January 9

Of one thing I am sure, namely that mine is a private mission to my time, and of quite independent and friendly character. It is to the fine minds both of clergy and laity, the priests of the New Gospel and their discerning followers; and I am to seek and be sought of them in private houses, by no means in public places.

Friendship is the only religion possible to moderns. Our God is a domestic God, and that fine sentiment which binds persons to each other is the only piety practical and efficient.

January 14

Labour educates the world. There is no education without it. Labour is the genius and god of this lower or outer world.

———

The age of insight and intuition is fast evicting that of observation and inference. From using contentedly the old eyes of a circuitous and painful logic, men are finding the superior power of a direct and instant intuition in all investigations of nature and spirit.

New eyes for discerning the old things! New instruments for the old implements!

It is easier to repair the eyes than to mend the spectacles.

———

The girls expressed great pleasure in their studies today. Dear maids, they have good faculties and have had slender justice from us amidst the vicissitudes of our life. I have always had a school in my brain for them, and furnished with all needful assistance; but the time has not yet availed me.

January 22

Carlyle has a broader and solider dramatic range than any living modern writer. What movement! What storm! It is as of the feet of grenadiers and the tramp of Napoleon's squadrons. Eyes! Who has eyes like his? And his sentences are a pellmell of Cheapside — all London agog, and the continent in the distance.

It is the Imagination a-merchandizing, all wares and advertisements of wares spread abroad, with ships, harbors, and banks and brokers, in the prospect. His sentences and paragraphs do an infinite business.

He sings no less than he fights and soliloquizes, and his sentences take any rhythms. Carlyle's energy is almost demonic, and even under his calmest and stillest sentences there seems to slumber a hell of fires that shall break forth and scorch and consume you as you read.

January 23

Thoreau came in while I was reading Thirwall's account of Pythagoras and of his aims, philosophy, and endeavours, and we discussed a little the possibility of reaching the people by means of a similar character in our day.

I was reminded by the perusal of the views and purposes of this illustrious teacher of our enterprise at Fruitlands, and of the many points which it had in common, both in idea and form, with the institution at Croton.

————

The Garrisons now rally under the watchword "No Union with Slaveholders," and, as a consequence, "Dissolution of the Union." Better step at once onto the firm ground, where they must plant themselves sometime to achieve complete victory — "No Union with the Union of Massachusetts" — that is, dissolution of themselves from the Bay State, and the organization of a government of free men if such there are among its population. That would be a step worth taking, and the only manly stand becoming the pioneers of freedom to New England.

Mem.: to sound the bravest minds at the Sabbath Convention in Boston next March. Revolution is inevitable, and it becomes the friends of good government and pure religion to take the initiative on this gravest of all popular interests.

————

Christianity, being first evolved by the Greco-Roman world in which art and war were the predominating ideas, partook as a matter of course of the genius of this people. And the polytheism to which they inclined, and which was indeed organic in them, was moulded into this new religion — which was a pure theism in the mind of its Jewish Author.

We have yet to free it from polytheism, and England and America seem the only countries in which it can emancipate itself from the old traditions.

————

Protestantism is far from being the true positive religion. Yet this is all of modern religion we now have. And it is all negative, and in some sort aggressive. It is *anti* — against some old-established form. It is restrictive. But the new and genuine faith is positive, peaceful. It is *for* a distinct and felt somewhat. It is constructive, and defines itself without a negative.

January 26

Heard Thoreau's lecture before the Lyceum on the relation of the individual to the State — an admirable statement of the rights of the individual to self-government, and an attentive audience.

His allusions to the Mexican War, to Mr. Hoar's expulsion from Carolina, his own imprisonment in Concord Jail for refusal to pay his tax, Mr. Hoar's payment of mine when taken to prison for a similar refusal, were all pertinent, well considered, and reasoned. I took great pleasure in this deed of Thoreau's.

February 1

The "Best Book in the World" is always the one you have just finished reading. Were it not so, I should pronounce this of Howell's *Letters*[1] transcendent. That it has one quality of the best composition, robust healthfulness and fair proportions, is a happy discovery; for among the many books commended to us again and again by their depth of thought, their large comprehensiveness, their sprightliness of wit, or playful humour, to say nothing of the graces of style as various as the mind itself, that is the Book of Books which breathes the air of health and colours every feature of sentiment and principle with bloom and freshness.

Such a book is Howell's. Written amidst the times of Bacon, it partakes of some of the humours of that period. It is as pure and intellectual as Shakespeare. It is the quintessence of humanity, and is pregnant with the flowers of civility. A book for the study of a gentleman.

[1] *Epistolæ Ho-Elianæ*, or *Familiar Letters*, by James Howell (ca. 1594–1666).

Emerson, among moderns, yields odors breathing of sylvan rather than of a courtly civility. In him we see more of the manliness of thought than of manners, and hold discourse with Nature rather than persons. Howell is a cultivated gentleman writing to gentlemen of his friendships and studies, and with the polished ease and gracefulness of conversation. He makes possible and beautiful the religion of friendship.

February 1

Walked to Walden with Channing. He admired the clear serene blue of the sky which, amidst the falling snowflakes, was almost as hazy as the summer heavens. The clouds piled above Wachusett in the west were magnificent, and some lying in buried repose about its base were worthy of the pencil of Rembrandt.

Altogether, our walk and conversation — especially at Goose Pond under the brow of the pine grove — was lively and suggestive and memorable. We talked of art and the new pantheism. We tried to name the gods whom some Angelo or Raphael is to paint. C. thinks pantheism is the only religion now left for us, and that the old Zoroastrian rites become us in so fine a Nature as ours here in this new world. The worship of the sun at dawn and at setting would at least promote the circulation of the spirits in which piety and the elements of a lively worship consist.

February 9

Montaigne's book is the only one, almost, which I wish were longer. Here is the perfection of speech — a mind thinking aloud, and faithful to the order in which the thoughts come into his head. I think his book the perfection of scholarship. He has achieved that most difficult of all arts, giving the natural history of his humour. One beholds the circulation of his blood, the beating of his heart. The whole man himself, the interior, appears in his pages — a natural gentleman, and so clear and elegant a mind. His learning illuminates his thought and is always pat, apposite, and proper. This is a rare man, Montaigne. Of all men, Emerson has most in common with him; and as I read I discern all along my friend's debt to this author. But how happens it that Emerson first found him out? Simply because he found himself there.

February 13

When a man's own culture falls behind that of his time, he is conservative. When it outstrips and enables him to over-see his time, he becomes a reformer.

February 23

Education and Government are one and the same. Government is best administered in the school-room — or, better, the family is the Executive of the Republic.

February 26

What must be the state of family life amongst a people whose literature has not yet given us a single volume of letters? Politics, sermons, the manual arts, merchandise, give us exhausting occupation but leave neither time nor spirit for the cultivation of friendship or those refinements which give to civility its charm and justify this human existence. See what Pliny did, and, if you can, think of Webster or Calhoun afterwards! The scholars and reformers, if followed into the house, shrink into ordinary if not hideous men.

March 2

The stalk and flower of our English speech is plucked only by boys. They alone who will read Ben Jonson or Beaumont and Fletcher shall see how solid and outspoken was the life of that period. It is refreshing to read these phrases of theirs. They admit us into an intimacy so entire with the thoughts and manners and speech of their day. I remember hearing the same words, and was indeed accustomed to use them, in my boyhood and native village, into which the refinements of the brisk town had not found the way. It lay so remote and secluded there on the mountains; neither was there a scholar to modify the homely speech of the people. They spoke the speech of Shakespeare and Beaumont and Ben Jonson. But now, if I would enjoy that pleasure of hearing my native tongue in its riancy and exuberance I must listen to the boys about our school-houses, or cast my eyes along the columns of the dictionary, there to recover the animal spirit which once sparkled and pranked itself forth in the buxomness and proud motions of our mother-tongue.

What we have gained in elegance we have lost in thought and expression; and in proof of this feebleness and paleness entailed on us it needs but to witness the effect of a great thought or the swelling of a passion, to see how the mind oversteps these conventional barriers and leaps into the ring with the boys and the mob, to make itself felt in genuine Mother-English.

The human body is itself the richest and raciest phrase-book; and it is at once a proof of the shallowness and indelicacy of our American authors that our rhetoric is so seldom drawn from this armory, and our speech partakes so little of the blood-warmth and the flesh-colours of nature.

March 8

"What are you doing, friend, there in your retreat?"

"I am thinking."

"Idler! Callest that 'doing'? Nothing comes, or can by any means come, of that nothingness."

"Stay, friend. Thoughts are the parents of deeds. Now I am ambitious of begetting an illustrious family."

March 14

I asked Thoreau if it were not proof of our inefficiency that we had not as yet attracted some fine soul, some maid from the farmer's hearth or youth from farm or workshop, to our houses, and there found a proof undeniable of having a positive and real existence here in this world, in this 19th century, in this winter of 1848, in this little centre of Concord, Mass. We may take it for granted that such youths abide near us, and that if these doors of reserve were once opened then would appear auditors and lovers of the truth, to whose voice we devotees daily listen and whose presence constitutes the charm of our days. It is true that neither by Lyceum nor other manner has anything like real intercourse been had between ourselves and our townspeople. . . . It is the office of a great life that it shine abroad and educate all within its neighborhood, and instruct, if not the adult, the youthful population who are nearest to it.

But between us and our townspeople only relations the vaguest, and in most instances of a character wholly fabulous, exist. We are ghosts and spectres, chimeras, rumours, holding no known relations to the fields and houses where we are supposed or seen to abide; and our dealings with men have an aspect ridiculous and to be made game of at the bank and bar-room. Our very virtues are mythological.

March 16

Art is but the record and memory of Nature, but of Nature's intentions rather than her performances. Art celebrates the victories of the mind over Nature.

March 24   (*Boston*)

Took a morning walk around the Common before breakfast. Passed an hour at Parker's,[2] where I met James,[3] who has spent some years in London and knows Wilkinson[4] and Carlyle intimately. He told me many things of both, and we had much to say on Swedenborg, of whose writings he is a student and whom he ranks first among modern minds. James intends to print a journal devoted to the views of Fourier and Swedenborg. His tract called *Tracts for the Times*[5] won him regard of the best people among us. I liked him well.

April 2

FRUITLANDS

"An air-castle," says Carlyle, "after all, that looks well at a distance but will secure no one from real wet and wind."[6]

But in the American's[7] case this fine lesson came from it: a measuring of his thought with the men and institutions of his time, and no less with the friends who approved and the few who

[2] Theodore Parker's house, 1 Exeter Place.
[3] Henry James, the Elder.
[4] J. J. Garth Wilkinson, a prominent English Swedenborgian.
[5] *Tracts for the New Times*, New York, 1847. The Journal to be called *The New Times*, which James was at this date planning, never appeared.
[6] Carlyle's comment, in a letter to Emerson, on Fruitlands.
[7] Alcott's.

joined in the enterprise. Also with the multitude, and their Church and State. Aloof in his conscience, his whole soul was in the work, and the shame and sorrow that followed was less for himself than for them and their supporters.

Three years in private seclusion and communion with Nature and himself restored him to hope and the service of mankind — a richer, a stronger, a wiser man for these lessons. Thus Heaven wins health from sickness and hope from defeat, when the patient is not defeated in the first principles.

Is it not much to front famine, nakedness, obloquy, insanity, family desertion, debt, alienation of friends, and be left to roam over the land an outcast, and a subject of pity, if not sometimes of contempt?

April 14

Not unless the whole of you goes into your sentences have you written anything. To maintain yourself in the full intense state requisite for writing is the most difficult of all endeavours.

But writing, as thinking, comes by the grace of God alone; and it is only the humble that receive the visitation of the Muses.

There can be no will in composition. Thought is organic, or else the productions of the brain are premature and monstrous. Only a great man can write greatly.

The spirit within is the only writer, but uses all the graces of culture as material ready to its hand.

August 15

We can no more dispense with the spirit of the old Hebraism than with our lungs. It is a part of the instruction of man, and must endure while man endures. It is one with the effluence of Jehovah, and the breath of life to one of devout soul.

If my E—— were but filled with it, then his fine Greek culture would shine forth and justify itself.

August 21

Emerson lived in and represented the life and time in which he lived, an historian of the past. But A. was not contemporary with him, though cast upon the same time, but dwelt solely in the future, leaving little or no impress on his time, or taking any from it. — A seer of the events and ideas of the next century.

Emerson will go down as a solitary person, the names of his friends known to posterity by their occurrence in his writings and not by any services they have rendered to entitle them to live in the memory. — They are names denoting the vague qualities of persons whom this writer knew, and so wove into his pages as a part of his own design.[8]

[8] The magnanimity of this statement is enhanced by the fact that Alcott knew something, though not all, of Emerson's debt to his own thought.

MUCH OF *Alcott's time was given during this year to Conversations at Salem, Hingham, Fall River, and his rooms in West Street. In February he organized The Town and Country Club of one hundred members, excluding women at Emerson's request. During July and August, while living at 1 Temple Place, he had the second clairvoyant experience — or, as he called it, "apotheosis" — of his life, and wrote with a steady sense of inspiration a strange manuscript called "Tablets," half mystical and half astrological, which bore no relation to his later book of the same title. This so exhausted him that he was obliged to spend two weeks at Concord for recuperation. In October the family moved to 11 Groton Street. At the end of the year Alcott began his Conversations "On Human Life" in the rooms of the Town and Country Club in Tremont Street.*.

1849

May 20

Clutch wheresoever about him he may, man cannot miss seizing hold of some symbol and correspondence of himself. Nature is put through, and forms and fructifies in, man's soul, wherein it takes root and finds its proper sap and nourishment.

All form is a limning of Spirit. Nature, in its ultimate, is throughout as faithful and finished a draught of mankind as matter can receive and retain of him.

The Spirit, which dictates, is alone competent to read the letter of things spiritual or sensible.

Revelation is God's word, Creation his work, the Spirit sole seer and interpreter of both.

Man's mind is a menstruum of the universe, and its only solvent.[1]

May 21

Philosophy, practically stated, appears just now to be subsistence minus bread and butter.

May 26

Today comes Henry Thoreau to town and gives me a copy of his book, just published by James Munroe & Co., entitled

"A Week on Concord and Merrimac Rivers"
— 12 mo. pp. 413.

An American book, worthy to stand beside Emerson's Essays on my shelves.

May 27

Read Thoreau's book all day.

May 28

Again read Thoreau, and admiringly.

June 24

To say that all things were once created out of nothing is saying nothing has been created, or is.

The assertion denies, as it undermines, the grounds of all existence, namely Spirit and God, as premise, and is puerile, atheistic, and impious. Spirit creates out of itself.[2]

---

[1] In this meditation Alcott is groping toward the doctrine of "Genesis" which was to become one of his most characteristic ideas. The fact is of some importance, therefore, that he wrote the passage just after reading, in E. P. Peabody's *Æsthetic Papers*, the article on "Correspondences," by J. J. G. Wilkinson.

[2] A second step toward the doctrine of "Genesis."

July 7

To Concord this afternoon, to pass Sunday with Emerson.

July 8

With Emerson. Also see Thoreau a little while. To Walden afterwards, discussing Genesis and the rest.

> The forest bees flew round to sip
> Sweet honey sage from sovreign lip.

Evening: I am at Hillside and sell my grass crop to Hosmer, the carpenter, for house repairs there. I sleep at Emerson's.

July 9

I leave at 10, and bring home "Hermes Trismegistus" — also MSS left with Emerson some months since and intended for my transcripts now.

This has been a refreshing time, and leaves now in the memory a sense of an eternity outlived with my friend, and ensouled by us mutually.

July 11

The most expressive faces owe their interest to their inwardness chiefly, and the depths and distance of their perspective — as a palace seen at the end of an avenue, or at some unexpected turn in the grounds. But I have seen faces frequently without distance or vistas, like houses without shrubbery and thrust into the street. The soul asks a background also, as well as courts the winding approaches. A human being is a creature too significant, even in his meanness, to be approached with rudeness, and is not to be seen sidewise or run against by the roadside.

July (undated)

And I, if I be lifted up, will draw all men unto me. — Christ.

Throughout nature's forms, heads symbolize sovreignty, spines subordination. Vices ascend in spirals — the serpent form the type and base of all forms else visible. Man, the serpent spiritual and ideal, being emulous of being lifted from the dust, he, of all creatures, is alone capable of rectitude and sole imperial self-rule under the Spirit. Nature is man recumbent and prostrate, himself treading upon the breast and dwelling here upon his overthrown torso.[3]

August 5   *At Concord, with Emerson*

All day discussing the endless and infinite theme in the study and while walking, the late revelation leading all the rest — Oken, Goethe, Swedenborg subordinated and sunk in their theories of the Creation as they seemed and were.[4]

September 1

Go to Concord, send Elizabeth home, see Thoreau a while, and sleep at Emerson's.

September 2

Pass the forenoon with Thoreau. We walk by "The Cottage" and discourse reclining on the hillside near the Indian meadows by the riverside.

Afternoon with Emerson. We walk to Walden and bathe. Emerson reads me the introductory paper to his book *Representative Men*, now nearly ready for the press, and we discuss Plato,

---

[3] The doctrine of "Genesis," fully formed though not yet clearly stated. The present phrasing of this doctrine is based to some extent upon the writings of the physiologist Lorenz Oken.

[4] The "infinite theme" and the "late revelation" are, undoubtedly, the Alcottian doctrine of "Genesis," to the formation of which Lorenz Oken, Goethe, and Swedenborg had contributed much.

On the same page with this entry there is pasted a slip of paper bearing, in Emerson's handwriting and written in pencil, the famous lines long afterward incorporated in the poem *May Day*:

> "A subtle chain of countless rings
> The next unto the farthest brings;
> The eye reads omens where it goes,
> And speaks all languages the rose;
> And, striving to be man, the worm
> Mounts through all the spires of form."

Emerson's thought that Nature "mounts" toward man is opposed not only to Alcott's theory of "Genesis," which asserts a universal descent, but to his own early teaching in the book called *Nature*.

Goethe, Swedenborg, and some others of his Representatives of the race. — Of Swedenborg especially there was much said, and of the Goethe and Oken morphologies, with my late experiences and their fruits.[5]

September 3

Mrs. Hosmer invites me to take rooms in her house near the Cottage for a fortnight or three weeks, to recruit a little; and I return to Temple Place.

September 9

A family day, the girls all at home again. Also arrange my things a little for going to Concord. . . .

September 11

I take the 11 o'clock train for Concord, take possession of my chamber at Mrs. Hosmer's, and arrange my things there. After-noon, see Thoreau, and come in early to bed.

September 12

Arise from a refreshing night's sleep to breakfast at half-past six with Mrs. Hosmer and daughter Sarah. Have a fair morning's intimacy with my papers, correcting and casting out many of them as inadequate and unworthy here. An after-dinner stroll about the grounds of my pretty Cottage near, once my daily haunt and still having some trace of my hands, and of my brother's also.

Afternoon, walk with Emerson by the riverside along the meadows behind Hillside and the Virginia fields, to pass the eve-ning with Emerson discussing Boston and the winter's entertain-ments, returning at 9 to my rooms.

September 13

A delicious morning, and a sweet night of sleep and dreams. After breakfast, walked along the railway and over the hills by Thoreau's and the Concord stream. Clear, cool, invigorating the sun and the morning moistures. After sipping of the heavens and

[5] The recent "revelation" of the doctrine of "Genesis."

the landscape for an hour or so, I came into chambers to papers and books till dinner time.

Yesterday, Emerson gave me a copy of his newly reprinted *Nature, Addresses, and Lectures,* being his fourth book. . . .

Afternoon, came Thoreau, and I read from my Journal of '47 a criticism on his book on the Concord and Merrimac Rivers — also notes on himself, Emerson, and Channing; and we walked afterwards to the Hallowell Place and along the riverside. Home to supper, and I to sleep again.

Thoreau [6]

(from my Journal of 1847)

"*March 16*

"This evening I pass with Thoreau at his hermitage on Walden, and he reads me some passages from his MS volume which he is preparing to print some day entitled 'A Week on the Concord and Merrimac Rivers.' . . . It is a Virgil and Gilbert White and Yankee settler all, singing his prose-poems with remembrance of his reading and experiences in the woods and road-paths by way of episode and variety — a portraying of a dreamland lying wild and yet unvisited here in New England, and still remote from everybody but the bold dreamer himself.

"It seems likely to become a popular book with our people here, winning at once the reader's fancy and his heart, inspiring a natural piety for nature and natural things, as surprising as it is refreshing. So sweet and robust withal, as if succulent yet, and promising a growth comparable to the scenes he communes with, and making everything foreign and artificial look cheap and trivial beside it — as if the rocks and mountains and the green earth had spoken in good earnest again, and so broken the silence they had sworn to keep till some brave heart should visit them. . . .

"The book is purely American, fragrant with the lives of New

---

[6] This passage of glowing appreciation is to be read with the fact in mind that Thoreau was an unknown man when it was written, and that no one — at least so far as Alcott knew — had ever before attempted a careful estimate of his thought and style.

England woods and streams, and could have been written nowhere else. It preserves to us whatever of the wild and mystic remains to us along our brooksides and rivers, and is written in a style as picturesque and flowing as the streams he sails on. . . . There is a toughness too, and a sinewy vigor, as of roots and the strength that comes of feeding on wild meats, and the moist lustres of the fishes in the bed below.

"It has the merit, moreover, that somehow, despite all presumptions to the contrary, the sod and sap and fibre and flavour of New England have found at last a clear relation to the literature of other and classic lands, and we drink off here the quintessence also of literature the coolest and freshest. Egypt, India, Greece, England, flow from the poet's hand as he scoops the waters for us from the rivers, or perchance surprises by opening sometimes a hive of wild honies before undiscovered or tasted in the woods. . . .

"Especially am I touched by this soundness, this aboriginal vigour, as if a man had once more come into Nature. . . . Moreover, there is business here for the naturalist's notice — facts abundant in these pages, of leaves, lakes, rivulets, and old fields and hillsides. Such animals and fishes as he can surprise! Plants and stones hitherto untabled in the books! And here the husbandman and huntsman are helped in their callings — the former especially, to see for the first time . . . the farms they call theirs and somehow cultivate, or desolate rather in their shiftless economics.

"Poems are here also, vigorous and rugged enough to defy Quarles or Donne, and as sound and seasonable as theirs; as if, in some mood of great exuberant frolic, the Muse had set the poet to rhyming the stumps and hedges into music, and he had done poems for Irishmen idealized at the gravel diggings, and all the animals were enamoured of the strains. Criticism, too, we have, of the like radical quality and toughness. Homer, Hesiod, Æschylus, and Chaucer have got some one to look a little into their merit now, and modernize and make them indigenous and home-felt once in Concord.

"I came home at midnight through the woody snow-paths and slept with the pleasing dream that presently the press would place on my shelves a second beside my first volume, also written by my townsman, and give me two books to be proud of: Emerson's *Poems* and Thoreau's *Week*."

September 17

Afternoon: bathe with Thoreau at the Fishing Place and write again to my wife in the evening, to send by Miss Sarah. . . .

Emerson is here this evening also.

September 18

Again taste the morning fresh along the Groton road, and return by the fine woods of neighbour Browne, for whom I chopped wood in the year '42, the winter before I went to England. Fruitlands seemed to lie off in the distant blue there, as I caught a glance at Wachusett in sight of it, and I will take a look at the spot before I return to winter quarters in town — if the mood favours and I can bring myself to walk so far.

But now the old sweetness comes for some hours while at my "Tablets" today, disposing the transcripts on Friendship and the ideal society, of which I am tasting so lavishly these September days here and have tasted in the early summer before. . . .

September 26

Walk by the factory and turnpike home. . . . Bathe at the fishing place. Emerson comes and invites me to pass some days with him.

September 27

To Walden and home by the Village. Dine at Emerson's and walk by Ed. Hosmer's. Afterwards back to supper.

Evening: talk on Plato and Plutarch.

I sleep at Emerson's.

September 28

This morning and forenoon, repair the thatching a little, and interior, of Emerson's summer-house, standing gracefully on the lawn and embowered now in evergreens set there by Thoreau and myself — the front gable seen from the south door of his house with its rustic lyre emblazoned and latticed window so pretty, a pleasure to see. . . . I built and endowed it so far with all the opulence of the woods.

Have an hour on my "Tablets," and a walk after dinner with Emerson.

About "Hillside" again, surveying the premises and the reminiscences they suggest of Antæus and the Earth.[7]

[7] That is, of the way he had regained his strength at "Hillside" after the defeat at Fruitlands.

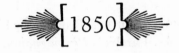

{1850}

IN THE middle year of the century the poverty of the Alcotts approached destitution. Mrs. Alcott was working among those who were poorer than herself; Anna was teaching school, and Louisa, though only seventeen, was assisting her; Alcott himself, whose contact with children was confined to his daughter's schoolroom, "conversed" where and when he could, with slight financial reward. In the early summer the entire family was taken down with smallpox. The tragic death of Margaret Fuller on the sixteenth of July startled and saddened all her friends, of whom Alcott was one of the most admiring. It became evident that Alcott's second attack upon the strongholds of Boston conservatism was not to succeed better than his first. His naturally social disposition found inadequate response. He turned inward, began to regard himself as a recluse, and spent much time in lonely musings on Boston Common. Some alleviation of his solitude was found in the increasing warmth of his affection for Emerson, in a new association with James Russell Lowell — whose powers and shortcomings he almost immediately saw — and in the companionship of Ednah Dow Littlehale, who was to be his daughter's biographer.

1850

January 1

I passed some hours at Little & Brown's, looking at their extra-fine collection of books. Larabie's *Physiognomy*, in four volumes, attracted my eye — the plates particularly. Here too I found the collected Works of the poet Wither, in three volumes, and read his poem "Fair Virtue" again — the book lost by me at Albany in 1844, with other books and MSS not recovered at this date, but whose loss I can never repair, for with these went my records of the British and Fruitlands experiences, and many valuable letters of that period.

January 4

Read from poems of Lowell's and passed this afternoon at Elmwood in Cambridge. Lowell read me some lines from a poem of his which he calls "The Nooning," and will print at about next midsummer. I must give Lowell's books more faithful reading before I may venture any criticisms. If as good as I find the poet to be, I shall like them quite well. He is about the heartiest and best-natured person I have met with lately. His ruddy health and flowing spirits render him the best of company; and one asks how he came by those qualities, so rare to be met with here amongst this severe and staid Puritan people. But the culture of the Old Countries has flowered into the brain of the present generation, and so softened the asperities and remoulded the manner of those primitive settlers as to suit the genius and temper of our times; and the best qualities native to the present American seem to have been engrafted with the best foreign elements upon the old primitive stock. Lowell is an example of this. He, of our young men of promise, is perhaps the most American, and yet would feel most at home in England or Germany of any young persons amongst us. With powers thus healthy and vigorous, and blessed with a fine animal basis, our poet would take life in London or Berlin quite freely, eagerly even, and find nothing very strange in it. His best endowment is his admirable health, and this is the Poet's endowment — felicity, health of mind and body. And, taken in its freshest and widest sense, it seems one with genius and sanctity, and to be the source and secret of art. For beauty, in its varied displays, is but the overflowing of life's tides, rising and spilling forth their forms and colours in rapture, in music, and song. Health is an art, and is one with inspiration. . . .

Lowell walked with me as far as Cambridgeport on my way home in the evening.

I found a note from Emerson awaiting me on my return, inviting me to visit him at Concord.

January 5

Set off for Concord to pass Sunday with Emerson. Dined with E., and saw Thoreau in the evening a while. Emerson is now writing on "The Modern Mind and Times," and the current of discourse set in that direction. But the best of intercourse is the intercourse, and the best of all conversation is the least reportable. Our amanuensis is thus unaccountably shy of us, or, by some freak of fancy or another, is absent altogether, and we get no services out of him when they would be most acceptable to us.

. . . Opinions were never at any former period of the world's history circulating with the speed and momentum and sure tendency, as of birds of omen, given them by the adventurous genius of our time. But these aerial passengers await obviously enough the organizing genius to bring down and acclimate the vagrants in the warm instincts of the mother nest and native country out of which they flew, till the season of cold be over and they venture forth again in rare adventures to the regions of snow. . . .

We must treat our friends as we do pictures and statuary — survey them from the perspectives of an affectionate idealism, or we get nothing out of this enterprise of friendship. A friend must be a creator and renew us often, to win and keep us.

I know of but one soul that can draw me near and make it necessary, in some sense, to abide in his neighborhood. And this emotion of the mind which I call friendship is the nearest that I have attained as yet to what men call religion, if it be not one with that venerable sentiment of the preference of Deity. It is only in the ebullience of love and genius that we snatch the new delights and discover first the brilliancy of the dove's neck. . . . Pure intimacies are illustrious, like the reflection of oceans and of firmaments. Introduce me to him, if you have found him, who casts pearls from his lips as stars ray forth from their centers.

For disputation, crowds; for rumination, woods; closets for thought; and for discourse, a single friend. . . .

January 6

We conversed all day and late again on the old themes. Toward night we walked to Walden Water and by Thoreau's hermitage, celebrated in some descriptive verses by Ellery Channing which are characteristic of the primeval virtues and sylvan beauty they sing so well.

. . . Concord is classic land; for here dwell the poets, the Americans *par excellence* and men of the future, whose names shall render Harvard and Yale, with their professors and halls, one day ridiculous. The names of Emerson and Thoreau and Channing and Hawthorne are associated with the fields and forests and lakes and rivers of this township, and here still reside the three first-named of them. . . . And 'tis at heart my own home. I must draw me closer to its bosom and my friends one day, for the cities cannot detain me long, nor the necessities that led me forth from "Hillside" a year since or more. It were well to breathe its air and feed on its landscapes again. The town is well enough, and yields its own proper enjoyments, and I find great content in it; yet, though the mind be a citizen, and love the urbanities as good and native and fit in their season, she delights the more in what Nature spreads abroad, and is still a countryman at heart. . . .

I am the richest of all men in this Commonwealth, I sometimes think, in possessing these friends of mine. I esteem them as the victories of my life. They are country and countrymen. They are lives and places and times, and stand for thoughts and things perennial and enduring:

> Olympian bards, who sung
> Divine ideas below,
> Which always find us young
> And always keep us so.[1]

[1] From Emerson's *Ode to Beauty*.

January 13

Woman is an allegory; a myth sleeping in a myth; a sheathed goddess and a blazonry; a Sphynx's riddle, devouring and devoured; an ambush and retirement, a nimbleness, a curiosity, a veil behind a veil, and a peeping forth from behind veils; a crypt of coyness, a goal of surprises, and an ambuscade.

But here comes the enemy in blazonries! Our Venus recoils, retreats behind the screen, and has escaped. And yet, lo! such is the art of this fine modesty, she stands yet the more visibly before the pursuer, and in her slipper, wrapped in blushing fears, tremulous, and in cypher, is found the plighted vow.

January 15

. . . Coming home from my call on Miss Bremer,[2] I met Lowell in Pemberton Square, and we walked together up Washington Street to Miss Peabody's. L. begged me to write my autobiography. And I shall attempt something of the sort presently, to clear my existence of the charge of unproductiveness which might be quite honestly preferred against it by those who are not in my secret.

January 18

Miss Littlehale [3] called in the afternoon, and I walked home with her. The company of intellectual women has a certain freshness and zest one seldom tastes from intercourse with cultivated men. Sexual qualities seem as needful to the propagation of thought as of human beings, nor do I like any man who never reminds me of the graces proper to women. It is these qualities that we love in a friend. The best of Emerson's intellect comes out in its feminine traits, and were he not as stimulating to me as a woman, and as racy, I should not care to see and know him intimately nor often.

[2] Fredrika Bremer, 1801–65, the Swedish novelist.
[3] Ednah Dow Littlehale, later the wife of the artist Seth Cheney, and the biographer of Louisa Alcott.

January 21

. . . The rhapsodist [4] declares what he must. There is no will in his utterances. As our best things overtake us sometimes in dreams, and profoundest thoughts often startle and awaken us at the midnight hour. "As the wind blows where it lists and we hear the sound of it but cannot tell whence it comes nor whither it goes, so is the voice of instruction."

February 1

It was during these months [5] that there came a period of surprising introversion unlike any former experiences of mine, and too remarkable, indeed, to be easily forgotten, yet not easily described. The state is faintly indicated in the following notes from my diary of that time:

"And this seems to be our apotheosis — shall we name fitlier by any other name what we see and feel as ourselves? . . . It is no longer Many but One with us, and we live recluse yet sweetly and sagely, as having made acquaintance suddenly of some mighty and majestic friend, omniscient and benign, who keeps aloof as if it were beneath some intervening umbrage, and yet draws me toward him as by some secret force, some cerebral magnetism, while he enjoins the writing of things he extends to me from behind the mystic leaves. I am drawn on by enchantment, and seem taking the leaves of the trees of lives then plucked for me, and to sojourn I know not whither through regions of spirit — some Atlantides, perhaps, of the mind, and Seats of the Blessed. And now come the old memories into me, and I fear, almost, this blaze of being. This survival of the foregone periods in me shall blot from the memory forever the spots and forms and names I so lately knew. . . . Far too slender is the thread that holds me to this Now, so that I forebode its snapping asunder with every inspiration."

February 7

Nothing in the world is so rare and precious as this grace of free and elegant discourse; but it is the late and loveliest flower

[4] In using this word Alcott is usually thinking of Emerson.

[5] The summer and autumn of 1849, when Alcott was working on his manuscript called "Tablets."

of all civility, and takes time to ripen. I do not think our people eminently social and gifted in conversation. We have no distinguishing social talents; we have no surpassing talkers. It takes a fine, full, flowing nature, and capable of abandonment to ideas, to give the accomplished discourser and show us a soul alive and intense throughout. We have no great thinkers-aloud, the spectacle of which is the finest game of the mind. Our Eastern temperament is reserved, stands fast and long in dissensions and thinks highly of differences and decorum, excluding from our culture the advantages of surprise and enthusiasm and the free play of the whole nature. It will be long, and in spite of our manners, before a Coleridge shall come to reveal the resources of the mind and show us the fine organ that Conversation is in the hand of a master.

February 12

Went to Concord with Lowell and dined with Emerson. It seemed, on discussion, quite feasible, and a thing to be — our *Town and Country Magzaine*, with Lowell as editor and the men we know as contributors to it. Emerson wishes to have it, and will print his best things in it; and with him and Lowell and Hawthorne as prominent and steady contributors the success of the work is sure. Each has things which, printed in any journal, would insure its popularity with a select and somewhat wide circle of readers. And I desire it no less for Thoreau and Channing, who are to be known and prized in literature but find no organ as yet, short of the printed book, by which they have come to speak.[6]

I value Thoreau's Commonplaces [7] more highly than the writings of any man whom I know save Emerson; nor can I be mistaken in my conviction, long cherished, of his certain fame, when the rare qualities of his mind, his freshness of fancy, and vigorous veracity of understanding shall have won their proper reward. A character of so much originality and probity of soul must prevail, and he is able and ready to wait his time.

---

[6] It seems more probable that the seed of *The Atlantic Monthly* was sown in this conversation than that it was, as F. B. Sanborn suggested, in the one held by Alcott with his English friends on July 21, 1842.

[7] Now known as his Journals.

February 13

Today I looked again at Little & Brown's a while, pleasing myself principally with inspecting some admirable anatomical drawings of the human body in five large volumes, folio, but forget now the author's name. — I can never satisfy my eye with looking at this mythos and crypt of spirit, the human form and its organs. Yet I should not care to witness dissections. It is the living integral whole that I care for, and the parts viewed always in their connexions. A gallery of statues is more significant and instructive than one of skeletons. . . . Every organ, when thus seen, is a noble myth of the life it enshrines, and, seen in picture or figure, becomes poetic and beautiful, and, its functions thus idealized, religious.

We call the Greeks wanting in that modesty which is proper to nature and the sign of innocency, and yet we nowhere find in nature forms so modest and faces so fair and godlike as they have left us in their marbles and paintings. And the modern nations, with all their fortune and prosperity in many things, have achieved nothing that can compare with the splendid and seemingly completed mythology of that ideal people. . . . As a people, this Saxon race does not, I fancy, supply finer, if it does as fine, figures, whether male or female, for the artist's choice. It would seem as if only idealists could propagate the highest forms of majesty and beauty, and that the Roman blood, in giving force and material power, had despoiled the human figure of the symmetry and ideal loveliness of which the Athenians seem to have been the highest and surest known representatives.

But this type seems reappearing here in New England, and we shall nowhere find a native American woman whose Roman physiognomy and figure would remind us — as would Fanny Kemble, for instance — of that formidable people. It is plain to me that Nature has charms yet lurking within her breast that shall one day rival all we know of the wondrous beauties of Greece, and that this New English people, after some centuries, will surpass all others in majesty and grace, as they must in power. . . .

Webster, our boldest type of the American man, is plainly a

cross of the Roman Briton with the American Indian, and with no trait of the Attic race. He has all of the intellectual qualities on a base of aboriginal stock — solid, columnar, formidable, but no comprehension of other than material interests and affairs, no idealist, but an understanding colossal and imperative, with the temperament and rhetoric of the Indian, and as ironic and enduring.

Our best and almost sole example of the nobler type, though not quite pure, is to be seen in the ideal and classic beauty of Emerson's head and neck, and the firm chiselling of the nose and lips; the whole contour of the figure and the motion of the intellect being as Olympian — the eyes particularly — as Webster's, and as American in his understanding — dealing with affairs in a style quite mercantile, as if he were born within a wall and had a Threadneedle Street in his brain, as well as with a world of ideas, and an imagination to illustrate and build thenceforth in visible shapes to the reason and sense.

February 14

This afternoon read at the Athenæum again.

Emerson came in while I was reading at the table, and we had some talk in the alcove on Garrison's part in last Monday evening's parliament at my rooms. E. said that he could never speak handsomely in presence of persons of G's class. And I, too, plead to the like infirmity, if infirmity it be; and while entertaining profoundest respect for the formidable talent and executiveness which works out principles to their issues, and can scarce over-rate these admirable qualities as practical equipments, I scarce never meet a person of this temperament with unmixed pleasure. The spirit and grain of this class is essentially discourteous, and there is fight and desperation in the blood, manners, and speech of the creature. He persists, and must, on precipitating every man he meets headforemost into the pit of his indignation, and sets his conscience forthwith to fork the poor victim into the flames raging in his own veins, impaling his prey there most unmercifully, as he were doing Satan's behest in the Lord's name.

. . . A poor creature may be so overloaded with the sense of responsibleness, so frightfully executive and instant and despotic in enforcing what he calls his "sense of duty," as to sacrifice the rest of himself in his endeavours to be faithful to himself and to others. For an overplus of conscience is quite as disastrous and fatal as a like excess of passion or of intellect in our mixture, and converts the talents and propensities instantly and inevitably into demons to victimize the possessor — or possessed, rather — and everyone who falls in his way. Only the good man and true and circumspect safely mounts the law and rides onward to victory. But neither of our prophets — Carlyle nor Garrison — seem to have now the complete mastery, and demonize in a style most Satanic, lurid, explosive, and damnable.

February 17

Afternoon, came Mr. Bowers from Lowell, inmate once of our family at Fruitlands. His Paradise seemed as far off as when I first knew him, nor had his theories of life changed essentially since then. This man is the first and only Adamite that has come to me these last ten years, during which every possible phase of human speculation has turned up here in these parts, and samples of all the zealots of history, broadly enough caricatured sometimes, have walked in modern costume over my threshold as if to claim sympathy, if not paternity, under my roof.[8]

A history of these men, their thoughts and doings, their vague longings for a terrestrial Eden, their pictures of an ideal society and adventures in endeavouring to actualize their dreams here in Yankee land and in some of the western states, would rival the stories of Defoe, Don Quixote, and the Arabian Nights' Entertainments. I know of no better material than could easily be collected from this period for a philosophical romance that should vie with Sir Thomas More's *Arcadia* [*sic*] and Plato's *Republic*. Extremes have met — the odds and ends and beginnings of all imaginable reforms, the chaos of a new cosmos.

Brag and gasconade, prophecy and blasphemy and preaching and contention and denunciation, Chardon Street and Bible and Groton Conventions, Abolition mobs and meetings of non-resisters and of women, Committees and Symposiums, Clubs and *The Dial*,

[8] In this and in the preceding selection Alcott gives the first clear evidence of his gradual turn away from the more radical men and measures of reform. His air of detached amusement suggests the influence of Lowell.

Fruitlands, Brook Farm, Parkerism, Conversations, and Emerson — these were significant aspects of the time, and elements of the biography of its ruling spirits, looming forth from the canvas bold and lurid and serving to illustrate their ideas, failures, and experiences.

March 1

. . . But there is a free spirit abroad that is educating us quite over, and out of what are usually deemed the means of grace and culture. It is but a few years since the creative and forming minds first met the people in the people's own meetings. I remember the feeling about Parker and Emerson and Channing. They were, but a short time ago, not only unpopular but obnoxious exceedingly. But the two first of these gentlemen get more invitations to lecture at Lyceums and before literary societies than any body else, and Thoreau has read papers quite recently before the people in our cities and towns with a decided acceptance. Even Phillips and Garrison and Pillsbury are now listened to with some respect, and their doctrines and measures find favor from a very excellent body amongst us.

Extremes are getting less extreme; conservatism concedes a little and reform softens somewhat; and one feels, amidst the transition of our time, the sure signs of an improved order of things.

March 5

. . . Our circle of purely literary men is very small here in Boston and vicinity, and a dozen or twenty persons at most, with such few women as would care for intellectual entertainment, would include every desirable element. We talked about some concert of this kind at Lowell's the other day, and found our list of names very brief and soon told. There was: Emerson, Hawthorne, Longfellow, Lowell, Clarke, Hillard, Weiss, Thoreau, Peabody, Bartol, Parker, Cabot, Sumner, Ward, Channing, G. B. Emerson, D. Jackson, Hedge — but one might not venture further with any safety or advantage.

I, for instance, should never meet some of these gentlemen, never see them in private, perhaps, but in so small a circle, and one so purely literary, intercourse would be quite possible, and oftentimes very stimulating. . . . Our Symposium Club contained about this number and was a fine whetstone for the wits, and served us higher ends than we were at all conscious of at that time of *Dials* and other the like endeavourings of the present genius. It was in its day an institution, and a good one.

March 8

This morning called on Charles Sumner, who declined reading us a paper.[9] Sumner's person and manners are very agreeable to me, but I have never yet been successful in getting through these fairly to the essential gifts and natural motives of the man. He is one of the pleasing spectacles that I like to look at once in a while, but see best at some well-defined angle and with the advantage of the best conventional glasses, to bring out the fine points and impart the species of pleasure proper to objects of this class.

I think him one of the purest samples of the new Bostonian — a gentleman of finer qualities than belonged to the men of our earlier day, to the Ticknors and Everetts; quite catholic, urbane, affable, of handsome gifts, and so far emancipated from metropolitan convention as to venture a little into fields of politics and benevolence and to close sometimes into the neighborhood of seditions and fanaticisms. Quite unpopular, yet holding a clear position, and indisputably of honor and influence.

I have never discovered any aptitude for ideas or signs of genius in him. He seems conventional, scholastic, commonplace, and owes his reputation mainly to a noble disposition and a fine person. His attainments are all of the Harvard cast.

March 9

Walked to Elmwood and passed an hour with Lowell. He read me some verses from the new edition of his Poems. They were all very pleasant to hear, yet his rhymes have not taken my fancy as I find they have the ear and heart of several good people of my acquaintance. I look for pure idealism in poetry, and do not, I suspect, accept any mixtures in compositions of this sort. Lowell does not seem to me to be an idealist. His fancy has not freed him

[9] Before the Town and Country Club, of which Alcott was the Secretary.

from the understanding and given him to unrestricted thought. There is a humming about the flowers, in an easy diction rhythmic and grateful to the ear, but honies are not secreted for us. We get the music and the motions, but the Psyche seems not quite fledged, and the imagination loses the expected delights of the true poem. His diction is more varied than that of any of our poets, and, within his limits, has a surprising fitness and adequacy, but the range is not wide, and I am constantly expecting more where so much that is quite select and pure is given.[10]

March 20

. . . A thoughtful man finds it less easy to relax and flow at any moment, according to the wishes of his company, than a man of mere sentiment who spends himself only on society and faces solitude as an enemy. Times change as we change, and habits are put on and off as garments; only longer periods are requisite to reclothe minds than bodies.

I am not as I once was. I am become recluse and thoughtful in the extreme, and an idealist, from having been a socialist and sentimentalist as extreme in days past. Children were once my companions. Time was when I lived almost exclusively with them, and was privileged beyond most men in being the centre of a lively circle. . . . I was the greater gainer, and those days were golden. But of late I have been drawn aside from this intimacy by pursuits and objects more intellectual and ideal. The diversion has come against my will and wishes, and by the force of circumstances. I have accepted and submitted against long-cherished hopes and endeavours, seeing it must be so.

March 21

I love nature much but man more, and enjoy the landscape and society only as these are meliorated by genius and remind me of the art which humanizes and liberates nature.[11]

[10] Another unerring estimate of a "new man," to be set beside Alcott's early remarks about Emerson, Thoreau, and Whitman.

[11] With this humanistic attitude, from which Alcott never again wavered, compare the "romanticism" of the entry, written in dejection, for April (undated), 1846, beginning "Forests were first dwellings." Closer acquaintance with Thoreau and Emerson only strengthened Alcott's opposition to their preference for the "wild."

March 23

Evening: Heard Parker, Phillips, and Garrison at Faneuil Hall on Webster's late speech in United States Senate on Slavery.[12] The speeches were eloquent for freedom and humanity, and expressed the sentiment of the freemen of New England, but a little more time must pass to enable the nation to discern the scope and tendency of affairs and Webster's true place, his merits and demerits as a statesman. I am incapable of becoming a partizan; and while I accept and am proud of the declarations of my friend who pleads the cause of civility and justice with an eloquence so fervent and convincing, I yet must cry for the awards of justice and civility to Webster, Clay, Calhoun, and the conservatives of slavery even.

March 28

My debt to Plato is greater, perhaps, than to any mind — greater than to Christ, I sometimes think, whose spirit is an element of humanity but whose genius I did not entertain and comprehend till Plato unsealed my eyes and led me to the study of his fair performance. It was in studies, however, for presenting the mind of Christ to the apprehension of my children in the Masonic Temple — a pleasure and a privilege greater than I can express — that I grew enamoured of the beauty and grandeur of his character, the delicacy and force of his genius, the simplicity and efficacy of his methods. Plato and Christ interpreted each other and the mind of mankind.

April 6

Further talk with my desponding wife on family affairs. Embarrassed on every side, with no possible means of relief. We are spared house rent by the kindness of Mr. May, but have no income nor present facilities for earning a support. I am less adapted

[12] Webster's last great speech, on "The Constitution and the Union," delivered on the seventh of March, 1850. The moderation of Alcott's remark on this occasion is the more remarkable in view of the fact that he had long been an ardent Abolitionist. Among the literary men of New England he stood almost alone in his temperate view of what even Whittier and Emerson considered an act of treachery on Webster's part.

to existing things than I was when, ten years since, I left this city to seek society and the means of support at Concord and, afterwards, my Paradise at Fruitlands.

It is a small matter, this of sympathy, support, and success, as far as I am concerned, since time and purpose overtake and avail themselves of the solitary and so-called visionary thinker's ideas at last, to compensate him for long neglect, it may be for deep injustice, at last. But to the thinker's family, if he have one, it is no small matter, but a serious; and for the wrongs it suffers there is, nor can be, no recompense.

May 27

Mrs. A. quite dejected, feeble, weeps from anxiety, is disconsolate, and cannot be comforted. . . . A crisis of some sort coming, and to be met. No income, no earnings, etc. etc.

Yet I will not permit myself to speak on this subject of family destitution, so complicate and intricate in its economics. Nor is it quite possible in the present incoherent and dislocated state of our social system to disentangle this crimson thread running through and reticulate in all its strands. . . .

Never was family placed under circumstances so favorable for suffering all the disadvantages, not to say ills, of the present state of so-called civilization as mine.

June 30

Lately there has been a good deal of conversation on family affairs, and especially on this mundane question of "ways and means." My illness,[13] following that of other members of the family, has given the occasion for it indoors and out, and every word comes to my wife's ears to add to her other numerous and overpowering discomforts. She tells me today of the gossip about my permitting her to delve for the family, and of my implied indifference to its welfare. And it must seem such to the outsiders,

---

[13] These words are Alcott's only allusion to the serious attack of confluent smallpox from which he was at this time recovering. The disease was contracted from immigrants whom Mrs. Alcott had fed in the garden. First the daughters were taken sick and then the parents, much more acutely. No help was received from any neighbor, nurse, or physician.

nor will any words of mine put fairer face on things. No explanation can take the place of deeds in their eyes, and I must stand for the time as a thriftless if not a heartless and incapable fellow. So let it seem; but let it not be so.

July 13

And all because I had one set of gifts and not the other, and fell so obliquely on my time that none caught my point of view to comprehend the person I was. 'Tis as disastrous to leave body as soul out of our regards. Mind is not always a merchantable commodity; and here's the Pedlar, July 1850, the pack of metaphysic that he is, set bodily, mystically, down in the best market in the world. Athenian times, yet without customer for his handsome wares.

July 21

The *Tribune* brings intelligence of the wreck of the ship *Elizabeth* on Friday last, on Fire Island, four miles east of the Long Island Light. On board were Margaret Fuller, her husband, and child, returning from Italy.

The noble lady gone down into the sea — fated, as she foresaw, to perish. "I see nothing but death before me. I shall never reach the shore." These were her last words, symbolical of the life she had lived of conflict for the truths she saw yet did not quite attain. So near her own friends and country, and yet to go down in sight of them to the silent and insatiate sea!

She had been more to many women — and to many men, I may add — than any woman else of these last years; nor is there any to fill and make good her place.

How sweetly she rests, now, from all those labours! A memorable life, as it was a memorable end.

July 26

Comes Emerson with Goodson, Professor of Music from Cincinnatti. He tells me (Emerson) that W. H. Channing and Henry Thoreau have gone to Fire Island in hopes of recovering the remains; also the work on Italy. W. E. Channing on the ground also.

September 2

Passed the morning in Louisa's school in Suffolk Street. Read from the *Pilgrim's Progress* to the children, with applications. I never go into a school without some regrets that I may not be there at my post. Had I a hundred and more little ones to meet daily, then would my cup be filled to overflowing, for the pleasure it would give me. . . . "Suffer the little children" etc. The passage has a modern pertinency of significance also.

October 12

Evening: Heard Jenny Lind's admirable singing at the Fitchburg Station Rooms, and for the first time in my life caught strains of melody. The "I know that my Redeemer liveth" and "The Herdsman's Song" were the more impressive pieces.

October 17

It was a pleasing thought, but fanciful, that of having Jenny Lind sing an evening for me — that is, for a school of children, say fifty boys and as many girls to be committed to my care to be fed, clothed, educated, for genius and usefulness. I envy the millionaires for the opportunities they own but will not use for humanity. That school would be able to purchase their souls for them and redeem the city some day. . . .

A few years given to teaching would be a pleasing close to a life like mine.

*T*HE REFORMING *zeal that animated Alcott during his English journey and at Fruitlands had, by the beginning of this year, cooled down. He was for a time a quieted if not a chastened man, with a deeper understanding of the slow processes by which all permanent human advances are made. Something of Thoreau's detachment and some realization of the patience of Nature is discernible in his thought. Boston Common seemed a better place than the Abolitionist meeting, and the fountain in the Common was accepted as a perfect symbol of the life that he would lead. But then, in April, came the arrest and trial and return of Thomas Sims, a fugitive slave. Instantly, Alcott was a reformer again, participating fully in the huge excitement of the time and serving eagerly on the Boston Vigilance Committee which was striving in various ways to save negro refugees from the clutch of the law. Henry James the elder began at this time to attract Alcott's attention; Henry Thoreau he admired more enthusiastically at every interview; but chiefly he was dominated, without knowing it, by the great preacher who rode the whirlwind and controlled the storm, Theodore Parker.*

1851

January 3   *Boston*

Foreseen and premeditated discourse seldom serves me for occasions, and I am happiest when left to the methods of intuition. The initial thought is all, and the rest follows according to the genius of the moment and the present company. The power comes, and comes only, when unsought. An abandonment to the instincts appears to be the state of mind necessary for the largest reception of the Spirit. Conversation is a gift of divine grace; and if the mind will but wait, it shall be filled and overflow.

January 9

Kindled my fires early. For comfort's sake, for company, and for my mother, who has been accustomed to the comfort, I am keeping an open fire in my room, and we both enjoy it very much. It brings along this advantage besides, of inviting exercise daily in sawing and splitting fuel to feed it, and this, with daily outdoor walking, is likely to renovate and intensify the spirits for study and discourse. It is a spur to health and briskness, and acts as friendly a part as the frost and shower-bath, during these studious days of winter.

Thought, to be vigorous and sane, and to tell its own firm tale to the end, seeks the precipitates of arctic climates, and to come fiercely upon us as a Hyperborean, bearded with rigours. A good clear thought is sane and startling, like an electric shock, and comes from a region of snow. I have always found the winter months friendly to the intellect. Then is the holiday of genius, and the advent of ideas. And of sanctity also, for Christendom dates from it; and the experiences of virgin minds confirm what I have thought about its virtues. Frost for thought, and heat for sentiment. . . . The mercury rides low to elevate the intellect.

January 10

'Tis a thousand pities that we have not caught the secret yet of daguerreotyping our thoughts as they are spoken in conversation. That would be a discovery worth while, and outlive all predecessors in the arts. Pity, especially for me, idealist and discourser born too soon, by half a century at least, for this Hermes to put the instant text into my hands from the cloven lips. If the pulses would but fasten our sensations on some indelible scroll, and become our faithful diarist from the first systole to the last diastole of their motions, that would be an autobiography and portrait of the invisible original worth having, and spare the writing of much nonsense and dullness.

And yet the printing of all our inanities, follies, and sins, is frightful to think of — nothing omitted or extenuated by the inexorable scribe! . . . Who would not shudder and arrest the hand that would put us verbatim into the text? Still I should like the benefit of editing, with omissions, the book of my acts and thoughts, which is never likely to be completed without such aid — my fifty volumes of MSS. testifying on every page to the indispensibleness of such a co-editor.

. . . I shall not say as good things, much less write as good, about the Memory and Plato's reminiscences, again, as I did today when conversing with my cousin, Almira Seymour, who came from her school to see and spend an hour with me. O for a Hermes to report us!

January 12

This Diary is taking the best of my time; and if it would take the best of me, and get an autobiography out of me, or help edit one, I should be content, and thank heaven for the performance. But I am not delivered so easily. Perhaps a Diary is the most difficult feat of authorship. I should be too happy if I had before me the transcript of a single day. But the best refuses to be put into the pillory of words, and to be gazed at, as multitudes stare at culprits, and mock, in the market-place. I can't help writing, nevertheless, criminal as it seems to ink the mind in this manner. I write, write, driven by the demon with the quill behind his ear — eloquent of a morning, always, in praise of ink; then tempting me of afternoons to silence and depose him, as Luther did, by dashing the contents of my standish into his face for riddance of him once and forever.

January 12

Blessed be Commons, whether for cities of merchants or for the metropolis of the Mind! Pasturage for all things and thoughts. I keep out of Washington, and but for the Post Office should avoid State street, where every sign elbows me off the pavement, and scowls at my impertinence at venturing to rise from the gutter. These ways are plainly not my ways, nor their thoughts my thoughts. But the Common seems welcome, and welcomes me hospitably, — outside the broad pavement, freed almost, and friendly, and the palaces, reserved and courtly, as if knowing their place, and respecting even a scholar's individuality, of an afternoon, if never earlier. — Inside is snow, and lively boys, and forage for the mind, everywhere. Commons, I say, for cities! They are as refreshing as sleep, and whet our wits by shifting and tireless perspectives; as that invigorates and strings the members for toil through the metamorphosis of dreams. We mortals must have Commons, and walk therein, whether citizens or country men, and by night or by day, by dream and idea. For these are resting places, and recreations for the restless and lazy inhabitants of the Mind.

January 18

Urbane and select as I am by taste and temperament I yet find very little refreshment from persons even in this Athenian society. The Conversations are taken with a better relish than any other viand, and are as stimulating as company can well be; they are the winter's entertainment for me, and I am all the richer for them when spring comes. But if I could plunge into fields and woods from my house every afternoon, Conversation, company, MSS., days, and dreams, would be all the sweeter and the more vigorous for it. Concord woods were more to me than my library, or Emerson even. They were more to him than they were to me, and still more to Thoreau than to either of us. Take the forest and skies from their pages, and they, E. and T., have faded and fallen clean out of their pictures.

January 18

Afternoon: at the Abolition meeting at the Tremont Temple. Very few persons seem sane and sweet as Nature is. The Common is the better abolitionist, clearly. Yet 'tis good to fall into the multitude sometimes, for the experiences it gives one. A little madness, a touch of it for once or twice, is quite worth having. It puts new faces on men and things, and makes us hospitable, humane, and merciful to the lunatic ever afterwards.

January 22

Thoreau passed this morning and dined with me. He was on his way to read a paper at Medford this evening — his "Life in the Woods at Walden"; and as refreshing a piece as the Lyceum will get from any lecturer going at present in New England — a whole forest, with forester and all, imported into the citizen's and villager's brain. A sylvan man accomplished in the virtues of an aboriginal civility, and quite superior to the urbanities of cities, Thoreau is himself a wood, and its inhabitants. There is more in him of sod and shade and sky lights, of the genuine mold and moistures of the green grey earth, than in any person I know. Self dependent and sagacious as any denizen of the elements, he has the key to every animal's brain, every flower and shrub; and were an Indian to flower forth, and reveal the secrets hidden in the wilds of his cranium, it would not be more surprising than the speech of this Sylvanus.

He belongs to the Homeric age, and is older than fields and gardens; as virile and talented as Homer's heroes, and the elements. He seems alone, of all the men I have known, to be a native New Englander, — as much so as the oak, or granite ledge; and I would rather send him to London or Vienna or Berlin, as a specimen of American genius spontaneous and unmixed, than anyone else. I shall have occasion to use him presently in these portraits. We must grind him into paint to help brown and invigorate Channing's profile, when we come to it. Here is coloring for half a dozen Socialisms. It stands out in layers and clots, like carbuncles, to give force and homeliness to the otherwise feminine lineaments. This man is the independent of independents — is, indeed, the sole signer of the Declaration, and a Revolution in himself — a more than '76 — having got beyond the signing to the doing it out fully. Concord jail could not keep him safely: Justice Hoar paid his tax, too; and was glad to forget thereafter, till now, his citizenship, and omit his existence, as a resident, in the poll list. Lately he has taken to surveying as well as authorship, and makes the compass pay for his book on "The Concord and Merrimac Rivers," which the public is slow to take off his hands. I went with him to his publishers, Monroe and Co., and learned that only about two hundred of an edition of a thousand copies were sold. But author and book can well afford to wait.

January 31

Another cold day. There is little or no snow in street or on Common; and, but for this biting cold and northerly wind, I should think it were March. It takes my time to prepare wood and build fires for us all. Yesterday, walking with Lowell from Federal, where I met him, to Washington Street, and very briskly too, I came near frosting my fingers, and my friend's beard was frozen stiff with icicles, as if he were Pan walking beside me.

I wish his beard became him better, and if I knew him intimately perhaps these saffron hues might seem becoming. There is an exuberant life in him, and here is the crop. I am reminded of Hyrcanean forests, and could fancy him quite at home in Russia. There is abundant iron and steel in him, much grit and road gravel and earth of brown and grey mould. One might establish potteries and razor factories to advantage on these premises. I said once that I caught a roysterer in his eye, and another seated on his chin, to scout Puritanism. A saner and merrier man one does not meet in Boston streets often, and with a right to his wit. If it ran deeper a little it would be humour, but it is now but wit, and a dextrous weapon of his good nature. One might call him "a comical fellow," and almost a gentleman besides.

On second thoughts I find I like his yellow beard very well; and he shall be Homer's Phoebus hereafter.

February 2

Busy days and prosperous for me and mine, as the philosopher reckons prosperity. I find it easier to accept our fortunes than does my family, which yet resigns and submits with a very good grace. Poverty, they say, is the philosopher's ornament, and the worldling's plague. I would take wealth if it came by any fair exercise of talents into my hands; and if I feel, sometimes, a little mortified on meeting a creditor with a civil "nothing" for his honest demand, I have yet to receive the first incivility from that class, to whose better knowledge of business I owe more than is put into the bill. A civil dun is one of the finest pieces of courtesy that I know of. It brings the parties always into the presence of an invisible, yet felt, third person, and puts both into unexpected and quite unworldly relations to each other.

*   *   *

The worst that I know of poverty is that it often confuses the mind, warps and embitters the hearts of parents, and is sure to touch the children at last. If my wife told us a tithe even of what comes to her ear from day to day, no father and daughters were in a fairer way to be spoiled than we should be. As it is, the consequences are none of the best. Paradise is not quite fixed at 50 High Street. Too much of the Serpent's cunning is as bad as none of it, they say. The babies should see the Adversary just often enough to recognize him instantly, and at sight, from any lesser personage; and, what is far more to the point, to discover that he is frightened far more by their presence than they need be by his.

February 9

During the extreme cold of the winter of 1844 I was at Fruitlands,[1] and kept within doors and at my pen from early sunrising to midnight and sometimes far on towards dawn, leaving my chamber for short times to provide fuel and water for bathing twice a day, at morning and again at sunset. I fed on fruits, biscuit, and drank water exclusively and often. Sometimes I was unable to relinquish studies, so delicious was thought to me, and sat up all night. I bathed in cold water, ducking head and shoulders for

[1] Alcott must have had the experience described below at the Lovejoy farmhouse, near Fruitlands, to which he and his family repaired on January 16, 1844.

several times successively to the bottom of the capacious tub in which I stood, and poured water by pailsful over the whole body, rubbing down briskly afterwards with crash towels, and practiced friction with the flesh brush. In the coldest mornings there was a crackling and lambent flash following the passage of my hand over the pile of the skin, and I shook flames from my finger ends, which seemed erect and blazing with the phosphoric light. The eyes, too, were lustrous, and shot sparkles whenever I closed them. On raising my head from the flood there was heard a melody in the ear, as of a sound of many waters; and rubbing the eyes gave out an iris of the primitive colors, beautiful to behold, but as evanescent as a twinkling. It was not easy to write prose while thus exalted and transfigured. I tasted mannas, and all the aromas of field and orchard scented the fountains, and the brain was haunted with the rhythm of many voiced melodies. I enjoyed this state for a couple of months or more, but was left somewhat debilitated when spring came, and unfit for common concerns. Most of what was written during this season of efflorescence [2] is now lost; but the sweetness was secreted in the memory and abides as a honey-combed era of my spiritual history.

March 2

Henry James [3] has been reading some lectures in New York, lately, on art, property, the Church, &c., of which last the *Tribune* of this week gives some notice.

James is one of the ablest men now speaking — bold, clear, comprehensive, deep, the champion of Socialism for this country, and armed with a certain club-logic which makes his thought more formidable than any other man's in the country. Sensible and well-read, capable to the backbone, he is a match, and more than a match, for any the ablest conservative of the present order. A Robespierre in argument. No man wields a logic so swift and fatal. A Nemesis in thought, which comes clothed in Rhadaman-thine rhetoric as terrific as it is inevitable. Such criticisms on life and letters and institutions have come from no mortal else in these latter times. Carlyle is meek in presence of this Samson Agonistes,

[2] The manuscript "Prometheus," lost at Albany in 1844.
[3] Henry James the Elder, 1811–1882.

whose very virtues have a certain virulence and bloodthirstiness that relate them to the axe. I would as soon attend an execution as one of his lectures. He is headsman of social evils, and shows his teeth with a grace to frighten one. There is a seven of them in him, and ready for service whenever he sounds the trumpet for revolution. I think him of the race of Ogres, and should not be surprised to learn that he breakfasted on a brace of civilians every morning, with scarlet wines, before he came to digestion and his pen.

Emerson told me that James invited him once to his house, but that J. said he feared to eat in his presence, for he "fed like the devil, and was ashamed to be seen at his orgies by any gentleman."

March 4

11 oclock, A.M., went to Cambridge. Dined with Lowell at Elmwood, and had a very good time of it. Lowell tells me that he purposes to sail for Rome early in June with his family, and to be absent two or three years. He has a good right to travel, and is a capital person to send abroad. So our journal [4] must wait till his return, unless Weiss or Higginson will take to the editing of it for us. Lowell is the more capable, perhaps, and travel will ripen him for this or something better on his return.

He spoke of writing a play, next time, to be historical — "New England for the Last Ten Years" or something of that sort — for which there are abundant materials, and would be greedy of readers, and if an acting play, all New England as spectators.[5] Lowell has an aptitude for this thing, and knows more about the times than any literary person of his years whom I happen to know. He unites extremes in his comprehension, and has a free and outdoor treatment of what he sees that fits him for this class of composition. A good historical play would be a novelty in our Athens, and a credit to our literature. . . . I wish him all the pleasure and fame he

---

[4] See the entry for February 12, 1850.

[5] The manner in which Lowell might have written such a play is discernible in the first part of his essay on Thoreau. Alcott deplored this essay, but his entry for February 17, 1850, suggests, in its amused detachment from movements in which he had once played an important part, that Lowell affected his thinking, for a time, rather deeply.

deserves, and a safe return to write it, and edit the magazine besides.

*   *   *

Lowell gave me a copy of his *Fable for Critics,* which, bating his treatment of Miss Fuller, is worth living a little while, till better portraits are drawn of the contemporaries he quizzes in it. Nobody has said better things of Emerson, Parker, Dwight, or Hawthorne.[6]

March 6

Emerson called today. I found him at the American House and dined with him. He lectured at Syracuse and Rochester lately, and goes to Pittsburg on the 16th inst. to read some new lectures — one on "Power," also on "Wealth," "Culture," and another on "Fate."

E. seemed in better spirits than usual. He had a good deal to say on the times and the spirit of the times. Boston was a base place just now. He was ashamed of it. Elliott, the Senator, deserved insult from every right-minded citizen for his late vote on the Fugitive Slave bill. Southerners were saints compared with him.

April 4

Thomas Sims, a colored boy, was last evening arrested by Marshall Tukey as a fugitive slave, and committed to the Court House for safe keeping.

There is great excitement in the city. The Court House is surrounded with chains and armed police to hold the prisoner in safe custody. It is a novel spectacle to our people, and excites the indignation of every one in whom sentiments of justice and humanity yet survive as the safeguards of manliness and of religion. The question "What has the North to do with slavery?" is visibly answered. Here it is in the Capital and the State has opened its Court of Justice (so called) not to protect and free, but to convict and remand the fugitive, who sought its protection and sympathy,

---

[6] Alcott says nothing here or elsewhere of the highly favorable treatment Lowell had given him in the *Fable.*

to slavery and all its horrors. A few scenes like this will show us where we are, and settle our destinies.

What is a republic, taking sides against itself? What are citizens who can stand and tamely see themselves insulted; the city police drafted as hounds of the Slave Power, to catch and keep their victims from rescuers? Such disgrace to the country, to the State, the city, to humanity, to the consciences of freemen, cannot long be borne with, nor silently. Redress in some way, but a redress at any hazard, and a rescue, not of this prisoner perhaps, of one fugitive, or several, but of the consciences and constitution of Massachusetts, the vindication of the rights of freemen.

This afternoon, attended a meeting on the Common called to discuss measures for action relative to this crisis. There was great excitement and earnest speaking. The true feeling pervaded the crowd, and good manners, throughout. — The meeting adjourned to convene at once in the Tremont Temple.

Evening. The Vigilance Committee met at Timothy Gilbert's rooms, Washington Street. I was elected a member of the body. Several gentlemen volunteered to beat the streets for protecting fugitives from being arrested during the night. Traversed the western portion of the city with John N. Spear, and visited the Watch House in Hanover Street. We met but a single watchman during our walk. Came home a little after midnight.

April 5

In Court Square. Sims' trial proceeding before Commissioner Curtis in U. S. Court Room. At Cornhill with Vigilance Committee. The excitement very great. Court Square filled with people. Had much talk with Channing (W. H.), Pillsbury, and others. The Court adjourned till Monday.

April 7

Returned to Boston early this morning and heard Robert Rantoul's argument on the Unconstitutionality of the Fugitive Slave Law, before the Commissioner. It was a sad spectacle. The Commissioner seemed to have made up his mind to face the moral sentiment of the people and carry his point at all costs. . . . I would not have been in his place for whatever the Nation has to give. He will share in the Nation's disgrace, one day.

April 8

Today and this evening at a meeting of the people in the Tremont Temple. The speeches earnest, humane, eloquent, and every way creditable to Massachusetts and liberty. Horace Mann Chairman of the meeting. Pierrepont, Palfry, and S. C. Phillips, W. H. Channing and Wendell Phillips in the evening, acquitted themselves nobly. Such vials of wrath as were poured and dashed indignantly on Webster and the abettors of this Fugitive Slave Law! There was no mercy for the recreant statesman, no shield from the moral indignation of freemen whose trust he had betrayed.

April 10

Heard Parker discourse this morning for a couple of hours and more on the sins of the nation in general and of the city in particular. The house was crowded, and his auditors would have listened unweariedly to his declamation for another hour. . . .

It was truly Roman, the spectacle. Victim after victim he cast grimly into the amphitheatre, to be devoured without mercy — President, Secretary, Senators, Marshalls, Sheriffs, Mayor, hunkers, the poor Commissioner Curtis. Such ignominy as he cast upon him and his kidnappers — scourging them, the city, the Nation! It was frightful. I commended his discretion in advising the women and children to bear with him and not scream as he called forth his spectres.

April 11

Today at Tremont Temple; at Anti-slavery Office in Cornhill; in Court Square, which was thronged with people, many from the country, and all awaiting Judge Woodbury's decision of Sims' fate — some to see the fugitive taken from the Court House and many to seize the moment for his rescue from the Marshall's custody.

Evening: at Washington Hall, where Garrison, Pillsbury, Wilson of the Senate, and others, made speeches. I left the Hall at midnight.

April 12

Walked with my wife to Court Square, and found that Sims had been taken away just before our arrival.

April 15

Sims' catching, keeping, and extradition cost Boston City three thousand dollars, it seems, or nearly that sum. It would be a handsome piece of honor and justice to withhold the payment of the assessment for this item of the tax-bill when it shall be claimed by the municipality, and take a freeman's place within the House of Leverett Street if it should be carried so far. I am tempted to try it. Certainly the prison could not be put to better use than the holding of honest men, to the discredit of unrighteous laws.

I had fancied till now that certain beautiful properties were mine by culture and the time and place I live in, if not by inheritance — namely, a City, Civilization, Christianity, and a Country.

April 17

It is plain where lies the virtue and strength of the country. Erase a dozen names, now the most feared and hated here in this neighborhood if not at Washington, from the Book of Reform, and things might take a more peaceful aspect. But no! The question of questions is put, and will not sleep till it get a definite rational answer. These men are for that, and only that.[7]

April 20

But bad laws are good things — profitable at least by proxy and consequence. So the Nation is debtor, it knows not yet how deeply, in the intelligence and the sentiments, to the discipline which this draconian schoolmaster, the Slave Law, and the events coming fast on its heels, are giving us — putting questions and torturing replies that never the Adversary had dared to thrust

---

[7] At the side of the page Alcott wrote "names: — ," as if about to make a list. It was probably a fear that his papers might be examined that prevented him from doing so.

otherwise upon a people civilized and in some sort Christianized before. The lesson is likely to be learned and remembered.

April 22

Theodore Parker told me today that he had given a month's time and more to this fugitive business, besides a thousand dollars. Moreover, had harboured a parishioner of his, a colored man and fugitive, at his house, during the recent excitement, to shield him from the law's clutch. And Christian Dr. G.[8] of Federal Street Church has denounced him as a traitor and infidel for his humanity.

Parker is most intrepid in his hostility to this infamous Bill, and report has it that he keeps pistols ready for service in his study. Lately he married William and Ellen Crofts[9] when they were about escaping from the city, by George Thompson's and the Abolitionists' countenance, for safety in England; and 'tis said that Parker gave to Ellen a Bible and to William a brace of pistols, with the expressed hope that both would use them as occasion offered.

April 25

It is one of the auspicious signs of these latter times that men are beginning to canvass and account for everything that turns up in the world. Nothing remains unquestioned. The popular enquiry is: "Who are you? What are you here for? Account for your existence. Show us, on penalty of forfeiting it, what right you have to be; and away with you if you don't do it." Even the devil, and his place and functions in the world, are under discussion, and he too will have to show what he is here for, or quit forthwith.

That is a question altogether new, first raised on its proper grounds, and poetically argued, by Goethe in the *Faust*. But now the thinkers everywhere are fast hold of it, and it must render up its secrets, so long hidden from the faith of men. Modern judgments seem to be far more tolerant of him than at any former

[8] Ezra Stiles Gannett — opposed to slavery, but not an Abolitionist.

[9] The name is usually given as "Craft." According to Parker's own statement, it was a sword and not a "brace of pistols" that he gave to the bridegroom.

period of the world. The devil's claims are fairly admitted, and his right to be here and take part in mundane affairs is unquestionable. Tolerance is taking the place of the old prejudices, and it is becoming quite evident that his presence is indispensible. . . .

The Lord needs — and so provides an agent for the administrative ends of morality — a whipper-in and Secretary. We should not know what nor where we were without such. The devil is a friend in the guise of an enemy. We need him to measure our strength and weakness, to prove our virtue. Life, for the most part, is a contest, a devil's duel, with seconds few or many to provoke and stand sponsors for us, to each according to his mettle and provocation. An imp or two, if no more, is pitted against every one of us — *is* one of us, if we knew it. To some there are seven of them, we read, and our merits and demerits are measured precisely by our management of the enemy, whether one or many.[10]

April 26

Left for Concord, to see to the transplanting of the apple-trees at "Hillside" and to spend the Sunday with Emerson. Found E. at work on Miss Fuller's Memoir, which he has undertaken to compile and have ready for the press by September. W. H. Channing is preparing his memoir also of Margaret, and the two are to be bound in the same covers. So we shall have the best that can be gathered now of this great woman. There is hope, too, of Samuel Ward's tribute to her memory being given in the same work.

Emerson is asked to read a paper on "The Fugitive Slave Law" to his townspeople, and intends doing so on Sunday evening next. His opinions will go to swell the tide of detestation which is overwhelming that odious statute and all those who uphold it.

Evening: We have had the Conversation on Webster, Union, Disunion, the Vigilance Committee, and the slave-hunters' work here in Boston.

[10] This meditation, clearly connected with the case of Thomas Sims, is the first of many in which Alcott wrestles with the problem of evil. For some time, in fact, he planned a book to be entitled *Adversaria*, in which he hoped to show that evil is not only necessary but ultimately beneficent. Thus he strove to retain the realism of Carlyle and also the optimism of Emerson, while advancing beyond both of them.

April 27

All the morning was given to conversation in E's study. After dinner we walked to Walden, and in the evening came Thoreau and Elizabeth Hoar and stayed till 10 o'clock. There was endlessly varied and miscellaneous discourse, which no man may well report. . . . A narrative is what I could never compass, and hanging were easier than testifying or telling a story. Heaven forfend me from a court and the lawyers! I can manage a myth to perfection, and revel forever in metaphysics. Without fables and ideas, what were the crass and craven facts of the understanding to such as I am?

May 31

Every spectacle has its lesson, and the Abolition and other Conventions, theirs. They show me the ultra-private person that I am, and how little in keeping with my habits is all that passes about me — the speakings, the deliberations, the hissings and applause — and how, with the intensest engagement in the idealism and import of the proceedings, I am no party in the pageant but the spectator and guest of the principles and tendency at the heart of it.

June 7   *Concord*

Rode to Concord this afternoon to pass Sunday with Emerson. An evening's talk.

June 8

Uninterrupted conversation till dinner. Afternoon, heard Huntington of Boston discourse on Christian Socialism at the Unitarian Church. Afterwards, walked to "Hillside." Evening, conversation again till bed time.

These days and nights in Concord with Emerson in study and field, beside Walden Water and woods, are differenced by nameless traits from all days and nights in my calendar of experience. There is nothing like them, nothing comparable. Perhaps I best describe them by saying that they make conversation and ideas possible, and the pleasures of friendship without stain. Like sallies into some fabled cloud-land, remote and golden, they seem, rather than actual scenes on *terra firma* — where minds divested of mortal forms sit sedate and aloft, discoursing free "on fate, free-will, and knowledge absolute."

Add that they have something planetary and astral, and, if I may say so moderately, show the place of our little planet in the solar system, as if the parties had got planted in the sun somehow and were looking through the Lord Rosse and Herschel telescopes at mundane concerns and the little people.[11]

On returning, it takes a day and a night's sleep to restore me to my place and poise for the customary rounds of study. Yet I like these visits to the sun and their great perspectives very well.

June 9

Walked to "Hillside." There is prospect of fruit — apples, peaches, cherries, etc., and a heavy crop of grass.

Dined with Thoreau. We had a walk afterward by the Hosmer Cottage, and back by the rail-track. T. tells me that he read his paper on "Walking" lately at Worcester. He should read this, and the "Walden" also, everywhere in our towns and cities, for the soundness and rectitude of the sentiments. They would have a wholesome influence. I sometimes say of T. that he is the purest of our moralists, and the best republican in the Republic — viz., the republican at home. A little over-confident and somewhat stiffly individual, perhaps, — dropping society clean out of his theory, while practically standing friendly in his own strict sense of friendship — there is about him a nobleness and integrity of bearing that make possible and actual the virtues of Rome and Sparta. . . . Plutarch would have made him an immortal, had he known him. . . .

June 27   *Boston*

This afternoon Emerson called, and we walked in the Mall and City Gardens, returning by the Fountain, which shot its crys-

[11] Elizabeth Peabody says that in Alcott's description of the solar system at the Temple School the children "were called on to imagine themselves placed in the centre of the sun, and to picture out the scene presented to the eye, supposing that organ strong enough to look through and beyond Herschel" — *Record of a School*, p.xxx.

talline peaks from the foliage as it were part of the globe itself. "Some glacier," as E. said, "alpine and admirable." We sat some time nearby and looked at it. Afterwards I took a cup of milk with him at the American House, where he stops tonight, and goes tomorrow to Lenox to pass Sunday with Hawthorne and the Tappans.

June 30

It takes much and strong love to free one from the fates that divide and distract him, and deliver him to Genius and virtue. How very few of the human race have been thus favored of Heaven, or by their own strength, to win the victory! — I suppose I have not enough of this love to unload myself, and so am left the pure mystic and idealist, coming never clean into the hearts of persons and things. Had I loved enough, then should I have prevailed, and have made my private purpose — fair and friendly as it was and is — dear, also, and irresistible, to the human race.

Give us, dear God, the all-prevailing love that drags us out of ourselves, our thoughts and theories, into the presence of the common day, and the warm embrace of mankind!

July 5

Came Joseph Treat to see me from Portage County, Ohio. He is one of the disciples of the Moral Sentiment, and as plain a piece of humanity as I have seen lately, being clad in brown linen and cowhide. A primitive sort of backwoodsman; a prophet of the John Baptist school, and a fearless Come-outer besides; yet catholic and kind, and for the whole of virtue and progress. I liked him very well, finding a genuine man's heart beating freely and warmly under his uncouth dress and address.

The more of this class the better for us. A crude giant is a far more instructive and agreeable spectacle than a flowering pigmy, and promises something for us when he comes to ripen. One of these Treats with an epic poem in his heart is of more value to the world than scores of puny civilians and religionists, who know no more of Mr. Greatheart than they have gathered from some fable of his exploits in *Pilgrim's Progress*, and have never discovered their image in the person of Mr. Feeble-Mind.

July 15

. . . Evening: came Emerson. We walked to the American House, where we talked of M. F. and her times. — Her genius was eminently urbane. She was a citizen and socialist, by virtue of constitution, or by womanhood; and here, in this particular, she was less American than Greek. Her intellect, alike with her disposition, was, of all persons I have known, perhaps the more [*sic*] civil and polite. There was a courtly air about her thoughts as well as her behaviour — a certain ripe and autumnal courtesy that loves great manners as the vine its clusters, and most becoming to the parlour as to the person. Her wit was ruddy, as her fine sense was sane and wholesome. She was Italian in her tastes, and, though an American by birth, she was never naturalized in her talents, which were Greek with a cross of Roman. I should say that she was Color, not Form eminently; and that both Englands, Old and New, were less part and parcel of her substance than Rome and Athens.

August 9   *Concord*

Left for Concord. Passed the afternoon at "Hillside" repairing fences and slept at Emerson's.

August 10

With Emerson till dinner. Afternoon, walked with Thoreau, and bathed in the Lake.

> "The blue eyed Walden there doth smile
> Most tenderly upon its neighbour pines." [12]

Thoreau read me some passages from his paper on "Walking" as I passed the evening with him, and slept at Emerson's again afterwards.

August 11

Thoreau rode with me to Cambridge, and we passed the forenoon in Harvard Library. I looked at the compartment of English Poetry (of the Elizabethan age), but found nothing of worth to bring home.

[12] From a poem on Walden Pond by Ellery Channing.

T. dined with me, and took from my library for perusal *"Rei Rusticae Auctores Latini Veteres: Cato, Columella, Varro & Palladius,"* for which I paid a couple of shillings at the London bookstalls, and am glad to find so good a reader for it.[13]

August 17   *Boston*

Thoreau has the profoundest passion for the aboriginal in Nature of any man I have known; and had the sentiment of humanity been equally strong and tender he might have written pastorals that Virgil and Theocritus would have envied him the authorship of. As it is, he has come nearer the primitive simplicity of the antique than any of our poets, and touched the fields and forests and streams of Concord with a classic interest that can never fade.

The lines "Lately, alas, I knew a gentle boy" are suffused with a sweet elegiac tenderness, as if the woods and fields bewailed the loss of their foraying friend and essayed to sing their grief in their murmuring leaves. So the essay on "Friendship" wears a sylvan sympathetic manner, and carries a heart of oak in its bosom — so brave, so self-helpful, so defiant, and yet so sternly kind and wholesome in its counsels. No man lives in so close a companionship and so constant with Nature, or breathes more of the spirit of pure poetry. And in this lies his excellence; for when the heart is divorced from Nature, from the society of living, moving things, poetry has fled, and the love that sings.

Channing stands farther from it, yet comes sometimes, in certain moods, as by some happy fate of the moment, into a closer intimacy that makes him passionately one with the heart of things; and then his song, as in the "Hymn of the Earth," touches us with a superhuman pathos, as we feel that he commands deeper elements of poetry than any of his contemporaries.

For Emerson, far more widely known, and assumed the first

---

[13] Thoreau's Journals contain some thirty references to these four authors, most of them showing that he used the original Latin of Alcott's volume rather than the translation — of Columella only — which he withdrew in 1856 from the Harvard Library.

Alcott, who could not read Latin, got from Thoreau certain notions about the ancient writers on agriculture which were more congenial to him than to Thoreau himself.

of our poets, was forbidden pure companionship with Nature. He dwelt rather in an intellectual grove, and looked at society from this his retreat through the glass of imagination, coming rarely into positive contact and sympathy with it through the heart and understanding, and set never a firm foot on the Yankee-land in which he nominally dwelt. He was a citizen of the crystal palace, but of no country because of all.

August 20

Consider how very few persons you shall meet who are sweet and sane as Nature is. One quaffs health, courage, genius, and sanctity from that cup, and is never satiated with it. Most wholesome these morning draughts; and what were the days, citizen and student that I am, without them? I make bold to say that the Common is the best saint, physician and reformer of the city it ornaments; and for this Sylvanus resident in town I can forgo the company of Urban and all his clerks, from Copp's Hill to South End.

October 6

Abby [14] begins her studies today, and with hope and courage. The child has fair talents, and good disposition. She opens life with prospects somewhat fairer than fell to her elder sisters, who, with gifts no less promising, have yet been defrauded of deserved opportunities for study and culture, by the social disabilities under which we have been struggling since the close of my Temple School. It was my hope in that, and afterwards in the Fruitlands endeavour, to provide the means of an improved culture in which my children might participate with others to the extent of an enthusiast's dream; but these plans were frustrated, and at the greatest personal hazard and domestic cost. Nor have years of toil and anxiety been adequate to repair the damage. — But the dear intent is all the dearer for its hurts and delays, and shall nevertheless fructify and ripen in some distant generation, of which it is the germ and seed. The dream cannot be smothered: —

"No, no, the work in hand, by meddling Time
Delayed, shall blossom yet, and bear
Its century-burdened flower."

[14] Alcott's youngest daughter, later called May.

October 18   *Concord*

Rode to Concord. W. H. Channing in the cars on his way to Brattleboro, and just from the Convention at Worcester, which he praised as admirable.

October 18

Very rainy. Discussed our old topics all day. Also heard some passages from Emerson's Memoir of Margaret, and thought what was read to me very characteristic and admirable. I wait for the rest of it. This portrait of his friend will be something to be proud of, and a credit of praise to both of them.

Of Margaret too much cannot well be said. None can say and demonstrate her talents and disposition better — her talents especially, for she gave to him all she thought and thirsted for as an intellectual devotee, and in the eagerness of a confidence that left little unrevealed of what was inmost and intimate of purpose. Intellectual she was in a fairer sense and fineness, perhaps, than any woman of our day, with a subtlety and saliency best exhibited in conversation, as becoming as it was brilliant and rare; and he, of all her friends, perhaps, best seized, and so can paint, its colors.

I fancied her, sometimes, some sacred bird, Indian or Egyptian, so Sibylline and changeful were the hues and motions of that powerful yet graceful neck of hers, and the tones of her voice as it were of an ibis, or else of Juno's bird. Imperial creature that she was, and, alike in ideal excellencies and bearing, mythological! Her fancy, too, of being a stolen princess committed to foster-parents, and of a crown somewhere awaiting her, was characteristic, showing the composite qualities of her memory, every way the most remarkable that I have known. The keeper of secrets she could not impart, with all her womanliness, to any one.

Afterwards: Saw Walden with Emerson. Also, Thoreau, in the evening.

October 29   *Boston*

E. P. Whipple sends me his card of admission to his lecture on "The English Mind," delivered by him this evening before the Mercantile Library Association at Tremont Temple. — The best of it was, to me, its display of memory, as he, the lecturer, standing, and without note or desk, recited it to the company sentence after sentence, paragraph after paragraph, the whole leaving on the mind an impression of a read esay from a printed page, so perfect was its compactness and continuity of thought and diction. It was like reading, or hearing read, Macaulay or Macintosh, and quite after their fashion. The statements and reflection were pure sentiment, and the piece creditable to its author, who has won some fame as an essayist and magazine writer; and has certainly a depth and comprehensiveness of reflection that I do not meet with in any others of the Boston stamp — a catholicity and fairness of perception that relates him to cosmopolitans and idealists. And I like him for this quality, as sane and creditable to its author, whom I have met sometimes since I came to town, and who has taken to me quite unexpectedly from the first interview.

His I call a reflective and lunar mind, which takes on the hues of setting, not of rising suns. There is an evening conservatism, an almost night-mare maze, that excludes the blaze of ideas; an eye, if one observes carefully, as of the filmed bird's — rather, of Nox, and the owls, to scour the purlieus of the oldest dungeons and towers of conservative intellect and show their interiors under the twilight of their reflections. I observe, too, a horizontal breadth of brain positively enormous: from which the eyes stand out hemispherically, and more, as in bold bas-relief; globular almost, as corresponding to the brain, and dipping behind the rim of day, as if peering on the nethermost depth of midnight; sublunar orbs, and opacous, like Plato's Gates of Horn. He sees best at a distance, and retreats from one to find his angle of sight. And then his hesitancy of speech has a certain glimmer about it, showing the nocturnal intellect that he is, and moon at the full. — But I am unable to bring him into the sun, and so leave him in his twilights, for the present at least.

November 4

Henry James advertises his lectures in the city papers, and is now come to town to read them. His audience will be small but intelligent and select, as was Emerson's, and essentially the same. But I cannot vouch for a very enthusiastic reception of him, or of his teachings. It would be too much to expect of our jealous and conservative Athenians. His themes, besides, are a little unpopular just now, and his bearing too consequential and knowing, as of a man with Kingdom-Come in his brain, to make friends with any but the votaries of logic unadorned and of royal Truth herself.

A voracious intellect, subtle, sinuous, clear, forcible, and swift, voracious of guile as a cormorant of its prey. A terrible logician, and audacious even to the verge of duplicity. A fearless sham-shower of all visnomies, as of Medusian heads and Satan's, to his company. There is nothing so formidable, in his way, on this continent, and an over-match for any man — unless, perhaps, Carlyle — in the two hemispheres. It were safer for pretenders of all grades and complexions to keep out of his way on pain of being gobbled down by this glutton of deceits and fierce friend of truth and plain dealing.

Perhaps this our New England is not quite the place for one of this Thracian mettle. Metropolitan New York were fitter, or the wild West. Or, being of the aquatic race, he should betake himself rather to the wide-weltering Atlantic, the Leviathan of wave-dividing continents. There, with room and verge enough, on mighty mischief bent, the dread ocean try . . .

James is, perhaps, the best-read of any American in those sovreigns of manifold thought — continents and seas each in himself — Swedenborg and Fourier, and needs all the room which these take and allow in which to move unencumbered and free, Our poor little junketing archipelagoes of speculation are all too shallow and obscure, too narrow, for this salt-ocean sailor and galleon of the times.

November 5

Henry Thoreau comes and passes the afternoon and evening; also sleeps under my roof. A very welcome guest, this countryman. I meet nobody whose thoughts are so invigorating as his, and who comes so scented of mountain breezes and springs, so like a luxuriant clod from under forest leaves, moist and mossy with earth-spirits. His company is tonic, never insipid, like ice-water in the dog days to the parched citizen pent in chambers and under brazen ceilings. Welcome then as the gurgle of brooks and drippings of pitchers! Then drink and be cool! Without this admirable glacier how would we stand the summer heats, how find shade under torrid climes? Our milk and meats would sour and taint, our butter melt, and our friendships dissolve into jellies. The world would get valetudinarian and consumptive. But here is a gelid man and valid, sane and salt, and will keep forever — a friend who comes never too often nor stays too long — comes, it may be, a little unwillingly too, and uncommuningly, as streams descend into the urbane vallies below, yet sighing as they descend, leaving their mountain sources behind.

November 10

Plato held that the philosopher might withdraw from the state when it was formed on an imperfect model, and the like freedom was clearly intimated, if not definitely enjoined, in Christ's teachings also. Moreover, 'tis the dictate of the instincts, and the duty imposed by the moral sentiment, that legislator and president of the royal law in every man's soul. The commandment is to "come out of whatsoever is illegal and base, alike in institutions and ourselves." Nor are we to wait for multitudes to accompany us. 'Tis our individual and personal outcoming from all evils and iniquities of every shade and name. Man is prior to, and the superior of, states. These are but the human pantry at best, stored at an immense cost. . . . Caesar's tribute-money must not be levied on God's treasury. An honest man is a brave man, and heroes can afford to live on nuts, as freemen, sunning themselves in the clefts of the rocks, sooner than sell, for the state's pottage of slavery and wrong, their inborn liberties. Manliness is all that maintains and makes states respectable. Man-keeping is the imperial economy. 'Tis a great age when the state is nothing and Man is all.

December 7   Concord

Concord. All day with Emerson and Ideas, the rain pouring outside also.

But now, as before, nothing remains reportable for these leaves — yet not lost, but, like some ray from the old stars, still blending, I doubt not, with the evening and morning twilights of my experiences, "flattering the mountain tops with sovereign eye."

Say whatever may be said in praise or dispraise of him, this is the master-mind of our country and time. Match him who shall from England, Germany, France! Nor shall Hungary's and Italy's Kossuth and Mazzini abase his titles. Far less is the American theirs than they are his. . . . Continents and countries have their equipments, and what were ours without Emerson? Take him from the population, from the Lyceum and Library, smite this Orion from our Zodiac, and what of national splendor and ideal significance is fallen! Emerson is as necessary to our hemisphere as the day-star and the evening and morning maiden who feeds her urn at its beams.

AS EARLY AS 1842, *under the influence of the English Transcendentalist J. P. Greaves, Alcott abandoned the belief upon which his early teaching had been based, that all differences in individual attainments are due to inequalities of education. The conviction increased with his years that such differences are determined at birth and are chiefly due to ancestry. The death of his brother Junius, in April, and the fact that both Ellery Channing and Lowell had recently urged him to write his autobiography, drew his attention to his own ancestry, and in June he set out upon a genealogical study which filled the next five months and took him for several weeks to his boyhood home — a visit to be repeated almost annually during the next thirty years.*

It is not clear how Alcott secured the funds for these extensive researches. In October the family moved to 20 Pinckney Street, on Beacon Hill, where the elder sisters opened a school and Mrs. Alcott took lodgers. In December Alcott began a series of Conversations in Boston on "Demonocracy." His receipts from Conversations — sixteen in number — during the entire year amounted to one hundred and sixty-four dollars.

1852

January 6

Emerson said fine things last night about "Wealth," but there are finer things far to be said in praise of Poverty, which it takes a person superior to Emerson even to say worthily. Thoreau is the better man, perhaps, to celebrate that estate, about which he knows much, and which he wears as an ornament about himself — a possession that Kings and Caesars are too poor to purchase. He can best describe the evils of wealth and the penury it often entails — on owner and trustee,

Whose opulent wants betray his poverty.

Eloquent, wise, and witty as were the orator's praises of Gold, and just to this transition period of civilization, the merchant's day as none ever before — still the moral laws were too faintly implied, and so left not without detriment in the auditor's mind. But there are lectures to come on "Culture" and "Worship" to soften and set things in their proper lights doubtless, and justify the whole to the conscience and intellect of good men of all times.

January 10

'Tis so easy to blame and denounce; but for truth's, for righteousness' sake, as for that of charity and good manners too, let us abstain from pushing this duty (if duty it be) very far or frequently. Even good men may damn themselves in denouncing the damned. And just now this virtue is blazing fiercely here in these parts, every one calumniating Webster as if his sin were not theirs also, and himself their proper representative and interpreter for today. A kindlier discernment, a broader comprehension, would show us that Webster, wise or wicked, is just the mixture and contradiction the country and the people are who denounce him — he, of all its statesmen, abiding steadfast alike to the spirit and letter of its compromises, the best representative and exponent of these Disunited American States. — And this is his merit and his blame, as 'tis theirs and the country's. Even the Abolitionists forfeit their claims to consistency by the severity of their blame.

March 9

Legislation comes too late, and sits frettingly on the citizen's neck. And this from the passions not being crushed and the appetites tamed to sobriety and self-will during the softer seasons of childhood and youth. A parent may enforce upon his child with impunity what the state cannot. Now this Liquor Law may be easily and rightfully enforced in every family as an act of legitimate parental authority, but when the state comes to legislate and proceeds to deal at once with appetites and passions, the right to do so is gravely questioned, and the privileges of excess of every name are pleaded as original and unalienable prerogatives of the citizen. — Begin at the beginning; or any beginning is impossible afterwards.

March 11

The child's body is a recollection of ancestral particles from seven generations preceding; and the like of its mind's memories also. All instincts are recollections of foregone lives.

October 30

Webster's funeral. The city in weeds. His death the gravest criticism on himself and country.

November 11

— Meet Charles Sumner today at his rooms in Court Street, and discuss the political aspects and prospects of the Country. — A man with a conscience and a clear head, and good for Massachusetts to have in the United States' Senate. His recent speech on slavery opens a new campaign of action for the old political parties as well as the new, and must modify our legislation on slavery in times to come.

November 13

Ellery Channing is here this morning.

5 P.M. I go to Concord. Clough is at Emerson's, and just from England.

A. H. CLOUGH,
FELLOW AND TUTOR OF ORIEL COLLEGE [1]

[1] Clough's calling-card is pasted into the Journal.

November 14

I pass the forenoon with Thoreau, have a walk with Hawthorne after dinner, and am with Clough and Thoreau at Emerson's in the evening.

November 15

Return with Clough to Boston by the morning train, and read at Athenæum. — Evening I pass with Dr. N. Shurtleff, antiquarian, at his house.

November 22

Horatio Greenough calls, and leaves his card of admission to his Lectures on Art. Also comes and passes the evening and discusses art — the symbolism of man's body, particularly.

November 23

This afternoon I hear Greenough's lecture on "Art" at the Music Hall Buildings. — An admirable essay, and far too metaphysical and fine for the few who came to hear. Also meet Longfellow and talk of Greenough.

November 30

Greenough is here all the morning, and discourses sagely on art and artists, to my great surprise and profit. He amazes by the subtlety and mysticism of his distinctions, no less than by his great American sense and solidity of perception.

December 18

Read Swedenborg's book on Generation.
Greenough dies today.

ALCOTT'S prolonged studies of his own ancestry led, in February, to membership in the Massachusetts Genealogical Society — in which he did not find quite the deep philosophical motives he expected. During the early months of the year he read Thomas Taylor's Hymns of Orpheus, *Aristotle's* Ethics *and* Politics *for the fourth or fifth time, Lyell's* Principles of Geology, *Swedenborg's* Heaven and Hell, *Bishop Berkeley's* Siris, *and the* Confessions of St. Augustine — *all in his own library. In March he began a series of Conversations on theological topics with the young men of the Harvard Divinity School, which not only brought him the acquaintance of Moncure D. Conway and F. B. Sanborn but gave him the pleasure of smuggling in his friend Emerson, contraband there for many years. Plans were laid in August for Alcott's first tour of Western cities, and late in October he set out from Pinckney Street with high hopes, and with eighteen dollars of Emerson's money in his pocket. He had never before been west of the Alleghanies, and was known there to very few. Cards had been sent before him to Syracuse, Rochester, Buffalo, Medina, and Cincinnati, advertising his willingness to converse upon Daniel Webster, Horace Greeley, Garrison, Margaret Fuller, Theodore Parker, Horatio Greenough, and Emerson.*

1853

Awhile at the Spiritualists' Convention which is sitting — or sleeping, rather — in the Masonic Temple; and volunteer some rays of what we called "sunlight," to find the same somewhat annoying to the recumbents. And so we desisted, and left them to their preferred lunacies.

This case of Mr. Feeble-Mind is a difficult one, always, to handle, and 'tis the more becoming and considerate, doubtless, to leave him — utterly unable as he proves himself usually to apprehend his condition — to stumble, if he must, into the ditch digged by his lunacy, and then convert his blunders sometime into blessings, if possible.

January 28

Read Isaac Taylor's *Ancient Christianity*, to find its extremest opinions are more modern, so to speak, than the most recent Transcendentalism — the Chardon Street, Bible, Antislavery, Non-resistance, Grahamites, Woman's Rights discussions not excepted. Some of these early Christian Fathers were unmistakable Come-outers, and of the rankest type; doubtless esteemed very unsafe persons to run at large in their day, as they certainly would be in ours — agitators, disturbers of the peace of Church and State, and far more dangerous than Garrison, Parker, or Gerritt Smith [1] now, because more profound and ideal.

It is always troublesome to know something, [2] and especially the having practical novelties at heart. Idealism, in Church or State, is ever the most pestilent enemy they know, and the most

---

[1] A New York philanthropist and Congressman chiefly known at this time for his part in the rescue of the slave Jerry McHenry from a jail in Syracuse. In this rescue Alcott's brother-in-law, Samuel J. May, had been as prominent as Smith.

[2] Apparently a covert reference to the Know-nothing Party, founded in 1852, which refused to take a definite stand with regard to the extension of slavery into the territories.

provoking. Nothing so felt and feared. Christ, the most ideal, the most courageous and catholic of historic minds, is of all the most mystical — and has been from the first, and still is, esteemed a heretic and a bad citizen.

February 2

These Parties steal one's integrity away. Always the Right is a majority of one against everybody, and presently prevails. An honest man is mightier than multitudes. All Christendom is not so much as Christ's whisper.

. . . The State is a coarse outline and hasty memorandum of the people's culture and aspirations . . . nor should good men obey the laws too well. Would the State behave as handsomely by me as my mother does, I would do anything, everything, for so fair a benefactor, even to my last crust and the end of my conscience. But am I to respect and serve willingly what is ugly and unlovely, not to say base and abominable?

February 3

Mixed people, mixed institutions: therefore, time, tolerance, and the long patience, suffering wheat and tares to ripen side by side as they sprang up in the field. That reform itself needs reforming which plucks up the man in rooting out his sins. Heaven's Kingdom comes not by violence but by persuasion.

. . . Love is the soft but mighty curb. Pure power sleeps in reserves, and is benign and beautiful. "Yet half his strength he put not forth." Reserves are God instinctive, and checks from within.[3]

February 6

To meliorate Nature and his temperament, man's homestead in Nature, is the office of civilization, the end of institutions. A genial, hospitable home, the clearing felled and planted from out

---

[3] A clear expression of the deeper wisdom that came to Alcott the Reformer in his ripening years. The final words may be a reminiscence of Emerson's now famous phrase "inner check," or — more probably — of Alcott's own reading in the religious literature of India.

the forest of the passions and protected from prowling beasts —
this is the backwoodsman's business and performance, fitting his
premises for receiving into its bosom the seed of a meliorated stock,
a manly mind fed from the vigorous virgin soil of cultured endeavor.

But man is scarce naturalized, far less acclimated, as yet, and
settled in his proper nature. With all natural and acquired advantages, superior tools and tendencies — the axe and spade and
ship, the drill of commerce and his wants — he remains but a
semi-savage and a beast, the victim of his imprisoned genius. Yet
these brute forces, these Indians of his wild nature, like the
aborigines of this continent, like the extinct animals, are passing
away, to date eras in the human geology.[4]

February 10

Henry Thoreau is here today. Also met Emerson at the
Athenæum. He has just returned from a lecturing tour through
the western cities — Syracuse, Buffalo, Cincinnati, St. Louis —
and speaks hopefully of the people in those parts.[5]

February 19

Good teaching is the temporary using of another's talents and
senses instead of one's own. "Lend us your mind for the moment," says the pupil, "that we may see how things look through
that prism." And he is the master who so serves his company that
prospects seen never before, nor surmised, become present and
memorable thereafter forever.

March 4

To take the beast out and put in the man — to tame the beast,
rather, and develope the man in the man, disqualifying him for
howling longer with the wolves or glutting himself with the

---

[4] This meditation, sharply distinguishing Alcott's thought from the "primitiv-
ism" of Thoreau and also from the expansive pioneering spirit of Emerson and
Whitman, should be compared with the entry for January 24, 1860. It was
suggested by a recent perusal of *The Principles of Geology*, by Sir Charles Lyell.
[5] At this time, probably, the first suggestion was made to Alcott of those
western tours which greatly extended his activity and influence in later life.

swine — that is civility, that is culture, freedom, and the pure humanity.[6]

April 13

Miss Littlehale is here with young Sanburn [*sic*] of Harvard College, a youth of fine genius and great promise. We discuss the subject of culture. Mr. Sanburn is one of my circle at Divinity Hall, though not yet a member of the class.[7]

May 8   *Concord*

All the morning in the library at the old game, discussing un-reportable things with Emerson — he reading me, besides, some sheets of his new book on England — and we walk afterwards to Walden, and home in season for me to sup with Hawthorne at "Hillside," where I pass most of the evening, and return to Emerson's to sleep. Hawthorne is preparing for the Consulate to which he is just appointed by President Pierce, and leaves pro-spectively for Liverpool, where he will reside, sometime in July, intending to be absent for four years certainly if not for five, and to visit the Continent meanwhile, perhaps passing a season in Italy before he returns to "Hillside" and the improvements he designs for it. The shrubbery there is becoming more luxuriant and grace-ful every season, and is fast showing the fit place for the setting of the new house he will build on his return.

July 1   *Boston*

Ellery Channing is here today, and discourses with rare good sense on life, literature, and literary men. And he permits me to

[6] It is possible, although there is no other evidence of his having done so, that Alcott had been reading certain lines of verse, now famous, which, when he wrote this passage, had been in print for less than three years:

> "Arise and fly
> The reeling Faun, the sensual feast.
> Move upward, working out the beast,
> And let the ape and tiger die."
> — Tennyson's *In Memoriam*, 118.

[7] Alcott's first mention of F. B. Sanborn, who was to be his friend and helper for the rest of his life, and also his first biographer. At this time Alcott was con-ducting informal classes at the Divinity School in Cambridge, by invitation not of the Faculty but of a group of students.

open before him my Collections, and dips with me here and there into the same, having the shrewdest suggestions for me as we run over the leaves together. His is a far wiser and wittier mind than most persons are aware of. . . .

Emerson read me something lately from a joint production of Ellery's and his which I was glad to know of, and the better pleased at the prospect of its being sometime published. It was excellent in design and performance, a sort of literary recreation, being transcripts of the friends' walks and conversations in Concord, their speculations and experiences by the fields and woods, along the streams and meadows, seasoned sagely with the pleasantries and learning of both — the whole, judging from the sample read to me, promising an entertainment as elegant and racy as anything in modern literature.

Channing's conversation I think far superior to anything of his printed, surpassing as well in subtlety as compass of thought that of most men I have known — while his humour, so rarely a talent of this New England blood of ours, is flushed with an admirable sense, the more stimulating from the unexpectedness of its caprices. He is the best of company, but only when he seeks company; the very worst when forced into it — if this he did not fatally dodge always and avoid as by instinct. The shyest and moodiest of mortals, never encountering but a single person at once, or absconding forthwith at the approach of a third lest his duplicities should be offended and himself nonplussed by numbers. — But I am not his draughtsman at present, and shall add only this, that he seems to me at once the most social yet solitary of men, snatching his pleasures by stealth always, and under disguises which his friends alone can excuse.

July 21

Emerson comes, and we go to Nahant, where we dine and pass the day, discussing many things as we survey the ocean from Nahant to Lynn.

August 7   *Concord*

All day with Emerson, having the old yet ever-new game of speculation parliamentary; also the ever-Walden walk, with discussions — not usual — on ways and means, the largest concernment being given to a purposed conversational tour for me along the great Canal towns, west: Syracuse, Rochester, Buffalo, perhaps Cleveland, also Medina — where I have relatives of my name — and so on to Cincinnati. This jaunt to be undertaken some time during the current autumn, and to be so managed as to defray its expenses and more, if the same can be made feasible and continue to seem desirable to me. I shall consider it well, and hope to have it so. The West is a new field for me, and Autumn an auspicious season for the species of entertainments in which I indulge.

October 23

Arrange the western tour with Emerson. E. pays my passage to Cincinnati — $18.00.

October 24

Return in the 9 o'clock train. Outfit, etc. for my journey.

October 25

Pack my things. Wilson sends my printed Prospectus of Conversations for the western cities.

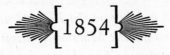

{1854}

*T*HE STORY OF *Alcott's return, in February, from his
first "Tour at the West" is known not from his but from
Louisa's Journal: "We were waked by hearing the bell. Mother
flew down, crying 'My husband!' We rushed after, and five white
figures embraced the half-frozen wanderer who came in hungry,
tired, cold, and disappointed, but smiling bravely and as serene
as ever. We fed and warmed and brooded over him, longing to
ask if he had made any money; but no one did till little May said,
after he had told all the pleasant things, 'Well, did people pay
you?' Then, with a queer look, he opened his pocket-book and
showed one dollar, saying with a smile that made our eyes fill,
'Only that. My overcoat was stolen and I had to buy a shawl.
Many promises were not kept, and travelling is costly; but I
have opened a way, and another year shall do better.' I shall
never forget how beautifully Mother answered him, though the
dear hopeful soul had built much on his success; but with a beam-
ing face she kissed him, saying, 'I call that doing* very well.' "*

Here is a perfect epitome of the man's entire life.*

Within a day or two Alcott was advertising a new series of
Conversations on "The Conduct of Life," to be held at Haver-
hill. Most of his week-ends, during the early spring, were spent
with Emerson and Thoreau at Concord, where many passages of
English Traits and of Walden, then in manuscript, were read to
him. At the end of May occurred the convulsion of excitement
over the arrest of the fugitive slave Anthony Burns, in the effort*

to save whom Bronson Alcott — although he says nothing of the matter in his Journal — was thought by his contemporaries to have played an active and heroic part. In June Alcott paid an extensive visit to the Transcendentalist Marston Watson at his estate called "Hillside," near Plymouth. The chief event of the summer, however, was the publication, on August 9, of Thoreau's Walden. *In September and October Alcott was again at Watson's "Hillside" for more than a month, working on various manuscripts, gathering apples, helping Thoreau at surveying, and considering Watson's suggestion that he make his permanent home there.*

1854

May 26

I return by early train this morning and meet the Vigilance Committee concerning Burns' rescue and measures for this exigency.[1] A full attendance, and many opinions expressed.

Evening: I am at Faneuil Hall. The meeting is large and the speeches very exciting. Phillips and Parker acquit themselves manfully. The meeting is adjourned in prospect of Burns' rescue. I return by Court Square, where I meet Higginson and witness some incidents of the unsuccessful attempt at the rescue.[2]

May 27

All day about Court Square,[3] in court, in counsel with Vigilance Committee; the crowd very large, and much excitement prevails in all classes.

[1] Immediately upon hearing of the arrest of Anthony Burns, the fugitive slave, Alcott had gone to Worcester to bring T. W. Higginson to Boston.

[2] A surprising understatement, due perhaps to Alcott's unawareness that he had done anything extraordinary, or possibly to a fear that his papers might be used as evidence against his friends. Higginson, who relates Alcott's conduct in *Cheerful Yesterdays*, Chapter V, considered him the hero of the occasion. For twenty years Alcott made no mention, in his Journal at least, of the part he had taken in the events at Court Square. But see the entry for February 9, 1874.

[3] The fugitive Anthony Burns was kept, after his arrest, in the Court House, under heavy guard. The purpose of Alcott and his friends in haunting the Square during these days was to effect a rescue of the prisoner from the soldiers.

May 28

Hear Parker this morning at the Music Hall. S. J. May is here, and stays with us.

May 29

About Court Square, and with Vigilance Committee at Tremont Temple. The trial proceeds, and the crowd is large and clamorous for the issues of the case.

May 30

In Court Square today, at Anti-Slavery meeting in Melodeon. Also meet Vigilance Committee. The country all in town.

May 31

Again in court, and at Anti-Slavery meeting.

June 1

Today about Court Square.

June 2

Witness Burns' rendition today sadly, and ashamed of the Union, of New England, of Boston, almost of myself too. I must see to it that my part is done hereafter to give us a Boston, a Mayor, a Governor, and a President — if indeed a single suffrage, or many, can mend matters essentially. So I shall vote, as I have never done hitherto, for a municipal government and a state. Possibly a country may yet be rescued from slavery. . . . Yet something besides voting must do it effectually.

August 9

Thoreau dines with me and gives me his book, just published.[4] We go to Southworth's and see his picture of Emerson.

August 10

Read *Walden*.

[4] *Walden* was, in fact, published on this very day, and Alcott was probably its first reader.

August 11, 12, 13

Read and re-read *Walden;* also the *Week on Concord and Merrimac Rivers* — books to find readers and fame as years pass by, and publish the author's surpassing merits.

August 27

Louisa leaves this morning for Syracuse to spend a month there with Anna, and I go to Concord at 4 P.M. to pass Sunday with Emerson and Thoreau.

August 28

Emerson reads me a chapter of his book on England. We walk to Walden and discuss the old themes again.

August 29

I dine with Thoreau, and come home afterwards.

*I*N THE early months of this year Alcott was hesitating, like a young man at the very entrance to life, as to what he should do for a livelihood. He asked advice of many persons, though chiefly of Emerson, and was given promises of assistance by many more, though Emerson did more than promise. He revived his earlier plan of combining the work of a pedlar with his Conversations; but he thought also of gardening at Concord, of working in a clock factory, of going to England as a purchasing agent for American bookstores, and — with a definite longing — of farming at Spindle Hill. His daughters wished, as always, to remain in Boston, but Mrs. Alcott wanted to move to Walpole, New Hampshire, in the valley of the Connecticut River, where her brother-in-law offered the use of a house rent-free. Accordingly, the family moved in July to Walpole. There for the next few months Alcott was happily engaged in farm-work, carpentry, conversation with his country neighbors, and writing. In October the family circle was first broken by the departure of his eldest daughter, Anna, for Syracuse, where she was to teach. One month later Louisa wrote in her Journal: "Decided to seek my fortune; so, with my little trunk of home-made clothes, $20 earned by stories sent to the Gazette, and my MSS., I set forth with Mother's blessing one rainy day in the dullest month in the year."

1855

May 12

Leave for Concord to pass Sunday, or longer, with Emerson.

May 13

We discuss the going to England, the missionary plan, and the gardening, all the forenoon — E. thinking less favorably of the first and liking the last best as a means of support for myself if not for my family. After dinner we walk to Sleepy Hollow. Ellen, Edith, and Edward with us. Mrs. Ripley comes and passes the evening. Also Elizabeth Hoar dines with us.

May 14

I call on Thoreau and Channing. Also walk about "Hillside." Dine at Emerson's, and we walk afterwards to the Baker Farm and Fair Haven. I return in the 7 o'clock train, a little dubious.

May 15   *Walpole, New Hampshire*

Meditating plans of life for the future — the working at the clock factories in Connecticut among the rest, if nothing better offers for me here.

September 3–8

This week is given busily to sodding, grading, and improvement of the grounds about the house — Mr. Farnham, man and team, assisting me.

There is profit in working with labouring men, and wholesomeness. Their wits are so handy and their senses so parallel to the world they work in and measure so well. Nor do I find myself out of place beside them, but one of them for the time, and as concrete as they are. 'Tis refreshing to yoke one's idealism with this team of tug-along-the-rut of realism, and so get practical wisdom out of it, and sanity.

October 5

Anna leaves for Syracuse by the 11 o'clock train. I go with her to the station and see her off. She leaves with good hope and courage, and will doubtless find good account in her new field of labour and usefulness. But it makes us all sad when so much goodness and grace leaves our house, though it may be to return soon again to us. I must add some little words which I put into her bandbox when she left us.

ANNA'S TABLETS

Avoid	*Take*
1. Late hours	1. Early bed
2. Close rooms	2. Daily walks
3. Superfine bread	3. Brown bread
4. People too many	4. Bath often
5. Suffering from diffidence	5. Pure amusements
6. Spending too little for self	6. Good readings
7. Routine	7. Heed conscience

November 8

Louisa has finished her book of tales which she calls *The Christmas Elves*, and Abby has illustrated it very prettily for her. I arrange and prepare the MSS. for the press.

November 9

This morning Louisa leaves to pass some time in Boston, and find a publisher for her book. But she is a month too late for a Christmas offering, and will fail, I fear, in getting it printed this season.

I am here now with my wife and the two girls, to make the most of myself and them in this little river town and its quiet population, with which I am scarcely acquainted — nor am I likely to be very soon. But we shall see what comes of a residence here as the months pass and the winter opportunities for intercourse come round.

THE WINTER months went quietly by at Walpole, with letters from Anna and Louisa, conversations with the neighbors that never reached a satisfying height or depth, and enthusiastic reading of the new book Leaves of Grass. In the early spring Alcott was again at work in the fields and in his garden, but the first half of May was spent in Boston and Concord, conversing. Late in the same month his third daughter, Elizabeth, was taken seriously ill with scarlet fever, contracted from the children of a neighbor whom Mrs. Alcott had tried to help. As in the visitation of smallpox six years before, no physician was called at first and no drugs given, the parents depending upon their own skill as nurses and upon such directions as they could find in the medical writings of Hahnemann, to whose homeopathic theories they were entirely committed. The father, at any rate, based much of his hope upon the fact that Elizabeth had "never tasted animal food." After a period of great anxiety the patient seemed to recover, but she never regained her strength.

In September came Henry Thoreau for a brief visit in the midst of a walking-tour, and on the thirteenth of the same month Alcott started for New York, taking several others cities and towns on his way. This journey, which lasted until the end of the year, gave him one of the happiest and busiest periods of his life; and his Journal for the period shows that the pressure of events

*and contact with interesting persons could enable him to write
even briskly. Remarkably adaptable in mind and mood, he passed
without difficulty and at once from the atmosphere of Boston to
that of New York City. Boston Common and Concord's Mill Dam
would seem, indeed, to have been temporarily forgotten by the man
who described Walt Whitman with humor, gusto, and graphic
power in the passages here first brought fully to light.*

1856

February 2   *Walpole, New Hampshire*

Emerson has made the lecture, and a public to listen to the
master and his chosen disciples. That were a victory worth a
life, since the lecture is the American invention, serving the
country with impulse and thought of an ideal cast and conquering
virtue. The Lyceums are properly *Emersonia,* and we must sub-
stitute the founder's name for the thing he has invented. . . .[1]

There was no lecture till Emerson made it. Plutarch's readings, now published as his "Morals," come the nearest, perhaps,
to something of this kind, since these fair fragments were briefs
of discourses made by the philosopher to assembled companies,
Athenian and Roman, and since collected for our entertainment
in good learning. But besides these we have nothing reminding
us of Emerson's utterances.

February 26–27

The interest taken in exploring expeditions and the Kane
discoveries, just now, will be transformed presently into the parts
unknown and far distant regions of mind and the moral nature
of man, for the survey and settlement of which these rough ad-
venturers, these facilities and implements, are the prepared outfit

[1] Few persons had better reason than Alcott to know that this statement was
exaggerated, for he had been a housemate and a collaborator of Josiah Holbrook,
the true founder of the American Lyceum, in the years when that institution
was beginning. It is doubtful whether Emerson did more for the Lyceum than
it did for him.

and manifold means available on the great and grand scale of the century they audit and prefigure so masterfully.

Bridge first and belt the globe, tunnel and grade earth and ocean, skate round the poles or steam round, mine and map the particles all round, and the planet will for the first time show a pretty little estate in prospect for the youth in expectancy when he comes of age to occupy and improve his inheritance — presuming, as we must, simply a power commensurate therewith, and cosmic as his titles and domains. The twentieth century should be able to produce an Adam with no Cain in his loins, this time, to curse posterity and blacken its prospects.

'Tis the age of conquest. By the new facilities the civilized nations are conquering the rest, the territories of matter and mind to match — this last invaded, or soon to be, by a speculation daring, demonic, as of the brute elements, the hemispheres taken tightly between fingers and thumb and made to spin or serve for pitch-coppers in the palmistries of the period.[2]

March 22

The man of the world is of necessity the temporizer and man of expediencies, or what will "go" at the time. His traits are a certain flexibility and adaptedness to circumstances, also the slurring-over or ignoring the moral sentiment, if necessary to carry his point, nor obtruding that sentiment on occasions, being by interest and habit a *lower-law man*. His will divided and demonized, the parts playing toward his interests, his Satan is ever ready to serve for the consideration, as himself shall incline and determine. Like pincers, he holds fast whatsoever he gets, nor will let go. Call him a vice, and so dismiss him with "Yankee" written on his frontispiece all over.

March 27

. . . This infant Young America, at the breast; her absorption, the Great West, Florida, Texas, California; presently all Mexico,

[2] One of the most characteristic of Alcott's utterances. Thoreau, at this time, was copying long passages about the "Kane discoveries" into his "Fact Books," Emerson was giving the exploiters of the continent his reserved and modified blessing; but Alcott never wavered in the Transcendental conviction that "conquest of nature" is only the beginning of man's task, that the real frontier lies within us, and that the true America is a country of the mind.

Cuba, South indefinitely, Canada north; pap and spoonmeats those named; — England intellectually for solids, and the Continental lores. And what else and beyond, who knows? — Then samples a few, most of them living, and last of her striplings: Webster, Greeley, Garrison, Greenough, Emerson. — Let's wait a little and see what shall come of so much promise and such great ambition.[3]

April 10

Garrison made the Convention,
Greeley made the Newspaper,
Emerson made the Lecture,
and
Alcott is making the Conversation.

These are all purely American organs and institutions, which no country nor people besides ours can claim as we can.

May 11   *Concord*

All day with Emerson, and a renewal of the old pleasures.

What is there comparable in this life to the meeting of a man face to face, though it shall be for moments only! Yet I find myself rich enough, with all my poverties, to dispense for months with these enjoyments without the sense of loss, and can live even in the solitudes without complaint. It has been a twelvemonth now since I met my friend, and still I meet him as if I had parted with him but yesterday, or not at all.

We walk with Ellen and Edward through the new cemetery at Sleepy Hollow, Emerson pointing out to me his family lot still rudely staked on the pine-grove mound, and I for the first time breathing aloud my wish of reclining sometime near my friend's memories,[4] finding a grave in the bosom of the little village which came nearest of any under the sun to being the home of my mortal

[3] It is evident here that Alcott has been reading *Leaves of Grass*, a gift-copy of which, in the first edition, had been in Emerson's hands for some eight months when this note was written. Never before had Alcott spoken boastfully of America's mere bulk, or of her powers of "absorption," and seldom had his writing been so incoherent.

[4] The grave of Alcott is, in fact, only a few steps from that of Emerson, on "the pine-grove mound."

parts. Sweet were this memory of mine, thus laid in calm repose not far from that of my benefactor and the friend of whatsoever is imperishable in me.

May 12

I see Thoreau, and Cholmondeley's magnificent present of an Oriental library, lately come to hand from England — a gift worthy of a disciple to his master, and a tribute of admiration to Thoreau's genius from a worthy Englishman.

Walk with Thoreau by the Cottage and Hallowell Place, and dine with him. . . .

Meet my friends and former neighbors in Emerson's parlours — Miss Mary Emerson, Mrs. Browne, Miss Jane Whiting, Mrs. Brooks, Mrs. Ripley, Thoreau, Sanborn, and many more, and talk pleasantly on Society — Emerson, Thoreau, Mrs. Emerson, Mrs. Ripley, Sanborn contributing to the entertainment.

Emerson praised the meeting after the company had gone, and said of it that Conversation was a power, and must become an institution.[5]

May 13

This morning . . . see Thoreau again. He lends me from the Cholmondeley Collection *The Bhagavad Gita,* or a Discourse between Krishna and Arjuna on Divine Matters, a Sanskrit Philosophical Poem, Translated, with copious notes, an Introduction on Sanskrit Philosophy, and other matter, by J. Cockburn Thomson, Hertford, England, 1855.[6]

May 20　　　　　　　　　　　　　　　*Walpole, New Hampshire*

Plant peas, corn, cucumbers, and melons in my little garden plot.

Human life is a very simple matter. Breath, bread, health, a hearthstone, a fountain, fruits, a few garden seeds and room to plant them in, a wife and children, a friend or two of either sex, conversation, neighbours, and a task life-long given from within —

---

[5] See the enthusiastic eulogy of Alcott in Emerson's Journal for about this date.

[6] Alcott had first read the *Bhagavad-Gita* in May, 1846.

these are contentment and a great estate. On these gifts follow all others, all graces dance attendance, all beauties, beatitudes, mortals can desire and know.

July 10

This day twelve month we left Boston and came here; and now I am familiar a little with the place, especially my little garden plot and the plants I cultivate and care for from day to day. I cannot say so much of my acquaintance with the people here, very few of whom I have met otherwise than in my walks to and from the stores and post office, or at my Conversations for a few times last winter. My garden has been my pleasure, and a daily recreation since the spring opened for planting, and promises the same for the month to come or more. Every plant one tends he falls in love with, and gets the glad response for all his attentions and pains. Books, persons even, are for the time set aside — studies and the pen. — Only persons of perennial genius attract or recreate as the plants, and of books we may say the same, as of the magic of solitude.

July 25

Bunting, the Englishman, reaps Mr. Willis's wheat before the door in our lane. 'Tis a pretty sight, but passing fast from us, superseded as it is by the cradle and horse-gear; and the coming generation will need commentaries to make plain Thomson's text and harvest-home.[7] The sickle rusts in garrets already, a memorial of a past pastoral time fabled of poets. Bunting tells me that reaping still prevails in England, many poor families in the farming districts gleaning their year's pittance of bread after the reapers in the fields — the work chiefly of women and maidens.

August 30

Attend a Conversation at Dr. B.'s[8] on "Spiritualism." . . . This apotheosis of idiocy and fatuity only serves to betray the latent atheism and dark superstition of multitudes in our time, and the need of some spiritual discernment and culture to detect and

[7] James Thomson's *Autumn*, line 151, ff.
[8] Henry Whitney Bellows.

banish these grim goblin gods here enthroned from the vacant popular mind. Yet the ghastly superstition is spreading fast and wide, and is to have its victims and its day. Nor need we wonder in the least at this calamity when we consider the superficial, not to say no-teaching of the multitude in the elements of metaphysics and of the spiritual life. The oracles are dumb; and if any proof need be cited in confirmation of the shallow infidelity and the current stupidity, it is to be found in the calling of this direst of all materialism of any people or time by the fair name "Spiritualism," and a "philosophy" besides.

September 1

The autumnal months, September particularly, have something of the Platonic affluence for me, and touch the imagination with ambrosial fancies, Attic ideas, as if Philosophy found herself for the time draped in a poesy the comeliest that Nature could confer on Genius to crown him lord and emperor of the flourishing year. Our Indian Summer, too, is but a snatch of the same Olympian strain, and celebration of the sovreign ripeness of autumnal virtue, the season's opulent ode.

September 10

This afternoon comes Thoreau, having been at Brattleboro, at Bellows Falls, climbed Fall Mountain with his pack from the river, and come down on the Cold Stream side, walking from there to our house, where he spends the evening and sleeps.

September 11

We discuss politics, Frémont, Garrison, Emerson, and the rest all morning in my study. Thoreau is persistently manly and independent as of old. His criticisms on men and the times as characteristic, individual, and urged with all the honest pertinacity befitting a descendant of the Scandinavian Thor. A man of a genealogy like his — Franko-Norman-Scottish-American — may well be forgiven for a little foolhardiness, if not pugnacity, amidst his great common sense and faithfulness to the core of natural things.

We walk after dinner over Farm Hill and to the Monument.

In the evening Thoreau reads Dr. Bellows' Historical Sketch of the Founder's Family, and takes all there is known of Walpole to bed with him, to be used for such ornaments of his jaunt this day as our traveller's humour shall dictate.

Seldom has a scholar's study circumscribed so much of the Cosmos as that of this footed intelligence of ours — nothing less than all out-of-doors sufficing its genius and scope, and this day by day, through all weeks and weather, the year round.

September 23　　　　　　　　　　　　　　　*Wolcott, Connecticut*

. . . I have not met lately, anywhere, so primitive a people and so simple as these relatives of mine. The housekeeping, the farming, the blessing at table, the thanks, the manners and turns of expression, the curiosity, the religion, are the same I had known at my grandfather's when a boy. . . . His very copy of the *Pilgrim's Progress*, London, printed 1725, an 18mo., much thumbed and soiled, turned unexpectedly forth from its slumbers on the hidden shelves of the smoked book-case sunk into the chimney over the mantle-piece, and which none of the family remembered having seen. To my surprise, moreover, they were quite willing I should claim it, containing as it did the autograph of my grandfather still legible, despite smoke and the dog's-ears:

> "John Alcock
> His Book God
> Give him grace there
> in to Look ye 1751"

It is the 120th edition, has the frontispiece of the author in wood, also of Vanity Fair. The last leaf is wanting.

September 25

I ride to Waterbury and dine with Wm. R. Hitchcock, a former patron of mine when teaching the Cheshire School. Here meet his son, a graduate of Trinity College at Hartford, and discuss theology, Bishop Clarke and his Broad Church Diet, etc. — I being taken as a heretic and seceder from the primitive faith. But, taught two catechisms — the Westminster and Episcopal —

in my youth, I chanced to like neither as I could wish, and have belonged to the Church of One Member, a creed of one sub-scriber, till now; and now free to secede from that if once better informed and feeling the duty incumbent upon conscience and faith — Christianity being older than Luther or Calvin and the Apostle's Creed, or the Apostles themselves. Christ himself kindly agreed to dissent from the superstitions of his fathers, claiming his privilege of private judgement in the matter of revelations and creeds; and is the Christ, and best interpreter of the oracles of the human heart because of this freedom and fine catholicism of spirit and deed — of no sect, but the friend of freedom for all.

October 4   *New York City*

P.M. To Brooklyn, and see Walt Whitman. I pass a couple of hours, and find him to be an extraordinary person, full of brute power, certainly of genius and audacity, and likely to make his mark on Young America — he affirming himself to be its representative man and poet. I must meet him again, and more than once, to mete his merits and place in this Pantheon of the West. He gives me his book of poems, the *Leaves of Grass*, 2nd. Edition, with new verses, and asks me to write to him if I have any more to say about him or his master, Emerson.

A nondescript, he is not so easily described, nor seen to be described. Broad-shouldered, rouge-fleshed, Bacchus-browed, bearded like a satyr, and rank, he wears his man-Bloomer in defiance of everybody, having these as every thing else after his own fashion, and for example to all men hereafter. Red flannel undershirt, open-breasted, exposing his brawny neck; striped calico jacket over this, the collar Byroneal, with coarse cloth overalls buttoned to it; cowhide boots; a heavy round-about, with huge outside pockets and buttons to match; and a slouched hat, for house and street alike. Eyes gray, unimaginative, cautious yet sagacious; his voice deep, sharp, tender sometimes and almost melting. When talking will recline upon the couch at length, pil-lowing his head upon his bended arm, and informing you naively how lazy he is, and slow. Listens well; asks you to repeat what he has failed to catch at once, yet hesitates in speaking often, or gives over as if fearing to come short of the sharp, full, concrete meaning of his thought. Inquisitive, very; over-curious even; inviting criticisms on himself, on his poems — pronouncing it "pomes." — In fine, an egotist, incapable of omitting, or suffering any one long to omit, noting Walt Whitman in discourse. Swaggy in his walk, burying both hands in his outside pockets. Has never been sick, he says, nor taken medicine, nor sinned; and so is quite innocent of repentance and man's fall. A bachelor, he professes great respect for women. Of Scotch descent by his father; by his mother, German. Age 38, and Long Island born.

November 1

I take the boat Thomas Hunt for Perth Amboy, and dine with Thoreau at the Springs, Eagleswood,[9] where I sleep. Thoreau is here surveying Eagleswood Estate for Mr. Spring and Company.

November 2

Evening: Thoreau reads his lecture on "Walking," and interests his company deeply in his treatment of nature. Never had such a walk as this been taken by any one before, and the conversation so flowing and lively and curious — the young people enjoying it particularly.

November 7

I am at Mrs. Botta's,[10] and meet Lawrence and wife, Dr. Anderson, Prof. Hackley of the Theological School, Mr. and Mrs. Field, Charles Brace and brother, and many more.

Henry Thoreau comes from Eagleswood and sees Swinton[11] the Scotchman at my rooms — he, Thoreau, declining to accompany me to Mrs. Botta's where he is invited.

We sleep at the Cure.

November 8

We find Greeley at the Harlem Station and ride with him to his farm, where we pass the day. He takes us to see his acres, his

[9] A famous spa.
[10] Anne C. Lynch Botta, 1815–1891, hostess and poet.
[11] John Swinton, 1829–1901, a journalist and social reformer.

ditches, the barn he is building of rubble-stones and cement, and tells of his crops, his purposed improvements, etc. But I doubt the wisdom of his farming and predict nothing of it. — A more tragic family I have never seen, and pity man and wife and children, I know not which the more.

Alice Cary [12] accompanied us, and returned in the evening with Greeley and ourselves to the City.

We sleep at Savery's Hotel.

November 9

We breakfast at Savery's, and cross afterwards to Brooklyn and the Plymouth Church to hear Ward Beecher. It was a spectacle good to see, and very impressive. His auditors had to weep, had to laugh, under his potent magnetism. His preached doctrine of justice for all men, for bond and free, the righteous and wicked alike, was broadly put home to North and South. Aisles, entries, galleries, every pew, every chair, was occupied. The praise, the prayers, the baptism of the babes — a dozen of them — all was silent, solemn, and devout. Thoreau called it pagan, and was restive under it; but I pronounced it very good, very well suited to priest and people, the best I had heard lately, and hopeful for the coming congregations.

Beecher has the good sense to leave out the old traditions, and speaks to the fact and the times in his own lively way, as much player perhaps as minister, and so tells on the multitudes. . . . His flowing spirits, his wit, his earnestness and impetuosity, are eloquent, and work the miracles. Perhaps of preachers he ranks first in energy and effectiveness, in unction and dramatic force; yet I class him among the lecturers rather — or, more truly, as a cross between priest and player, I should say, with the fervour and quaintness of both. An Idealist he is not, nor a man of genius in any sense, but of versatile talent, a keen intelligence, broad humour, and lively human sympathies. His health is perfect, the gift of few in these days, and his western training, with the prestige of his ancestry and name — in these lie the secret of his power and popularity.

[12] The poetess, sister of Phoebe Cary.

We walk to the Mannings and dine. Here find Mrs. Tyndall,[13] from Philadelphia, a solid walrus of a woman spread full many a rood abroad, kindly taking the slaves' and Magdalens' parts and advocate for general justice and equality in all relations. Also Miss Margaret Sedgwick, very curious to see Thoreau and measure the man for herself.

After dinner we call at Walt Whitman's, Thoreau and I, but, finding him out, we get something from his mother — a stately sensible matron believing in Walter absolutely and telling us how good he was and wise as a boy, how his four brothers and two sisters loved him, and how they take counsel of the great man he is grown to be now. Walt was always, she says, for the weaker against the stronger, and the umpire in all disputes. She invited us to call early tomorrow morning, when we should be sure of finding him at home and glad to see us.

Evening: There is company at Mr. Manning's, and we discuss "the Wild in Character," Thoreau being our representative of it and spokesman against the humanities present or absent. The talk is spirited and talented. Behemoth [14] takes the woman's part to perfection, for woman's wild honesty and ways, she being the kindliest piece of cumbrous candour and common sense I have happened to meet for a great while. Thoreau's savage was the more agreeable and certainly the more possible person of the two, she insisted, than the blessed Christ of my painting, of whom she could make nothing but a "fancy man," very insignificant in her eyes, as he must be to all sensible people and sane everywhere. It took good manly meat to make a man.

November 10

This morning we call on Whitman, Mrs. Tyndall accompanying us to whet her curiosity on the demigod. He receives us kindly, yet awkwardly, and takes us up two narrow flights of stairs to sit or stand as we might in his attic study — also the bed-chamber of himself and his feeble brother, the pressure of whose bodies was still apparent in the unmade bed standing in one cor-

[13] The mother of General Tyndall, who was related to John Tyndall, the English scientist.
[14] Mrs. Tyndall.

ner, and the vessel scarcely hidden underneath. A few books were piled disorderly over the mantel-piece, and some characteristic pictures — a Hercules, a Bacchus, and a satyr — were pasted, unframed, upon the rude walls.

There was a rough table in the room, and but a single window, fronting Ellison Avenue, upon which he lives, his being the middle tenement of a single block of three private dwellings and far out on Myrtle Avenue, in the very suburbs of the city of Brooklyn.

He took occasion to inform us three, while surveying his premises aloft, of his bathing daily through the mid-winter; said he rode sometimes a-top of an omnibus up and down Broadway from morning till night beside the driver, and dined afterwards with the whipsters, frequented the opera during the season, and "lived to make pomes," and for nothing else particularly.

He had told me on my former visit of his being a housebuilder, but I learned from his mother that his brother was the house-builder, and not Walt, who, she said, had no business but going out and coming in to eat, drink, write, and sleep. And she told how all the common folks loved him. He had his faults, she knew, and was not a perfect man, but meant us to understand that she thought him an extraordinary son of a fond mother.

I said, while looking at the pictures in his study: "Which, now, of the three, particularly, is the new poet here — this Hercules, the Bacchus, or the satyr?" On which he begged me not to put my questions too close, meaning to take, as I inferred, the virtues of the three to himself unreservedly. And I think he might fairly, being himself the modern Pantheon — satyr, Silenus, and him of the twelve labours — combined.

He is very curious of criticism on himself or his book, inviting it from all quarters, nor suffering the conversation to stray very wide away from Walt's godhead without recalling it to that high mark. I hoped to put him in communication direct with Thoreau, and tried my hand a little after we came down stairs and sat in the parlour below; but each seemed planted fast in reserves, surveying the other curiously, — like two beasts, each wondering what the other would do, whether to snap or run; and it came to no more than cold compliments between them. Whether Thoreau was meditating the possibility of Walt's stealing away his "out-of-doors" for some sinister ends, poetic or pecuniary, I could not well divine, nor was very curious to know; or whether Walt suspected or not that he had here, for once, and the first time, found his match and more at smelling out "all Nature," a sagacity potent, penetrating and peerless as his own, if indeed not more piercing and profound, finer and more formidable. I cannot say. At all events, our stay was not long, and we left the voluminous Mrs. Tyndall . . . with the savage sovereign of the flesh, he making an appointment to meet me at the International tomorrow and deliver himself further, if the mood favored and the place.[15]

November 20

Swinton comes and we cross to Brooklyn and dine with Whitman. I am well paid for this visit, and bring home spoils for great uses.

November 23

I am at the Woman's Convention, and hear good speeches from Elizabeth Jones and Wendell Phillips. The Convention is well attended and orderly, the spectacle impressive. There are public women as there are public men, gifted and official, equal to the platform, the profession, the public occasion, and gracing them well — the spokeswomen and presidents of their sex. If any is disposed to question it, and its pertinency, let him sit here for ten minutes and see how becomingly, how ably, this Convention is conducted — Lucy Stone presiding, and discretely, over this mixed body. . . .

Their ways, just now at the outset, may not be theirs always, but bad imitations of our worst ways — mistaking as they may, in their novitiate, the coarse instrumentalities as best, of convention, speech, resolution, petition, denunciation, the mob appeal,

---

[15] There is no indication in the Journal that Whitman kept this appointment.

With the entries for November 7–10 compare the Walden Edition of Thoreau, VI, 295–298 — i.e. Thoreau's letter of December 7, 1856, to H. G. O. Blake. It is remarkable that the "sensuality" in Whitman of which Thoreau makes so much is not mentioned by Alcott either here or elsewhere.

F. B. Sanborn, in his edition of Thoreau's Letters and in his *Memoir* of Alcott, gives a grotesquely false rendering of the present passages about Whitman.

for the truer and more potent persuasions of the parlour, the conversation, prevailing manners, . . . the suggestions of literature, religion, and of pure art. Not that woman shall not use any armour, but use it in a superior and womanly way. The Convention if she will, the ballot, the pulpit, the professorship: all these are hers if she will grace them well or show man how to become them better.

Whatsoever a woman can do better than a man, that she is bound to do, and that she has things to do is presumable from the fact of her being not a man but a woman, and fitted to do them in ways inimitable by us. There is no danger of confusing sexes or spheres. . . . Absurdities are short-lived, and, during their reign, promote the criticism that unmasks them at last. The Bloomer is an experiment at a convenient costume; and when, presently, good taste superadds the comeliness, and some graceful woman the ornament of her person, the sex will adopt it and thank the genius to whom they owe their freedom from the present fetters.

November 25

This morning I breakfast at Dr. Bellows'. Henry Ward Beecher, Fanny Kemble, Mrs. Kirkland, Charles and Mary Brace and brother, are of the party. 'Twas a breakfast quite memorable, and worth the eating. The viands were sumptuous; the vessels costly; the apartments, the decorations, the cheer, elegant all and in keeping, yet subordinated to the company — my part and interest in the feast, in the spectacle, being of the supersensual and human sort — if indeed and in fact the brilliant Lioness of the Royal Isle seated at the banquet could be esteemed human and fairly civil.

Such voluminous flesh-foldings; such gluttonous orbs; limbs Herculean, Cyclopean more, and blazoning! The destinies here, for once, merged and were embodied visibly in the form of woman. All was power and pathos and a sight to see!

The conversation was spirited and discursive, Dr. Bellows prompting his guests to good things and sayings. Beecher at his right; on his left Miss Kemble, myself, and Mrs. Kirkland next opposite; then the Braces three; our hostess, Mrs. Bellows, and children at the foot. Tickets inscribed with our names designated our plates and places for us. I shall not venture here upon an elaborate account of dishes or of entertainment where all was solid, of course, and savory . . . 'Twas a feast of meats, and became the company well.

Beecher and She had most of the talk, as was proper. Players both, they discussed texts and audiences, told anecdotes, compared notes, diverted presently to western life, to Beecher's home there, Theodore Parker, the metaphysic of memory and of second-sight — in which last neither were metaphysical or posted profoundly, it seemed. I in my turn and time here having a tilt at the theme also, the rations aside, with the monster mermaid or whatever it was.

We sat down at 11 and rose at 1, all leaving then but Beecher. Miss Kemble was courtly enough, nor indisposed for the talk, saying, as she was about leaving the room, glancing the while at her bosom and with a significant toss: "Now, Mr. Alcott, I am a true woman, in spite of the seemings." Undoubtedly. . . .

Her eyes are dark, dire, the orbs fatally rolling; and she tosses her head scornfully at the passionate passages in the talk, like Margaret Fuller though less royally. If one will get some notion of her head and bust, let him look sometime at the Hercules and imagine a suitable mate for him. She wears her hair cropped behind and dressed most like our sex. 'Tis raven and grizzled somewhat. In person she is tall, but so bulky as to appear short rather. Her complexion is dark, slightly freckled, and her features tauric and coarse. I think she was in colours, and wore jewels.

December 12

Today fair and sunny, and I walk for two hours in the Park. Walt Whitman comes, and we dine at Taylor's Saloon, discussing America, its men and institutions. Walt thinks the best thing it has done is the growing of Emerson, the only man there is in it — unless it be himself. Alcott, he fancies, may be somebody, perhaps, to be named by way of courtesy in a country so crude and so pregnant with coming great men and women. He tells me he is going presently to Washington City to see and smell of, or at, the pigmies assembled there at the Capitol, whom he will show up in his letters from there in some of the newspapers, and will send me samples of his work by mail to me at Walpole. It will be curious to see what he will make of Congress and the Society at the Capitol. Walt has been editor of a paper once, at Brooklyn, and a contributor to the magazines sometimes. If a broader and finer intercourse with men serves to cure something of his arrogance and take out his egotism, good may come, and great things, of him.

December 28

There is company [16] in the evening and a Conversation, Walt Whitman being the observed — he coming in his Bloomers and behaving very becomingly, though not at home, very plainly, in parlours, and as hard to tame as Thoreau or any Sylvanus, or train in good keeping with the rest. Longfellow, Maxwell, Rice, Mr. and Mrs. Goodwin, Miss Parmalee, Miss Sedgwick, and many more are of the party, and the Conversation is spirited and metaphysical.

[16] At the home of Samuel Longfellow.

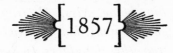

{1857}

AS HE APPROACHED the age of sixty Alcott began to accumulate a modest fame. His acquaintance was wide, and rapidly expanding; he had long been closely associated with persons of high distinction; his earlier heresies had either been forgotten or had become orthodox, and his present opinions, though seldom taken seriously, were at any rate "harmless." Already venerable in appearance and possessed of a majestic voice and an utterance remarkably fluent, he commanded an increasing respect wherever he went. On the verge of old age he was beginning to succeed.

After the excitements of New York City, Alcott felt that Walpole was somewhat dull, although he was able to organize a few Conversations even there. February found him again in New York, and for two weeks in March he tried to storm the citadel of New England orthodoxy, Yale College. The immediate result of this effort was that the students were publicly warned in a Chapel sermon against the "new philosophical infidelity," but far more important was the intellectual awakening of William T. Harris, then an undergraduate, who was to become Alcott's ablest follower and expounder. In April two weeks were spent at New Bedford with the Quaker poet Daniel Ricketson, friend of Thoreau, and in May Alcott visited Thoreau's friend Blake at Worcester and spent a few days at Concord with Emerson. As the

summer advanced, however, the alarming condition of his daugh-
ter Elizabeth, who had seemed a year before to be in a fair way
to recovery, called him home. Mrs. Alcott took the invalid to
the seashore in August, leaving her husband at Walpole with
his mother and his three other daughters. In September, "Orchard
House," at Concord, with its twelve acres of land, was purchased
for $945, and Alcott addressed himself at once to the necessary
carpentry and repairs. In spite of the assurances of the physicians
who were at last called in, it was by this time evident to the father
and mother that Elizabeth had not long to live. In November,
however, Alcott started westward on another conversing tour.

1857

February 5   *Walpole, New Hampshire*

This evening I meet my neighbours again at the Parsonage
and treat of Village Life, its opportunities, advantages and duties.
Lathrop and some of his parishioners help us a little in our discussions; but the rural, the pastoral, are foreign to the culture and
keeping of our people, native as they are to the genius and affections of refined men and women everywhere, and traits of the
most advanced civility and piety as well. Still our fields and
streams, garden and orchard, our youths and maidens, the home
life and occupations, await their poet, being as yet unsung. Only
Thoreau and Longfellow have ventured any strain, and these,
too, celebrate the wild, the Indian, the beast, the bird, the forest
and the savage, instead of the tame and tender, the genial sentiments and dear humanity of private life. And so we wait for the
pastoral poet to be born and sing.

February 6

Fruitlands was an adventure, reckless perhaps, for planting
a Paradise in good faith here in honest Yankee mould, and of
realizing the pastoral age in more than pristine simplicity and
tenderness in the lives of devoted men and women, smitten with

something of the old heroism for holiness and humanity. But it was too soon, and they too frail to sing and serve it so — the grand ideal of all lofty yet humble life to all, and enjoyable forever.

April 1   *"Woodlawn," New Bedford*

At Mr. Ricketson's, 2½ miles from New Bedford, a neat country residence surrounded by wild pastures and low woods, the little stream Acushnet flowing east of the house and into Fair Haven Bay at the city — the hamlet of Acushnet, at the "Head of the River" so-called popularly, lying within half a mile of Ricketson's house.

His tastes are pastoral, simple even to wildness, and he passes a good part of his day in the fields and woods or in his rude "Shanty" near his house, where he writes and reads his favorite authors, Cowper having the first place in his affections.[1] He is in easy circumstances and has the manners of an English gentleman, frank, hospitable, and with positive persuasions of his own. A man to feel on good terms with, and reliable for the things good and true; mercurial, perhaps, and wayward a little sometimes, but full of kindness and sensibility to suffering; something of a poet, too, singing the common things around him with a genuine love and tenderness reminding one of Cowper and, in the best lines, of Wordsworth. He has just written some papers, and printed in the *New Bedford Mercury* newspaper, on the antiquities of that place, of which he intends to make a book soon, illustrated with maps and portraits — the genealogy of the primitive families, and the local history of the district.

His ancestors were among the original settlers of the district, and were gentlemen of good estates. They were Quakers, and the traits of that sect survive in him, as, indeed, in the best families here. He tells me most of them, by intermarriage if not direct descent, spring from this formidable persuasion.

R. has a pleasing wife and two very agreeable daughters —

[1] An exact description of Ricketson's Shanty is given by Thoreau in his journal — entry for April 10, 1857. See also *Daniel Ricketson and His Friends*, pp. 350–354.

also two sons, the eldest a seaman, the youngest a promising student. The family friendly and hospitable to excess.

We talk on men, times, and things; on Emerson particularly, as a representative of American Ideas; on Thoreau, as scarcely less so, and walk to the "Head of the River," returning to dinner.

P.M. We ride into New Bedford and see Weiss [2] about talking here some evenings while I stay. He approves the design and will move at once in the matter. We return and get early to bed.

April 2

All day with R. and family. He reads verses and passages from his Journals. The day cold and snowy.

Henry Thoreau comes to tea. Also Ellery Channing, who is engaged here on the *New Bedford Mercury* newspaper, and all talk till into the evening late.

April 3

A.M. In house and shanty, Thoreau and Ricketson treating of nature and the wild. Thoreau has visited R. before and won him as a disciple, though not in the absolute way he has Blake of Worcester, whose love for his genius partakes of the exceeding tenderness of women, and is a pure Platonism in the fineness and delicacy of the devotee's sensibilities. But R. is himself, and plays the manly part in the matter, defending himself against the master's twistiness and tough "thoroughcraft" with spirit and ability.

P.M. I walk into the city and see Weiss, who has seen his friends and commends me to the "Arnolds," where he hopes to hold our Conversations. . . . Channing returns with me to "Woodlawn" to smoke his pipe and joke with Ricketson in the shanty. R. has made his house a pleasant retreat for the poet, and here he spends many of his afternoons, and sleeps.

April 11

Evening: We meet again, and discuss — assisted slightly by the company — "Home and the Family," from 8 till 10. Our theme is inviting, and some of the best passages are pointed and pertinent, the whole evening being very agreeable to me. But

[2] John Weiss (1818–1879), a Unitarian clergyman and author.

Ricketson criticises my shortcomings all the way home, and abusively.

I think him half right, and tell him so, in this matter of method and concision about which he complains so eloquently; but say that the law of Conversation is less fixed and rigorous than is the logic of premeditated thought and composition. . . .

April 25　　　　　　　　　　　　　　　　　　　　　*Boston*

4 P.M.: I dine at the Parker House. The company [3] meets for social convenience on the last Saturday of the month, and is quite literary and select. I find today, and seated — all but Longfellow, who comes in just after me — Agassiz, Emerson, Prof. Peirce, Lowell, Sam. Ward, E. P. Whipple, Tom. Motley, John Dwight, Ed. Quincy, Woodman. Prescott and Richard Dana Jr. are sometimes of the party, and Quincy is Lowell's guest for the day.

The Conversation is for the most part colloquial. Only one passage on the Generative Ideas, suggested by some assertion of mine on the necessary priority of man and the animals to the earth, afterwards put by Agassiz for the votes, gives it a philosophic and general turn, and tries the strength of heads present unmistakably. Ward, Whipple, Dwight, Lowell, Peirce, Emerson for the Ideas, clearly; the rest for Agassiz and his Facts in preceding or contemporaneous order of outworking to the senses.

Of the persons whom I had not before met, Prof. Peirce interested me for depth and comprehensiveness, interpretation and scope of his logic upon this nut of the Genesis. But, 'tis plain, with Agassiz I shall neither make heads nor mend — he the analyst, the observer — Ideas, as he views them, being inferences from observed facts and generalized therefrom, not their patterns and predecessors in the creative order. Purely Aristotelian, his genius plays the naturalist habitually, never the spiritualist, nor can. Such breadth of brain and horizontal over-capping the ears, globe-shaped, yet not ensphered nor astral, takes temperamentally to anatomic and mundane studies — to the forces and forms following, not leading, the sun. Breadth and bulk idolize,

[3] The "Saturday Club," founded in 1855, of which Alcott came to be regarded as an "after-dinner member" — a fact of which Edward Emerson seems to have been unaware when he wrote the *Early Years* of the Club in 1918.

always, but cannot idealize, power. So Whipple's comprehending breadth of phrenology come of the reflected lunacy of his intelligence, as of the gibbous moon glimmering gray upon the hemisphere it over-rides.

May 4   *Worcester, Massachusetts*

Evening: I hear Fanny Kemble's reading of *Henry Fourth*, and am astonished at the brute power, the terrific fates imprisoned in this ponderous woman. The depth of voice is appalling, and the transitions amaze one at her flexibility of organs — the hoarse notes the more particularly, and the grimace is in keeping with the general expression. A fearful creature, untamed, untameable. She is not artist, having no ideas but only forces; is driven by passion, and without free election to guide and harmonize her wayward energies. There is no rest, no company in her, no communion — see how impossible is any meeting for her, any conversation in the true sense! All is mimicry, and the impersonation of an egotism unapproachable, yet multitudinous and antagonistic — a kingdom divided against itself.

May 5

To Boston this morning. Find Mrs. [sic] Kemble at the station, and assist her about seats, she wishing to pay for three — two for herself and the other for her servant. She asks me to ride in her carriage to the Parker House, and speaks of American manners on the way with the true English feeling. She presents me with a fresh orange flower, and asks me to call and see her.

May 10   *Concord*

Louisa goes to church with Ellen and Edith. I sit in the summer-house and walk about the grounds, plotting improvements with Emerson of his estate — the site for a wood-house which he intends building, the lines for his paths, Mrs. Emerson and the children approving or dissenting as they come out and catch the designs thus rudely scored with my cane on the lawn and garden. His place has few advantages by nature and situation, and is hard to ornament well. The chief attraction is the summer-house, which is now embowered in a pretty coppice of pines and larches, the front gables being seen from the south door of his mansion and from the Lincoln road in passing. But the thatching is much dishevelled. I recommend laying the latticed roof here and training grape vines over it, thus making a rustic arbor for a poet's pleasance and his press of inspiration, or bower for contemplation, for entertaining the Muses or any company he lists. . . .

Young men may write books, but the old and mature read and remember the books. Time alone ripens the substance of the mind, as the season its fruits, and mellows them. The best apples do not fall till winter, keep the longest, surviving all others, and the winter itself. The choice fruit of a man's life should be housed in his book. It were the better if posthumous, shaken from an orchard of honours, the seeds of immortality at its core.

September 22

I leave for Concord and close my bargain with Moore for the place,[4] the papers to be drawn by S. E. Sewall.

Sup at Thoreau's and sleep at Emerson's.

September 23

Thoreau surveys the place. He makes 12 acres and 66 roods of the estate.

Terms — Orchard and Buildings	$600.00
Woodlands 11½ acres	345.00
	Dolls. 945.00

October 29

The new magazine, *The Atlantic Monthly*, is published today — No. 1, for November — which I get at Stacy's and find pleasant reading.

4 "Orchard House" and grounds.

ALCOTT'S WESTERN journey of this winter was cut short at Cincinnati, in January, by news of Elizabeth's rapid decline. The father watched through many nights beside the dying girl, feeling to the full the sorrow of farewell, but his daily life went on with its now habitual serenity. In March Elizabeth died. One month later Anna became engaged to John Pratt of Concord, son of the head-farmer at Brook Farm.

The renovation of "Orchard House" filled the summer with hard, congenial labor. Most of the alterations were planned and overseen by Alcott, much of the actual labor was done by his own hands, and his minute record of what was done fills a hundred pages of the Journal. "Orchard House" as it stands today is his in every important sense, and bears the mark of his mind and taste. It is perhaps the most successful of his undertakings. At a time when few Americans valued anything for its age he showed a deep respect for his old house, he learned its history from the town records, and he loved the thought of its antiquity. So eager was he for the precise execution of his idea that he seems, at times, to have lost even his long-suffering and monumental patience, for he admits that the house cost him "much quarrelling and deep disgust" at the "unconquerable stupidity" of carpenters and joiners. He expressed his sense of responsibility by quoting from Thomas Fuller the words: "He that alters an old house is tied as a translator to the original."

In July, although the work was not yet finished, the family moved into the house most closely associated with their name. Since their marriage Alcott and his wife had moved some thirty times. Here they were to remain for many years. Here too Louisa, although she was never fond of Concord, was to write the most successful of her books. From this house came most of the books that Alcott himself published. And here, on the grounds that Alcott sodded, planted, and gardened, was to be the scene of his final triumph, the Concord School of Philosophy.

Early in December Alcott started westward, in response to an invitation from W. T. Harris, now the ring-leader of a remarkable set of philosophers in St. Louis. He conversed at Chicago, Cincinnati, and Cleveland, and at the very end of the year he first crossed the Mississippi.

1858

January 23   *Concord*

I am at home again, having been absent at the West since November 11, 1857 — conversing at Syracuse, Rochester, Buffalo, Cleveland, Cincinnati, pausing for a fortnight or so in those cities and retaining pleasant recollections of interviews there, with prospects of renewing the same when the season of lectures and winter's evening entertainments comes around. I bring home besides some small pecuniary gains. I find my family well, save my child Elizabeth, who is wasted to the mere shadow of what she was, and feeble exceedingly, though more comfortable than I had reason to fear from the family letters. All are anxious, very, and doubting sometimes her final recovery from this extreme debility and emaciation of body.

I have a sweet and tender interview, this morning. She knows the perils and talks resignedly of the change, desiring the passage rather than remaining longer with us. She says, "Sleepy Hollow is a lovely spot to be laid away in, and I shall love to go there, Father, with you, when I feel stronger some of these sunny days."

I asked, "Have you thoughts of your not recovering sometimes?"

"Yes; nor have I believed otherwise for a long while past. It will be something new in our family, and I can best be spared of the four."

I said, "I shall see Dr. Geist and hear what he says of your prospects, Elizabeth."

" 'Twill be as well one way as the other; with me as with the rest of you."

I inquired, "Have you some notions of your state after the change?"

"Not so clear as I could wish, but you will have me none the less, and I prefer going as soon as may be." — She seems to have anticipated the possibilities, and has busied herself lately, in better moments, in disposing of her little things as gifts to friends: to Anna, her desk, &c.

The day is mild and cheerful. I spend it mostly in the house, with my wife and girls, and am with E.

January 24

In Elizabeth's chamber. She has a cheerful morning busied with her little needleworks and conversing a little sometimes.

P.M.: At Emerson's. We have the adventures west, lecturing and the lecture system, the present posture of the country, &c. Accompany him and his children on their Sunday walk to Walden, which we cross on the ice, and into his woodlot opposite, returning late.

Evening: We are at Thoreau's, my wife and myself, for an hour. Thoreau has been lately to Lynn and read some papers of his in drawing rooms to a good company there.

January 30

4 P.M.: I go to the Parker House, and sit till 8 with the Club. Present:

Agassiz	Ward
Longfellow	Hoar
Holmes	Dana
Whipple	Woodman

The Conversation is spirited, turning chiefly on Personal Identities; the distinctions, physical and metaphysical, between man and beast. *I* would have discriminated more fully and finely between the threefold forces of *brute, human,* and *divine,* in whose admixture and interplay life itself consists; but the company were unused to such analysis, and talked to the senses the more becomingly, as naturalists and observers can. — Holmes I meet for the first time today.

Leave at 8, with Judge Hoar in his private carriage, and reach home at half past eleven to sleep.

February 4

Elizabeth is downstairs and sits awhile in the parlor. Dr. Geist comes up at noon, but she sees him unwillingly, and refuses medicines, desiring rather to pass away. He speaks cautiously, yet thinks her recovery possible still, and to be hoped for nevertheless.

Evening. Thoreau is here, and talks much on his favorite themes of wild life, on Emerson, and Blake of Worcester particularly.

February 8

I write Diary all day.

February 9

I am at the Orchard and planning repairs. Also at Emerson's for an hour or more, discussing our privileged theme largely.

Evening: I sit with Elizabeth in her chamber, talking on the little things in which she retains an interest. Today she is comfortable, and has come out of 3 days' silence and suffering.

February 10

I see carpenters George, Hosmer, McKee, and Benjamin, mason, about repairing my house.

February 12

Copy Diary. 1 P.M. comes Emerson and asks me to accompany him home to tea. We talk late on intellect and individualism, discriminating the latter from Personality.[1]

February 13

I work on my MSS. Also take Rufus Hosmer to see about moving the smaller building at the Orchard.

February 15

Elizabeth is down stairs this morning, and talks pleasantly about herself with us. I write Diary all day again.

February 16

Ah, my child! But so much goodness is worthy of heaven and its beatitudes, nor may I selfishly interpose mere human wishes into the commanding designs of the All-Good and Fair. Possibly this precious fruit must be plucked away that I may divine the better those living symbols spreading around me still, remaining and spared to gladden my heart and homestead for the residue of my sojourn. So my child passes on and awaits dutifully the father's arrival to possess the Paradise with her, if he may be so worthy.

I sit with her through the night.

March 13

Bricklayer builds the west parlour fireplace, fashioning it after my design, the bricks projecting from the jambs and forming an arch. Garfield trails mason.

---

[1] In a letter of 1868 Alcott wrote: "I can only ask you to distinguish finely that in yourself which differences you from other persons essentially and that which unites and makes them one with yourself, also makes you one with them, indissolubly and forever. The unity is the Personality; the difference is the Individuality. . . . We must grow into and become one with the Person dwelling in every breast, and thus come to apprehend the saying 'I and my Father are one' — that is, perceive that all souls have a Personal identity with God and abide in him."

This idea, central and controlling in Alcott's whole career, was never quite accepted by Emerson during forty years of amicable controversy.

March 14

This morning is clear and calm, and so our daughter Elizabeth ascends with transfigured features to the heavenly airs she had sought so long. She died at 3, passing beyond our mortal grasp. She lived a short, innocent, and diligent life with us, and has an early translation.

Sad offices for the departed. Call on Emerson.

P.M., Thoreau calls, and Mr. and Mrs. Emerson.

March 15

All day is beautiful for the final rites. 3 P.M. Dr. Huntington comes. He reads, at my wife's urgent request, the King's Chapel Burial Service, and prays afterwards. Our friends Mr. and Mrs. Emerson and Ellen, Henry Thoreau, Sanborn, John Pratt, his sister and mother, and others.

We deposit her remains in the receiving tomb till we select our family lot in the cemetery.

First carriage, Mr. Alcott, Mr. Emerson, Mr. Thoreau, Mr. Sanborn.

Second carriage, John Pratt, Dr. Bartlett.

March 16

Breakfast together sadly, and with dear Elizabeth's mementoes before us. It was Anna's birthday and she has her sister's desk with other gifts.

My wife and Abby go to the "Orchard."

Evening: Pleasing memories of the dear one, and a night of good refreshing sleep.

March 17

Today comes McKee with his men and begin repairs on the house.

April 4

Look over Hawthorne's books, and find few in his library for me.[2]

[2] The Alcotts had taken rooms for a few weeks, while the renovations at "Orchard House" were proceeding, at their former home next door, now called "The Wayside." One of the rooms they occupied had been both Alcott's and Hawthorne's study.

But the room is attractive. It suggests memories of busy days spent within these walls, and pleasing experiences in times past, when Thoreau and Channing and Emerson sometimes honoured me with their sittings. Here, too, I have written pages of Diary, letters to my wife when she was absent at Waterford in Maine, met my children at their morning conversations and studies, had some thoughts, besides nameless family satisfactions, trials — these last faded for the most part into undistinguishable colours in the memory. . . .

Then my dear departed child was here, around whom so much of my home delights are gathered as to their image and spring.

April 7

Anna returns from Mr. Pratt's, and reveals John's affection for her simply and beautifully. John comes also, and we speak together about it. I think well of him, and doubt not of his power of being the good friend and companion of my good daughter. Still, the thought is more than I am ready for at this moment.

September 3

Madam Mary Emerson dines with us and passes the afternoon. She gives me sundry biographical facts and incidents concerning Emerson's early days, and of his father and grandfather.

Madam E. is Emerson's aunt. She is now 84 years of age, sprightly, entertaining, and a lady of much wit and genius. Of a theological family, she has been a reader of theological works, and is metaphysical in her tendencies and a match for any theologian. Dr. Price is her favorite author, and the thinkers of that connexion. Emerson has frequently read her letters in my hearing, and spoken of her with respect and admiration of her genius.

She is passing the summer here at boardings in town, and likes to see her friends at her rooms in the village. Henry Thoreau calls sometimes, and the Emersons. She asks me to visit her, which I shall if I can command the mood and the hour desirable.

September 18

I walk down Hawthorne's lane with my wife, surveying our place from that perspective, and seeing how the prospect will be opened and improved when the barn opposite is removed to give full view of the willows by Mill Brook and of the landscape beyond. It seems the fittest spot for a house, protected so by the hills on all sides round from East to West, and enjoying the South so pleasantly. And the house standing quietly apart from the roadside to give room for the overshadowing elms to lend their dignity and beauty to the scene and bring out its homely aspects; the brown porches, many gables, architectural chimney tops; the hills through which winds the grassy lane, rising in the background green with pines, with orchards on the slopes down to the wayside, and beside the lawn.

'Tis a pretty retreat, and ours; a family mansion to take pride in, rescued as it is from deformity and disgrace by these touches of grace and plainkeeping which I have contrived to give it against journeyman's jibes and joiners void of taste or carpenter's skill. But my points are gained, and we have a house and grounds combining many advantages of comfort and tillage, and estates of content. 'Tis more than I deserve, and surpasses any thing I have dared to ask of those who know and value us aright.

November 5

Again to the village and back. Thoreau comes home with me and stays to supper. Good company always and present in Nature, and the best of her. An out-of-doors man, and with doors opening on all sides of him, slides in slides, to admit her to his intelligence. His senses seem doubled and give him access to secrets not read easily by other men. His observation is wonderful, his sagacity like a bee and beaver, the dog and the deer — the most gifted in this way of any mind I have known, and the peer of the backwoodsman and Indian.

He stays and discusses matters and men for an hour or two, and admirably. I suspect he deals better with matters, somewhat, than with men, but masterly with either, and anything he meddles with or takes seriously in hand. I am proud of him. I should say he inspired love, if indeed the sentiment he awakens did not seem to partake of something yet purer, if that were possible, and as yet nameless from its rarity and excellency. Certainly he is better poised and more nearly self-sufficient than other men.

November 29

Today I become 59 years of age. I make preparations for going West.

Evening. I meet some company at Emerson's and we discuss Private Life. Present are Henry James and Sam. G. Ward from out of town; then Thoreau, W. E. Channing, Sanborn, G. Brooks, Mrs. Brooks, Mad. Emerson, Mrs. Emerson, the Pratts, Miss Thoreau, Miss Ripley, Stacy, and others of our townfolk. James takes a prominent part in the talk, and embarrasses our theme, as well as the harmony of the evening; and for the sentiments he utters is called to account by Madame Mary Emerson, whose gifts of speech and mode of handling poor James win the admiration of the party and thanks of everyone present.[3]

December 24   *Chicago*

I have letters from Louisa and Abby from Boston. Read *Atlantic Monthly* for January — Lowell's "Shakespeare" paper and Holmes's "Professor." Men of wit and good parts like these cannot fail of amusing their readers, and along with their fine sense, to afford them entertainment and instruction. Still I am disappointed at not getting more of the last, and find myself doubting whether the show of rhetoric and parade of phrase do not over-ride the substance and disguise the matters of which they treat so learnedly and do know so much.[4] Holmes is subtle, but I cannot call him wise. He betrays a certain stolen information which might be taken for sagacity, surcharged as it is with sense, and the spoils of curious observation on life and manners, metaphysics and the arts. He knows too much. And Lowell fails to affect one for the better. The folly is too large an ingredient in the wit, so we do not taste the wholesome wisdom we promised ourselves from the draught of brilliancy and beauty they pour for us. I miss the earnestness which earns respect and confidence, and is the secret

---

[3] The story of this encounter is vividly told by Edward Emerson in his *Early Days of the Saturday Club*, and also in his book *With Emerson in Concord*.

[4] Alcott's suspicion about most of his writing contemporaries, certainly including Emerson but not Thoreau, was that they were rhetoricians, phraseologists, more concerned with manner than with matter.

and charm of eloquence; the faith implied, which wins faith from the listener, and confirms the speaker's, the writer's, veracity.

This magazine is far superior to any other literary journal and well deserves the interest and circulation it receives.

December 28   *Journey Westward*

We pass several places, some of them called cities, along the road. These consist of a few rude dwellings, imbedded in mud at this season, standing in the open prairie country. Here and there a pretty coppice of timber is seen, a clump of trees along some straggling stream of turbid water, sparse cornfields and log-hovels, the general landscape looking slovenly and dismal enough. Wild, and spreading indefinitely into the distance, the prairie is yet tame and monotonous, and the eye takes flight into the over-spreading sky to get relief from the sameness, and fancy prospects above and beyond the horizon of sedge and sward extending far into immensity. It is an ocean of grey grass, yet without the grandeur of waves and mountain crests to awaken the picturesque and delight the imagination. There are no images, and the speech of the people at the stations seems flattened, with sudden startings and awkward leapings into the regions overhead, for fit figures of expression. A residence here for a generation or two must have a marked effect on the speech of the population and the prairie dialect become as distinguishable as the Yorkshire or the Yankee.

At Alton I caught sight of the river Mississippi, yet it caused some effort of fancy to make good its claim to the name of Father of Waters. One needs include its broad valley, its tributaries, and tablelands, to comprehend its significance.

⚛{ 1859 }⚛

*T*HE FIRST *weeks of the year were spent in St. Louis, where Alcott was in daily contact with a group of thinkers, containing several remarkable men, later known as the "St. Louis School of Philosophy." This group was at the time possessed, as one of them says, "with a sort of philosophical fury." Its thought was prevailingly Hegelian, and the members were interested in Alcott not as a reformer but as a metaphysician. He was deeply impressed by this first contact with systematic thinking, so different in method from the Transcendentalism of New England, but his stay was neither profitable nor wholly pleasant, and he was glad to reach home late in February.*

Alcott's health and strength had been seriously impaired by the arduous tour of this winter and he was obliged for some time to husband his energies. In March he returned to the books he had already perused many times — the Bible, Plato, Aristotle, and Swedenborg. April brought him the wholesome labors of the garden. In May, greatly to his satisfaction, he was chosen Superintendent of the Concord Public Schools at an annual salary of one hundred dollars, and he set immediately to work upon an almost embarrassingly conscientious performance of his duties. On the eighth of the same month he was profoundly impressed by his only meeting with John Brown. The summer passed quietly, with much interchange of thoughts and views between Alcott, Emer-

son, and Thoreau. In October Concord was greatly excited by the startling deed, the trial, and the execution of Captain John Brown. Echoes of Harpers Ferry resound in the Journal until the year's end.

1859

January 4   *St. Louis*

I return by the Levee along the Mississippi, seeing the steamers, mound, the people, all novel and strange to a New Englander, and show me how purely Eastern I am, how little I have in common with the wild life of the West. I seem to be older than this wilderness, its trades, its rough ways, and look about me here for the mankind, the landscape of which I am part and parcel, as if I had been thrown upon these banks by some mishap and some centuries too soon.

March 4   *Concord*

At home again and thankful for its privileges and opportunities, all the more pleasurable after the privations and discomforts of loafing about that slovenly West. The respite and leisure are charming. To me, a country becomes attractive and habitable by the civility it practices, the sympathy it excites and organizes in its population, society being the costliest product of its grounds and complement of the landscape. I perceive that I am neither a planter of the backwoods, pioneer, nor settler there, but an inhabitant of the Mind, and given to friendship and ideas. The ancient society, the Old England of the New England, Massachusetts for me. Perhaps I am older than those, than any present civilization, and have come down from primeval times, the worshipper of the primitive convictions, not acclimated well and a resident in these ages of bronze and iron.[1]

Sometimes experiences are like nightmares and not to be shaken off the next morning. So with multitude and masses. They

[1] Compare Emerson's remark in his journal for 1838: "Alcott is a ray of the oldest light."

betray and perplex us exceedingly. Do but sally forth into that wild country for but a month's jaunt about it, and you shall come round home, whatever you were at starting, the Cynic confirmed, the Skeptic and the Sloven, in spite of yourself. Even the sanest mind in the soundest body, standing in that solitude vast of beasts and their synonyms, the human populations, shall forthwith deny deity and humanity there, conceding the fact of man's fall and of nature's debasements in consequence.

March 12

Own is properly the loss, the absence, and cypher of One. To own anything is to appropriate it to Self, and to abstract it from Unity and God. Hence Self is Ownhood, or the lapse and loss of Godhood out of these into the evil and the wrong.

Nature is Soul divested of Personality, and a divorce from Unity.

March 14

Clear and bright morning, the sun shining again, and the birds sing early in the grove behind my house, as voices of the pines and of the slumberers beneath them and far beyond.

Elizabeth.

She withdrew a year since from us, and went Thither. Yet still the light of those mild eyes abides as a presence, a countenance attending me, and a friend ever since and through all my days. Blessed be the memory, blest and blessing me always!

March 23

After a long abstinence from me, Ellery Channing reappears at my door today, comes in, and talks on Emerson's position and the cost of it. Yet he shall unsay and most likely deny his words, next time he comes to see me. In all my intercourse with C., I remember having angered him but once, and then by intimating the distinctions between a man and his moods, saying that I had known a mood once claiming to be a man, while it was but a mood and no more — a thought too personally impersonal to be mistaken by him or forgotten at once. He seems to have been arrested on the way to existence, caught by Fate at its portal, and held fast by some Caprice, so never getting free deliverance from the loins of the Nature he reverences into the proper world of love and humanity.

April 4

Write to my mother and mail my letter. Returning from the Post Office, I meet Emerson, and he comes round by my house, and I accompany him in his walk around the Triangle, he flooding me all the while with fancies fair about his lecture on Clubs which he is composing for his Boston course. He asks me to dine with him next Sunday.

April 7

Sanborn comes to invite my acceptance of the office of *Superintendant of the Concord Schools.* The town has appointed a committee of nine, Sanborn Secretary, and they invite me to have the visiting and general care of the Schools, and report to them at their monthly meetings. I incline to take this trust, if the committee will make it suit my wishes, and allow the freedom of action desirable.

April 11

Comes Thoreau and sups with us. We discuss thought and style. I think his more primitive than that of any of our American writers — in solidity, in organic robust quality unsurpassed, as if Nature had built them out for herself and breathed into them free and full, seasoning every member, articulating every sense with her salubrities and soul of soundness. He is rightly named *Thorough, Through,* the pervading *Thor,* the sturdy sensibility and force in things.

May 8

This evening hear Captain Brown speak at the Town Hall on Kansas affairs and the part taken by him in the late troubles there. He tells his story with surpassing simplicity and sense, impressing us all deeply by his courage and religious earnestness. Our best people listen to his words — Emerson, Thoreau, Judge

Hoar, my wife — and some of them contribute something in aid of his plans without asking particulars, such confidence does he inspire with his integrity and abilities.

I have a few words with him after his speech, and find him superior to legal traditions and a disciple of the right, an idealist in thought and affairs of state. He is Sanborn's guest, and stays for a day only. A young man named Anderson accompanies him. They go armed, I am told, and will defend themselves if necessary. I believe they are now on their way to Connecticut and farther south, but the Captain leaves us much in the dark concerning his destination and designs for the coming months. Yet he does not conceal his hatred of slavery nor his readiness to strike a blow for freedom at the proper moment. I infer it is his intention to run off as many slaves as he can, and so render that property insecure to the master. I think him equal to anything he dares, the man to do the deed if it must be done, and with the martyr's temper and purpose.

Nature obviously was deeply intent in the making of him. He is of imposing appearance, personably tall, with square shoulders and standing, eyes of deep gray, and couchant as if ready to spring at the least rustling; dauntless yet kindly; his hair shooting backward from low down on his forehead; nose trenchant and Romanesque; set lips; his voice suppressed yet metallic, suggesting deep reserves; decided mouth; the countenance and frame charged with power throughout. Since here last he has added a flowing beard, which gives the soldierly air, and port of an apostle. Though sixty years of age, he is agile and alert, resolute, and ready for any audacity in any crisis. I think him about the manliest man I have ever seen, the type and synonym of the Just.

May 10

The sentiment of neighborhood once centered itself in the School, and was bounded by the district lines. These little territories were so many jurisdictions of their own, and the school house was the common gathering place. Owing to the prevalence of local causes and larger interests, our affairs are losing something of the social and family character they once had; but the old names serve to mark the new things — in some cases the old divisions. We cannot let them pass away. They sound as then, and have a Puritanic accent still. They connect us with the venerable names of Bulkeley and Winthrop, and Butterick and Merriam, and Conant and Hosmer, and Barrett and Melvin, and many more — with their descendants and the living population and the landscape we know so well.

May 18

Call on my way home at Edmund Hosmer's and converse with him on his favorite themes of Church and State. A dreadful dissenter this man, but thoughtful in his way and cynical still, I find, though mellowing some with age, and getting to be a little companionable. Admires Cromwell and George Fox, and reads Carlyle.

June 9

Sanborn, Henry Thoreau, and Allen take tea and pass the evening with us. We discuss questions of philosophy and the Ideal Theory as applied to education. Thoreau is large always and masterly in his own wild ways. With a firmer grasp of the shows of Nature, he has a subtler sense of the essence and personality of the flowing life of things than most men, and he defended the Ideal Theory and Personal Identity to my great delight.[2] . . .

Sanborn is a graduate of Harvard College and a scholar. He is sensible and manly and commands the respect of all who know him. He has a popular and prosperous school here, and attracts scholars from good families. He thinks highly of Parker and accepts his methods of thinking and modes of reform. In politics, he is a Republican, and something revolutionary in a quiet way — perhaps abetting Captain Brown and the Emigrant Aid measures. I think he is brave, and likely to do good service for freedom if necessary.

June 20

I know no better way of proving one's professions of democracy to himself than by laboring a day or two beside plain

---

[2] By "Ideal Theory" is meant the Platonic theory of ideas. For "Personal Identity" see, above, the first footnote in the Journal for 1858. The present passage gives valuable testimony regarding Thoreau's relation to Transcendentalism.

men, and finding what you have in common with them. It is the best test of our humanity, and of the degree in which all are one of the people. A wise man shall find something of the best in every man he thus meets over the spade, and discerns the basis of that true aristocracy in which all believe.

July 3

Thoreau comes and stays an hour or two. Students of Nature alike, our methods differ. He is an observer of Nature pure, and I discern her as exalted and mingled in Man. Her brute aspects and qualities interest him, and these he discriminates with a sagacity unsurpassed. He is less thinker than observer; a naturalist in tendency but of a mystic habit, and a genius for detecting the essence in the form and giving forth the soul of things seen. He knows more of Nature's secrets than any man I have known, and of Man as related to Nature. He thinks and sees for himself in ways eminently original, and is formidably individual and persistent.

July 24

Dine with Emerson and pass the afternoon. E. has sprained his ankle and is crippled for some weeks and confined to his house. We discuss times and men comprehensively, with the usual spirit and general agreement. Perhaps I should say that he is the only mind I meet face to face and without possibility of misapprehension, cramp, or collision. It is a rare privilege.

August 5

Emerson rides down and asks me to dine and spend the afternoon with him tomorrow. Is getting better of his sprained ankle and about again. His crutch does not become his genius, and irks him greatly, even to something akin to impatience and ill humor. He tells me that he has never known any restraint of limb or liberty before, nor a fever or sickness of any sort. He is now nearly 60 years of age, and has the countenance of a youth.

August 7

In study arranging papers till 1. Then dine with Emerson and pass the afternoon pleasantly in his room. These interviews, coming not too often, are so much the more attractive and profitable to me, and I enjoy and prize them too highly to seek them too often. I can conceive of no greater misfortune than never to have partaken of this fellowship, or to forfeit its continuance by any mistake of mine. His friendship has been from the first, and still is, a religion and a culture to me, without which I should have been left much alone and unfriended on this planet. Nor can ı estimate its value to me. I esteem it the greatest prize and privilege of my life, aside from my mother and family. Without it, these would have been far less to me than they have been since I made his acquaintance. And yet we meet but seldom. Perhaps often enough.

August 21

Henry Thoreau is here and spends the evening conversing in his remarkable way on Nature and naturalists. I think him the naturalist by birth and genius, seeing and judging by instinct and first sight, as none other I have known. I remark this in Thoreau, that he discerns objects individually and apart, never in groups and collectively, as a whole, as the artist does. Nature exists separately to him and individually. He never theorizes; he sees only and describes; yet, by a seventh sense as it were, dealing with facts shooting forth from his mind and mythologically, so that his page is a creation. His fancy is ever the complement of his understanding, and finishes Nature to the senses even. If he had less of fancy, he would be the prose naturalist and no more; and had he less of understanding he would be a poet — if, indeed, with all this mastery of things concrete and sensible, he be not a poet, as Homer was.

September 4

Dine with Emerson and pass the afternoon. We talk broadly of life's problems and performances. He is in a more passive mood today than is usual with him. I carry him Vaughan's *Hours with the Mystics* [3] to read.

[3] By Robert Alfred Vaughan, published in London, 1856 — a brilliant and influential book which Alcott valued highly. It contains several passages about Emerson.

September 28

Of Americans, Thoreau speaks and writes the strongest English, and, in departments of thought relating to Nature and its expression, his speech surpasses that of any writer I have met with for its robust truthfulness and vigour. Nothing can be spared from his sentence; there is nothing superfluous or irrelevant, but all is compact, solid, and concrete, as Nature is.

October 23

Read with sympathy and the sense of the impossibility of any justice being done him by South, North, by partisans, people, by the general mankind, the newspaper accounts of Capt. Brown's endeavour at Harper's Ferry, now coming to us and exciting politicians everywhere, and everybody. This man I heard speak early in the season here at our Town Hall, and had the pleasure of grasping his firm hand and of speaking with him after his lecture. This deed of his, so surprising, so mixed, so confounding to most persons, will give an impulse to freedom and humanity, whatever becomes of its victim and of the States that howl over it.

October 30

Thoreau reads a paper of his on John Brown, his virtues, spirit, and deeds, at the Vestry this evening, and to the delight of his company I am told — the best that could be gathered on short notice, and among them Emerson. I am not informed in season, and have my meeting at the same time. I doubt not of its excellence and eloquence, and wish he may have opportunities of reading it elsewhere.

October 31

Think much of Capt. Brown and read the newspaper reports with an eagerness and sadness unusual. This is too noble a man to be sacrificed so; and yet such as he, and only such, are worthy of the glories of the Cross.

November 1

Thoreau goes to read his lecture tonight at the Music Hall, and again on Monday night at Worcester.

November 2

Read newspapers with curiosity and interest concerning Capt. Brown. Mrs. Child is said to have gone to Charlestown to take care of him, having got the Governor's assurance of safety there and protection.

Brown's trial is over. The jury bring him in guilty, and he is sentenced to be hanged on the second of December.

Sanborn takes tea with us and tells us many things about Brown, all to the credit of the man and hero.

November 4

Assort my Baldwin apples and get them ready for customers.

Thoreau calls and reports about the reading of his lecture on Brown at Boston and Worcester. Thoreau has good right to speak fully his mind concerning Brown, and has been the first to speak and celebrate the hero's courage and magnanimity. It is these which he discerns and praises. The men have much in common: the sturdy manliness, straight-forwardness and independence. It is well they met, and that Thoreau saw what he sets forth as no one else can. Both are sons of Anak, and dwellers in Nature — Brown taking more to the human side and driving straight at institutions whilst Thoreau contents himself with railing at them and letting them otherwise alone. He is the proper panegyrist of the virtues he owns himself so largely, and so comprehends in another.

November 9

Thoreau calls again. He thinks someone from the North should see Gov. Wise, or write concerning Capt. Brown's character and motives, to influence the Governor in his favor. Thoreau is the man to write, or Emerson; but there seems little or no hope of pleas for mercy. Slavery must have its way, and Wise must do its bidding on peril of his own safety with the rest.

November 19

Dine with Sanborn. He suggests that I shall go to Virginia and get access to Brown, if I can, and Gov. Wise. Thinks I have some advantages to fit me for the adventure. I might ascertain whether Brown would accept a rescue from any company we might raise.

Ricketson from New Bedford arrives. He and Thoreau take supper with us. Thoreau talks truly and enthusiastically about Brown, denouncing the Union, President, the States, and Virginia particularly. Wishes to publish his late speech, and has been to Boston publishers, but failed to find any to print it for him.

November 27

4 P.M.: Go to Emerson's, take tea, and spend the evening talking about Capt. Brown, the times, metaphysics, and men.

November 28

Evening, at Town Hall. A meeting called there to make arrangements for celebrating by appropriate services the day of Capt. Brown's execution. Simon Brown, Dr. Bartlett, Keyes, Emerson, and Thoreau address the meeting, and Emerson, Thoreau, Brown, and Keyes are chosen a committee to prepare the services proper for the occasion. Sanborn is present also.

Thoreau has taken a prominent part in this movement, and arranged for it chiefly.

November 30

See Thoreau again, and Emerson, concerning the Brown Services on Friday.

We do not intend to have any speeches made on the occasion, but have selected appropriate passages from Brown's words, from the poets, and from the Scriptures, to be read by Thoreau, Emerson, and myself, chiefly; and the selection and arrangement is ours.

December 1

Again see Thoreau and Emerson.

It is arranged that I am to read the Martyr Service, Thoreau selections from the poets, and Emerson from Brown's words. Sanborn has written a dirge, which will be sung, and Rev. Mr. Sears from Wayland will offer prayer.

I copy the passages I am to read from the Book of Solomon's Wisdom, David's Psalms, also from Plato.

December 2

Ellen Emerson sends me a fair copy of hers of the Martyr Service.

2 P.M. Meet at Town Hall. Our townspeople present mostly, and many from the adjoining towns.

Simon Brown, Chairman.

Readings by Thoreau, Emerson, Bowers, Keyes, and Alcott, and Sanborn's dirge is sung by the company, standing.

The bells are not rung. I think not more than one or two of Brown's friends wished them to be. I did not. It was more fitting to signify our sorrow in the subdued tones, and silent, than by any clamor of steeples and the awakening of angry feelings. Any conflict is needless as unamiable between neighbors, churchmen, and statesmen.

The services are affecting and impressive; distinguished by modesty, simplicity, and earnestness; worthy alike of the occasion and of the man.

December 11

Thoreau calls, takes supper, and passes some hours, conversing on Emerson and the times. Tells me something of Redpath,[4] the Englishman, who has been here during the past week gathering information for his Life of Brown. His book, *The Roving Editor*, speaks freely of slavery and of the South. Perhaps the portraits are overdrawn sometimes, and tempered with prejudices unjust to all parties.

December 13

Meet Wendell Phillips at Emerson's. He comes from Brown's funeral, and tells us much of the family at Elba. He is to speak on Saturday evening at New York City, for Brown's family, and hopes nothing will defeat Emerson's speaking then also. Beecher, he says, declines.

---

[4] James Redpath (1833–1891), though born in Scotland, began his active life as a writer for the *New York Tribune*. He is remembered chiefly as a reformer and as founder of the Boston Lyceum Bureau.

❄{1860}❄

THE JOURNAL of this year is a first-draft rather hastily written. Alcott was absorbed at the time in his work as Superintendent of the Concord Public Schools, doing much more than was expected of him and very much more than he was paid for. He visited, on foot and frequently, all the schools of the township, often walking many miles in a day and speaking to the children whenever he could. His annual report to the School Committee was no less surprising in its range of thought and warmth of enthusiasm than it was in its unprecedented bulk. In March he planned and triumphantly managed a school festival, saying "We spend much on our cattle and flower shows; let us each spring have a show of our children." Probably he had not been happier since the days, twenty-five years before, when his Temple School was flourishing. Anna was married in May. Louisa was beginning to win a modest reputation with her stories. In December the youngest daughter, May, went to Syracuse to work as a teacher.

1860

January 11

Emerson, Alcott, Thoreau, Channing, Wasson, Sanborn, and

7

Hawthorn, which comes to [six] persons.[1] Opened once a week for conversations, without form, and from 7 till 10 in the evening, at private houses.

January 24, Evening

My wife accompanies me to the Lyceum this evening, and we hear Higginson lecture on Barbarism and Civilization. He defends civilization against Thoreau's prejudice for Adamhood, and celebrates its advantages — of health chiefly, among the rest.

After the lecture Thoreau and I go to Emerson's and talk further on it. Anna Whiting is there. I ask if civilization is not the ascendency of sentiment over brute force, the sway of ideas over animalism, of mind over matter. The more animated the brain, the higher is the man or creature in the scale of intelligence. The barbarian has no society; this begins in sympathy, the perception and sentiment of personality binding the general in one. Thoreau defends the Indian from the doctrine of being lost or exterminated, and thinks he holds a place between civilized man and nature, and must hold it. I say that he goes along with the woods and the beasts, who retreat before and are superseded by man and the planting of orchards and gardens. The savage succumbs to the superiority of the white man. No civilized man as yet, nor refined nations, for all are brute largely still. Man's victory over nature and himself is to overcome the brute beast in him.

[1] The words "and Hawthorn" are written in pencil, as an afterthought, and the word "six" is deleted and "7" inserted.

February 8, Evening

Thoreau and his lecture on "Wild Apples" before the Lyceum. It is a piece of exquisite sense, a celebrating of the infinity of Nature, exemplified with much learning and original observation, beginning with the apple in Eden and down to the wildings in our woods. I listened with uninterrupted interest and delight, and it told on the good company present.

February 17

I ride to the village and bring home the *Atlantic Monthly* for Louisa, whose story of "Love and Self-Love" appears in this March number, to encourage and lead her to some appreciation of the fair destiny that awaits her if she will be true to her gifts as she has begun. Her mother is greatly delighted, and partakes largely in the good fortune herself — a heroine in her ways, and with a deep experience, all tested and awaiting her daughter's pen.

I am pleased, and proud of thee.

May 23

Anna's wedding day, and a day of fair omens, sunny after showers of the days past. Apple blossoms luxuriant, and a company of true and real persons present to grace the occasion. They come together at eleven: Mr. and Mrs. Pratt and daughter Caroline, the grandparents Bridges, Mr. and Mrs. Emerson, Mr. Sanborn, Mr. Thoreau, Mr. Bull the magistrate, Mr. May and son Edward — Mr. May representing the hearth and Mr. Bull the State.

It is a pleasing and impressive spectacle. Mr. May's address and prayer admirable. All persons spoke of its fitness and beauty.

Ah! Anna —

Joy and sorrow mingled together in a blended sentiment of hope and fear for the good child, who has behaved so beautifully through the whole of this friendship and taken it as an invitation from the springs of love and delight. I cannot yet write about it.

They leave at half past one for Chelsea, where they will live at present with their grandparents.

May all good and grace attend her and him! [2]

June 1

Set trees on the hill, and some firs given me by my neighbour Moore before my door, working steadily all day.

The Anniversaries of the various societies and persuasions have been holding during the week in Boston. I thought of going down, but the reports coming from day to day do not invite me, and so I stay here and ornament a little spot as the better use of myself, perhaps.

I have had a time of frequenting these meetings, and of speech-making, and should be tempted now, were I present, to take some part in most of them. — Yet not the part of dissonance and individualism, which distracts and disjoins, but of agreement and of conciliation, about which the parties care less to hear. [3]

June 17

Emerson is in town today and at the commemoration services for Theodore Parker at the Music Hall. I should like to have attended, but could not conveniently. Parker, latterly, had gone a little aside from my ways of thinking and speaking, though ever for freedom and the higher rights. I respect him, and do not see how the country can spare him. None to take up and carry forward his work. Still the land is rich with promise, and abounds in all kinds of talent ripening into something almost genius.

[2] Of this occasion Louisa writes in her Journal: "The dear girl was married on the 23d, the same day as Mother's wedding. A lovely day; the house full of sunshine, flowers, friends, and happiness. Uncle S. J. May married them, with no fuss but much love; and we all stood round her. . . . We had a little feast, sent by good Mrs. Judge Shaw; then the old folks danced round the bridal pair on the lawn in the German fashion, making a pretty picture to remember, under our Revolutionary elm. . . . Mr. Emerson kissed her; and I thought the honor would make even matrimony endurable, for he is the god of my idolatry."

[3] Alcott's theological doctrine of "Personality" slowly modified his social and political thought. He came to condemn most radical measures of reform as "Individualistic," because he thought they dismembered society by ignoring that "Personality" which all men hold in common.

I think I have felt him less than most of my contemporaries of active powers and habits; but I find he has been much to many excellent persons all over the land, and, had he lived, might have perhaps founded a more happy and saner sect of religionists. Perhaps will now.

Too much work killed him, and he had such an egregious appetite for information and for doing that he had lived several lives, and died older at 50 [4] than any man of his time is likely to do.

June 28

Hawthorne and family arrive at Boston in the Europa this morning, and come up to Hillside to dine — himself, wife, and three children.

P.M. Emerson calls and invites me to meet Hawthorne at his house tomorrow evening.

Evening: We call at Hawthorne's, my wife and I, and see them all. He looking well, and full of thoughts of "Hillside" and the repairs he wishes to make on the buildings and improvements generally in the grounds. Asks my suggestions and counsels. I shall delight to assist him and build for him in my rustic way, restoring his arbours if he wishes.

June 29, Evening

Eat strawberries and cream at Emerson's with Hawthorne, Thoreau, Sanborn, Hunt the artist, Keyes, and Cheney — a party made to welcome Hawthorne home to "Hillside" and Concord. Talk mostly with Hunt, who is here taking Miss Forbes' picture. He seems vivacious and full of faculty. I have seen none of his works, but should think there was genius in him.

Come home with Hawthorne at half past 10.

---

[4] Theodore Parker was, in fact, several months short of fifty when he died, in Florence, on May 10, 1860.

In the earlier years of Alcott's association with Parker his admiration for the great preacher was higher than the present passage indicates. The two men had much in common. Alcott came to feel, however, that Parker's talent lay rather in public speech than in private thought, and that his methods in social reform were too violent.

ALCOTT IN HIS STUDY AT "ORCHARD HOUSE,"
ABOUT 1875, WITH VOLUMES OF HIS JOURNALS
ON THE TABLE

July 1

Hawthorne comes down the lane from a walk behind my house, and expresses great admiration of my place — house, grounds, and the good keeping of all the parts with the landscape. Wonders the artists have not been here to sketch.

July 24

Work all day on the slope and in the orchard for my sod-plot and strawberry bed. Sod the bank for a terrace under the large Baldwin apple trees and by the tomatoes.

Slope the grounds generally.

July 25

On the terrace sodding and forming; also make a trellis.

My wife makes a most palateable and wholesome beer of pyrola, spruce, and hops, which I drink these days to great profit, drinking less water, and find I have more than usual power of labor and enduring the heat.

August 14

Hawthorne is here in the evening, and tells me young Howells has been to see him. He is from the West, and has written verses for the *Atlantic*.

August 21

Pull up my pea sticks and pick the rest of my red Astrachans — good for eating.

Also thank Jackson for his book on the mountains. Thoreau is here in the evening and tells me of his trip to the Monadnock with Channing lately. He is always entertaining, and draws my wife and girls to hear what he says when he comes to see us.

August 22

Emerson comes, and we look about my garden and grounds. He tastes of my apples and carries away some of them, and mint, to Edith. Invites me to supper, and we discuss the Platonic genius, the *Atlantic* Club, his essay in the *Monthly* on "Culture," in which I tell him of passages and phrases of mine [5] — to which he gen-

---

[5] These are not now discoverable.

erally assents. Says he shall do me ampler justice if he survives me, or if he does not.

November 6

At Town House, and cast my vote for Lincoln and the Republican candidates generally — the first vote I ever cast for a President and State officers.

It stands for one, and an Independent Mind.

November 7

Lincoln elected, doubtless; and Andrews certainly Gov. of Mass. At Emerson's Lyceum listen to speech of Sumner on Lafayette.

November 8

Gather leeks, parsnips, and turnips. Abby May [6] is here, and dines at Emerson's. I meet her there after dinner, and she reads a letter addressed to her by a friend on Transcendentalism and with special reference to Emerson and myself — a subtle and sensible criticism on us and the times.

November 11

Thoreau is here and discusses the suffrage. Thinks a freeman cannot vote for the President, candidates, etc.

December 15

Call on Thoreau, who has returned from Waterbury where, with a severe cold on him,[7] he read his lecture on "Autumn Tints" to the Lyceum on Wednesday evening.

December 25, Christmas

In village again. See Emerson a moment at his house, and G. Bradford.

P.M.: Thoreau is here and talks about Emerson's last book.[8]

[6] Mrs. Alcott's cousin.
[7] The beginning of Thoreau's fatal illness.
[8] *The Conduct of Life.*

Thinks it is moderate, and wants the fire and force of the earlier books.

I told E. today that his essay on "Worship" gave us the worshipful temperament but not the worship. The "Fate" and "Beauty" are perhaps best. I think he must write out and complement the "Worship" to the superstitions and wants of our time in another essay.

Certainly a simple devout soul, maid or man, will not find what she seeks in that essay.

*A*LCOTT BEGAN *to think that he might make a book out of his Journals, in Emerson's way, and worked during the winter at a manuscript which finally became* Concord Days, *published in 1872. Throughout the winter and spring he conducted Conversations in his own town, but his chief concern was still his work as Superintendent of Schools. The second school festival, given in March, was for him a personal triumph, and one thousand copies of his elaborate Report for the year were published and widely distributed. In the early weeks of April he gathered contributions from his literary townsfolk for a "Concord Book" in which local scenes and events were to be celebrated, but this came at the time to nothing.*

The illness of Henry Thoreau, who went to Minnesota for his health in May and returned in July unimproved, was a constant anxiety. In July Alcott sprained his ankle, so that his reading for the year was more extensive than it had recently been. Mostly from his own library he read or reread, in whole or in part, Cowley's Essays, *Varro on Agriculture, Norris of Bemerton, Pordage's* Mundorum Explicatio, *Samuel Daniel, William Law, Jakob Boehme, Walton's* Lives, *Hegel's* Philosophy of History, *Marsh's* Lectures on the English Language, *Howell's* Letters, *Wood's* Athenæ Oxonienses, *Petrarch's sonnets, Lord Herbert of Cherbury, Selden's* Table Talk, *and Roger Ascham's* Schoolmaster.

Late in April came the opening guns of the Civil War, and Alcott, though he remained "the serenest man in Concord" and was to all appearance mainly busied with his garden, was deeply stirred. He had little to say about the conflict at any time, but it is clear that he thought it a necessary and a holy war. The women of his family worked night and day for the soldiers. After the shocking defeat at Bull Run in late July Alcott's thoughts were seldom far from the armies. Even his gardening, in which vegetables took this year the place of flowers, was affected.

1861

January 28

Channing writes tenderly of Thoreau's confinement, and I see him this morning and find his hoarseness forbids his going out as usual. 'Tis a serious thing to one who has been less a housekeeper than any man in town, has lived out of doors for the best part of his life, has harvested more wind and storm, sun and sky, and has more weather in him, than any — night and day abroad with his leash of keen senses, hounding any game stirring, and running it down for certain, to be spread on the dresser of his page before he sleeps and served as a feast of wild meats to all sound intelligences like his. If any can make game for his confinement it must be himself, and for solace, if sauce of the sort is desired by one so healthy as he has seemed hitherto. We have been accustomed to consider him the salt of things so long that we are loath to believe it has lost savor; since if it has, then "Pan is dead" and Nature ails throughout.

I find him in spirits — busied, he tells me, with his Journals, and, bating his out-of-doors, in his usual working trim. Fair weather and spring time, I trust, are to prove his best physicians, and the woods and fields know their old friend again presently.

February 2

Evening at Emerson's; topic *Education*. Very bad walking, but we have a good company: Sanborn, Channing, Stacy, Bartlett, Mrs. Emerson, Brooks, Bigelow, Miss Bean and others. Fewer parents and teachers attend than I had hoped. I suppose they do not know precisely what I mean by Conversation, and so do not come in. Then almost every evening has its call: — The Lyceum, the Social Circle, the Farmer's Club, teachers' and prayer meetings, &c. About thirty have attended from the first, and some of our best people. Thoreau has been unwilling to risk himself since the first evening, being still confined to the house. Emerson has been present when in town. Hawthorne never goes out. I have never seen him at any lecture. I have dined once with him at Emerson's since he became our neighbor, and chanced upon him, by some mistake, at his house occasionally.

February 4

Call on Thoreau and take tea. He is busied about his MSS. and hopes to be out again soon. Has been classifying and arranging his papers by subjects, as if he had a new book in mind. I wish him to compile his Atlas of Concord, for which he has rich material, and the genius; but he must work in his own ways and times, sure to give us something worth waiting for, and surprising, when he shall print a book. With eyes abroad like his, Emerson's, and Hawthorne's, Concord life and landscapes should yield their contributions to the literature of our times and keep its good fame fresh in the memory, and fair as ever. I believe Hawthorne is writing on England, and Emerson is adding his paragraphs for lectures and essays as usual. I wish the spot may own me also, for something worthy of it, sometime.

February 11

Evening. Take tea with Emerson, and talk much on the Mind. He is curious concerning the memory and imagination as marvels of intelligence, these faculties being less discriminated and defined in metaphysics than any. . . . The Platonists have felt their prime significance from the first, and have done most to give them their due place and importance in the scale of thought.

February 15–16

At Emerson's a little while, and tell him something of my last month's work. He says he must come and hear some of the paragraphs, hopes they are as good as I intimate, but doubts, as is his wont; thinks the design excellent, capricious as it appears; the portraits likely to be better than the rest. I give him my list of heads, ancient and modern. He has tried his hand at many of them — Plato, Swedenborg, Goethe, Montaigne, Carlyle, Coleridge. But his Plutarch — if he have one — I have not seen, nor his Thoreau, Garrison, nor Phillips. I have always suspected his Swedenborg owed something to his nameless neighbour, but he has the best of rights to the uses of whatsoever his genius can convert into substance or colouring for his portraits, since none can claim any property in the picture as it comes from his hand. Genius puts unsuspected virtues into the pigments it honours, tints every feature with touches of life, the gloss of personality.

Perhaps Emerson draws profiles best. He seems to have been instructed by Fate, and assisted far more than by felicity of genius, which makes strokes transcending Fate, dashing off portraits, in sport, as from the sun's palette itself.

He names his book "Traits," that is, strokes, at England and Englishmen — himself only less English by some few generations and so overdrawing their features and fashions as none at home had done for them. The profile is fine, but the portraits and personalities not so fine. — Some intermediate colouring, some solvent of common sense in the sentiments, by a subtler alchemy than even his imagination could compass and command, leaves the picture unfinished, the parts perfect. Marvellously individual, but the personality somewhere at fault nevertheless, and it remains but a sketch and unfinished.

February 17

The snow is melting fast and the ground beginning to appear. I get glimpses of Hawthorne as I walk up the sledpaths, he dodging about amongst the trees on his hilltop as if he feared his neighbor's eyes would catch him as he walked. A coy genius, and to be won as a maid is, by some bashful strategem, and as difficult of approach as Channing, only less capricious, and having nothing of impudence in his bearing. His avoidances have a certain reasonableness, nothing sullen or morose about them, and excite a pitying affection, as if he were their unwilling victim and would gladly meet you if he dared disobey the impulse that dogs him to solitude and study.

I hear he is writing a book on England where he spent his four years' consulate, and must have suspected if not seen much to tell of in his way of romance or sound history. His tastes and habits are friendly to this kind of composition. The old country should be a rich bait for his antiquarian appetites, and every way relishing. He seems not at home here in his temperament and tendencies. His English name, I suspect, designates but in part the stock he springs from. I am sure of his coming into Britain with William the Conqueror, and that there runs a drop of dingy Roman life in his veins, exclusive of the Saxon and the sunnier qualities of the British race. See how he behaves, as if he were the foreigner still, though installed in his stolen castle and its keeper, his moats wide and deep, his drawbridges all up on all sides, and he secure within from invasion. Nobody gets a chance to speak with him unless by accident. He never calls on any one, is seldom seen outside of his gate, and spends most of his time in his tower with book and pen and the solace of the weed. Still he has a tender kindly side, and a voice that a woman might own, the hesitancy is so taking, and the tones so remote from what you expected.

February 25

Anna comes up to pass a week or two with us.

Evening: Louisa reads several chapters of her book entitled Moods.[1] It is entertaining and witty, her characters are drawn in lively colors, and there are several fine scenes. The chapters on "Nemesis" and "Herbs" are especially excellent. The book has merits, and should be popular. Her discriminations are metaphysical; there is a variety of character and a wealth of fancy expended in it; nor is it the less attractive to us for the personal and family history, but slightly shaded, scattered along its pages. She writes with unusual ease, and in a style of idiomatic purity. Her

[1] Louisa's first long story, published in 1864.

culture has come from the writing of letters and the keeping of a diary, chiefly.

March 1

Blake and Brown are here.[2] They come to see Thoreau, who has walked out with Channing once or twice in the last days, and seems a little better. These men have something of the disciple's faith in their master's thoughts, and come sometimes on pilgrimage to Concord for an interview with him. This confidence in persons, this love of the mind, enthusiasm for a great man's thoughts, is a promising trait in anyone, a disposition always graceful to witness, and is far too rarely seen in our times of personal indifference, if not of confessed unbelief in Persons and Ideas. I know of nothing more creditable to Thoreau than this thoughtful regard and constancy by which he has held for years some of the best persons of his time. They are not many, to be sure, but do credit alike to him and themselves.

March 4

Thoreau calls with Barker, who is passing the winter here, having left Leominster where he had been preaching for a year or two. Thoreau is impatient with the politicians, the state of the country, the State itself, and with statesmen generally; accuses the Republican party roundly of duplicity, and ends by calling me to an account for my favorable opinions of Seward and the Administration which takes charge of the national affairs today.

March 9

Evening.

Emerson comes and stays till 10. He asks me to read him some Sketches from my Book of Men and Opinions.[3] He prefers the moderns, and I choose Goethe, Carlyle, Thoreau and himself, ending by reading the Illusion verses. I fancy these are better than

[2] Harrison G. O. Blake and Theodore Brown, both of Worcester, the first a teacher and the second a tailor. Blake was the first editor of Thoreau's *Journals*.

[3] Never published under this title. Some of the materials of it are to be found in *Tablets* and *Concord Days*, as well as in the Journals. They consist of character-sketches, somewhat in the manner of Carlyle. Alcott sometimes called them "heads."

he expected to find them, and give him some slight hope of me. I had read nothing of mine to him for many years, and these heads with much diffidence.

None hears but to admire the stately wisdom and ornate beauty of Emerson's diction. Then in speaking he pleases, practising a sort of hesitancy between the readings of his paragraphs, as of the spring of locks or choice of keys at the showing of cabinet specimens; seems sensitive at the delay sometimes, and the negligency, as it were, of another — as anxious as we are to get sight of each as it comes forth from the separate drawers, yet hesitating till the gem is out and glittering, so glad to see and admire, and the setting as the jewel itself.

A magic showman, it must be confessed; voice mostly, and without gesture of any kind, and an organ of marvellous compass and cryptic tones like Milton's, giving forth exquisitely the subtle sense he brings from his breast — now hurling this on the ear, or now it dying away like the roar of waves on the ocean shores, or else the whisper of zephyrs in the summer's evening. He works wonders with it. And it suits the sentiment he would speak, and idea, fitly and aptly. One can imagine what the Greeks meant by Mercury and the oracles. And, but for the time he has fallen into, he were a Greek, and member of the Symposium of wits described by Plutarch, or speaker in the Platonic dialogues.

April 15

News comes of Gen'l. Anderson's Surrender of Fort Sumter, and of Pres. Lincoln's call for 75,000 Volunteers.[4]

April 16 and 17

War threatens, and unforeseen issues.[5]
Read newspapers.

April 18 and 19

The Concord Company of 40 men, under Capt. Prescott, leave for the War. The town raises $4,400 for these volunteers. A meet-

[4] This entry is in red ink.
[5] In red ink.

ing in the evening at the Town Hall. Judge Hoar presides, Sanborn Sec'y. Speeches made by Hoar, Emerson, Keyes, Simon Brown, and myself.

Trouble in Baltimore.

May 1

I plant some early potatoes today, and begin to plot my garden for the season. It is a pretty spot, and, in a good sense, a part of myself. Without a garden, I should be out of place in the country. Certain prime duties seem to belong to every countryman and among the most becoming are the keeping of his conscience and garden; if the caring for some little spot be not the condition of preserving his integrity. The mind needs to come into tender relations with the earth and treat that most intimate of all spots with something akin to piety, since a personal presence is diffused through every part of it, and divinity there awaits to meet us always. It should be the first duty and the aim of the State to insure to every citizen a homestead, and of the Church to see that it be well kept.

May 22, 23, 24

In my Garden. Plant sweet corn, beans, cucumbers &c., and copy some. At Hawthorne's. Find him walking on his hill-top. He says he can think of nothing but the state of the country. He wishes to go to the seaside and recruit for a month or more; says he likes Concord as well as any place to live in, but remembers London with pride and could spend his life there delightfully. Wonders if some means cannot be devised to bring us oftener together, and seems to feel the want of more society than he has here. He says he sees nobody, has been down to the Club meeting but three times. Emerson has called once or twice, Channing but once, since he came to the "Hillside." I doubt whether he has met Thoreau at all, and I have failed of seeing him, Hawthorne, save by accident when I have been over there.

June 7

I take it as one of the best pieces of good fortune that I was born in the country and brought up in the arts of husbandry under the eye of a skilful farmer, who gave me early to my hands and the uses of tools, so that from a child I have known what to do with them — the axe and saw, the rake and hoe having been as it were parts of me from my earliest remembrance. I came as naturally to the spade, the plow, the scythe and sickle as to book and pen.

June 14

THOREAU

Call again to inquire about Henry. He is still near St. Paul, and writes that he is finding some new plants in those parts and enjoying the freedom of the country house and wild life where he is staying, but says nothing concerning his health, from which we infer a change for the better.

The West opens a new field for his observations; and to one whose everyday walk was an expedition into some unexplored region of Concord in search of novelties, though his track had been taken but yesterday, that wilderness must have surprising attractions. . . . I know not to whom that wild country belongs if not to this old explorer, and think it has waited with an Amazonian patience for his arrival. . . . His visit must have been predestined from the beginning, and this lassitude of these late months only the intimation of his having exhausted these old fields and farms of Concord of the significance they had for him.

August 6

I look into Hegel's *Philosophy of History*, Sibree's translation, published by Bohn, 1857. I find the book much too dry and crabbed for my taste, as I have found nearly all books claiming the merits of system; but it contains valuable information and repays perusal. Hegel has the advantage of writing later than his masters, and of drawing largely from them all, borrowing oftentimes from the best, and I think without due acknowledgement. I do not find anything better than Plato or Behmen have for me, and read best at first hand what I wish to find, being sure of falling upon it in the pages of these masters.[6]

[6] Alcott's brief encounter with Hegel and with "system" was almost certainly due to the influence of W. T. Harris and the St. Louis group.

November 21

Hawthorne comes to my house and sits for half an hour, but diffidently, and as if he were wishing to rise and leave at the first easy pause in the conversation. This is the second time he has called since his living next door, and very likely to be the last. He looks at my books and I give him a Road-Book of England as these were in 1780.

November 29

I am 62 years of age today. Write at length to my mother and send her a little money. For myself, I am content to be poor, but for others how gladly should I have been rich in gold, houses and lands, and whatsoever adorns life and the landscape!

Give my wife a blank book for Journal, with her favorite motto from the Golden Sayings of Pythagoras written on the title page.

December 2

Dine at Thoreau's with Sanborn. Thoreau is lively and entertaining, though feeble and failing. He does not conceal his impatience with the slowness of the present Administration and its disregard of honor and justice to the free sentiment of the North.

We hope Congress, which assembles today, will spur the cabinet to do its duty, and better represent the demands of the country.

{ 1862 }

THE JOURNAL of this year is made up, for the most part, of rough notes, never revised. Several absorbing interests prevented Alcott from giving as much time as usual to his daily jottings. The work of his school superintendency, involving the preparation of a voluminous "Report" took much time. From January to April he toiled with great enthusiasm at an essay on "The Garden," and in the summer he wrote his long essay on Emerson, his most satisfactory extended piece of prose. During the summer, also, there was much gardening and carpentry done at Orchard House. The decline and death of Thoreau, for years a close friend of all members of the Alcott family, brought deep sorrow. Meanwhile, the news from the seat of war was not good. In December Louisa went to Washington and, soon after, entered the Union Hospital at Georgetown as a nurse.

1862

January 1

Orchards are generous as well as grateful, and in times of war especially should they intimate the courtesies of peace and of fraternity. Mine is thus disposed, and after the day's business about my paper on "The Countryman in his Garden," I take apples and bottles of cider to my friends Hawthorne, Emerson, Channing.

Also to Thoreau, and spend the evening, sad to find him failing and feeble. He is talkative, however; is interested in books and men, in our civil troubles especially, and speaks impatiently of what he calls the temporizing policy of our rulers; blames the people too for their indifferency to the true issues of national honor and justice. Even Seward's letter to Earl Grey respecting Mason's and Liddell's case, comforting as it is to the country and serving as a foil to any hostile designs of England for the time at least, excites his displeasure as seeming to be humiliating to us, and dishonorable.

We talk of Pliny, whose books he is reading with delight. Also of Evelyn and the rural authors. If not a writer of verses, Thoreau is a poet in spirit, and has come as near to the writing of pastorals as any poet of his time. Were his days not numbered, and his adventures in the wild world once off his hands, then he might come to orchards and gardens, perhaps treat these in manner as masterly, uniting the spirit of naturalist and poet in his page.[1] But the most he may hope for is to prepare his manuscripts for others' editing, and take his leave of them and us. I fear he has not many months to abide here, and the spring's summons must come for him soon to partake of "Syrian peace, immortal leisure."

January 2 and 3

Gardens and orchards plant themselves as by affinity of neighborhood about our dwellings. It seems as if we preserved their seeds in us, and they became ours by birthright. The first of privileges, the ornaments of our homesteads, the charm of the landscape, the place of pleasures, they almost subordinate us personally, and make us their accidents. We build our houses and plant trees about us and esteem ourselves fortunate in the enjoyment of the products of ancient orchards and gardens and vine-

---

[1] An expression of Alcott's disappointment that Thoreau never abandoned his primitivistic feeling for the "wild," never shared Alcott's humanistic preference for the partnership between man and nature which produces the garden, the orchard, and the New England village at its best.

yards from which generations have plucked the ruddy clusters, the spangled fruits. . . .

Apples have other virtues than those that nourish merely. They refresh the spirits by their taste and perfume. "The sweet and tart ones are alike strengthening to the heart, and, to any troubled with hot infirmities, are a singular help." Lord Bacon reckons pearmains among the cool cordials. Apples had once the reputation of being good for immortality. They are still good for virtue and wisdom. A dish of the choice kinds standing in one's study shall perfume his composition and rejoice his temper whensoever he tastes them. He may snatch wildness from the woods, shrewdness from the market-place; but for subtlety of thought, for strong sense, grace of diction, for ideas, he best betakes himself to conversation with orchards,

> Where on all sides the apples scatter'd lie,
> Each under its own tree,

or to his bins in winter.

January 4

Gardens and orchards distinguish man properly from the forester and hunter, who are such by ascendancy of the savage and animal life. The country, indeed, as discriminated from the wilderness, is purely of man's creation. His improvements are the country; the savage has none. Nor are farms and shops and cities more than civilization in passing and formation. Civilization begins with ideas, and the garden and orchard show the place of their occupant in the scale — these dotting the earth with symbols of piety and humanity wherever they touch its face. It is by mingling his mind with nature and transforming the landscape into keeping with himself that he generates the homestead and opens a country to civilization and the arts.

Gardening, properly considered, is the blending of man's genius with natural substance. It is the intermingling of mind with matter, and a conversion of the earth into man through the mind, the hands assisting. The gardener thus distinguishes himself as man cultivating the ground by choice, not from necessity and in bondage to his wants. He deals duteously with it by humanizing it, so to speak, and subdueing it to his designs and taking it into his picture. The woods do not belong to art nor civility till they are brought into keeping with his thoughts, nor may they encroach upon us by nearness. Graceful in the distance and stately as they are, they appear melancholy and morose when crowded around our dwellings. Like unkempt savages nodding saucily at us, they need to be cropped and combed into comeliness before they are fairly taken into our good graces and as ornaments of our estates.

January 6

Louisa goes to Boston to learn further about her proposed Infant School. James T. Fields has written that he will aid her in money and books if she will open it at once, and Mrs. Fields invites her to pass a month at her house in town. I wish she may succeed in her teaching and gratify her friends by the undertaking; yet while her heart and genius are in her books and studies I can hardly hope for any great success in an art that demands the freedom of every gift for attaining its ends.[2]

January 22

Gracefully the seasons come round, weaving into the fancy, if not the faith of most of us, the old world's ritual, as a religion of engagements. They task us as they come. We are calendars and weather-glasses. We take our seasons and stints from the sidereal signs and aspects. The months sway us. What if we must take our March and September equinoctially? Will our April fail to distil its mystic moods with the fertilizing rains? Then our winter brings its hoary ideas, and brown October shall be our Golden Age, of orchards and their ambrosia.

[2] Louisa made this final effort to teach in a Kindergarten sponsored by Elizabeth Peabody. Her Journal for the month reads: "Don't like to teach, but take what comes; so when Mr. F. offered $40 to fit up with, twelve pupils, and his patronage, I began." Four months later she wrote that her labors had "ended in a wasted winter and a debt of $40 — to be paid if I sell my hair for it." At the end Fields said to her, "Stick to your teaching. You can't write." To this she answered: "I won't teach, and I can write; and I'll prove it."

January 26

I take tea again with Thoreau. He is no better, as busy as ever with his books and manuscripts, enjoys his friends, and seems anticipating his summons at any moment.

April 4   *Boston*

Emerson and Mr. and Mrs. Botta from New York breakfast with us. I see Louisa afterwards and arrange with C. Barnard to lecture at his rooms on Sunday evening on Early Education and have Conversation after it; also to speak to his children on Sunday afternoon.

See Fields at his office and arrange with him about my Garden paper for June No. of *Atlantic*. Dine at Parker House. At Athenæum and bookstores. Take tea with E. P. Whipple, where I meet C. Leland,[3] editor of *Con. Monthly*, and once a pupil of mine in Philadelphia. He remembers the readings from *Fairy Queen*. After tea go to Bartol's and see some good people: Whipple, Mrs. Howe, the Fields, Dr. and Mrs. Rogers, Conway, Alger, and many more. Some gentlemen read and Mrs. Howe reads. I read also some verses from Herbert, "How Fresh and Clean."

April 20

At Emerson's and read my "Rhapsodist"[4] to him. Declines the praise, but accepts some of the traits, and says proper to be read for private circles, not to be printed. I fancy he is content with it if the shades be added and the praise tempered some. See Thoreau for ten minutes, sitting but feeble.

May 4

Channing is here and we see Thoreau together. He is confined to his bed and has not many days of his mortality to give us. Channing is sad, and Thoreau's death must be a great desolation to him.

[3] Charles Godfrey Leland, at this time editor of *The Continental Magazine*. See Alcott's Journal-entry for April 28, 1834.

[4] Alcott's essay on Emerson, privately printed in 1865, and published in 1882 after Emerson's death.

May 6

Oversee some hired men about work on my grounds, taking out pipergrass and preparing ground for ploughing. Channing comes in the afternoon and informs me of Thoreau's decease this morning at 9, peacefully. Emerson calls also.

May 7

I am at Mrs. Thoreau's. She tells me about Henry's last moments and his sister Sophia showed me his face, looking as when I last saw him, only a tinge of paler hue.⁵ 44 years last July.

It is the departure of many persons from our population, and leaves the town greatly the poorer in virtue and expectation.

May 8

I am in the village arranging about Henry's funeral at the church. Mr. Emerson wishes to read an address on Henry, a brief sermon. Channing writes some verses, and I will read appropriate passages from Henry's books. Mr. Reynolds will pray and read from the scriptures; the verses will be sung by the choir.

May 9

Again in village, and leave word at school for teachers to dismiss their schools for funeral. 2 P.M., Anna and Louisa accompany me to the church.

READINGS AT HENRY'S FUNERAL⁶

"As surely as the sunset in my latest November shall translate me to the ethereal world and remind me of the ruddy morn-

---

⁵ "One of his [Thoreau's] noblest and ablest associates was a philosopher whose heart is like a land flowing with milk and honey; and it was affecting to see this venerable man kissing his brow when the damps and sweat of death lay upon it, even if Henry knew it not. It seemed to me an extreme unction, in which a friend was the best priest." — William Ellery Channing, *Thoreau: The Poet-Naturalist*, Revised Edition, Boston, 1902, last paragraph.

⁶ The following passages were selected by Alcott, who does not name their source, from "Thursday" and "Friday" of Thoreau's *Week*, and were read by him at the funeral with a considerable rearrangement to suit the occasion. At the end of them Alcott read also Thoreau's poem *Sic Vita*.

The exercises at Thoreau's funeral were suggested by those which Thoreau himself had arranged for the Concord services in honor of John Brown.

ing of youth; as surely as the last strain of music which falls on my decaying ear shall make age to be forgotten, or, in short, the manifold influences of nature survive during the term of our natural life, so surely my friend shall be my friend and reflect a ray of God to me, and time shall foster and adorn and consecrate our friendship no less than the ruins of temples. As I love nature, as I love singing birds and gleaming stubble, and flowing rivers, and morning and evening, and summer and winter, I love thee, my friend."

"There have been heroes for whom this world seemed expressly prepared, as if creation had at last succeeded; whose daily life was the stuff of which our dreams are made, and whose presence enhanced the beauty and ampleness of nature herself where they walked."

"A more copious air invests the fields and clothes with purple light, and they know their own sun and stars. They have the heavens for their abettors, as those who have never stood from under them; and they look at the stars with an answering ray. Our present senses are but the rudiments of what they are destined to become. Every generation makes the discovery that its divine vigor has been dissipated and each sense and faculty misapplied and debauched. The ears are made to hear celestial sounds; the eyes to behold beauty not invisible. Did not he that made that which is within make that which is without also? May we not see God? It is but a thin soil where we stand. I have felt my roots in a richer ere this. I have seen a bunch of violets in a glass vase, tied loosely with a wisp of straw, which reminded me of myself."

Hawthorne and family, Blake and Brown from Worcester, J. T. Fields and wife and Alger [7] from Boston, and many of his townspeople and children of the schools attend the funeral. He is laid in the burying-ground back of the meeting house, near the North Primary School House.

Afterwards interred in Sleepy Hollow Cemetery, next to my lot and opposite Hawthorne's. [8]

---

[7] William Rounseville Alger, author of *The Solitudes of Nature and Man,* Boston, 1866, which contains a thoughtfully adverse passage about Thoreau, and some remarks about his funeral.

[8] This sentence is written in another ink and in a slightly different hand.

May 19

Garden

Also sow beets, spinage, and parsnips.

Emerson brings me books left me by Thoreau:

Bhagavad Gita 2 Vols., translated by Thompson and given to Thoreau by Chelmondly [*sic*] of England.

Budism [*sic*] 2 Vols., *Eastern Monachism* and *Manual of Budism*, translated by Hardy from E.[9] MSS., also from Chelmondley.

June 8

Go to Emerson's at four and dine. We discuss Thoreau a good deal. He is about publishing his address on Thoreau, with additions, in the August number of *Atlantic Monthly*.

After dinner, read my "Garden." He commends abridging it and printing only what is really mine. Offers to look it over some time and mark the good passages. I incline to have it by me and add from time to time, and so make it good.

September 24

Pres. Lincoln issues his Proclamation of Emancipation, putting a new face on the war and a step in the right direction — a policy definitely declared.[10]

October 26–28

Read *Atlantic Monthly* and find papers for me are Emerson's, Thoreau's, Agassiz's, and Wasson's. Wasson's are much to my taste, both as regards theme and treatment.

Also examine myself and doings, to find how little I have to show for life of near sixty-three years. — A deplorable lack of early discipline in expression that leaves me lame at last.[11]

[9] Eastern.

[10] Lincoln's Proclamation of Emancipation was not, in fact, issued until January 1, 1863. In the document here referred to he merely announced an intention to issue this decree.

[11] This is one of Alcott's very few confessions of the sort — brought on, perhaps, by the fact that all the men whose work he had been reading were well known to him and that they were all college-bred. His own essay on "The Garden," though most carefully worked, had recently been rejected by J. T. Fields.

November 4–8

Rains and snows. I read indoors — Emerson's books generally, and compare their aims and opinions; the first more hopeful and fresh, the latter more confident and prudent. Together, they stand out distinctly from the times, and will be read more intelligently by the next generation.

December 7

(Notes for Conversations, 1862–63)

ON NATURE

"Grey, dear friend, is all theory; but green are the golden threads of life." — Goethe

Nature is impersonal, and a part of parts. It is not a whole; neither has it the Unity that belongs properly to Man, who alone has Personality and a will, and thus gives the name of "Universe" to Creation. . . . Nature is Many; Mind and Man, its representative, is One, and the synonym of the All, or God.

———

Like Homer, Hesiod, and the earliest poets, Thoreau saw and treated Nature as a symbolism of the mind, as a physiological theology. His mysticism is alike solid and organic, animal and ideal. He is the mythologist of these last days — reminds more of the ancients in his mode of seeing and saying than any recent naturalist and poet.[12]

———

Magnetism, rightly viewed, appears to be, in human subjects, the return of the varied to the embryonic state, and a partaking of the humors and caprices of the mother Nature — an appliance of the soul to the nipples of Nature, and a visceral experience.

———

The Greek gods had the infirmities of men, and hence stood nearer to men than if they had been conceived as perfect. So the

———

[12] This confident assertion is the more valuable because it comes from one who knew not only what Thoreau wrote but what he said. It supports the opinion that the main purpose of Thoreau's observation of Nature was mystical and transcendental.

Christian view aids the weakness of man's conception by the humanities of the second person in the Trinity.

The Greek gods were men ennobled by the attributes of poetry, exalted by art and religion, never monstrous, as were the Eastern, but shaped in accordance with the ideal of the human figure.

Our gods are partly pagan — composites of Greek, Roman, British; and the process of humanizing them, modifying their forms and attributes from the Puritans, is fast going forward. Ours are not our own. Hebrew largely. Not in accordance with western genius.

———

Life is the passage of the soul out of itself, and the birth of itself into the bodies of nature, which it generates in its flow. The flux is ecstasy; the ebb is fate.

{1863}

*T*HE CHIEF *events of the year are narrated in the selections themselves. After Louisa's recovery her literary successes began, but she was never again entirely well. Alcott spent much time in the writing and revision of an essay on Emerson called "The Rhapsodist," intended for the* Atlantic Monthly *but left unpublished, at Emerson's request, for many years. William T. Harris of St. Louis, after a period of silence, began once more to correspond with Alcott. F. B. Sanborn, as the new editor of the* Commonwealth, *published several poems written by Alcott in the Fruitlands period, and also his essay on "The Garden," now called "The Countryman." In September died Alcott's mother, at the age of ninety.*

1863

January 8

Letters come from Louisa, giving lively descriptions of hospital scenes. She seems active, interested, and, if her strength is adequate to the task, could not better serve herself or the country. But I fear this will end in her breaking down presently.

January 14

Telegram comes from Georgetown announcing Louisa's illness at the hospital.

I leave by the noon train, take the Norwich route from Boston to New York. We are befogged at Hellgate and do not reach Jersey City till noon.

January 15

Take the cars at 6, ride all night, and reach Georgetown on

Friday morning, 16th

Find Louisa ill of some hospital disease, and decide to bring her home while she is able to journey.

Telegraph to my wife.

P.M. See Mrs. Walter R. Johnson and Miss Donaldson at their house in Washington.

Mrs. Capt. Dana invites me to stay with them at their house in Georgetown while I remain in these parts.

I pass the night with them.

January 17

Louisa hopes to feel equal to undertake the journey by Wednesday, though the doctors dissuade the effort. But I see not how she is to gain strength or spirits by remaining here.

January 18

Write to my wife and see Louisa's patients in their beds. Horrid war; and one sees its horrors in hospitals if any where.

January 19, evening

Murdoch reads for the soldiers in the Senate Chamber. I sit near the President. He has a strong face, and is more comely than the papers and portraits have shown him. His behavior was good, and I respected his honest bearings. I wished to have had an interview, but am too anxious about Louisa, and without time to seek it, nor has he to give. This is not the moment for seeing any one, nor the Capitol to advantage.

January 19

Look for Louisa's box sent from Boston, and her pay at the Paymaster's; but get neither.

January 20

Rains detain us here. Doctors consent to Louisa's leaving.

January 21

Miss Dix prepares good things for Louisa's comfort and meets us at the cars in the city. Misses Kendal and Thurber, nurses at the hospital, accompany us north. We leave at 6 and ride all night, all day Friday, and reach Boston too late to take the cars for Concord. Pass the night at Thomas Sewall's. Louisa greatly spent, and alarmed. Miss Stevenson comes to see her. She rests some during the night.

January 24

We take the cars at 4, and reach home.

January 25

Dr. Bartlett is called. He pronounces the fever typhoid, and speaks hopefully.

January 26, 27, 28

Wait on L. Also ride to Chelsea and apprise Anna of her sister's condition.

January 29, 30, 31

Watch and wait on our patient. Mr. Pratt sits with me through the night.

February 1

Get some rest from my long watchings. Her symptoms are encouraging, though the delirium rages with the periods of fever.

February 4, 5, 6

Louisa's fever abates, and she comes to her right mind. I am with her parts of the nights, reading at intervals and conversing.

February 18, 19, 20

Wait on Louisa through the day and watch parts of the night.

February 22

Louisa comes down stairs to breakfast.

March 22

Louisa leaves her chamber and begins to clothe herself with flesh after the long waste of fever. I am with her more or less every day.

March 28

Go to Boston and meet the Atlantic Club after dinner. Emerson, Agassiz, Holmes, Lowell, Norton, Whipple, Ward, Dr. Howe, Appleton, Weiss, the Conways, are there. I talk with Lowell, Whipple, Weiss, Norton, and Holmes.

Come up with Emerson at 6.

John brings me the news of the birth of a grandson.[1]

April 2

Meet Agassiz at Emerson's. He is here to lecture before our Lyceum. We talk about the order of Nature and plan of Creation. Emerson, Conway,[2] and Channing are interested, and the two first named take part in the discussion. I find unexpected coincidences, if not confirmations, of my theories of Genesis in his classifications.

The lecture is listened to with profound interest. He is eminently the teacher in his department. After the lecture, meet many of our people at Emerson's, and have further talk with the

[1] Frederick Alcott Pratt, son of Anna and John Pratt. From Louisa's letter to Anna: "We were all sitting deep in a novel, not expecting Father home owing to the snowstorm, when the door burst open and in he came, all wet and white, waving his bag, and calling out, 'Good news! Good news! Anna has a fine boy!'

"With one accord we opened our mouths and screamed for about two minutes. Then mother began to cry; I began to laugh; and May to pour out questions; while Papa beamed upon us all, — red, damp, and shiny, the picture of a proud old Grandpa. . . . Father had told every one he met, from Mr. Emerson to the coach driver, and went about the house saying, 'Anna's boy! Yes, yes, Anna's boy!' in a mild state of satisfaction."

[2] Moncure D. Conway.

Professor. With his knowledge of the facts of the world, what might not an Idealist like myself accomplish for the mind! [3]

April 16

Came up at twelve. Rains. Miss Peabody sends me a note urging me to modify the *Rhapsodist* and offer it to Fields.

Evening: At Emerson's, and talk on Personality, in which I think him deficient, his Individuality overpowering, and he only saved by his liberating imagination from Fate. [4]

June 14

Henry James writes expressing his pleasure in Louisa's Sketches. He sends her his new Book entitled *Substance and Shadow*. It is a bold criticism on the hollow faiths of our time, and an attempt to place Swedenborg at the head of modern theologians. James is the only mind I know equal to an attempt of the sort, and is more deeply read in Swedenborg than any one I know. I am not ready to accept all his conclusions, though given in a commanding way and fortified by a fierce logic whose terms are irresistible. Still it appears to a subtler sense than his how fatal is the sophistry that underlies all his statements; and he deals error largely with his truths.

August 5

My mother was ninety years of age on the 20th of June last. She has reached a term beyond all her long-lived family, save a brother who lived to see ninety-two. She has outlived her five sisters, and is the only surviving member of her house.

I have always felt how much we all owed to her; how in our home quiet and good order reigned because she was there; and how her influence was diffused for good throughout the rural neighborhood into which she brought so many excellent qualities of heart, good sense, serenity, to sweeten and soften any rudeness of

---

[3] Based upon the Transcendental belief that every fact of nature is an emblem, symbol, or analogue of a spiritual or intellectual truth.

[4] That is, from fatalism. This controversy, already of long standing, was never settled. Alcott contended always for a personal Deity, self-conscious and purposive, but Emerson felt "a profound need of distinguishing The First Cause as super-personal." For Emerson's comment upon the present discussion see his journal-entry for April 17, 1863.

that district. She had the best influence over my father too, who, of all his brothers, appears to have been the superior man. He left us at the age of 58, just when the head of a family feels the deeper interest in his children, as they are about taking parts in life and beginning to reward him for all his painstakings. He was sensible, having all the plain virtues, with few of the faults of the district where he was born, where he lived and died. Cheney's medallion head of me shows his best features, and may be adopted as his portrait idealized in that of his son. I imagine he gave me his mechanical genius, his industry, his love of order, sense of justice, and his bashfulness. If life has been a delight, the disposition that made it so my mother gave me, she being one of the best-tempered persons I have ever known. And now she is passing away. It was my hope to have had her here with us when that translation came. And now she may have withdrawn from us before I can see her face again. Yet its serenity can never pass from memory. I am sure the transit will be peaceful, and the reward great. Lovely gifts and graces depart with her.

August 26

Redpath sends copies of Louisa's book of *Hospital Sketches,* a neat green-covered 18mo. of 100 pages, handsomely printed, and likely to be popular, the subject and style of treatment alike commending it to the reader, and to the Army especially.

I see nothing in the way of a good appreciation of Louisa's merits as a woman and a writer. Nothing could be more surprising to her or agreeable to us.

September 11

P.M. See Emerson and talk about Thoreau's letters to Blake, which we agree Blake should edit. There are some forty or more, and, as Thoreau wrote always with consideration on his own themes, these must all be good for printing. A few might be added to the collection, written by him to Emerson, Cholmondeley, Ricketson, and perhaps other persons.

I find but a note or two of his among my papers.

Collected, Thoreau's works would make as many as seven volumes. They might be arranged in this order when printed, beginning with the two already published, the titles running thus:

Volume   I   The Week
"   II   Walden
"   III   Excursions
"   IV   Morals
"   V   Politics
"   VI   Letters
"   VII   Poems

I have seen two photographs of him, and a crayon head by Rouse.

Emerson's memoir of him should precede and preface the series.

September 27

I have lately revised my paper on Emerson, shortening it, adding a touch or two, and now lay it aside for such use as time may intimate.

P.M. Abby walks with me to Walden. We find the old paths by which I used to visit him from "Hillside," but the grounds are much overgrown with shrubbery, and the site of the hermitage is almost obliterated.

October 13

Locke sends for me to come and speak to himself and family at the funeral of his little son, a child of seven years, who died suddenly of diphtheria. I prepare to leave in the morning.

October 14

To Boston early. See Fields and leave my paper on Emerson with him to read and print in the *Atlantic* if he finds it suitable.

Go out to Locke's at 12 and pass the afternoon and night.

Evening: His friends and neighbors come in and we talk on Life, Death, and Immortality.

October 15

Locke's neighbor Bicknell asks me to attend the funeral of his daughter tomorrow. The young maiden died shortly after Locke's child, of the same disease. I have known them slightly, and shall gratify the wishes of their parents in being present tomorrow.

Leave early for Boston, and go out to Anna's, where I dine and pass the night. Give my little grandson a ride in his wagon. He bids fair to grow and be somebody.

October 16

Early to Boston, and breakfast with Fields. We have much talk about Thoreau's MSS., all of which he desires to have properly edited and printed — the volume of letters at once. I give him my distribution of the books as enumerated on a preceding page.

Fields praises my "Rhapsodist" paper and wishes to print it in the *Atlantic,* but thinks it were courteous to get Emerson's consent before he prints.

If not printed in that Journal, the paper is good as one of several papers which I design to publish as a Book of Characters sometime. Thus I have the thread of sketches for

Thoreau
Carlyle
Hawthorne
Channing
James
Marg. Fuller
Higginson
Wasson

and some few others might be included possibly.

It would please me much to make a book in which these persons were treated in the manner in which I have done Emerson. My "Forester" paper [5] would form the thread for Thoreau, and the reports of my Conversations on him, Hawthorne, and Channing, serve for completing their portraits. The others I have known less, but have, I think, the key to their manners and genius, and should like to try my hand and see what came of it.

Fields speaks admiringly of Louisa's book. He will like to

[5] Alcott's essay on Thoreau called "The Forester" had appeared in *The Atlantic Monthly* for April, 1862.

print "Plantation Sketches" in the *Atlantic* if she goes to Carolina to write them as she now thinks she may, teaching the freedmen on the plantations meanwhile. She has a book in manuscript ready to be submitted to his reading with a view to having it printed.

Also Redpath is asking her for the MSS. of another story, wishing to print it at once.

October 24

Send apples to Anna for her winter use — Baldwins, Sweetings, and Northern Spys.

The *Commonwealth* contains a notice of Thoreau's book [6] just issued by Ticknor and Fields, and a copy of which Fields gave me when I was last in the city. It contains essays first printed in the *Dial, Democratic Review, Atlantic Monthly,* and makes a delightful collection. We cannot enough admire the genius of this townsman of ours, nor will measure our delight at the acceptance which his contributions to literature are finding from scholars and naturalists as they read his papers. Our little town has the merit of nursing the genius of two minds who, more than any the country has produced, have given to it a literature and a fame it waited long to obtain.

November 10

My cask of cider comes from the mill, and I set it in my cellar. Sanborn also will have a barrel made from my apples.

I find this drink answering to the old countryman's commendations, and since I became the owner of an orchard have varied my drink, which for many years was water only. The juice of the apple seems native to our New England constitutions, and, taken moderately, as every drink should be, is wholesome for the winter months. In spring comes the hop and pine beer, and I take cocoa with my meals — never coffee or tea. Fruit, apples chiefly, are a favorite dessert, and taken before as after a meal.[7]

[6] *Excursions.*

[7] It will be seen that Alcott's thoroughly temperate views concerning drinking did not turn him against the favorite tipple of his native region. Nor did he attempt to defeat the improvement that nature makes in cider with the process of time. When Louisa was writing *Moods*, and could neither sleep nor eat for days together, her father fed her, she says, with his "reddest apples and hardest cider."

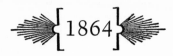
*A*S ALCOTT *approached old age his thought tended more and more to emphasize likenesses rather than difference, and to find grounds of agreement rather than reasons for controversy. His religious beliefs grew simpler. Although never quite "orthodox," he discovered ever more correspondencies between his own faith and that of Christian believers. He deplored the "atomic atheism" of Ellery Channing, continued his long-drawn debate with Emerson about the "Personality" of God and the hope of immortal life, and began to speak, when invited, from liberal pulpits. Occasionally he even found himself able to attend church services conducted by other men.*

After the death of Hawthorne, following closely upon that of Thoreau, Alcott realized that his social circle was narrowing, but his own conviction that he himself would live to extreme old age — perhaps to a full century — prevented any sense of haste.

1864

January 4–8

Compiling my "Friendship,"[1] sitting in the parlor, to save fuel these pinching times. Louisa's story of *A Hospital Christmas* comes in this week's *Commonwealth*. Abby goes to Boston weekly,

[1] Published in *Tablets*, 1868.

taking lessons of Rimmer at the Lowell Institute and modelling at home. She has done a fair head of her mother. . . . My wife over-burthened with household cares, and little to do with. Alas! I wish, for her sake and my children's, I could have had a pair of profitable hands and marketable wits. But no! not too much was to be given to any son of Adam, and I must pay the cost of such gifts as I have by the lack of such as I have not, in something like dependence on others. I wish I may use these in this direction to their comfort and my own credit. But 'tis a cross, when there is so much that gives comfort to the weary and heavy laden, that I may lay my hands on so little.

February 13

Evening, pass with Emerson, at his house, where I sup, and stay till 10. As age steals over me I think I am drawn more closely to my friends, and to this noblest of any I have known still more tenderly, though I should blush almost to speak in words what I now write. We talked last night about the longevity of friendships, and I declared — what is perhaps the burden of my Essay — its personal immortality. Certainly if immortality inhere in anything, we know it must be in persons; and to question the continuance of a connexion like the one I here intimate would be an impiety, if not an atheism, which I am the last of persons to espouse. If I have known life, I have known it not alone but in and through the reciprocation of it with a friend. What had it been to me, had he been a stranger during all these thirty years past!

February 28

Pass Sunday evening with Hawthorne. See him seldomer than I would were he more disposed to seek his neighbors. He complains of indisposition to write and speaks of going forth soon to recruit.

March 13–20

Survey my papers and read miscellaneously. Also see Emerson and talk on youth and age. My friend indulges in futurity[2] less than myself, and speaks with less assurance than I could wish.

---

[2] Belief in a personal immortality.

I know not what felicity of humor, what strength of wit, can add weight to the faith my mother gave me, and question whether any shall take it away.

March 27–31

The reading of Renan awakens my dreams of public culture and a perfect society once cherished and attempted in practical endeavors both in my Temple School and at Fruitlands. Those efforts still commend themselves to my judgement, and, I must think, partook as largely of the spirit and ideas of the Nazarene Teacher, as any known to me in my time.

I find *myself* in this life, and feel a nearness to the young Idealist most brotherly. Nor am I to be deterred from saying this by any superstition still clouding the minds of Christian men and women, few of whom are competent to judge in any case. If I love the Christ they speak of, and interpret him in a sense more personal, less doctrinal, than most persons of my time, it may chance that Christianity is mine also. Names are important, but the Spirit is most so. I am not emulous of taking the Christian name while it stands for so much the lovely Idealist knew nothing of — so disparaging to him and his true friends and disciples.

May 1

My little grandson spends more or less time with me in my study daily. He has many arts and accomplishments for his age, is a gymnast and rhetorician, a lover, a gentleman, and a wit already, has an eye for portraiture, to say nothing of his other attainments, and is an endless delight to the household. To conceive his acquirements as originating in nature and dating from his birth into his body, is to me an atheism that human stupidity alone could entertain; an idiocy which our shallow metaphysical culture could alone have made possible in these days of such marvellous material knowledge, such victories over the natural forces.

May 19–20

News arrives of Hawthorne's death, at Plymouth, N.H. He left home a few days since, too feeble it seemed to me to undertake a journey, and had reached Plymouth, where he died yesterday morning. I saw him last at his gate a few days before he left.

He seemed unequal to meeting anyone, and I had but a word with him, he asking me if I was well only. I had my little grandson with me.

May 23

Attend Hawthorne's funeral. The day is serene and suitable for a poet's sleep. Many distinguished persons came to pay their last honors. The Atlantic Club walk beside his remains to the grave.

Emerson	Longfellow
Holmes	Agassiz
Norton	Hillard
Dwight	Judge Thomas
Whipple	Greene
Alcott	Lowell
Judge Hoar	Fields

May 23

Fair figures one by one are fading from sight. Thoreau, once the central figure in our landscape, has disappeared from it, and Hawthorne no longer traverses his hill-top near my house. Only Emerson and Channing remain of our village circle. I meet the first familiarly, though seldomer than I could wish, but catch no more of the last named than a glance as he passes by my door once in a long while, or crosses my track in the streets. Lately he has avoided my glance, my house too — whether from some pique of his, or from what cause I know not, nor does he know any better than myself. Capricious man that he is, the victim of his moods, whimsical as any spoiled child, and holding his best friends on his own terms or none — may take offence at you know not what, and be off missing for a month, for a twelve-month, unless you take him as he chooses to have you — always walking and talking from behind his mask, and resenting any stroke of candor on your part, as if that were breaking faith with him. Ever

> "The enemy of the strait road,
> To whom the honest sun
> Most like a traitor showed."

August 2-3

Wendell Holmes sends me his book of poems. 'Tis beautifully printed and tastefully bound in Ticknor and Fields' best manner. I find much good poetry in the volume. I am charmed by the melody of his lines; his cadences delight my ear and my eye is pleased by the exceeding fitness and sparkle of his imagery.

In his note accompanying the book, he points to verses for my special reading: "The Chambered Nautilus," "The Voiceless," "Contentment," "The One Horse Shay," all fair samples in his best vein, though for my reading "The Old Man's Dreams," "To My Companions," "Daily Trials," are as good. And "The Pictures" from Occasional Poems, the Vignettes, are all new to me, and justify his fame as a gifted poet.

Such fluency of spirits as these verses everywhere show I have not found in the works of any American besides. Yet I cannot say the author impresses one as being youthful, but as an old man's son rather, and witty by ancestry. I know not what contrarious bloods were dashed into his genius to flirt and flash there, nor by what good chances he was spared from being smart only by his surprising subtleties of wit and allusion. I should say the Frenchman, for one, prevailed over the rest, to give him the saliency of spirits, the glib speech, and make him the agreeable companion, the delightful songster, he is.

His genius seems iridescent — if I may thus express it — rather than magnetic, as if he were the culminating sparkle of high born wits and courtiers, the blending of courtly bloods on several sides of ancestry.

I write thanking him for his book, and expressing my hope of meeting him soon with opportunity of dwelling at length on its merits.

September 5-9

Emerson spends the evenings of Monday and Thursday with me. He distrusts the present Administration perhaps less than myself, yet wishes another man than Lincoln were available in the coming election. And we alike agree that we must vote the Republican ticket to help save the country from ruin.

September 22

Cattle Show. Fair display especially of apples, grapes and pears. And the speaking is good, Agassiz making a strong plea for the State Agricultural School.

Certainly 'tis an accusation of our civilization that so few graduates from our colleges take to agriculture as the most elegant and honorable of the arts, uniting with the accomplishments proper to it those of the gentleman and the scholar, no less. Whoever adorns and enriches the smallest spot has not lived in vain; and Virgil sings for him still.

I meet Agassiz at Emerson's, and have some words with him on agriculture as a means of human culture. But I fail to find in him the scope of thought on the ideal side of things which his eminent natural knowledge implies. Roomy as he is, there is not the space for ideas that one could wish for, and he, the man, is thrust too compactly into his frame to speculate much outside of it. Nor he alone. 'Tis the tendency of the time, every department of thought as of practice suffering for lack of faith in persons and ideas — an all-pervading atheism now paying the costliest penalties that a people can pay for their infidelity to both. We have been growing cattle and cotton instead of men and mind, and are now defrauded of all.

October 29

Richard Randolph of Philadelphia writes from Marlboro House in Boston, enclosing what he is pleased to call his "matriculating fee for admission to the College of Emerson and Alcott." He adds that he hopes to meet me sometime in Philadelphia, and sends his respects. He was here a year ago, and I suppose desires to come again. He seems to be a man of piety, culture, with excellent aims, and disposed for forming wider and more congenial friendships. He writes verses and reads mystical books, and is, I judge, a gentleman of good social position. I will keep his money and pay him the visit he asks at the first opportunity. It seems he expects as much from Emerson.

November 6

Work a little on my fence and about my grounds, preparing for having these ploughed and manured, perhaps planted in the Spring.

November 7

Attend our annual Town Meeting and vote for Abraham Lincoln as President, also the State Republican ticket. We have no choice left us between Lincoln and Jeff Davis, to vote for McClellan being to support the Rebel Rule and the ruin of free institutions.

December 20

Dine with James.[3] He talks freely of our priests and scholars, complains of their subserviency and disloyalty to the hour. Even Emerson and Phillips fall short of his mark. James has a trenchant wit, deals damaging blows on all sides, hates pedants, priests, and fine folks with a refreshing passion. I respect his sincerity and wish his thought the largest audience. Brave, benevolent, earnest, he would break the heads of not a few of the popular idols by his formidable fist, to clear the temples for the purer worship.

December 25

Louisa's book[4] is published, and her mother gets a copy as a Christmas gift with a note.

"I am happy," writes L. "very happy tonight, for my five years work is done, and whether it succeeds or not I shall be the richer and better for it because the labor, love, disappointment, hope and purpose that have gone into it are a useful experience that I shall not forget. Now if it makes a little money and opens the way for more I shall be satisfied, and you in some measure repaid for all the sympathy, help, and love that have done so much for me in these hard years. I hope success will sweeten me and make me what I long to become more than a great writer — a good daughter. And so God bless you, dear mother, and send us all a Happy New Year."

The mother almost completes the reading before she sleeps.

December 26

I read Louisa's book with admiring interest, and think I am not overestimating its merits when I say that she has succeeded better in her treatment of the social problem than did Goethe or

---

[3] Henry, the elder.   [4] *Moods.*

George Sand, justifying its laws to the moral sense without their lapse into murder or adultery. Her style, too, is vigorous and clear, suited to the dignity of her theme, her characters being forcibly drawn and making a deep impression on the imagination and heart of her readers. She has written a better book than she knows, opening for herself, I trust, a career of wide usefulness, if not of permanent fame as a novelist and a woman.[5]

December 30

James reads his lecture on Carlyle to our Lyceum. My wife enjoys it greatly, the hearty manner of the lecturer and the anecdotes are so exceedingly characteristic and witty, his estimate of the man's genius and influences so discriminating and just. A heartless intelligence worshipping force, he intimates, and incapable of apprehending moral excellence.

James has known Carlyle more intimately than perhaps any American, tells his anecdotes of more than one interview with the terrific talker with great good humor and naiveté, giving his broad Scotch accent as well as his words and sentiments. Everybody enjoyed his lecture — Emerson even more, perhaps, than any.

[5] Alcott's opinion of *Moods* shows no hint of that moral disapprobation which other readers of the book were soon to express. It reveals the absurdity of the allegation that Louisa based certain episodes of her story upon some sort of amatory affair between Charles Lane and her own mother.

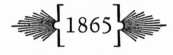

{1865}

*O*NE OF ALCOTT'S *chief concerns during this year was with
the reform of preaching, which had interested him since
his arrival in Boston thirty-seven years before. He himself appeared rather frequently in New England pulpits. In April he
attended the National Unitarian Convention at New York and
spoke in favor of an itinerant rather than a settled clergy. He was
deeply pained, in April, by his loss of the Concord school superintendency, in which he had worked with keen delight and mani-
fest success. This was another of those many rebuffs, to him quite
incomprehensible, that had defeated his best efforts to serve his
time. He found his peace in a return to simple things — to play
with his infant grandson and to the improvement of his house and
grounds.*

*The main events of the year were the death of Lincoln, Lou-
isa's first trip abroad, and the visits of W. H. Channing and W. T.
Harris. Alcott labored at the manuscript of his book called* Tablets.
*He began the building of the famous Orchard House fence, made
of twisted boughs found in the Concord woods. His fame was
growing. Newspapers referred to him as "Emerson's master," and
as "The Sage of Concord."*

1865

February 13

Take tea and pass the evening with Emerson. He has just returned from his lecturing tour West; has been at Chicago, Milwaukee, Erie, and other places.

E. thinks his lecture on "Character" should content people. I tell him it will not satisfy the religious mind, and needs the complement of Personality to stand good for the Universal Faith. He claims "Nature" as the best word, on the whole, for the All, and is not disturbed by any scandal of his pantheistic notions, or idealism.[1]

March 5   *Boston*

Hear Freeman Clarke at his Church of Disciples. Louisa goes with me. Earnest, devout, sensible, the services, the sermon, good doubtless for the pastor and people, but for me, formal, and far too Hebrew, touched beyond truth and nature with numerous allusions to Jesus, and not adapted to the wants of New Englishmen of today. — Let us have the facts and figures in modern phrase, without this fulsome laudation of the past.

I must own myself no Christian if this be Christianity ripe and robust, tolerant, and apt for the needs and issues of this hour. No youth, man or maid, would write love-letters in this sentimental strain suited to Biblical times. Clarke is a priest, in spite of his humanity and culture, of the ancient type.

April 10   *Connecticut*

Gaylord drives me to Spindle Hill. I see the old homesteads of my father and grandfather, cousins and neighbours; dine with James Alcott, and return to Terryville. I am sorry to find it gives me little pleasure to see these old haunts and people, all now in ruins and seemingly unrelated to me as I am.

[1] On May 6th of this year Emerson wrote in his journal: "*Talk with Alcott;* assured him that character was the result of pagan morals."

April 11

Come to Hartford, and stop with Charles Cheney. Dr. Bushnell comes and dines with me. Compare views ethical, philosophical, and theological, finding good agreement except the place of Christ — he deeming him the abnormal being, I, the normal. The interview is mutually agreeable.

April 13   *Concord*

Fast-day. Hear Reynolds at his church, and see Emerson, telling him about the Convention, Bushnell, and my journey.

He tells me I am not re-elected Superintendent of the schools, owing to some informality in the transaction. But I am disposed to serve the town nevertheless, without compensation, lest the schools suffer.[2]

April 14

To Cambridge and see the proofs of my Essay.[3] Looks tasteful and elegant — paper, designs, and all promising fair. Go into Boston and see Anna and Freddy. Thence out to Medford and dine with the Stearns. After dinner ride with Mr. and Mrs. Stearns to the printing office and give final instructions about our book. Home at 7.

April 15

Appalling news of Pres. Lincoln's assassination in the Washington theatre last night, by Booth the actor. Sec. Seward also stabbed and his sons, nor likely to survive. The country is in woe, all men sorrowing at this calamity. The Chief Magistrate falls a martyr to his adherence to justice and republicanism. The sacrifice is doubtless to knit us in closer and more religious bonds to God and the right, and redound to the preservation of our national honor and glory. None but the hand of a traitor to liberty and

---

[2] Alcott did not, in fact, return to his visitations of the Concord schools for ten years, and he was never re-elected. The "informality in the transaction" of the present year was due, almost certainly, to a political "deal" rather than to any well-founded dissatisfaction with his work. No Superintendent was chosen for the year, but in 1866 Dr. Joseph Reynolds was elected as Alcott's successor.

[3] On Emerson, privately printed at the expense of Mrs. G. L. Stearns.

the foe of mankind could have struck this blow at the life of both.

See Emerson, who feels smitten with shame at the event.

April 19

At the National Funeral. The Town all at the Church. Reynolds and Rattray make prayers. Sanborn contributes a dirge. Emerson and Judge Hoar make addresses. Also Rattray speaks. 'Tis a solemn occasion, and the words spoken and sung fitting and eloquent.

Perhaps the nation's head and cherished idol need be stricken down by the slaveholder's bullet to rouse the people to vigilance lest their liberties go down also by a too easy complaisance with their enemies after all these sacrifices. President Johnson promises justice strict and swift to be visited upon these fratricides.

May 25

Delightful day.

Write my note to Mrs. Emerson to accompany the copy of the Book [4] which I give her on this, her husband's birthday, he being 62 years old today. Mrs. E. answers with thanks.

May 30

Emerson comes and expresses pleasure at the birthday gift, is charmed with the style and elegancy of the type, binding, ornament. Will like to talk further about the text. Invites me to tea.

After tea, he reads me his lecture on "Character," as revised, to which I give generally my hearty assent. Perhaps something more of warmth of coloring, a Godhead more personal, would have pleased me better; but 'tis his, and as the deification of his intelligence, admirable.

July 4

Emerson comes and spends Independence evening.

The Republic now begins to look sweet and beautiful, as if honest patriotic citizens might walk upright without shame or apologies as in years before this rebellion.

[4] Alcott's essay on Emerson.

The day is celebrated in the cities north with true joy, and may rightly own its name now.

July 17

Harris comes and spends Tuesday and Wednesday. I find him a profound master of Hegel and the German thinkers, able to apply their dialectic to life, literature, art, society, and a man for whom a great future is opening. He gives hopeful accounts of Brockmeyer, the German genius, and other members of his St. Louis circle; reads me papers of his own on philosophy, and hears many of my paragraphs, the oracles particularly, speaking of them all with enthusiasm, and predicting a success, if I print them, with readers of all classes. The Personal Sketches also interest him deeply.

I take great pleasure in this young man, now but thirty, a graduate of Yale, native of my state, and a successful teacher. My wife tells me that he reminds her of myself, at his age, and when she first met me at Brooklyn, Conn. I take him to see Emerson, and they have sympathy about authors and opinions.

July 18

Louisa leaves this morning for Boston, to sail tomorrow in the steamer *China* for Liverpool, with Mr. and Miss Weld, with whom she is to travel as companion to the German baths and other places on the continent. They purpose taking the train from Liverpool to London, and from thence the steamer to Rotterdam and up the Rhine stream, seeing France, perhaps Switzerland and Italy, before they return — England and Scotland too, if nothing interposes with their plans. It is a fortunate chance for Louisa, a good deal worn with literary labor, and desiring some diversion to recruit her paling spirits and fancy. I trust all will prove propitious and that we may find her restored to us refreshed, enriched and polished, for the future literary victories which I am sure she is to win. But her departure leaves us saddened, and, for the moment, disposed to blame the good fortune that takes her from us, almost the fair winds that waft her over the waves. Write to Anna, who must feel deeply the separation.

But time brings resignation, and restores more than it takes.

July 24

Emerson is here in the evening. Tells me that Fields declines printing his lecture on "Character" in the August number of the *Atlantic* as he had engaged, and had the MS. set in type, but fears the popularity of his Journal will be injured if he prints it. I fear it will ruin him if he does not print it, and his magazine too. The case is put in like straits as regards the *North American*, Fields owning that Journal also, and would decline, though Norton and Lowell wished it printed therein. Well, *he* can print his own book at his own risk, and let publishers spare their good name.

July 28

Miss Thoreau tells me that Fields wishes to print Henry's political papers, and that she has them nearly prepared for the press. These will come at the fitting moment and be widely read. The Letters are just out, and I have a copy sent me by the publishers. It shows Henry in his relations to friends, and is the most remarkable addition to epistolary literature that we have had; a book likely to be read and prized as are Marcus Antoninus, Pliny, Plutarch, and the delightful works of that class, for years to come. Indeed, I may say, the book is unique for the weight of wit, the high moral tone, the surpassing insights, and the fast hold it shows alike on thoughts and persons. The style, too, is as remarkable as the rest, and altogether proves the remarkable gifts of the man and the author. Thoreau is sure of living while New England survives and Nature continues to interest mankind.

July 29

Such a series of bright benign days — a season of such — I have never known, as if Nature, partaking of the temper of the country, had also begun her cycle of reconstruction to intimate her sympathy and delight in the brilliant prospects and peaceful reign of our new republic.

Personally, too, I am rejoicing in the season as propitious to our adventurer, who is today, we trust, fairly across the seas, and crossing the Island, admiring the country and the landscapes, and with her searching senses scrutinizing the manners, speech, and lineaments of that English people. We suppose she reaches London today.

August 8

Spooner from Plymouth calls and talks about Thoreau's letters with enthusiasm. Wishes Thoreau's hermitage, now standing in the north part of the town, replaced at Walden as a memorial of Thoreau. I tell him if nothing better is done I can raise a column on the spot, of rude workmanship — some grotesque shaft cut from the woods in the neighborhood, perhaps, and inscribed with his name.

September 30

Read young James'[5] notice of Louisa's book in the *North American* for July. Find it of a popular cast, flippant, and undeserving — the blame far overbalancing the praise, and the paper intended for popular effect.

October 19, 20, 21

About my front fence, making the gates and setting the posts of the same from the knotted oaken sticks with cedar stretchers and paling, working them out in grotesque designs, the effect both from house and grounds being picturesque and appropriate. Neighbor Gowan thinks it unlike that of any other man's in the world, and pronounces it "as good as anybody's," by way of praising it. It promises to be durable, too; and the cost is inconsiderable. A carpenter would have spent much longer time in planing and nailing his pine stuffs, to set me something in a straight line like my neighbor's pickets, scandalizing the landscape; and the painter must have followed him with some tint that nature and art alike disown. Now, my work will delight my eyes whenever I step out of my house, adding a new charm to the spot. Besides what pleasure the building has given me! I hope to add the ornaments of a summer house behind the apple trees on the slope and build grape trellises in various parts of the grounds.

[5] Henry James the younger (1843–1916).

October 29

Read newspapers. The *Antislavery Standard* of yesterday contains Lowell's Paper in the *North American* entitled "Thoreau and the Transcendentalists," which is a mixed affair, with much that Lowell should not have written about the men and interests which he treats. I have never been able to regard Lowell, with all his ability and his eminent sense of wit, as in earnest and deeply principled in what he speaks and writes. Thoreau and his class certainly are wide of his range and perception.

December 24

E. P. Peabody spends the day with me. Still the same sympathetic, serviceable, and knowing woman whom I have met from the first. The good purposes that she has furthered and brought to consummation during the last thirty years, who shall find out and properly celebrate? I think her one of the most generous souls that I have known, and a part of the life of New England.

EARLY IN February Alcott started Westward for his second visit to St. Louis, urged thereto by his friend W. T. Harris. The impression made by this visit was much more favorable than that gained seven years before, and Alcott returned to Concord in March with the definite opinion, which he never changed, that Western minds and audiences were in many important respects superior to those of New England. Perhaps the chief influence of the St. Louis group upon him was to give him a new respect for systematic thinking as opposed to the intuitive and spasmodic affirmations of Transcendentalism. This is shown in a renewed effort — not unlike that which he had made as a young man under the tutelage of the Scotchman, William Russell — to reduce his own philosophical thought to a clear system. The same influence somewhat increased that independence of Emerson which he had always felt — for Emerson, whatever else might be said of him, was not "systematic."

In July Alcott learned that he had been elected an "auxiliary" of the St. Louis Philosophical Society, and he became deeply interested in Harris's proposal of a Journal of Speculative Philosophy. *December found him again in the Western city, busily engaged in Conversations with his philosophic friends.*

1866

February 9   *Westward Bound*

This prairie country fails to interest me as I ride. One mile is like every other. Nothing breaks the prospect, and the faces seen at the stations seem transcripts of the dismal landscape. So one grows indifferent to the prolonged mud-level, and wishes to reach the end of it.

I reflect that here was the home of the Great American President. Here grew up the honest, upright Chief Magistrate, continuing to snatch from these dead levels, the plain poor images about him, a speech eloquent with native sense and humanity that universities could not have given. 'Tis true there were skies above, the great river flowing seaward, the wild adventures of the pioneer, the excitements of river and road, to fashion him into the Man he was — the anecdote, the epigram, the argument, the sentiment, that went home to the heart and head of a Nation and made him the first real ruler of a Republic. It seems a victory won from circumstances least favorable to the growth of a character like his; and yet how much of him seems indigenous, and could not have sprung into life elsewhere — a large-hearted, loyal soul, with a plainness and slovenly greatness that the West favors.[1]

February 9   *St. Louis*

3 P.M.: Arrive at St. Louis, and ride out to Harris' residence, on Salisbury between Ninth and Tenth Streets, where I am to stay while in the city. Meet with a hearty reception from my friend and family.

Evening: Harris takes me to an informal meeting of the Philosophical Society at Mr. Hill's rooms. Here meet Brokmeyer,[2] President of the Society, Dr. Watters, formerly professor in St. Louis Medical College, Dr. Hall, Mr. Hill, Counsellor at Law, and others. I receive a friendly greeting, and we discourse on *Faust*, Hegel, Fichte, eastern and western life and thought.

[1] Compare the entry for November 7, 1864. Until the death of Lincoln, Alcott — and Emerson as well — had regarded him with a reluctant toleration.

[2] As this extraordinary person, Henry C. Brockmeyer, spelled his name in several different ways, it will be as well to follow the vagaries of Alcott's spelling.

Brockmeyer interests me as a man of original genius. His thoughts on Goethe's *Faust* were surprisingly fresh and new; also on the prairie life as influencing the common sense of the resident.

My friends have arranged for my meeting them at Mr. Hill's room on Tuesday and Thursday evenings for discussing philosophy, and have a popular course on Wednesday and Friday evenings at private houses, as the company find most convenient. Plainly, they propose to hold me busy while I am with them, both in public and private interviews. My wish is to compare views generally with them — philosophical, literary, social — and meet, in such ways as open naturally, any who may care to see me.

February 9

The Society meet at Harris' for comparing thoughts a little — Brokmeyer, Watters, Hall, Hill, Martling, Kroeger.

I unfold my hierarchy of lives, or descent of souls from pure being, the Person, through mind; thence by lapsed minds generating matter, as seen in the scale of organized bodies; from idea to atom — nature being the surplussage of mind, and man the relic. . . .

Say this, loosely: Nature is the waste man. The soul instinctively frees herself from all superfluous matter generated in building forth her own body, and, from this surplussage of substance, organizes in descending series the natural kingdoms. . . .

Much questioning all round, and attempted reconciliation of theories. They tell me I am a Hegelian in spirit if not in form, and seem disposed to claim me as of their master's school. I am more desirous of seeing than of saying, and think far better of the gift of divining than of reasoning — of the seer's sight than of philosophizing; if, indeed, these are not essentially of one and the same divine genus.

February 10

Call with Harris on Dr. Watters. He has lately returned from the army, having been engaged in the hospitals during the war. Is deeply interested in philosophical physiology, and hopes to publish an original work before long, building the body from the soul and generating nature through the mind. This is an idea cherished by him for some time, and his studies have all been brought to bear during these last years to working it out practically, in aid of science and humanity. His friend Dr. Hall has like ends and studies, both being students of Hegel.

P.M. Meet the St. Louis Association of Teachers, and speak on the ideal teacher, his traits and methods. Two hundred teachers are present; one-third ladies. They appear intelligent and eager to hear. Harris appears to be an influence. The Superintendent of the schools did not particularly impress me.

Dine at Burnam's Hotel with Dr. Watters, and pass the evening with Harris. He surprises me by his enthusiasm and purposes. Thinks of translating — aided by his friends here — most of Hegel's works. Has already completed the Logic, Aesthetics, parts of History of Philosophy, Philosophy of Nature; and will simply write an introduction to the study and genius of Hegel.

February 11

We call on Mr. Kroeger, member of the Philosophical Society, and student of Fichte. Find him genial, enthusiastic, and able; less of an Hegelian than some other members, but catholic and hearty, taking part in political affairs too. Writes for the St. Louis journals. Is, besides, Treasurer of the City.

February 12

Write to my wife, and converse with Harris concerning men and measures for promoting thought in philosophical studies. Here are Harris, Brockmeyer, Kroeger, Watters, Howison, Tafel — all men of good ambitions and given to earnest thinking. I am to find whether theirs is not a task the East has failed to complete, whether these men are not to carry forward and complement the thought of New England.

February 16

At Brockmeyer's room. He reads a paper of his on Government, and talks about politics, his part in the Missouri troubles, his colonelcy, representing his county in the St. Louis legislature, etc. But I cared less for these than for his criticism on Goethe and philosophy.

Evening: Hoarse as I am, I talk to a good company gathered at Kroeger's house. The conversation takes a theological coloring, though professedly on "Home"; for here, I find, as in eastern circles, religion steals into any high discussion, refusing to be held aloof, and the sectarians persist in having all told that one may have thought in his heart. Kroeger knew how to manage his neighbours, and, though Howison spoke like the schoolman he is, and Harris like the dialectician, the Puritan persisted, and drew out his questions interminable. The clear sailing came at last, however and the evening was voted suggestive and wholesome.

February 17

If wanting in the courtesies of conversation, these western minds take every freedom of tart debate and drive home the argument at a fearful rate. Custom, traditions, what we call deference to authorities, they hold as embarrassing and set them rudely aside, ignore them altogether. 'Tis refreshing to see, and worth the journey. Nothing better for dissolving superstitions than beholding at first sight. I think every divinity student, at least, should take three months of his course out here with these loaded brains dealing directly with things. He might then return and graduate with some prospect of touching men and times about him, instead of speaking to antediluvians and Hebrews. I see not what chance of a hearing the mere scholar and bigot has here in these free wild parts. And though I value the reserves more than most, loving the sacred names and persons as I find few of my contemporaries, this free, frolicsome, slovenly sense of able earnest men has a formidable attraction, and carries the logic of an argument seldom reached by our well-behaved populations. One can spare the courtesy for this candor, the caution for the conviction — discretion being here the worser valor, and too slow in the race. After the thought will follow the manners, and this new New England will compete in all things with the land of its ancestry, the school of its culture.

February 18

Evening: Brockmeyer and Hill are at Harris's, and we discourse on the vision of Reminiscence and Immortality. I give also my image of the ideal community, instancing our Fruitlands adventure.

February 25

2 P.M. Speak to the Spiritualists on the revolution now in process in religious philosophy. Is not this spiritualism, poor as most of it is, and a misnomer withal, the only religion that may rightly claim to be of American origin? Its chief claim is that it is breaking up the old superstitions and preparing the way for a positive faith.

March 17   *Home*

Good and enjoyable are home, an open fire, family satisfactions, after these dreary days of travel and spent spirits. Yet I shall doubtless venture again into those wild parts. . . .

See Emerson, and talk over the western world, where he has been lecturing for a month or more.

April 8

It is claimed for Hegel that his dialectic is an organism of the spirit, like the mathematics of nature, completing for mind what Plato and Aristotle attempted in their way. Certainly the uses to which Harris and Brockmeyer put it were surprising to me, and almost persuaded me that Hegel's claims are valid.

April 9

Meet Emerson. He tells me that he has advertised to read some lectures in Boston, a series of six on Saturday noons, including his papers on the powers of the mind, some of which he has read to me at several times during the years past. Of course we are not anticipating a system of thought from him, but a series of brilliant suggestive paragraphs on mind and nature, involving a deep philosophy.[3]

May 14

"Full many a glorious morning have I seen
Flatter the mountain-tops with sovereign eye."

[3] No such remark about Emerson is to be found before this in the Journals. The influence of the St. Louis school and the recent readings of Hegel is already apparent.

Thus wrote Shakespeare, and thus might any poet write, celebrating a morning like this rising above my hilltop and shedding lustre on the apple orchards now in bloom and the fields in green. I fancy our Louisa may be eyeing in Shakespeare's isle one of his lustrous mornings, and rejoicing in the spectacle. May all good fortune attend the maiden abroad, and bring her home to the embraces of Summer and ourselves!

July 20

I receive Louisa at the station, 12 M., and bring her to our door. She returns in health and with deepened experiences. Brings agreeable memories of foreign lands, agreeable persons, and is delighted to be at home again, as we are to have her with us. The reunion is all that she could desire, the family being now all under one roof with a summer and autumn of fellowship in prospect.

Of the ornaments and gifts she brings I have my share in Raphael's "School of Athens" and Stirling's *Secret of Hegel*. To her mother she brings an olive-wood album of pressed flowers gathered by her own hands at various places on her journey, and inscribed with these lines:

> As children in the summer fields
> Gather each flower they see,
> And hurry back with eager feet
> To lay it on their mother's knee,
> So I, by ruin, lake, and lawn,
> Found flowers in many lands,
> And gladly hasten home to lay
> My little nose-gay in your hands.

August 14

Emerson spends the evening with me.[4] The Oriental Scriptures, we agree, are to be given to the people along with the Hebrew books, as a means of freeing their faith from the Christian superstitions.

---

[4] The two friends were seeing more than usual of each other at this time, and Emerson was thinking even more highly of Alcott than he had formerly done. See the passage of enthusiastic praise in his Journal-entry for August 12 of this year.

September 16

Sumner wishes to spend a day or two in Concord presently. Has been reading Thoreau with curiosity, and would like to visit some of his old haunts in wood and field.

September 22

Thoreau can take no second place on the roll of heroic fame, nor in literature — he of all his contemporaries writing closest to his time and clinging fastest to the truth of life passing about him. Nearer than any to nature, and, when he became interested in men, with a strength of outline that cast other writers into the shade. Witness his account of Capt. Brown, by which that martyr's fame will be transmitted to posterity. Rare artist, portraying the one brother-hero of his time.

*R*ELIGION, *theology, and preaching are the main concerns
of this year. Alcott's profound dissatisfaction with the existing orthodoxy had been growing ever since his first arrival in
Boston. His charge against the religion of his day was, simply,
that it was not sufficiently religious, and his complaint against
the conventional Christianity was that it ignored both the spirit
and the teaching of Jesus. For thirty years these opinions had
isolated him and minimized his influence, but now in his old age
he began to find about him a host of others, young and old, who
thought much as he did. It became evident that Dr. Channing's
thought was not yet dead, that the harvest of Transcendentalism
was still to be gathered, and that the mind of Theodore Parker
was still marching on. The Free Religious Club and its organ, the
Radical, gave Alcott precisely the sense of association he always
sought, and was obliged for the most part to do without. With
this support he spoke out more vigorously on the deepest themes
than had recently been his custom. He tried, with some success,
to draw Emerson into the same current of thought. He revived
the old plan for a publication of "the Bibles of the Nations" upon
which he and Emerson had worked in earlier years. He wrote for
several religious papers and magazines and spoke from many pulpits. Once more he turned back to natural science for analogues
of the spiritual life, and read all that he could find of the writings*

of Thomas Henry Huxley. Once more he interrogated the great local scientist, Louis Agassiz, with no satisfactory results. He hoped to go forth as a missionary into the towns and cities, preaching the true religion, and in the meanwhile he toiled at those final chapters of his Tablets *which were intended to express his central doctrines with unmistakable clarity. In the midst of such hopes and labors it was a comfort to have the assurance of no less a judge than W. T. Harris that he was, after all, a systematic thinker.*

1867

March 3

If the Greeks received their gods from Egypt and Phœnicia, Rome hers from Greece, and we ours from Rome, Judea, and Britain, by the law of interfusion we must ripen into a fresh faith with its pantheon, surpassing all predecessors.

If, as New Englanders, borrowing ours from the Jew long since, and taking it at second hand from the Puritan Fathers, Judaized to the extent their hearts permitted, it were surprising if we set at once aside a creed thus inborn and become almost a second nature. Some of us, doubtless, would have chosen descent from a race, rather, whose divinity was original and less judicial, domineering, and austere. I, for my part, while acknowledging due indebtedness for all that is natural and good in what was so prized by them, could have wished the genial Jove had succeeded to their grim Jehovah, and bequeathed us a smiling Olympus instead of this blazing Sinai.

March 4

Harlequin in bands and book has nearly played out his part, here in New England, with all sensible people. We have had the drawl of sacred names till sacred names no longer seem sacred, and it were more becoming to fall into a silence about them that were eloquent in their praise. If infidelity, indifference, scepticism, sweep secretly throughout Christendom, 'tis but the binding spell of these dreary delusions about one whom the love and admiration of all good men will not let pass away. We weary of this crape dispensation, this display of "O' Clo'" [1] at the slop-shops, and are intent on getting into plain brown homespun or superfine Saxon forthwith.

April 1

The New Testament writers seem unable to free themselves from the national bias. Capital saints and annalists they were for their time and nation, but Jewish Puritans, strong for Jewry against all the world. Nor do I think Jesus wholly free from the characteristics of his race, as any one will see if he reads the Gospels with open eyes.

April 2 and 3

A nation of come-outers from all nations, we partake of their genesis and genealogy, time fast fusing us into a social polity commensurate with the boundlessness of our geographical position and relative weight among the old nations. Some time hence we shall become one people. As yet, New England is England on this side of the Atlantic. The West is American if any part of the population may claim to be, and is fast gaining ascendancy in national affairs.

Of New England men, Thoreau came nearest to being indigenous; Emerson next; the first inheriting a tinge of the French or Latin turn of thought, the last a bias of Attic if not of Persian cast, with a twist of British understanding that does not acclimate itself without the motherly prejudice for the other hemisphere.

Were New York City American, it were proper to name Walt Whitman the representative American; but injustice would thereby be done to its Broadway, of which he may rightly claim to be the frontispiece and head.

Beside these three I know of no others who may aspire to represent the New World.

August 8

At Emerson's, and meet Weiss and Wasson. We consider the aspects of religion and its instrumentalities. 'Tis thought much

[1] The street-cry for "Old clothes!"

may be done by private clubs and conversations for inspiring a nobler divinity into the students, thus complementing the defects of the teaching at the schools.

This, we hope, is the first of future meetings here at Emerson's or at my house. E. Cabot to be invited to join us at our next sitting in September, and others to be added from time to time.

The books of thought, the Bibles of the races, specially invite the deepest study, and the more in our times of liberal literature when a comprehensive knowledge of the past attainments of mankind is essential to comprehend the present. Homer, Zoroaster, Vishnu, Gotama, Confucius, Mencius, Mahomet, the mystics of the Middle Ages and of times later — one cannot be called educated in any sense corresponding to his advantages who is not familiar with the thoughts of these planters of schools and of religions.

August 30

Read at Athenæum an able paper on American Literature in the *North British Review*, writer's name not given. He speaks appreciatingly of Longfellow, Lowell, Whittier, Emerson. Calls me the "brilliant talker but nebulous writer," and all true enough, omitting the first adjective.

September 2

Huxley Again

I wish to learn the last conclusions of science on matters pertaining to life and organization, believing that as nature is thoughtfully studied and read ideally it will be seen not as the analogue merely but the creation of man.

I see not how upon any other hypothesis the existence of matter can be accounted for. . . . Not the forms merely but the materials of natural things are preconceived, we think, in man's mind, and put forth as the nature we see externally. Nature is mind in solution — the waste or spent man. Without man matter were not, nor nature.

September 12

See Emerson. He declines signing Lucy Stone's Appeal for Woman's Right to Suffrage, but will write and send her his views. I write and send her my signature. I say:

"Gladly sign your appeal, assured that woman is soon to have her place in the State with every right of the citizen. What ideal republics have fabled, ours is to be. Nor need we fear the boldest experiment which the moral sense of the best women conceives and advocates."

November 9

The village tailor sends me a new suit of black. They fit me quite as well as my person, which might have been fashioned otherwise to advantage. Still, I am happy in believing those who clothed me originally gave me their best.

November 12–13

I used to be over-sensitive at the thought of meeting companies for conversation. And though I still come before such, or join such, with diffidence, I have learned that the fittest preparation is a free and open mind that can take company as one finds it, and speak out of the mood of the moment and occasion. Conversation is a game of the One with the One in the many — the speaking out of the sincere to the sincere in all.

December 3

In the evening comes young Quincy (Josiah), the brilliant saint of my Temple group in '36, and reads a rousing lecture on the defects in our system of Common Schools, insisting that heart and head should have positive guidance. The same ethical ascendency of tone appears in his observations and criticisms, and so far as teacher may take credit for right sentiments and skill in speaking these, I had that satisfaction.

A double one, too, in his case, since he showed most forcibly defects in our schools which, through the six years of my superintendence here, I steadily pointed out and urged upon my townspeople for amendment, as my several reports abundantly show.

{1868}

*THE YEAR was marked by much activity in the Free Re-
ligious Club, by the growth of a happy friendship between
Alcott and Ellen Chandler, a young teacher in Framingham, and
by the publication of Alcott's first book,* Tablets, *and of Louisa's*
Little Women.

1868

January 8

At Emerson's after the lecture. A long sitting, chiefly discussing religious reform. I insist on Personal Theism, and the
need of instrumental action for planting it. Can he further such?

January 14

Evening: Hear Emerson lecture on "Eloquence" before the
Lyceum, and, if not eloquent in the popular, he is in the true sense
— the rhetoric of transparent winged thought charming his auditors. I think his dramatic genius surpassing, and for the ends of
the noblest morality. While he lives and speaks the Lyceum will
preach the purest doctrine taught in our times, falling short of
the highest only by limitations of the speaker's temperament.

April 28

Letter from Walt Whitman, with his paper on Personalism in the *Galaxy*. Is pleased with my letter of Jan. 19, last. This Personalism is in the same grand vein of the Democracy, and he promises a third on Literature.

Say what men may, this man is a power in thought, and likely to make his mark on times and institutions. I shall have to try a head of him presently for my American Gallery: Emerson, Thoreau, and Walt. If there be an ideal Personalism, so is there an actual individualism, of which Thoreau and Whitman are prodigious impersonations — Walt for institutions, Thoreau for things. . . .

Write to Whitman and send him my *Emerson*.

Read "Personalism" again after day's work. Verily, great grand doctrine, and great grand Walt, grown since I saw him in his Brooklyn garret in 185–. Greater, and grown more open-eyed, as perhaps ourself, since then. Another American beside Thoreau and Emerson.

June 21

Evening: Hear Father Hecker speak at Town Hall. He gives his experiences in passing through various sects into the Romish Church, instancing his life at Fruitlands with us in 1843. Gives me the interpretation of his terms, and I find little difference of faith between his and mine. I would have mine in fresh fair forms, without his historic accompaniment.

October 14

Louisa has letters from Col. Higginson and wife praising her new story [1] as natural and eminently American. This is high praise, and should encourage her to estimate, as I fear she has not properly, her superior gifts as a writer.

Today the Hawthornes leave their house for a residence in Dresden, Germany.

October 16

Gather apples.

[1] *Little Women.*

October 17

Snows and freezes.

Read letters. Not an eventful life this of mine has been externally, but internally, rather, and not without significance. I may never report it adequately by lip or pen. And whether it shall interest any one sufficiently to make something out of it from my MSS. remains to be seen. I think I am not deceived in believing that I have lived true to my ideals and had their exceeding great rewards.

*A*LCOTT HAD *been much encouraged in his somewhat be-*
lated authorship by the favorable reception of Tablets, *which*
went promptly into a second edition. In working during the present
year upon the manuscript of his second book, Concord Days, *he*
intended at first to use only the Journal for the year as a source.
No particular relation to this Journal is discernible, however, in
the book as it stands, the materials of it having been drawn from
a much wider period of time.

There is little to distinguish the year from its predecessors
unless it be the comfort and the freedom from economic stress
that had come to the Alcott family with the success of Louisa's
recent books. Miss Chandler of Framingham was a frequent visitor
at Orchard House, and an eager correspondence sprang up between
her and the "Concord Sage."

In November Alcott started Westward again, taking several
cities on his way but with St. Louis as his destination.

1869

March 6
Louisa has had good success in her last book *Little Women,*
part first, of which four editions have been sold, and her publishers today send her their check for $228.00, as their second

payment, having paid her $300.00 last December. They have part second in press, and hope to find as ready a sale for it as for the first. The press generally commends it highly, and the young folks write expressing their admiration.

March 21

Johnson [1] reads his discourse on Pantheism at the Horticultural Hall this afternoon. He has a fruitful theme and is capable of treating it profitably to his auditors. Nothing like Comparative Divinity for forcing the mind from traditional teaching. Like travel, it opens out new and distant aspects of the globe on which men live, and shows their relationships in thought and purpose. Christianity cannot suffer by comparison with the faiths of the races. Its advocates need to learn its affinities with all religions and to discriminate its special merits, claiming no more than belongs to it.

As a religion for the heart it stands preëminent and alone, a revelation of the common brotherhood of the races. We must look elsewhere for a religion for the head. And where but to Plato's philosophy? The culture of the world today were as incomplete without the infusion of the Attic mind as it would be without Christianity: nor has this been virtually denied in all the colleges of Christendom since the advent of Christ. Indeed Christianity, as such, has done little directly for pure intellectual culture. The influences have been indirect, not organized and brought to bear systematically upon the mind. The Classics still maintain their high place.

March 23

Write to Miss Chandler:

" 'Tis much to have the company of Plato in these pinched times of ours.

Plato for thought,
Christ for action.

"Happier for us were the two happily blended in life. O, for thought to float the mass of traditions off the minds of

[1] Samuel Johnson, a clergyman of Salem, much interested in "comparative religion."

men and give them to action and ideas worthy of those masters of both! Now men run all to hands — nothing left for head or heart. Let us pray for new heads, as heretofore for new hearts, nor cease, though it were for a century."

March 31

Evening. Take tea and spend the evening with Emerson. He appears to be more engaged in purely literary matters than formerly. I find him less familiar with my world than I could desire. If above Boston, he yet leads its upper circle, and is becoming popular. Carlyle has just sent him the first volume of the new edition of his Collected Works. It is time that we had Emerson's.

April 11

Greenough, a worthy free thinker whom I first met at the Groton Union Conversation in 1840, spends the day with us. He finds comfort, in my wife especially, for his weary spirit laden with poverty and neglect.

His case recalls that of many who entered heartily into the social hopes of that period and took their disappointments sadly. To me that desolation was of short duration, becoming productive of joy and a fresher delight in life. I came presently near to the beatitude of those who were poor enough in spirit to inherit the earth thereafter. Outwardly it was the most thriftless period I have ever experienced, when I went knocking at the doors of my acquaintances seeking sympathy for my lost Paradise, and found the "no admittance" uncivilly blazoned on their front as I left their thresholds. To be pitied by one's friends for his simplicity is an experience that not everyone profits by. I believe I did, and am the wiser and happier man.

April 25

. . . I can hardly conceive of anything more conducive to my spiritual advantage than the experience of those years at Fruitlands and return to Concord. I think I may say that my defeats have proved victories. I did not plant the Paradise geographically as I fancied I might, but entered spiritually into a fairer Eden than I sought to people with human kind.

April 30

. . . Louisa's *Little Women*, Part II, has been most favorably received and generally praised in the reviews. She has made friends of the New England girls, and is deluged with notes of thanks and admiration by almost every mail. Her publishers are exulting in the pecuniary success, having sold thirteen thousand copies and are now putting a sixth edition to press, confident of selling twenty thousand before Christmas. This is most encouraging. She takes her growing repute modestly, being unwilling to believe her books have all the merit ascribed to them by the public. Her health is by no means yet restored. She writes but little, but has various literary works in thought — among others a novel embodying our family adventures which she entitles *The Cost of an Idea*. If written out with the dramatic genius with which she is gifted, the story will be a taking piece of family biography, as attractive as any fiction and having the merit of being purely American. She is among the first to draw her characters from New England life and scenes, and is more successful in my judgement, in holding fast to nature, intermingling less of foreign sentiment than any of our novelists. Her culture has been left to nature and the bias of temperament and she comes to her pen taught simply by an experience that few of her age have had the good fortune to enjoy — freedom from the trammels of school and sects, helps that her predecessors in fiction — Hawthorne, Judd, and Mrs. Stowe — had not.

May 5

. . . The only rightful ownership that man has in the landscape is born of his Genius, and partakes of his own essence as thus mingled with the substance of the soil and the structure which he erects upon it.

May 8

Write to Ricketson acknowledging the receipt of his book of verses entitled *The Autumn Sheaf*. Homely and plain almost to baldness, he yet treats of home life and the simple things of nature with sincere and not ungraceful sympathy, reminding some-

times of Burns and Cowper. His tributes to Thoreau are tender
and touching. I wish his verses may prompt our young authors
to something truly pastoral and American, instead of taking
foreign themes and leaving our life and landscape unregarded
and unsung.

It would not be far from the truth to say that — with the exception of Whittier, Channing, and now Ricketson — New England has produced little pastoral, idyllic — Thoreau hardly attaining to the music of humanity but chanting that of nature,
loving the wild and the savage even, with a sylvan rather than
urban affection. I am looking for the Genius of the home and
household, the orchard and garden, of childhood and youth, the
simple, innocent, the charming humanities, to complement the
wild, untamed, impersonal, and thus perfect nature in character.[2]

I do not intimate these as wholly wanting in our recent literature, but as subordinated unduly to custom and convention, deficient in the modesty as the vigor that constitutes excellence of
the highest order, whether in letters or life. Omit the human and
the copula that unites mind and matter is wanting; we have neither
refinement of mind nor of affection, neither the grace of manner nor strength of thought that enters into true culture. The
Muse must humanize nature and exalt mind into that ideal symmetry in which man's Personality is adequately revealed. If Thoreau, Emerson, Channing, seem bachelors of humanity while espoused nominally to the Muse, each falling short, in his degree, of
the heartiness that woos and wins all mankind, it is because the
fusion of thought with sympathy is incomplete.

May 9

. . . After all I am here most at one with thought and myself, surrounded by my friendly books, and free to follow the
mood of the moment, — read, write, meditate. Yet how little
comes of it, after all! There are these voluminous Diaries, and
how little of life is transcribed upon their leaves! Spectral intimations of the life that passed. Was it the mere accident of finding,

[2] Here one discerns most clearly one of the major ideas conveyed by Alcott
to his daughter Louisa — an idea which had recently found triumphant expression
in *Little Women.*

when a boy, hidden away in an old oaken chest, my mother's little Journal, that set me out in this chase after myself, and continued it till fixed by habit, and now become a natural part of the days — like the rising and setting sun?

August 7

As predicted, the eclipse came on this afternoon. Compared with that of 1806 it was disappointing. That was total. I remember it well, for I dislocated my shoulder-blade throwing stones at it. I was then six years of age, and at school. We boys, myself and schoolmates, were dismissed on account of the darkness, and amused ourselves in pelting the phenomenon. I, in my assault, misadroitly fell to the ground, and turned my shoulder-blade in falling. My friends may interpret the omen, if they will, as prophetic of the boy's fate — tilting at the sun and always catching the fall. The accident is less remembered from the pain of the dislocated joint than pleasure of the sport, and I suppose I am to toy with the sunbeams as long as I am dazzled by them.

August 24

. . . I should qualify my own practice to the extent of giving a scholar the advantages of a collegiate education, after fitting him to use books to profit. My own children, being daughters, and taking their education from the events and experiences of our varied life, have learnt from direct contact with life itself, and, while deficient (as I am) in what the schools profess to give, they have a native strength and grace that schools cannot impart or essentially foster. Louisa is praised for her fine command of the English tongue, and May for the air and expression of her drawings. She is commended by the masters in art. They doubtless owe much to their mother's strength of mind and good spirits. — A good education comes from calling forth the native gifts, and enabling the owner to use these with facility in the callings for which they were intended.

August 26

. . . I hope to spend most of my remaining days here on this loved spot, so largely now of my own creation, and where I

have had, on the whole, the most profitable and agreeable occupation since our married life opened — a home, in a sense, that neither
"Hillside" nor the Cottage at Germantown or at Hosmer's could
be said to have been. My wife and Louisa are less attached, but
Anna and May partake of my own love of it, and cannot think of
leaving it — much less letting it pass into the possession of
strangers.

August 29

. . . In writing to my friend, whether man or woman, and
to a maiden more especially, I may not express all I would, lest I
shall be taken to imply more than I meant and offend the delicacy
of the sentiment which I feel, as if it were no sentiment and were
to be measured by the understanding solely. Surely we are the
most reserved of peoples, fearing to declare openly the private life
we live — if, indeed, we have such. Our Puritan culture has
doubtless had its check, and still holds it hard on us. One comes
under the shadow of its eclipse as he nears New England — the
neighborhood of Boston especially, where it seems central and
almost total. Manners, trade, literature, pale under the shadows,
benumbed and obscured thereby. What book of light and liveliness has grown up under its influences?

It was a happy chance that placed the author of the first volume
of American letters published, out of its blighting atmosphere.
And strange that it should have been written by a recluse, yet so
fresh, and so private, with such touches of kindliness and humanity,
that all men and women delight in his letters, showing a generous
heart and fireside companionship that has hardly found elsewhere
its way into our literature. Thoreau's Letters are throughout
American. They never remind one, local as they are, and written
within twenty miles of Boston, of its exclusiveness or reservedness.

September 4

I read notices of Louisa's *Little Women* from all parts of the
country, and, with one or two exceptions, all are not only highly
commendatory but place her in the first rank of writers of fiction.
These notices are numerous, coming from all the principle cities
and from many of the towns where newspapers are printed.

It is an honor not anticipated, for a daughter of mine to have won so wide a celebrity, and a greater honor that she takes these so modestly, unwilling to believe there is not something unreal in it all. The public has not mistaken, I am persuaded, and if she regains health and strength she will yet justify all her fame. I, indeed, have great reason to rejoice in my children, finding in them so many of their mother's excellencies, and have especially to thank the Friend of families and Giver of good wives that I was led to her acquaintance and fellowship when life and a future opened before me. Our children are our best works — if indeed we may claim them as ours, save in the nurture we bestowed on them.

October 3

This last week has been sunny and Indian, only the maples along the brookside suggesting the coming winter. Only a slight frost as yet. The grapes hang temptingly in ripe clusters from the vines, and the apples redden the boughs in the orchards. One is never saturated with sunshine, and tastes the three seasons under the ripened rinds of these fruits. Certainly the sun does his best to put all skiey virtues into them; one tastes the choicest of heaven's juices distilled for human repast. Apples and grapes ripen at the same time. I imagine these were, as they still are, God's best and onlys — all others but vanities. Berries are only grapes of the woods. Pears are Adam's apple tickled by man's art; and peaches are Eve's. These the fruit that preserves most of Eden's flavor and bloom. Pears plainly are gentlemen, and peaches ladies: men and women, less elegantly. It is remarkable, besides, that the apple and the grape have been tipples from Adam, first of gardeners, down to Noah, first of vintners, and his mellow descendants of our time. 'Tis the ever-old-new story clothed under other leaves, of tasting wantonly of divine delights. A sip of felicity is the most that mortals may safely take from any goblet.

October 11

. . . If women will only use their own tools simply and skill-fully they may carry the world. I don't like to see them taking to our ways as if all power lay in these. The platform and pulpit are efficient organs, but parlor and pen are still more so, and graceful for women. An enthusiastic, intelligent, and earnest woman's eloquence in the parlor is irresistible.

Let the women cultivate conversation and their day is sure to come.

October 17

Everything concerning the author of *Pilgrim's Progress* is interesting to me, since the book was the first work of genius that attracted me as a boy, and became one of my bosom companions, taken into the field oftentimes, and read while my ox team rested, or myself, from the corn rows I was weeding. It was to me what Homer is to the classic student, and probably had a greater influence in forming my character and style of thinking than any other book in our tongue. Its homely speech became in some respects the model upon which mine was formed, though the dialect of my neighborhood was akin to that of its author. I did not own a copy of it, but borrowed and kept long a fine Edinburgh edition with fine engravings, from a cousin, and was probably the most devoted reader in all that district of plain farming people, whose chief reading was the Bible and almanac. I know very well that there lingers in the minds of mere scholars the prejudices of the collegian against the illiterate tinker, but if the universal estimation of a book is to be taken as a test of its merits, Bunyan must take his place with the great minds of the English nation, and his book takes rank with Shakespeare and Milton.

October 21

. . . Call on the Thoreaus. Madame is as talkative as ever about village matters, and Miss Sophia tells me that she has almost consented to have a book of selections made from Henry's papers. A volume of Natural History and one of Morals might be compiled from these, of great value and interest. Higginson has been named to arrange the first. Henry made the remark during his last illness that "Mr. Alcott would be a suitable person to publish his Religion." It would please me very well to make the selection from his papers.

October 24

. . . Emerson calls to see Miss Chandler, and the evening passes pleasantly. The company of young people is preferable to that of the elders generally, sensible young men and women interesting me as when I too was young, and is only second to that of cultivated scholars and fair women. When I shall become indifferent to these and the charms of children I shall know that I am growing old, and may as well withdraw from the scene.

November 9

Read Lowell's *Under the Willows and other Poems.* He has singular skill in verse, and rises occasionally into the realm of poetry and pure idealism. Yet he does not inspire with the spirit of the lyric ardor and enthusiasm, — not even in his "Commemoration Ode," which is rather skillfully wrought verse than nobility of sentiment. No, I cannot class him as a poet, one of the masters of ideas and song. In common sense, keen wit, fanciful humor, he is hardly surpassed by any of our American scholars, but in high imagination, and the dignities of moral sentiment, essential to the pure poet, he appears to me to be deficient. The *Fable for Critics* and *Biglow Papers* are as yet his titles to fame. Like all bookish men, he fails of touching life to its deepest issues.

November 15

The Radical Club [3] meets at Dr. Bartol's. Potter reads a masterly paper on "Christianity," defining its several forms and creeds, and some points of his Essay are discussed by Dr. Bartol, Wm. H. Channing, Dr. Clarke, Mrs. Howe, Wasson, Weiss, and others. The discussion became too personal to be attractive and edifying to me. I express as much, and regret that a theme so ably opened should have been thus dragged down to personalities. Our culture was narrow and our dialect sectarian. What we should seek was the unity underlying all differences of sect and races. It was discreditable to a company like this to be bandying Puritan or even Christian epithets and exaggerating our real differences. Place the best representatives of the great religions of

[3] The later name of the Free Religious Club.

the world in our places in the room, and they would be found in better agreement than the present company.[4] The revelation was One. Each race, sect, individual received it according to culture, temperament, condition, and we should not claim superiority over others, but find in all the universality of the truth. It was too late to claim for Christianity what other revelations had not. All religions were partial forms of the Absolute Religion, and we should no longer set Christianity above the rest.

November 21 P.M.　　　　　　　　　　　　　　　　*Syracuse*

Attend a temperance meeting and speak by invitation. The advocates of temperance, here as elsewhere, appear to be dealing with the subject superficially, and I fear I am a poor advocate for the measures which they propose in their popular meetings. The most practical measures, in my judgment, would be to create the sentiment that should lead the towns to own the hotel and elect their innkeeper as a town officer, holding him to their pledges upon his honor. A town has the morals of its inhabitants within its keeping, and should not, like Cain, seek to be excused from being its "brother's keeper." It should take the penalty of its guilt of neglecting the ignorant, the weak, and the wicked, and be held to the strict account.

December 1　　　　　　　　　　　　　　　　*Cleveland, Ohio*

Miss Thatcher's Drawing Rooms are filled with a curious company, and I speak at length of New England Authors — Emerson, Thoreau, Hawthorne, Margaret Fuller, Ellery Channing, Longfellow, Lowell, Holmes, Whittier, and, by request, of the author of *Little Women*. In a popular Conversation one does not venture deeply into metaphysical discriminations, but treats of living traits and personal anecdote chiefly. I am less conversant with Holmes, Lowell, Longfellow and Whittier, but of the others I have many characteristic peculiarities to tell, and am sure of interesting any thoughtful companies. Thoreau and Hawthorne are especially attractive, and Channing scarcely less so. But I am tempted, I find, to dilate so largely on Emerson that the others

[4] Compare Emerson's Journal for March, 1868.

get less justice done to their gifts and attainments than were becoming in a promised grouping of my portraits.

As to Louisa, I find I have a pretty dramatic story to tell of her childhood and youth, gaining in interest as she comes up into womanhood and literary note. Yesterday in the schools I was called upon to tell her story, most of the scholars being familiar with her book and curious to learn what I might tell them about her history. I am introduced as the father of Little Women, and am riding in the Chariot of Glory wherever I go.

December 2

. . . Write to Louisa, telling her of the enthusiasm with which her book is here received, and the admiration felt for the author — all of which she will be slow to accept, cannot even comprehend.

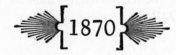

*A*LCOTT'S WESTERN *tour of 1869–70 lasted four months, took him to fourteen cities, and earned him over seven hundred dollars.*

Louisa's dream that she might "pay all the debts, fix the house, send May to Italy, and keep the old folks cosey," was rapidly coming true. To fulfill one item of it, she sailed for Europe in the spring with her sister May. What she had not foreseen in her early dreaming was that when financial success came her health would be permanently gone.

The effects of prosperity are obvious in the Journal. At the age of seventy Alcott finds his health to be excellent, and a slight trouble with his hearing is soon in large part cured. He enjoys his gardening as much as ever, although he now hires an assistant and plants flowers for beauty rather than vegetables for food. He begins to think of buying a horse and buggy, probably more for his wife's convenience than for himself. His thoughts recur to a plan, already of long standing, for a school of philosophy at Concord. Even in his choice of books there is a new freedom and amplitude. He turns again to Charles Dickens, whose Pickwick Papers *he had read with delight during his earlier days of prosperity at the Temple School. He discovers his English counterpart, Leigh Hunt, whom he thinks not only an excellent writer but a wise man. He considers going to San Francisco for conversation, and so "belting the continent with talk."*

Late in October Alcott started on another Western tour, beginning at Spindle Hill.

1870

March 31

To Boston with my wife.

Give Louisa a pocket book and May a mirror for their travels.

We bid them farewell with fear and hope. Deserving girls! They are now being rewarded for their toils and sacrifices in childhood and early womanhood. If Louisa can recover lost health and spirits and May gratify her thirst for art, then God be praised, and our cup will overflow. We commend them to the good Providence that has brought them firmness and fortitude hitherto and made them strong and true. The sea and land must smile propitious on their voyage and travels and bring them home safely.

April 1

The girls take their morning's train by Springfield for New York. John accompanies them to see them aboard the Steamer *Lafayette* which sails tomorrow for Havre, stopping at Brest, where they purpose landing and travel leisurely through France, Switzerland, and thence into Italy to spend the coming winter. They take leave of Boston under fair omens. Louisa's *Old Fashioned Girl* is to be published tomorrow, the day of her leaving the country. Twelve thousand copies have been sold in advance of publication and four thousand are now in press. They are abundant in funds for their travelling expenses and their companion, Miss Bartlett, speaks French and Italian, besides having been abroad and is familiar with the difficulties of foreign travel.

April 15   *Plymouth*

P.M. Leave for Plymouth to pass a day or two with Watson, whose house and grounds I always enter with pleasure. He is one of my friends who has built a world for himself out of our common materials, and adorned it by a calling in harmony with his disposition and gifts.

We have many reminiscences of past years of Come-outerism of which most of our colleagues are now cured — though most, if not all, acknowledge their deep indebtedness to that period and its fruitful experiences. It only needs that one survive its extremes to glean world-wisdom.

April 16

Walk about "Hillside," planted by his own hands twenty years ago and now a rural Paradise.

Watson is a successful florist and gardener. He has business communication with most parts of this country and of Europe. "The Old Colony Nurseries" have a wide fame. Could it have been "The Concord Nurseries" we should have complemented Thoreau and Channing, and given to college culture what it needs, though Emerson and Hawthorne were ornaments of the landscape. I think it is an accusation of our culture that so few graduates from our schools and colleges take to agriculture, leaving gardening, building, adorning the landscape, authorship, to the rare few whom college nor books could not sophisticate nor spoil. Agriculture and man-culture should have each its due place in civilization. Thoreau loved and respected the world in which he lived. His spoils were ideal, and left nature unharmed. Homer and Virgil were but elder singers of the old song, ever rhyming its periods in his ear, and were sung by him to a more modern air, wild or soft as he piped to his mood. But his contemporaries for the most part forgot their Greek and Latin periods, or recited them as exercises of their school days merely.

> One harvest from the field
> Homeward brought the oxen strong;
> A second crop his acres yield
> Which he gathered in a song.[1]

[1] Inexactly quoted from Emerson's poem "The Apology."

May 2   *Concord*

To Boston and see Niles concerning Louisa's books, which are having a large sale, The *Old Fashioned Girl* having reached 27,000 since the date of its publication, April 2nd, and *Little Women* is in the 48th edition, both books finding favor with the reviewers. Also see Loring, who is about publishing a second edition of *Moods* without consulting her as he should have done. But, having right of property, he persists. It was her intention to restore the text and print a second edition as originally written.

Meet Jas. Freeman Clarke and tell him about my Western tour. He confirms my assertion that the West is more hospitable to ideas than the East, less the victim of tradition.

May 3

Sanborn comes and breakfasts with us. His family have left Springfield for the summer. I cherish the hope of his returning to reside here in Concord. With Sanborn and Harris as neighbors, what might I not hope for! My cup would overflow. Concord is the proper seat for an Academy of Philosophy, Literature and Religion. Here should be founded the Divinity School to which young men and women might resort for the inspiration and insight which our colleges fail to cherish. And here should the journals and newspapers representing the freshest and ripest thought, the aspiration and enterprise of the country, be edited.

. . . Peter Hutchinson ploughs my garden. I shall not willingly relinquish the pleasures which the cultivation (even in my poor way) of a garden and orchard afford day by day. I cannot hope to enjoy the garden which has been celebrated so lovingly in my printed essays,[2] but only some shadow cast here on this plot wherein I have sowed seed now for the last seasons and harvested therefrom my scanty crop. 'Tis salutary and wholesome, this sowing in soils in summer time, as it is in souls all winter long, and the harvest is alike rewarding. I wish my crop from my garden may prove as prolific and wholesome as from the field of the West.

[2] In *Tablets*, Boston, 1868.

May 5

Plant garden, Carney helping me. Formerly I was loath to let any set hoe or spade into the soil, but now I submit and consent to have seeds dropped and covered by other hands than mine. And this man, Carney, has proved himself a faithful and capable servant during the several years past. I employ no other. He is the most sensible Irish laborer living in our town; knows his business and place, is companionable, with opinions worth listening to but never obtruded offensively. I deem it a privilege to labor beside a sensible man and compare notions and things. Ireland and China have something for us it were well for us to hear and respect. Romanism and Confucianism are yet to gain a hearing from us.

May 23 *Boston*

P.M. At the Celebration of Marg. Fuller's 60th birthday held at the rooms of the Woman's Club. The company is worthy of the occasion. Clarke, Hedge, Channing, Cranch, Mr. and Mrs. Spring, Miss Peabody, Higginson, Mrs. Cheney, Mrs. Howe, bear eloquent testimony to her exalted character and genius. Emerson is unable to be present, having a lecture to give in Cambridge, and I am too hoarse and ill conditioned to speak fitly.

I know not whether I may call her friend or acquaintance. Though an assistant in my school, we were seldom there at the same hours, and saw one another less often than I wished, but my instinct served me in place of more intimate acquaintance.

If I might characterize her in a word I should say she was a *diviner* — one of the Sibylline souls who read instinctively the mysteries of life and thought, and translate these in shining symbols to those competent to apprehend them. Her conversation gave a far better measure of her remarkable powers than her writings, wherein she seemed constrained and ill at ease. I saw her oftenest at the sittings of the Transcendental Club where she was sure to say extraordinary things, surprising to all who heard her, and where she was oftener the leader, while at the same time one of the most eager listeners in that eager circle. She drew all towards her by her potent and fascinating magnetism. Her scorn was majestic, her satire consuming, her wit the subtlest of any I have known.

She had the intellect of a man inspired by the heart of a woman, combining in harmonious marriage the masculine and feminine in her genius. We have had no woman approaching so near our conception of the ideal woman as herself.

It was my misfortune to have met her not always under the best circumstances, and to have fallen under a cloud after she left my school, so that I have not escaped the feeling that she never quite fathomed my secret — wise as she was, and seeking subjects for her divination. But better than most — more truly than any, unless it were Emerson and Channing,[3] she comprehended my drift and purposes, and bore testimony to these when many of my former friends were staggered at my course, and those who knew me not took sides against me. It was a fate disastrous not to her alone but to her country whose shores she so nearly touched, that she sank in sight to disappear forever.

May 26

. . . I seek a Personal Church planted in the faith in a Personal God, but find my friends speak hesitatingly about that — believers in Law rather and an impersonal theism which virtually annihilates a Deity.

They may plant free platforms for pleading popular reforms, hold conventions for discussing secular and sacred themes, and thus do good service; but a Church for meeting the deepest spiritual needs of mind and heart they are not likely to organize. They are too individual for that, and can associate for popular ends only.

I consider this movement [4] a stepping stone from the old creeds to the newer. But they are likely to overstep the mark and plunge into Positivism or something worse. In pleading for science they discredit religion in its divine sense, and sink divinity in humanity.

June 7

. . . Inquire the price of a through ticket to San Francisco, and am told it is $130. One can see the Pacific in a week's time.

[3] Probably W. H. Channing (1810–1884).
[4] The Free Religious Association, founded at about this time as a branch of Unitarianism, "to encourage the scientific study of theology and to increase fellowship in the spirit."

Nothing will suffice, it seems, but for me to belt the continent with talk. And once at St. Louis I am nearly half across it. . . . Every New Englander should see California. The stream of thought follows the great lines of travel. The traffic in things introduces ideas. Should travel and talk agree with me as in times past, it would be a good service done to open an ideal communication between East and West. I might then be ready for seeing Old England again, meeting Louisa and May there, under better advantages than I had at command in 1842. Such dreams are pleasing, and time may bring them to pass. I am not averse to travelling and adventure. While occupants of space and time we cannot well afford to be indifferent to their illusions.

June 8

Miss Chandler writes that she will come to Concord on Saturday the 18th and pass Sunday forenoon with me.

When young women cease to interest and charm me I shall know that it is time for me to withdraw from this world. And yet without youth what were any world conceivable? Heaven must be populous with damsels and beautiful boys, babes, and children. I see no room for old people.

June 10

To Boston. Leave a note for Fields thanking him for the gift of Hawthorne's *English Notes,* which I have read and find pleasant reading for these June days. Hawthorne had eyes for facts and the skill to deal with life and living things as only poets can. He loved England a little too well to be quite just to his native land, and seemed as much of an Old Englishman as New. He always appeared to be regretting the transplanting and unwilling to fix his roots in our soil. If his themes were American, his treatment of them is foreign. He stood apart, having no stake in our affairs, and, though calling himself a Democrat, sympathized apparently with the Absolutism of the Old Countries. I think his democracy was an idealism and the fruit of his temperament. He had not full faith in the people, and feared republicanism because it had. Of all our literary men, he openly espoused the side of the South, and was tremendously disturbed at the

Northern victories. I believe he seldom or never voted, actually, throughout the long struggle with slavery. He was an observer, rather, and held aloof, practically fearing to take a responsible part. In all this I think him true to his convictions and a strictly honest man, if not a patriot.

Mr. Hawthorne's excuse for his "morbidness and gloom" has, so far as this was inherent in his temperament, the show of truth. He strove by disposition to be sunny and cheerful, but these traits were not native in him. He was constitutionally grave and melancholy, and only by shafts of wit and a flow of humor could he deliver himself for the moment. There was a soft sadness in his smile and a reserve in his glance that told how solitary and isolate he was. He never seemed to be one of his company while with it.

June 10

. . . I read Dickens when he first appeared as an author — his *Pickwick Papers, Nicholas Nickleby, Oliver Twist* — and recognized his genius in portraying low-life English characters. His later works I have not read. Perhaps he has influenced the literature of fiction more widely than any contemporary of his. He brought his readers into living sympathy and communion with his characters, and dealt with life and manners in a real way. His caricatures always tell. Louisa has been an admiring reader of his works, and her method and style has been doubtless influenced by his example. If she has any trait in common, it is in her dealing with American life as he did with English, bringing men back to nature and reality.

June 19

A June morning and Miss Chandler brings another. Such charming company is rare here in my retirement, and I enjoy it like the taste of strawberries, the fragrance of roses. She interests one by her graceful deportment, social accomplishments, literary tastes, and devotion to good objects. A successful teacher in the Framingham school, she infuses a fine moral into the lessons, and wins the confidence of her scholars.

I confide my best thoughts naturally to her judgment, and find it easy to meet her in conversation. Her correspondence has been gratifying. She has almost taught me to write a lively letter.

The friendship of young women has more of sweetness than that of young men. We ancients need both. Our sons and daughters serve us to finer issues than we know. But they are near, and of us. We separate ourselves from them with difficulty. Youths and maidens delight us by giving us perspectives, and relating us sympathetically with all mankind. I am not a man entire till I have been transformed into womanhood, and can translate my boyish life into a girl's, to trace therein and thereby the genealogy of my affections and intellect.

"Either sex without the other is but half itself." It is the transformation that complements and completes the sexes.

Emerson calls to see Miss C., and invites her to tea this evening.

June 24

Niles[5] give me a copy of Leigh Hunt's *Seer, or Common-Places Refreshed* — a charming book. Leigh Hunt has the delicacy and playfulness of a woman, and whatever he touches takes on the hue of his genius. A more delicious book for summer reading will not be laid hold of anywhere. It is truly "Common Places Refreshed," and good to read in these June days especially. What a delicious essay, for instance, is this on Strawberries! One can taste them as he reads his pottled page. And the quotations are refreshing. It suggests Covent Garden and its strawberries in their season, as well as my neighbor Moore's, now in full luxuriance across the way. My only association with the first is the little children who swarmed about me, devouring my pottle with their eyes, and even getting most of the contents by their importunity. Ours are not inferior in size or taste. But I taste none like the wild ones plucked from the meadows of my native place, while the dews were on them, and the bobolink sought to decoy me from her nest in the grass when I approached it. The cream, too, was fresh from the full udders, and filled the bowl to the brim. Was anything so delicious to eye or taste! Herrick had tasted and sung its charms:

[5] Louisa's publisher.

You see the cream there naked is,
Nor dances in the eye
Without a strawberry
Or some fine tincture like to this
Which draws the sight thereto.

Clotted and dancing in the eye truly! Strawberries and cream! One is not married without this tribute of summer. What shall one offer bride and bridegroom from the fruits of the seasons like this? Ah, June is the month for nuptials, and this is the country.[6]

June 28

To Boston and home again, reading at the Athenæum and seeing Niles. He shows me his accounts with Louisa for the year past.

There will be due on the first of July, for six months percentage on her books, $6000.00. He has paid her, on these, Dolls. 12,292.50.

He thinks no American author has received so much during the current year, and says her works are selling better than others at present. It is unexpected success, and she deserves it and may well enjoy its fruits abroad. She seems to be finding favor also in England, where *Little Women* and *Old Fashioned Girl* have been printed.

July 3

. . . Yet a Diary is the most instructive of all writings, even though it record poorly the life of any man, however simple or wicked, revealing the story of the human heart without fear or equivocation.

July 19

. . . We meet Emerson and he tells me that Collier has written inquiring about his (Emerson's) giving readings in our proposed Parlor Courses in the Western cities. He says that he will be too busily engaged in preparing his Cambridge lectures, which open in February.

[6] A passage to be read in connection with Emerson's assertion that Alcott had "no senses."

But whether any one join in this venture or not, 'tis clear that the way is fairly open for me, and that I am to sow, if not reap, the first fruits. Perhaps Providence prefers rather to divide labors, assigning one to the East and its University and sending the other to broader and fresher fields of the West.

He certainly can do more for the University by giving it the benefit of his name and services than any American scholar. What other institution is roomy enough to open its doors to a mind like his? Besides, he has found himself, he says, most at home before an Eastern audience. And though well received at the West, he is plainly a better New Englishman than pioneer, is less American than his company. A Bay-State Scholar, he has much of the Old Englishman, and something of the assumption and air of blood and culture peculiar to Boston and Cambridge. If less of these than most of his class, 'tis owing to his wider acquaintance with mankind, and richer culture. Yet anywhere out of New England he would appear strange and an exile. To him the continents are but suburbs of his individualism, and Boston his birthplace. I remark the like in his chosen friends and acquaintances — a certain adherent provincialism underlying all their cosmopolitan studies and professions which renders them exclusives at heart if not in bearing.

In his case, the trait is heightened and the more apparent from his sensitive temperament and literary training; and we find his excuse, if any is needed, in the faith that this very delicacy and refinement of exclusiveness serve as native shields of his genius, without which his works could not have been produced. The like may be affirmed of Hawthorne, and in lesser degree of Thoreau, who, unlike Hawthorne, took refuge under a brusque and somewhat defiant manner — at heart as diffident and fine-strung as either of his neighbors and townsmen.

July 31

. . . The other day a poor infuriated dog ran just before me across the side walk and threw himself madly into a cellar to be slain by a howling crowd that followed him. Were the fountains flowing within reach of the thirsty creatures, such scenes would seldom occur. Mad dogs are innocent of tasting stronger liquors than the fountains afford when both are within their reach. And both mad dogs and mad-mankind accuse our civilization.

I pass, too, as I ride into the city and return, squares of newly built tenant houses erected on lands which the high tides can hardly fail to overflow and every rain inundate — near a slaughter house moreover, rendering them unfit for human dwellings at any season. The capitalist doubtless pleads his legal right to use his money or lands in any manner he please, and the poor occupant perhaps considers him a benefactor in furnishing a shelter even in such unwholesome quarters, while he can pay his rent for it; though his wife and children, if not himself, fall victims to his surroundings, unless they chance to be sound and virtuous.

Cities, like Cain, may not hope to shield their crime by legislation, excusing themselves from being their "brother's keeper" thereby, nor hold any guiltless who disregard, for gain, the health, comfort, or virtue of a single citizen.

1871

*A*LCOTT'S TOUR *of this year — lasting four months, covering seven States, and earning over eight hundred dollars
— was in all ways successful. His most popular theme, "Concord
and Her Authors," was often converted, upon request, into a discussion of Louisa's childhood, domestic virtues, and methods of
literary work. Thus he helped to spread the East Westward, and
to extend literary reputations.*

*At Jacksonville, Illinois, Alcott found a man of his own sort
in Dr. Hiram K. Jones, a physician, who had long conducted
there a large and enthusiastic "Plato Club," and who was to be a
central figure in the Concord School of Philosophy. Indeed, that
School first emerged from the realm of dreams and wishes during this tour, in the course of which Alcott was promised five
thousand dollars for the support of his beloved project. Much encouragement was given by Mrs. Mary Adams, the "Sibyl" of
Dubuque, one of the most vivacious, independent, and yet devoted
of his feminine admirers. At Quincy, Illinois, he spent some time
with the "beautiful and interesting ladies" of the "Friends in
Council," who were also to send their delegations to the Concord School in later years. On the whole, his Western tours were
beginning to resemble a triumphal progress.*

*In June the famous father, recently from the West, met his far
more famous daughter, who had been for more than a year in*

Europe, at the Boston docks. Little Men, *published on the day of her arrival, had already sold fifty thousand copies. At home again in Concord, Louisa complained that "people come and stare at the Alcotts."*

In July occurred the death of Samuel J. May, Alcott's brother-in-law and friend of forty years, whom he called "God's chore-boy." In the same month came William T. Harris, now a man of renown, on a visit to Orchard House — of which he was later to be the owner. Alcott worked for the rest of the year upon the manuscript of his Concord Days.

1871

March 5

. . . I take tea with Emerson and pass the evening. No man enjoys more any success of a friend with the public, or gives a more hearty sympathy by words and deeds. Yet he will not take without question my report of success at the West. I suppose I paint *en rose*, and must be taken with large abatements. But I cannot be mistaken as to the friendly reception which I have received wherever I have been, and may take an honest pride in having made the acquaintance of so many excellent persons as I journeyed. Names have their significance; and when one can refer to the "Round Table," the "Plato Club," the "Friends in Council," the "Philosophical Society," "The Journal of Speculative Philosophy," there rises before the imagination a culture and society to pique the curiosity and invite inquiries about that world at the West.

March 6

Call on the Thoreaus, and tell them of the interest felt by many persons in Henry's character and writings. They are disturbed by Lowell's paper on Henry, lately published in his book entitled *My Study Windows*. Lowell should have better known Thoreau in the qualities for which he was so remarkable and admired by his friends. There is truth at the root of his estimates, and just enough to give credibility to them; but Henry's merits will survive all disparaging criticism, and justify his life and writings to unprejudiced minds. By temperament, Lowell and he were opposites save in wit and humor, which played truly with their Genius alike, and neither could appreciate and delight in the other save by contrast. The cynicism of the one was only more graceful and polished than the other's; and if any preference is to be given to the manliness which both exhibit in their life and writings, the higher qualities of character, Henry compares favorably with the poet of Cambridge; nor was it quite becoming in the latter to attempt the measure of a character so unlike his own.

May 7

Emerson has been gone some weeks with a party to California, where he has lectured and met with a hearty reception, as he must wherever he is known. Significant, this belting the hemispheres with ideas. Like stars in the firmament overhead, the forces must surrender to ideas, mechanism to intelligence, thus overbridging matter with Personality. His is the most penetrating glance those cliffs and shores have met, and the results of his observations will appear in his future writings. Eyeless travellers never leave themselves, though they traverse the globe and survey every mote and pebble as they go. It is the pair of eyes behind the eyes that see and circumscribe the world outside.

May 25

Mow the lawn, already verdant and tall with grasses. The boys indulge their fancies in tedding and cocking the hay. Pity the poets, that the charms of haying and reaping are gone from our landscape! The compensations scarcely atone in improved implements for the poetry and pleasure which these occupations once promoted. But the march of invention is a gain to humanity at large, and we accept these improvements. Liberating hands for higher labors indicates the march of civilization, and gives the head to thought and improvement of manners.

July 18

Emerson calls on Harris, and we have conversation for the moment, sitting in my arbor on the hilltop. — We are at his library in the evening and have further discourse on the Hegelian thesis of Being. Emerson's categories are those of the imagination, not of pure reason. The Hegelian logic is strange and unintelligible to him, as it is to myself; but I see what marvels it performs in the hands of a master like Harris, and owe it a deep respect.

July 19

I ride to Concord with Emerson. He tells me that his *Parnassus* will make a big book like Dana's and Longfellow's. He praises Wasson's Sonnets, which I first brought to his notice when they appeared in *The Radical*. Hereby this anecdote:

Writing to Wasson at the time and praising the sonnets, saying they reminded me more of Shakespeare's than any modern sonnets, Channing (Ellery), on reading my note, cooly advised me to "burn it," and I in return commanded him to "find the door forthwith" — which he did, and did not enter my house afterwards for two years or more, and then reappeared to pay his respects to my wife, which he has followed up till the present, usually taking tea with us once a week, and addressing himself chiefly to the women-folk, seldom coming into my study as before. Whim, thy name is Channing.

July 25

Last night I dreamed of walking with Dr. Channing,[1] and as we descended the hill, I asked him what interested him now; to which he replied that the signs of the times seemed auspicious for furthering spiritual illumination and culture, and he had been wishing a school of Divinity were established, especially for bright young men and women, remarking that New England thought had led now for a quarter of a century, and it was time it began to

[1] Dr. William Ellery Channing, who at the time of this dream had been dead almost thirty years. Psychologically considered, the dream may have been Alcott's self-justification for his early disagreements with a man whom he deeply respected. Compare the entries for Week viii, ix, and x, 1837.

organize and cherish itself in this its highest form for the enlightenment and discipline of its preachers and teachers. He asked me
what I thought of it.

I said, "You anticipate a design of mine, which seems fitting to
round off my days here," (as I observed that he looked old and
somewhat infirm) — "the drawing together here at my house
during the summer months, if not the year round, such bright
youths of both sexes as would enjoy communion of thought and
sympathy of purpose with the advanced thinkers of our time, meeting them at proper intervals for conversation and study of the great
masters of the past. I remember how ardent was my drawing
toward some such supposed ideal friend, and how I was led provi-
dentially to visit my brother May at Brooklyn, and through him
was introduced to Boston as teacher of the Salem Street Infant
School, and presently made *his* acquaintance, much to my delight,
he more than any mind at that time answering to my ideal."

The doctor seemed surprised at this personal turn of remark,
and added that my design seemed opportune and very desirable,
if it could be carried out in practice. He hoped Boston and Cambridge might by this time have wiped the theological dust from
their eyes, and were ready to smile on my adventure, if not adopt
the suggestion, so far at least as to invite myself and others whom
he discovered were in sympathy with the association of young
students, to professorships in the Harvard School of Divinity. Why
a separate establishment?

I said, perceiving the Doctor still clung to his city and de-
nomination, at least practically and socially: "The young students
look elsewhere for what they seek. They, indeed, have quoted
us in their graduating essays, read our books in preference to
most others, and the late graduating class propose to visit Emerson and myself tomorrow for the very conversation about which
I was speaking. They say there is something in the atmosphere
of Cambridge, classic as are its shades, that paralyses and ob-
scures, and that Concord somehow seems delightfully classical,
as if the Academy, the Lyceum, were transplanted from Athens,
and the Orchard overshadowed the new School of Divinity."

Here the colloquy came suddenly to a close, by my wife appearing bearing a pail of water in each hand, tugging them up the

lane, leaving me to wonder where I was and why I was permitting her to do what belonged to me. — And on this hint, I awoke to find my Academium [*sic*] was all a dream and that the Orchard well was dry, the water having failed during these days of drought, and my Castalia was elsewhere. It is on the morning, however, when Harris is expected, and the discussion must clear up the mystery of the dream.

July 26

Read [to] Harris notices printed in the newspapers and journals of my *Conversations on the Gospels* when these appeared in 1836, with Emerson's criticism on my MS. "Psyche."

It seems incredible that such things should have been written on these views of children, and that the writers were but speaking the sentiment of Boston on my book.

Emerson's criticism on "Psyche" is a frank criticism of a friend on a friend's book, and at this long time afterwards appears kind and yet just. Fortunate for me that it came, and withheld the MS. from the press, though it disheartened me from taking my pen, for years afterwards, beyond my Diary. My style was vicious in the extreme. The introduction to the Conversations, which even he thought well of and praised at the time, is far from being natural, and offends me now. I shall not reprint it in a second edition, if the book comes to that. It was not until after the Fruitlands adventure that I came to the style which has won for me commendation from scholars, and from Emerson especially. The diction of *Tablets* comes nearest my notion of good writing, and charms me as I read — though I may not more than whisper this to my page as I write.

Of our best writing, I judge Emerson and Thoreau the great masters. After these, Lowell and Higginson. Weiss dazzles by exuberance of metaphor, though rich in thought. Wasson perhaps lacks fancy and inclines to measure in his prose, though his sonnets are the best written in his time. Bartol is terse and brilliant and comes nearer my type than the others named. Channing writes better lines of verse than any contemporary, if subtlety and exquisiteness of sense and melody are considered.

September 16

Walt Whitman sends proofs of his Poem lately recited before the American Institute, New York.[2]

It is characteristic of the man both in conception and execution. Even the spacious size and type of the printed document affect the metropolitan and continental. I am not sure, on reading, if the ponderous catalogue of productions celebrated in his lines does not impose upon the fancy, and question whether if the whole array were reduced to honest prose, the effect would not be lost.

November 11

Emerson is here trying his wits on Shakespeare's and provoking mine. But what can I tell him of Shakespeare? Who knows what he is, and why he was here to do what he did, if Emerson does not? He thinks him a miracle of intellect, and professes to have no clue to the secret of his genius. Jesus is an accountable fact in history; Shakespeare not.

December 15

Emerson comes to report his Western experiences. He has read in parlors and spoken in pulpits at Quincy and Dubuque, given a lecture in Chicago, and enjoyed his tour highly. . . .

Altogether, he seemed to confirm my favorable impression of the docility and strength of thought of the parties with whom he came into communication — and gave a hopeful account of the West. — Yes, and we here in New England begin to feel its thought and enterprize reacting on ours.

Westernize is a verb meaning *progress.*

[2] "Song of the Exposition," first recited September 7, 1871.

$\Longrightarrow$ **{1872}** $\Longleftarrow$

A MONG the events that interested Alcott during this year
were: the death of Thoreau's mother, the felling of timber
on the ministerial woodlot at Concord, the visits of Ellen Chan-
dler, the suggestion that Thoreau's Journals be published, and the
burning of Emerson's house. Early in September Alcott paid a
visit to Spindle Hill with Louisa, hoping that she might make
it the scene of a story. In the same month his Concord Days *was*
published. Emerson and his daughter sailed for Europe and Egypt
in October. A few days later Alcott set out on another Western
tour.

1872

January 18

I cannot resist the conviction, — a little humbling to New
England pride — that the West, in everything properly American as distinguished from English and the provincial spirit of the
East, is taking the lead, dispatching matters, whether of thought
or of practice, in the broader and more liberal method which our
century dictates.

Philosophy is published at St. Louis. Education finds there also
its most liberal advocates. The Western colleges favor a more

thoughtful culture than either Harvard or Yale, and divinity becomes the less sectarian and exclusive as one leaves sight of the Eastern cities. In business, the enterprize of the West is already conceded.

February 7

Hear Emerson's lecture on "Immortality," which he reads before our Lyceum. The supremacy of my friend's intelligence surprises me with every illustration of a public nature that I am fortunate enough to witness. Our people heard with eager interest, and what they did not apprehend clearly they were charmed into loving and admiring as something in itself lovely and charming. Could we have more preaching of this kind, our churches would stand for far more than they now do, and divinity have name and deserved repute. I could not but think our village preacher must have received some hints not only of a nobler doctrine but of a nobler method of address.

February 12

. . . The naturalist cannot urge the study of nature too strongly, nor pursue it too religiously as a ground of certainty in his sphere of observation, nor should the plea of the idealist be less vigorously urged for metaphysical researches on their proper grounds. Together, these exhaust the field of thought and of study, doing justice to the hemispherical forms in which truth is revealed in its whole to the mind.

March 30

Emerson has advertised Conversations on Literature to begin in April, the topics not named as yet. This is new with him, the method of Conversations, but becoming, and even more, his gifts, than lecturing.

June 12–13

I accompany Mrs. Adams[1] to the Unitarian Picnic at Walden Pond. See several of the young preachers, who express sympathy with the growing Idealism, and the hope of a spiritual Church.

[1] Mrs. Mary Adams of Dubuque, Iowa.

Mrs. Adams suggests that visitors to Walden shall bring a stone for Thoreau's monument and begins the pile by laying stones on the site of his hermitage, which I point out to her. The tribute thus rendered to our friend may, as the years pass, become a pile to his memory.[2] The rude stones were a monument more fitting than the costliest carving of the artist. Henry's fame is sure to brighten with years, and this spot be visited by admiring readers of his works.

July 24

Emerson's house is burned, but his library and MSS., furniture, goods, etc. are mostly saved unharmed.

It will be a trial to him, rooted as he has been to his familiar apartments during most of his married life and residence in Concord. Here I first visited him soon after making his acquaintance, October 1835. In these now charred drawing rooms and library I have met many friends, and not a few distinguished persons, since then.

Louisa and May bring home today some papers rescued from the attic, but mostly legible.

July 28

Emerson has taken his family (Mrs. E. and Ellen) to the Old Manse where they will abide while his house is being repaired. I walk there this afternoon, taking his father's "History of the First Church," and Rantoul's "19th April Oration," which are in a state for binding. He is not sure that he had copies of them in his library saved undamaged from the fire.

Fortunate that the Old Manse, built by his grandfather and afterwards occupied by Dr. Ripley, now opens its apartments for his reception. There he has passed portions of his life, at times — wrote his "Nature," and lines read at the dedication of the monument here, April 17, 1836:

> By the rude bridge that crossed [*sic*] the flood,
> Their flag to April's breeze unfurled,
> Here once the embattled farmers stood,
> And fired the shot heard round the world.

[2] The cairn thus begun has continued to grow from year to year.

We walk about the grounds, to the monument, and river. He takes me into the attic, still primitive, and with inscriptions of his father and others on its walls. The ancient spinning wheels there remind me of my mother's and sisters' wheels and spinning — they spinning and weaving home clothes for garments for our family.

I must have worn homespun garments till I reached the age of fourteen or fifteen, and later for working dress on the farm.

Mrs. Emerson and Ellen take me to the ruins on my return.

The repairs must cost considerably more than the insurance can cover. But his neighbors will contrive to make up the difference in some way that he can accept, giving him a better house than he had before.

August 25

Call on Emerson at the Manse. He has passed some days at Rye Beach and returns improved somewhat in spirits, though not restored to his usual condition. Thinks Sumner has made a mistake, and commends Phillips' letter. Says he wrote Sumner some time ago, urging him to hold himself high above all party considerations, and renounce, if he had entertained, any ambition for the Presidency.

Emerson has his prejudices, and is not a little influenced (in my judgment) by others' opinions, with the rest of us. I sometimes think him to err on the side of positiveness, and wish him more open to persuasion alike in religious as in political matters. I am, perhaps, more likely to err in the opposite direction.

August 30

Louisa hands me a chapter of her new story, to be entitled "The Cost of an Idea," [3] to read. It is her account of Fruitlands, in which herself, then a child, and her sisters, had their parts. It surprises one by the boldness and truthfulness of the strokes, and if other parts of her tale are told in this dramatic and sprightly way, her success in this, as in former efforts of the pen, is assured.

[3] This chapter was published as "Transcendental Wild Oats" in *Silver Pitchers*, 1876. "The Cost of an Idea," which was to have been a fictional account of Alcott's life as a whole, was never completed.

October 23   *Boston*

I call on Professor Tyndall at his rooms, and have a half-hour's interview. The Professor expresses his admiration for Emerson's genius, and his indebtedness to him alike for ideas and illustrations, his gratification at seeing him before he left for Europe yesterday, and at the Manse on Friday last at Concord.

I proposed my question of the temperamental colors for his investigation, with my hope that he will give us the law of complexions, voices, etc. He says despairingly, "Ah, no, you know not what labor and genius that demands!" Well, if not Tyndall, some idealist, which perhaps he is not, will take that task in hand and solve the problem.

I have but a moment to see the great man. He is sent for and takes his leave to prepare for his next lecture. But I am pleased to have seen him in private for this short time, and for the privilege of hearing and witnessing his brilliant lectures on light and heat.

November 16

I am not philosopher enough to know whether I am philosopher in the strictest sense of pursuing a methodical habit of thinking.

But if so competent a judge of method as Harris finds a logic in it, calls it "dialectic" or by any name known to philosophy, then I suppose I am entitled to the praise which he bestows on my thinking.

December 7   *Fort Dodge, Iowa*

If less culture here, there is not apparently less character. Many of the better educated and gifted come from New England schools and universities and have given tone and spirit to the population. For conversing I rather prefer a Western company before an Eastern. There appears a disposition to deal with things at first hand, a certain robust handling, rough perhaps but ready and respectful, that more than compensates for the daintier and more decorous book-training common to Eastern people.

RETURNING TO the East in February, Alcott found that his recent book, Concord Days, *had run nearly through the third printing. His effort to establish his friend Harris in the Department of Philosophy at Harvard was unsuccessful. Early in the spring the whole body of Thoreau's papers, filling three trunks, was put into his hands for preservation and administration. In the spring, also, his daughter May left home to study art in London. In the month of May Emerson's return from Europe to his new house was merrily celebrated by the whole town. For two weeks in June and for several days in November Alcott was in Wolcott, Connecticut, walking over all the territory he had known as a boy and observing the many changes that had taken place. Some anxiety was felt during the summer for Mrs. Alcott, whose mind was temporarily clouded. In December Alcott attended the funeral of Agassiz.*

1873

January 19   *Muscatine, Iowa*

Hear a poor discourse in the Methodist Church in the evening. Patience with the preaching almost everywhere! Vague, far from life, Biblical mostly, and sectarian. One wonders how the audiences can derive any intelligible ideas of their place in Creation or their human origin and destiny. But not always thus. Speak with thoughtful persons privately on religious matters and you find them taking, or disposed to take, deeper and better views of themselves and the world of matter and of mind.

Could I come disguised, or commended by the more liberal-minded in the several sects, I doubt not that my words, spoken in pulpits or private houses, would find general acceptance with sectarians even. Such, thus far, has been my experience — as ready acceptance, perhaps even more cordial, with orthodox than Unitarian or Free Religionist. What were the worth of preaching if it failed to bring people into sympathy and unity?

February 19   *Concord*

To Boston. See Niles. He tells me my *Concord Days* has gone to a third edition and the last nearly sold. It has been received with almost universal favor, and is a success in the "bookseller's sense," a book running to a third edition being likely to run to five in a year or two.

March 17

Longfellow[1] takes me to Cambridge and to dine with him. After dinner we call on his brother Henry, and find him in his study, glad to meet us. He said he had not been in Concord since Hawthorne's funeral, and showed us crayon heads by Joreston of Hawthorne, Emerson, and Sumner, drawn in 1846. He asked me to dine; but, having just dined with his brother, I declined.

After tea we call on Henry James, and spend the evening. James introduces the topic of the new anodyne, Euthanasia, and we are led into a lively discussion of life and Genesis. James seems too individual in his habit of thinking to comprehend universals. His method is negative and finite rather.

I sleep at Longfellow's. His sister, Miss Longfellow, a very charming hostess.

---

[1] Samuel Longfellow, 1819–1892, the clergyman, biographer, and hymn-writer, with whom Alcott was more closely acquainted than he was with the more famous elder brother.

March 18

We call on President Eliot. I commend Harris to him as a desirable person for a professor or lecturer on metaphysics, and give many facts of his history. He should be attached to the College, if not fixed here in Concord for our school.

March 21

Call on Miss Sophia Thoreau, Henry's only surviving sister. She is about disposing of the homestead, and to live with her friends in Maine. She wishes to commit to my keeping her brother's manuscript journals, charts, maps, a few letters, all contained in three trunks; and which in case of her decease are to become mine for such disposition as I may designate. The journals not to be public, nor copied for publication by anyone. Besides these, she gives me a bookcase constructed by him from driftwood, and a parcel of books.

April 4

P.M. Thoreau's journals, manuscripts and such books as his sister wishes to have in my care come to hand. They are sent in three trunks, the MSS. and the books, with a bookcase made by Thoreau himself. I am to hold them sacred from all but Thoreau's friends, allow none to take them away for perusal, subject to his sister's pleasure during her lifetime, and if I survive her, then they become mine for quotation or publishing. Many volumes may be compiled from them, and will be when his editor appears. I house them under lock and key safely in my attic. Along with the books are maps and surveys of local value.

April 6, 7

I look into Thoreau's books and find some valuable volumes. These especially: Wright's *Provincial Dictionary*, 2 vols., Bartlett's *Americanisms*, Loudon's *Encyclopædia of Plants*, Winthrop's *Journal*, Belknap's *American Biography*, Paley's *Works*, Locke's *Essays*, Stewart's *Philosophy*.[2]

[2] From among these books Alcott selected several for his own library, according to Thoreau's expressed wish. The dictionaries of Wright and Bartlett and Winthrop's Journal were so chosen.

There are volumes of manuscripts concerning the Indians, of literary character, from which several volumes of equal interest with those already compiled by himself and published may be compiled. The maps and surveys, of which there are —— are of local value. Also several letters which should be published in a second edition of the *Letters*.

April 25

May leaves by the early train for Boston, expecting to embark tomorrow in the tramp ship for Liverpool, and thence to London to study her art in the galleries and enjoy herself socially in the metropolis, returning perhaps in the Autumn.

We part with her with sadness, yet mingled with joy that she is going to her wonted haunts and congenial prospects abroad. She has earned her opportunity by faithful services at home. She spends the day and night with Louisa in Boston.

May 26

Again plant garden. The day is delightful, apple blossoms beginning to appear. Having been carefully pruned, my orchard should be productive of the seasons' favors.

Leave for Emerson a copy of *Concord Days*, bound in flexible covers, with illustrated title page, and photograph . . . a gift on his 70th Birthday. (Yesterday.)

Evening: Sanborn is here and informs me that Emerson arrived in the *Olympus* this morning, and will be here tomorrow at 12 M. The arrangements are all made, handbills posted, and the bells are to be rung announcing his coming.

The suggestions of presenting a study chair, a copy of Shakespeare, bookshelves, have been surrendered, as also an invitation to address his townsmen in the Town Hall. The latter is to be left to his option. We think we show the greater delicacy in conducting him to his gate and quietly retiring, leaving him to his family.

May 27

The village bells announce Emerson's coming by the 12 train. Then comes a telegram, that he will arrive here at 3:30 P.M.

The procession in carriages and on foot await him at the Station. Mr. Hudson receives and conducts him to the barouche. Sanborn conducts Ellen, and Mrs. Forbes and family take their seats in a second carriage.

Mr. and Mrs. Sanborn, Louisa and myself, take our places in the procession of carriages following the Concord band, Judge Hoar, Mr. Reynolds, Mrs. Hoar beside us, and other carriages abreast behind. Then Emerson and Ellen, Will. Forbes, in their open barouche, the schoolchildren and footmen in the rear. — All march down Main Street and Lexington, to the triumphal arch over the street by his gate. He passes through between rows of children singing "Home Sweet Home" and other melodies. After alighting and meeting his family within, he reappears at his gate, and thanks his neighbors for "this trick of sympathy to catch an old gentleman returned from his wanderings, being unmistakeably the old blood surviving to compliment him." The whole company then give him three hearty cheers and retire, leaving him to the privacy of his home. Thus the whole village honor their returned townsman, and it is good to see the enthusiasm illuminating their faces as they look and shout lustily at his gate.

'Tis a charming spectacle. Whatever doubts any may have had respecting its agreeableness to him, were instantly dissipated by the hearty response and cheer with which he returned this expression of his townsmen's regards. It was a surprise to him. "What meant this gathering? Was it a public day?" Ellen could not contain her joy at the compliment thus shown to her father. Standing in her carriage she smiled thanks all round to the friends waving their handkerchiefs, all happy to catch a glance from her eye. Both seemed in fine health, browned by travel, and in the familiar spot again. The prettiest sight was at the gate, the children singing as the open barouche passed under the arch, ornamented with laurels running up the columns, and the word "Welcome" surmounting it. I did not hear his speech distinctly, but trust someone gifted with a faithful memory will preserve it.

It is a novelty in the history of this our historic revolutionary village, this honoring scholars publicly. It stirs the latent patriotism which has slumbered unfelt perhaps in the old citizens, descendants of the patriots of 19th of April, and now rekindled at the fame of their townsman.

We are not given to sensational demonstrations — pride ourselves rather on the still currents, like the flowing of our river — but occasions like this make good the old renown. Much honored abroad, especially in England, the guest of Carlyle, Tennyson, Max Müller, Lord and Lady Amberly, and other noble, distinguished people, he returns to receive this spontaneous testimonial of respect and affection from his townsfolk, old and young. And his family are all present in his restored house to fill the cup of his satisfaction.

I repeat, nothing could be more appropriate, more delightful — the brilliant May day, blossom-freighted, the procession, the music, the flowery arch, the manners of the man, — a bright day in his, and the memories of his friends and admiring neighbors.

May 29

This morning call on Emerson. He returns with improved health and happy memories of places and persons visited. Carlyle, he says, still plays his old game of satire on men and things generally, for which he has a remarkable gift, appears young while professing to age. He met Max Müller also and speaks of him as an agreeable man, less German than he expected, with an English wife and pleasant children. Browning, Lord and Lady Amberly, Arthur Helps, Leckey, Froude, besides several distinguished persons. Speaking of Englishmen, he remarked that, contrary to his former impression, the cultivated classes spoke better English than cultivated Americans; and their manners were more refined. England was full of scholars and gentlemen and women.

June 5

In Washington Street I meet the poet Whittier and exchange compliments hastily, he saying, "Everybody likes your *Concord Days*. Put Emerson's reception by his friends into your next Days." It was heartily spoken.

A certain courtesy, I think, is due from contemporary authors to one another respecting their works. I readily excuse silence, where one cannot praise, only blame, another. But praise is always in fine keeping with friendship, as with the courtesy due from one man of letters to another. That code which carefully abstains from speaking to an author about his book, from a mistaken delicacy, appears to me wanting in real sympathy and refinement of courtesy; and to the extent in which it is practiced, vitiates the truest literary fellowship. Even where authors move in different walks of thought, the haughty manner that disdains to recognize humble merit, is, of all things, unworthy of the true scholar and the gentleman.

June 9

Under Louisa's supervision our housekeeping for the last fortnight has sped quietly and tidily. And it is gratifying to find that she has lost nothing of her practical cunning while engaged in writing stories for the million.

Today comes a housekeeper to relieve her of household cares, and give her days to writing again if she choose. Surely that is practical power which can turn hands and heart to practical matters, serving others and herself. Her practice bears out and complements her theories of *Work*[3] beautifully.

June 13   *Waterbury, Conn.*

P.M. Mrs. Bassett drives me to Wolcott by way of Gaylord Alcott's, whose grandmother, my cousin Riley Alcott's wife, gives me the veritable copy of *Pilgrim's Progress* borrowed so frequently when a boy and reluctantly returned after faithful perusal, to the committing of its dramatic parts to memory, and often playing them off as pastime. How hearty were my thanks to have it in hand at the age of 73, and bring it away as mine! I owe more to it than any book in existence. How glad then on opening it at noon spells, or rainy days, and dwell delightedly on its pictures of the pilgrim's progress to the celestial city![4]

June 15   *Wolcott, Connecticut*

Ride to Church on the "Hill" with James and cousin Selina. Mr. Orcutt gives a thoughtful discourse, partly extemporaneous, less of the old type than I usually hear from country preachers. His audience is very small. I recognize hardly a dozen

[3] The title of Louisa's most recent book.
[4] The book is still in Alcott's library at Concord.

of my age and time, and these age and toil have rendered infirm; the younger less sprightly and promising than I was accustomed to meet when I attended here in my youth. *Then,* the house, much larger than this, was crowded. Every pew below, the galleries above, showed numerous heads, old and young, and when the congregation poured out of the house at noon, or after services, the green swarmed with the attendants. Sunday was a great day in those times. Every family was out in its best attire — homespun chiefly, but something to be proud of nevertheless; and old and young were put upon their best manners as well. Primly all sat in their seats, listened to the services — the younger expected to remember the preacher's subject and repeat his text on returning home, to find it in their Bibles, and keep Sabba' day "till sundown" devoutly. Very primitive too was the custom of taking sprigs of fennel, caraway, and dill, to eat in "meeting time." The "tithing man" always seated in the galleries to see that mischief was not astir there among the young folks, the fennel and dill passing compliments of a kind not always warranted by true devotion. It is true that I caught sight of the dill today in the hand of a venerable lady whom I knew when much younger, but this and the tithing man appear to be nearly obsolete now, along with the habits of that earlier day. Then the elders had the front seats, age being the only distinction in the seating. I believe this custom still prevails here. That of walking with shoes and stockings to be changed at some private place on the road and appearing with clean outfit in meeting, appears to have no adherents now.

The primitive Meeting House, built at the organization of the Church in 1773, was burnt some years ago. A smaller one now occupies the place. That was without steeple or bell in my day. It was a plain two-storied edifice with galleries all around the sides and end, pews below and above, the singers' seats ranging the whole front, and the fashionable sounding board above the elevated pulpit, with the deacons' seats below, the minister having his nail for hanging his hat just over the deacons' heads. Venerable man he was, and greatly feared by the youngsters, reverenced by the elders of the congregation, his prayers neverending, like his sermons; his text twice repeated at the opening, and again at every head following of his discourse, to the "twenty-fifthly" and the "application" after that. The choir, too, had its chorister and pitchpipe. "Old Hundred" I hear, "Coronation — " tunes that country voices found difficulty in performing, the pitch oftentimes to be given anew.

How picturesque were the roads with the congregation returning in all devotion down the hillsides homewards, afoot mostly, on summer days, with coats on their arms, in shirt sleeves, the women with fan and handkerchief in hand, — when fairly along changing their Sunday shoes for every-day ones. Upon reaching home, exchanging Sunday clothes for work-day garments, to take an early afternoon meal mostly prepared on Saturday. Then the Bible and Catechism, the children finding the text, and reciting their Catechism — all play forbidden till after sundown. Yet Sunday evening for the young men and maidens was the most attractive hour for courtship; nor was this frowned down by the old folks, who found it convenient to retire in good season, leaving the house wholly to the young folks and hours uncounted.

August 3, 4 .*Concord*

I am favored with an early perusal of Channing's *Thoreau: the Poet-Naturalist, with Memorial Verses*, pp. 357.

The publishers, Roberts Brothers, only await the favorable time for issuing the work.

Perhaps few now living stand in as intimate relations to the author as my wife. Previous to her present illness, her table was spread for him twice at least every week, and her afternoon and evening given to him unreservedly. As he takes but two meals daily, the last meal is most important to him, and his company is, for the most part, agreeable alike to her and myself. Since Thoreau's decease, he has been at my house more frequently than before. And of all Thoreau's contemporaries he has the best right, as well by kindred tastes and pursuits as by intimate companionship, to draw his portrait.

Reading portions to my wife, we are struck with its exceeding picturesqueness and literary faithfulness. The book must surprise its readers. It is the tribute of a poet and a friend to poet and friend. Neighbor of his and a daily companion for many years within doors and without, he has caught his marked peculiarities of genius and speech, drawn a sketch which his friends will accept as lifelike and admirable. Fortunate for Thoreau as for his readers, this new presentation will make him better known far and wide.

August 9

Have a letter from Mrs. Adams of Dubuque, advocating in her Sybilline manner the importance of Conversations and Clubs as organs of educating the people; far more facile and available, as well as potent, than Church or State instrumentalities. She deemed these missionary tours of mine the opening of new institutions, and to precede our "Concord Academy."

"You know," she writes, "I have perfect faith in the ultimate establishment of your university. But, my dear Mr. Alcott, it will plant and develop itself far better than anything we can imagine for it. Will a 'Pilgrim Philosopher' establish a stationary Academy? The beauty and significance of Jesus' life and teachings were destroyed by St. Paul establishing it as a scheme of redemption in places, giving into charge of Bishops, writing the Law, having a 'Head Centre' at Rome. Wherever two or three are met together to exchange thought, commune with Spirit, seeking the conditions for light, there is a branch of your university. Like Heaven, it is not by time nor space. God alone can examine candidates for your freshman class. Divest the ideal of your university of time and space with these limitations. Where two or three are gathered to converse, there you will ever be. We cannot bodily go to Concord, Mass. When we secure the right conditions you are with us always. Whoever establishes a club room, a pillared portico (secluded, yet with a promenade passing it), plants a grove near, with the library and gallery in the centre, has established the conditions for the higher education. *That is all money can do.* I shall work untiringly to establish clubs for Conversation with libraries attached. I will leave the rest to Spirit."

August 10–11

We are having almost autumnal days, cool nights and mornings, with golden sunlight tinting field and wood. The landscape before my door is charming: the new-mown meadows fringed with woodlands, the willows gracefully adorning the lane, and the farm-houses showing their white coloring across the brook.

Such rural scenery deserves description by scholarly pens. A Thoreau, a Channing, best know how to do it justice. And no spot in New England, none possibly in our country, has had justice done it like Concord and its surroundings. The rural Muse has walked these fields and woods, along these streams, mounted our hills, and sung the over-hanging skies, the manners and habits of our persons, and caught their features in every variety of mood, fixed these in books which must live as long as letters delight and Nature charms her lovers. If Hawthorne and Emerson, familiar with these scenes, have not intimated their presence in their pages, their readers have the inspiration, and the Concord type is impressed indelibly on all their writings.

Would that I too might prove myself not insensible to their charms! Might they color and fashion my thoughts, and prove that I too am favored to belong to those to whom the rural Muse has vouchsafed some portion of her favors. Had Homer, had Goethe, better promptings from nature than our landscape affords? . . . Only the genius to feel and wit to fashion forth the sense is wanting, and of this our little village has not less than many surrounding cities.

To one of an ethical turn like myself the landscape has special attractions. One likes to climb for his satisfactions. . . . By taking a few steps I mount my hill-top, pine-covered, and oversee Mill Brook in all its windings along the meadows from Merriam's Corner to Emerson's house — Hawthorne's only hidden by the shrubbery on his hill.

Few houses in our town are so shielded and favored with forest trees . . . and the elms in my yard have the reputation of being primeval. They become the house itself, and the grounds from which they rear their trunks to overshadow the mansion. An owl haunts one of them. It may symbolize the mystic wisdom of the occupant — the twilight lore of the bird of the night — though the squirrel also finds his haunt therein to symbolize in turn the sprightly wit of the tenant of the chambers.[5] For what

[5] Louisa.

were a house without the significance of sun and shade, motion and rest?

August 22

. . . Yesterday Emerson accompanied me home from the Post Office to take Hamerton's *Intellectual Life* to peruse, attracted perhaps by the title chiefly, and being still a stranger to Hamerton's genius and writings. He ought — if I may say so — to like the author. But his canon of criticism is so severe that I can hardly hope as much. He complains of Channing's *Thoreau,* though conceding the originality and genius of the compiler, while impatient of his want of discrimination.

I tell him we should have nothing if not this, with all its deficiencies, and can afford to be content with a tribute so hearty and affecting. It is not often that so much of the privacy of genius finds its way into literature. The work is compiled in the fashion of the old scholars. Sayings and doings, the geography and daily life, are dealt out to the reader, and he feels himself in the presence and home of the subject.

August 24

Leigh Hunt is one of the most enlightened and liberal-minded of modern scholars, hospitable to all persuasions and schools of thought yet belonging to none; or, more properly speaking, so inclusive and embracing as to include the common ideas upon which all are founded — and was therefore a true member of the Church Catholic and Universal.[6]

October 28

Evening, take tea with Emerson and renew the pleasures of our early fellowship in a free and affectionate conversation, returning at near 11. Such interviews revive past delights and prefigure future ones. Of human fellowships this, opening at a fair period of our lives and continued by a choice husbanding of senti-

---

[6] In Leigh Hunt Alcott seems to have recognized a certain intellectual likeness to himself. Similarities of another sort were suggested by the unsympathetic persons who, after the appearance of *Bleak House* in 1852, occasionally called him "Skimpole."

ment, meeting only when fellowship was spontaneous and for the most part a surprise to both, is an experience to cherish in the memory and possession forever. Rhetoric fails to celebrate it. Better cherish as a sweet and silent joy, diffusing itself over the countenance and telling better than words can speak its own preciousness. If religion be other than Personal and one with the purest friendship, I must affirm that it is yet a stranger in my breast and I am without a God to love, reverence, and experience. "When shall we meet again? Where?"—are questions religion never puts to the heart, since friends divinely related never know separation.

October 29

Evening . . . I have thought it might fall to Sanborn, when events may call for it, to write my biography, and remember that, some years since, I intimated the like and made a minute to that effect in my Diary at the time. The other evening Emerson intimated his intention of doing the same, since none but himself, he said, could do it fit justice.[7]

Yes, Emerson for the ideas, and Sanborn for the facts. But one must ascend for one friend or other to tell the whole story fully.

December 18

To Cambridge, and attend the funeral of Prof. Agassiz, who died last Sunday. The funeral is as private as possible. Dr. Peabody reads the King's Chapel Burial Service, and there is appropriate music. Appleton Chapel is filled with a congregation of friends of the deceased from the city and surrounding towns — distinguished persons in the various professions, scholars, and many women. By favor, I find a seat between the Emersons, Ralph and George B., and am able to hear the reading distinctly.

Agassiz was perhaps the most distinguished citizen, and his loss the greatest the country suffers. I saw him last, and took his hand, at our Concord Cattle Show, last October.

---

[7] According to F. B. Sanborn, Emerson kept for years a special notebook of memoranda for the biography of Alcott he expected to write after his friend's death.

December 25

. . . And Louisa, in her story, makes the best of her materials. Here follows her extravaganza.

"Transcendental Wild Oats."
by Louisa M. Alcott.

*   *   *

Very few modern readers will readily place themselves in the ideal position to apprehend the high moral which animated and gave body to this social adventure.[8] I did not find the ready response even at the Radical Club which the experience of some present led me to expect. From the extreme Individualists I could not, of course, count upon their acceptance of results so fatal to their notions of self-sovereignty.

We shall hardly have any like experiment attempted within my time by any enthusiastic extremist, and it needs some time to pass to set this endeavor in its true light.

[8] As a matter of fact, Louisa's rather frivolous account of Fruitlands gives little suggestion of the social and philosophic ideas that actuated the experiment.

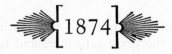

A YEAR *of earnest thought, eager talk, and wide journeying. The gradual failure of Emerson's powers had become apparent even to Alcott, but he himself showed little sign of age. His former interests remained, and new ones were added, chiefly by sympathetic sharing in the lives of younger persons such as his grandchildren, his daughters, Ellen Chandler, F. B. Sanborn, and W. T. Harris. A teacher and father still, and still an inveterate "hoper," Alcott looked forward out of a time already prosperous and happy toward yet better things to come. His one chief hope, for the Concord School of Philosophy, moved a little nearer to realization.*

Alcott's religious thought tended steadily in the direction of "orthodoxy." By a route less theological than metaphysical, he approached the "Trinitarian" point of view. W. T. Harris, who regarded Alcott as his intellectual father and yet had a deepening influence upon him, instilled in the elder man an ever greater respect for systematic thinking. This freed Alcott from his Transcendental moorings and increased his philosophical independence of Emerson.

In October Alcott started Westward on a more extensive tour than he had yet undertaken. His Journal for the rest of the year records chiefly his movements from place to place.

1874

January 5

Method is everything, in reform as in teaching in the schools; and for this reason the great reformers and teachers of the past have been practical if not theoretical methodists. Pythagoras, Plato (whose method was Socrates' idealized), Aristotle — all taught methodically, and disciplined the minds of their pupils in dialectic and logic, as the crown of their efforts. Jesus and Paul had their methods, the schoolmen theirs. We moderns are deficient in method, and, so-far, powerless. We need practical skill and discernment, the studying of the ancient dialectic, or the art of accosting the mind by a knowledge of its laws of thought and volition. We teach only by obeying the mind's processes. To prompt thought by thinking in accordance with its own laws — in this lies the art of teaching. To think with, and not against, is the master's art and method. Short of this is vain jangle and logomachy. . . .

The true logic, the ideal dialectic, walks abreast of the mind as a friend and prompter, a guide, not as an antagonist. . . . "He that is not against us is for us" [1] said Jesus to the sons of disputatious temper, herein declaring the persuasive law and divine method of influence. . . . I have never seen any attempt to set forth the method of Jesus by stating its grounds or by comparison with other methods. Its power is apparent in his treatment of multitudes, or dealings with persons singly. How salient and how subtle, undermining the premise of his antagonist's assertion at a stroke, convicting if not convincing him out of his own mouth! It was the intuitive method, the dialectic of the Spirit. He spake thus effectively because he obeyed the laws of thought, "knowing what was in man" by intuition, not by "letters." [2]

[1] The record of this remark in the Gospels is radically different: "He that is not with me is against me" (*Matthew* XII, 30, and *Luke* XI, 23). Alcott's misquotation — which may fairly be said to be more Christian than the original — is highly characteristic of all his later thought about teaching and reform.

[2] Alcott's increasing realization that his own and Emerson's thought was deficient in "dialectic" was probably due to the influence of W. T. Harris and the St. Louis group of philosophers. But here he comes round to a justification

January 10

We are, with slight deviations, copies of our ancestors. Family traits descend from generation to generation, over-riding climate, callings, intermarriages, culture. I am not yet persuaded of the truth claimed by certain theorists that types become intermingled and by circumstances blotted out. Rather it appears that, like ideas, their types are permanent and persistent, superior to outward accidents or physical conditions. Souls are typical, and mould bodies into forms corresponding. The types may vary, but never extinguish themselves. And the time approaches when persons will be classified by their spiritual characteristics as we now define their complexions, their voices, physiognomies.

February 9 *Boston*

Walking with Sanborn this forenoon, we met Louis Hayden [3] near the State House (he is now messenger of the General Court) and I asked him to relate the particulars of what he saw of my part in the attempted rescue of Sims [4] in Court Square.

He says that he saw me come up the Square from Court Street, approach the western door, pause there a moment and survey the beam of timber that had been used for breaking through the door, then ascend the steps and enter, glance up the stairway leading to the room above where Sims was confined, then retreat slowly and cross the Square and accost Higginson, who was standing aloof and alone at a little distance from the door. He did not hear what passed between us. The crowd then rushing up the Square from the Faneuil Hall meeting and the city police marching in directly after it, he lost sight of me. Bachelder, he says, had been shot only a few minutes, and on the spot where I had stood at the foot of the stairs. I was the first to enter inside the courthouse door, and had I been a few moments earlier might have been shot also,

of his own method on the ground that, like the method of Jesus, it has been "intuitive" and has followed the logic of the heart if not that of the head. With this conclusion Harris certainly agreed, if indeed he did not actually suggest it.

[3] Lewis Hayden, a negro, had been a prominent agitator against the Fugitive Slave Law.

[4] Really Anthony Burns. Alcott's memory, usually exact in such matters, has confused the two cases, in which he took at the time an equal interest. See the entry for May 26, 1854.

as the bullets had been flying over the balusters down to the entry, and into it from the assailants outside.

He does not tell me about his part in this assault, nor that of his colleagues, though it has been rumored that he shot Bachelder and possibly wounded Higginson in the melée at the door. Nor have I spoken with Higginson about the matter since the event. On accosting him at the time in the Square, I said "Why are we not inside instead of being here?" And he replied, "Because there are none here to accompany us!" — and we separated, the police appearing and the crowd dispersing as the former marched round the Court House.

I had an obscure instinct stirring within me that to die was about the best use that could be made of a freeman at that crisis, and felt that the wrong man had fallen on the wrong side. Had the victim been one of us, the sad fortunes of that day and of the country afterwards might have been less disastrous. It seemed the moment for a sacrifice to be laid on the altar for the rights of freemen and the salvation of the Republic. And I felt, I remember, ashamed to return, erect and breathing, to my house, as I had left it. Moreover, I restrained myself with difficulty from rushing into the phalanx as it marched its prisoner down State Street, hoping thus to provoke a movement that might set the indignant citizens, standing on the pavements and watching the spectacle, upon the bayonetted platoons, and rescue the slave from being returned to his doom. An innocent victim or two then falling might have spared the bloodshed and woes that followed.

But the nobler deed was reserved for the nobler victim, the hero of Harper's Ferry, and, the sacrifice completed, the slave and the Republic were freed. But our city would gladly blot from its annals the degradation and disgrace of that doleful day.

February 23

After dinner attend Canon Kingsley's lecture on The First Discoveries of America. Redpath asks me to introduce the speaker to the audience, but I decline. It were more becoming for a person better known to Bostonians than I am.

I am given a seat near the speaker, and listen with interest to his lecture. His account of the Norsemen suggests striking traits in Henry Thoreau's character and bearing, confirming his descent from that stalwart race. Kingsley should become acquainted with Thoreau's writings, if he have not already found them. Plainly, he has strong sympathy with the persons he describes.

February 24

Louisa and I call on Canon Kingsley at Parker House. He meets us cordially and speaks with interest of Louisa's works, which are much prized, he says, by his daughter, who regrets having an engagement in Cambridge but wishes to meet Louisa before she returns to England. Mr. Kingsley wishes to visit Concord, and will gladly pay us a visit on his return from California in April.

On my naming Bishop Alcock as one of the architects concerned in building Henry VII's Chapel, he invites us to find him at Westminster Abbey when we visit London, and view that miracle of art and mausoleum of the great and good in English history.[5]

Speaking of the name now spelt "Alcott" in this country, he says it retains the ancient spelling in the Old Country, that it is Norse, and that he has family relatives of the name. The family is of Sussex, and highly respectable.

February 28   *Concord*

Hallowell sends me a cheque for thirty dollars for my Horticultural Hall lecture in the Sunday Course. It comes quite unexpected, as I had not bargained for any other remuneration than the opportunity of speaking. Coin comes so seldom into my palm that I have long esteemed it almost superfluous . . . because mine by providential distribution alone. And here in New England services like mine seem to be less valued than at the West.

April 6

Attend a Town Meeting. New streets are proposed and named. Of these, a street leading from the Fitchburg Station to Brister's

---

[5] Charles Kingsley had been appointed Canon of Westminster only a year before he met Alcott. Less than a year after that meeting he died.

For Alcott's earlier feeling about Westminster Abbey see his Journal-entry for July 4, 1842.

Hill, intersecting the Walden Street, is to be named Thoreau Street — a compliment of his townsmen associating him henceforth with the village and his route across the fields, when living, to Walden Pond. — It was proposed to name it "Emerson Street," but Emerson modestly deferred the honor and proposed bestowing it upon Thoreau. I said: "We would not name one street Emerson, but all in the village, were this possible, to signify our respect for our fellow-townsman." Himself and Thoreau have given it a celebrity abroad that no other town of like population enjoys, its Revolutionary fame being almost eclipsed by their literary renown.

April 9

HARVARD COLLEGE LIBRARY

I am always overmastered by the presence of a venerable library, and set to thinking whether access to such when a boy would have furthered my progress in learning and wisdom. I feel at home in such retreats and about college grounds, assuming quite naturally a certain inborn title to their honors and advantages. Possibly the knowledge, too, that here trod ancestors of my name, and received their degrees, may have some secret influence.[6] . . . Yale College in like manner affects me when I visit it, more than one of my mother's kindred and name having shared its privileges and honors. An early acquaintance with scholars and the study of languages would doubtless have been a facility in after life. In defect of this I have striven to master the best thoughts of the best authors in my mother tongue, and the mastery of that also.

April 26

One's Diary includes how many incidents and particulars interesting to himself only! And of these he cannot determine the significance at the time of writing. It must be a rich and stirring life that yields something daily worth recording. . . . I am well aware of the sterility and inconsequence of mine, as of the in-

---

[6] The oldest Harvard diploma known to be in existence is one granted in 1676 to George Alcock, of Bronson Alcott's paternal line.

significance of the report. It shames me that long practice has not taught me the art of portraying myself and surroundings. Sixty years at least should have given me the master's pen. Beginning to write at ten years of age, and to think a little, I should have more to show for all my painstakings.

Today I read Shakespeare's *Coriolanus* — and who shall hope for success with his pen or thought after such consummate strokes of the great master's? One feels his best record is insignificant — a born blot, and no more.

April 29

Art has to do with the beautiful alone — beauty in nature and beauty in mind. It is not mere imitation, but creation. It is nature completed. It is mind in its becomings, and, in that sense, mind complementing itself and its ideals.

May 7

It is a wise Providence, doubtless, that withholds from me an abundance of gold and silver, since I should be tempted, I am certain, to spend it lavishly, and foolishly perhaps, in ornamenting and beautifying ampler grounds and structures than I can expect under present favors to possess. My little has sufficed to give me much satisfaction, and I have made the most of it alike for gratifying eye and hand, for comfort and employment. Home is handsomer to me than had it been wrought out artificially by others' ideas and handiwork.

May 8

Brooks sends me a ticket to Emerson's lecture to be read at the invitation of the divinity students on Tuesday evening next at Divinity Hall, Cambridge.

Since meeting the students at my Conversations at their rooms in 1853, I believe Emerson has not been invited to the Hall. His address delivered before the Senior Class in Divinity Hall Sunday evening, July 15, 1838, sounded the note of the New Divinity which these students now find in the ascendant, which has modified in larger measure than is known to most the theology of the modern pulpit and the literature of our time. It was then deemed "the latest form of infidelity," [7] and the professors thought it right to warn the students and the community at large of its dangerous tendencies both by personal declamation and by the press. Unitarianism and Orthodox Trinitarianism have alike denounced, while being partly converted to, its statements.

May 17

The Person is the pre-supposition of all things and beings. Nothing were without this premise. I am because God is; nor am I found save by his Presence in my consciousness, and incarnation therefrom. From my soul spring forth my senses, reflecting itself in natural images. My body is my mind's idol. From the beginning I was, and survive all things beside myself. Personally immortal, time deals my periods and dates me by its revolutions. I am born and die daily.

> Would'st know thyself and all things see?
> Become thyself, and all things be.
>
> Now, now, thy knowing is too slow.
> Thought is the knowing in the now.
>
> Depose thyself if thou would'st be
> Drest in fresh suit of deity.
>
> Out of the chaos rose in sight
> One globe's fair form in living light.
>
> Were God not God, I were not I.
> Myself in him I must descry.

June 8

Miss Sophia Thoreau dines with us, having come from Bangor, Maine, where she resides, to visit her native town. She wishes to present her brother Henry's "Indian MSS.," with sundry books of his, to Concord Library. The Indian MSS. number a dozen volumes, and will be a valuable addition to the Library.[8] Henry's

[7] The title of an address by Andrews Norton in which the theological implications of Emerson's Divinity School Address were vigorously condemned.

[8] These manuscripts did not finally come into the possession of the Concord Public Library.

Diaries she thinks of committing to the care of Mr. Blake of Worcester, a friend and disciple of Thoreau's and a fitting person to edit selections from them. The Diaries are sure to be published entire sometime. We wait for the editor who shall undertake this labor from love of Thoreau and an appreciation of his admirable genius. The man may not yet be born suited to accomplish this task in a manner worthy of the author and his subjects,[9] but Thoreau's character and genius are to win increasing favor as the years pass, and he is an enduring factor in our literature and life. Witness the interest of my correspondent, Mr. Cook, of London, in his genius and works.

The "Diaries" are now at Sanborn's. His library — what has not been distributed — is in my garret. From this I am to select suitable volumes for the Concord Library.

June 28

Dine at Sanborn's with Charles Dudley Warner. Mr. Warner is literary editor of *The Hartford Courant* and a journalist of considerable celebrity as well as the popular author of some humorous books: *My Summer in a Garden, Saunterings in Foreign Lands,* etc. He seems a well-informed and liberal-minded man, interested in modern life and ideas, and exerting a good influence on the taste and thought of Hartford and the State generally.

The Hartford Courant is a newspaper of ancient celebrity, and has always maintained its good repute throughout the State. It was among the earliest newspapers that came into Wolcott while I was a boy of 12 years of age, being then brought by a post-rider once a week from Hartford, and left at the doors of our neighbours on Spindle Hill. This, with *The Columbian Register,* published at New Haven, were the first newspapers that I had the pleasure of seeing and reading. It was our custom to interchange these, the neighbours subscribing and the papers passing from family to family for perusal in turn. Being war-time, we boys read with eager curiosity the news concerning the battles, Indian skirmishes, etc.

After dinner we ride to Walden and bathe. It is a luxury to

---

[9] Bradford Torrey, whose complete edition of Thoreau's Journal appeared in 1906, was already thirty-one when Alcott wrote this entry.

bathe in this classic lake. I had not done so for several years, and last with Emerson. After bathing we contribute severally our stone to Thoreau's cairn. The pyramid is insignificant as yet; but could Thoreau's readers add theirs the pile would rise above the treetops to mark the site of his hermitage. The shrubbery is now grown above the cellar, yet its traces are still visible and the path to the lake bears the marks of frequent footsteps. I recall with pleasure the hours spent within his hut, with the hopes and projects of that romantic period in our literature and social history.

July 13

. . . The suggestion may have weight that Thoreau, being of Scandinavian origin — or, properly, Teutonic, rather — finds a ready acceptance with the freer and less traditional minds of our time. . . . And it seems a happy circumstance that he should have been a native of Concord, born near the battle-field of the War of Independence, and the companion of some of the first and wisest of New England scholars. His friends and neighbors, these, representing a school of thought more purely American than any heretofore, to which his own life and works added some of its richest productions.

July 14

. . . Plants are found to owe their health and growth to the sun, to be affected by the absence of light; and we may reasonably infer that animals and men are not less influenced, this influence being modified measurably by sensibility and thought upon their instincts. Even sleep, though possible in the light, appears to be lunar chiefly, and affiliated with light as reflected from the sun — the reflex of the day's experiences, dreaming being lunar or semi-solar. Plants too have the like, but instinctively. And somnambulism and clairvoyance appear to have a similar origin.

I have observed the like law affecting the temperaments and dispositions of men and animals, the lighter — that is, the sunnier — being of a more wakeful and sprightlier genius than those of the darker complexions; the latter being drugged more deeply with the sluggishness of melancholy though oftentimes awakening by contrast of moods to a preternatural brilliancy, but fitful and passionate. I know not if the minerals are not subject to the influence of color.

The more of sun, of the solar beam, mingled in the atoms of bodies, the sprightlier the possibilities and quicker the thoughts, thus discriminating genius from talent or secondary intelligence, and the scale of proportions traversing from fair to the darkest hues: children of the light, sons of the morning; offspring of the darkness, descendents of night — of solar or lunar temperaments. Of course the extremes include the intermediate lights and shades. And figure and voice are embraced also. Light is the symbol of intelligence in all tongues, and darkness of ignorance not less.[10]

July 15   *Boston*

Find at Burham's a copy of Locke's *Essay Concerning the Human Understanding.* It is of the same edition as one first read by me while peddling in Virginia, that having disappeared from my library during our numerous movements from place to place. I gladly bring it home with me. It is of the New York edition of 1818, published by the Harpers, and bears the marks of usage, as my copy would have done by this time. I pay fifty cents for it, and write my name on the title page as I wrote it at the date of my first reading, 1822 —

Amos B. Alcox.

Whatever may have been my views at my first perusal, and afterwards while teaching at Bristol and Cheshire, later studies led me far from Mr. Locke's sensationalism, to pure idealism.[11] I shall be curious to find how the author treated the subject of ideas and the Personality from his standpoint in the understanding and

[10] This meditation is a fair example of Alcott's wildly-guessing and vaguely-suggesting habit of mind, possible only to one who has preserved wide areas of ignorance and a certain gay and adventurous irresponsibility of thought. He has no notion of any check upon his conjectures other than an inner warmth of personal conviction. He shoots without aiming, and with a blunderbuss, into the thicket — and so, occasionally, brings down good game. Thus, the present adumbration is not out of harmony, to say the least, with the most recent researches in the photoperiodicity of plants and animals.

[11] Alcott's turn against the sensationalism of John Locke was in large part caused by his reading, in 1833 at Philadelphia, of Plato, Kant, Berkeley, and especially of Marsh's edition of Coleridge's *Aids to Reflection.*

the senses. The best representative mind of his nation, it is not surprising that his philosophy has held it fast till almost the present hour, and this against the idealism of Coleridge and Carlyle. Berkeley, an Irishman, found only ridicule, and the Scotch thinkers wrought mostly on the surfaces, ignorant of the depths of the Italian and Greek Idealists. Let us believe that America has something to add to the speculations of the latter.

September 13

An old author calls old age "The House of Forgetfulness." If old in years, I have not found this infirmity of memory creeping over me as yet, and am pained to learn that my friend Emerson confirms its truth too openly to be questioned. It must be mortifying to one of his accurate habits of thought and speech and his former tenacity of memory to find himself wanting in his once ready command of imagery to match his thought instantly. I remember when the least hesitancy in another was painful to him in the extreme, so facile was his genius, his rhetoric so fit and so brilliant.

It has seemed as if I should be first to fail. I do not yet find, however, any serious decline of faculties, and think myself as capable of work as at any period of my life. . . . Only within these last few years have I allowed myself to cherish any faith in my literary skill, and that I might yet write something that could not die. It may be a mere dream still. . . . I know of no ambition, next to that of being a good man, that inspires me like that of literary excellence.

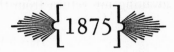

{1875}

ALCOTT RETURNED to Concord in April after six months in the West, having conversed in twenty-eight towns and cities. He found that he had been elected during his absence to honorary membership in the Harvard Chapter of the Phi Beta Kappa society. The celebration of the centenary of the Concord Fight, on the 19th of April, was to him an exciting affair, but his Western experiences tended to make the East seem rather tame. Anything in the nature of tedium was prevented, however, by a brief excursion to Providence, where Alcott had long had a group of influential friends, and by a highly successful series of fourteen Conversations in Concord itself.

1875

April 4   *Concord*

. . . I question whether many of my acquaintance will take without large allowance my estimates of the intelligence and gentility of western people. Need I remind them that not a few of the intelligent and cultivated settlers are from New England, and carried their attainments with them to plant cities and institutions wherever they settled? I regard the more thriving and cultivated portions as new New England, and, in many respects, an improvement on our population.

April 10

Among letters awaiting my return from the 'West I find the following:

> Harvard College
> Cambridge, Nov. 18, 1874

A. Bronson Alcott,
Sir,

I have the honor to inform you that at the last annual meeting of the Phi Beta Kappa Fraternity, Chapter Alpha of Massachusetts, you were duly elected an Honorary Member of the Fraternity.

> I am
> Your Obedient Servant
> F. E. Anderson
> Corresponding Secretary.

I return the following note of acknowledgement:

> Concord April 1875

F. E. Anderson
Sir,

On returning lately from an extended conversational tour at the West, I find your note of November last, informing me of my being made an Honorary Member of the Phi Beta Kappa Fraternity, Chapter Alpha of Massachusetts.

The honor thus conferred is as surprising to myself as it is prized by me. To be associated with so distinguished a fraternity of scholars and with our oldest university adds dignity to any name, and certainly to one who has always considered himself but remotely entitled to either.

With thanks and proper acknowledgements for this unexpected privilege of fellowship,

> I am, sir,
> Very respectfully,
> Yours,
> A. Bronson Alcott.

I have a very pleasant and flattering reminiscence of my first introduction to Harvard College. It was on Phi Beta Kappa Day, and soon after my becoming acquainted with Emerson in 1835. The usual procession of members of the Fraternity was being formed to pass into the Church where the annual exercises were held. Standing near Emerson and dubious as to whether I should follow after the procession and find a seat, he suddenly seized my arm, saying "We will not mince matters. You are a member by right of genius," and took me willingly along with the rest to a seat near the Orator, receiving my thanks for this unexpected generosity.

May 1

Home is home; yet I should enjoy a wider and more intimate association than opens for me here in my immediate neighborhood and throughout New England. Life seems a little tame after the closer fellowships of the last months at the West. With Longfellow and Johnson at Cambridge the other day we had snatches of conversation, only too short, and which rendered my last evening with Emerson, by contrast, somewhat disappointing. The old themes and the new dragged the more heavily. Was I still the visionary enthusiast, whom he must check by his moderated sense and less hopeful mood? Or was he in the subjunctive? Enthusiasts carry their ideals into age, themselves youthful still. Is my Tithonus being touched with age? To suspect this were almost an impiety. Yet my friend complains of growing old, says that his memory is gone, and that his Diary has few entrances in these late days. Does he exaggerate, as the rhetorician must? I have known not a single scholarly acquaintance whose memory of words was ready and retentive like his. His mortification must be extreme if the facts be as he states. I observe, however, in his conversation, how aptly he suggests by circumlocution his loss, his opulent vocabulary serving the while.

Let us concede the fact that we are ancients unmistakably. If one plead to infirmity of memory, the other may to that of hearing, though both may still attempt fellowship with satisfaction.

I should add the qualifying circumstance that Emerson falls latterly into his more subdued tones in conversation, and renders our intercourse the less satisfactory to myself.

May 11

May purposes to try her hand again at molding a bust of me, and yesterday I ordered a cask of artist's clay for her. Her former attempt she considered a failure. I may not hope to be in better physical condition than at present, and a successful head by her would be a compliment to us both. One surely should be flattered with having art and romance take his name and honor themselves thereby.

May gives me the following account of her cash receipts for pictures sold during the year past.

For pictures —	$1,558.85
And for Drawing Lessons —	718.00
Dolls	2,276.85

June 9   *Concord*

Miss Goodwin, Ellen Emerson, Cary Cheney, dine with us, and Mrs. Cheney joins us in the afternoon and takes tea. On rainy days like this my study fire attracts its worshippers. Miss Amy Goodwin is one of May's "amiable" associates.

Born at the Cottage and of nearly the same age, May takes kindly to her early playfellow, who is also a native of Concord but now residing in Cambridge. I met her father, Rev. Mr. Goodwin, then a colleague of Dr. Ripley's, on my first visit to Emerson in 183–. He was a most estimable man, and liberal preacher. Emerson thought highly of him. So did Dr. Ripley — more favorably of him than of his relative. I remember the Dr. telling me when I was taken by Emerson to the Manse to be careful of taking too deeply of the heresy of Transcendentalism, though he "could not tell what that was."

The old Church was then standing, and I attended Sunday services with Emerson, sitting in his pew with his brother Charles. The sermon does not remain with me, but I remember the rattling of the seats inside the pew doors after prayers — the sounding board over the pulpit. It was a genuine Puritan perch, and Emerson, Transcendental as the Dr. deemed, appeared in no wise above his fellow worshippers, seated or rising. The grace said at his table, the Scripture readings and devotions, were not wanting in unction or humility. A wedding service of his at the Middlesex Hotel *did* transcend, happily, any services of the kind that I had

Central Part of Concord as it appeared in 1836.

The old Church was then standing, and I attended Sunday services with Emerson, sitting in his pew with his brother Charles. The sermon does not remain with me, but I remember the rattling of the seats inside the pew doors after prayer — the sounding board over the pulpit. It was a genuine Puritan parish, and Emerson, transcendental as he then seemed, appeared in as wise a robe.

A PAGE FROM ALCOTT'S JOURNALS

(With an engraving, pasted in, from John Warner Barber's Massachusetts Historical Collections, *1839)*

witnessed in Puritan Connecticut; and had I not brought an assured faith along with me such charming words and ways would
have converted me, I doubt not, to the new ideas.[1]

June 16

Read at Athenæum and at bookstores. At Colesworthy's find
a copy of Burgh's *Dignity of Human Nature* — a book which,
next to *Pilgrim's Progress,* interested me in my boyhood, was borrowed and read and copied and returned to its owner — an aunt
of mine — to be re-borrowed and perused again and again. The
title, the treatment — so simple and plain in general and detail —
gave a charm to the subjects discussed unlike anything coming under my eye in a community where few books were to be found,
and these of secondary importance. My aunt happened to have a
taste for religious and ethical books, and I was fond of borrowing
for my Sunday readings and noonings.

Besides this book I found Hervey's *Meditations,* and read that,
less pleased, perhaps, with the sentiment than with the rhetoric,
which left its rhythm and style perhaps in my ear and doubtless
influenced my style of writing for a while at least. Later, I read
Milton's *Paradise Lost,* and still later Goldsmith's *Vicar of Wake-
field* and *Deserted Village,* Thomson's *Seasons,* and Cowper's
Task.

I judge that I owe more to *Pilgrim's Progress* and Burgh's
Dignity than to the other books named — more, probably, than
to any read by me during my boyhood and youth. How largely
these served to form my character and early opinions I cannot determine now.

August 26

Meeting Emerson on my way to the Post Office, he tells me
that his new volume of essays,[2] long advertised by his publisher,
is nearly ready for the press. Alluding to the Conversations, he
says that he finds himself silent in companies of many persons,

---

[1] Compare the entry for April 29, 1839. The fact is that Alcott was already,
at that time, "converted."

[2] *Letters and Social Aims.*

"whereas you have all your guns at command and are sure to carry the day. But you have not your best things recorded in your Journals, I am sure, and when you are fairly withdrawn I shall have the good things of yours to show in mine."

Not disconcerted, I said: "But suppose you should chance to withdraw before me? How then?"

"Why, then Ellen shall have my papers."

Very well; as fate and chance determine. Any contemporary of his may well be proud of a portrait from his hands, and I have ocular knowledge of more than one already drawn on his pages — having been permitted the privilege of looking into his Journals years ago, when our first intimacy prompted to such favors.

September 15

I return [from Boston] with Emerson. His new volume of essays, he tells me, is in press, and will appear in October. *The Parnassus,* he says, has proved his best literary venture pecuniarily. He has received from his publishers one thousand dollars for sales. His other books have a slow sale and yield him but small income.

October 7

Lord Houghton, Monckton Milnes, honors us with a call this morning, accompanied by Emerson, whose guest he is for a day. Carlyle gave me an introduction to his Lordship when I was in London, but I failed in finding him. He had become known to some of us here in New England by his volume of Poems, published in 1838, of which, he tells us, a new edition is soon to be issued. Emerson first met him in Paris during the days of the Revolution of 1848. He makes but a short stay in this country, but speaks with appreciation of American ideas and institutions. As he expressed an interest in "The Record" of my School, having, he said, read the book when it first appeared, I present him with a copy of a new edition; also with copies of *Tablets* and *Concord Days.* We take him to "Wayside." . . .

A plain, affable nobleman, we are alike gratified and honored by his call.

Should it be found practicable for me to accompany Louisa, next Spring, to England, we should seek him, with the scholarly friends with whom he is associated. Carlyle, he tells us, is somewhat infirm of hand, but fresh and forcible as ever in thought and manner. — Of Hawthorne and Thoreau he inquired with much interest.

It were not unbecoming republicans to consider whether befitting titles have not charm for the fancy, and do not give to the social life of a people a certain idealism which favors true nobility of character. I find my good wife and daughters feel somewhat ennobled by having been honored with having a Lord pass their threshold. And in Lord Houghton's favor it may be said that his verses had especially delighted her, being read and often recited by her in charmed moments.

I asked Freddy what he thought of Lords. "Were they different from ordinary people?" "They behave better," he answered. And surely His Lordship fulfilled the boy's fancy by his gentlemanly manners. It was only the national taste that gave the title to him and only plain "Mr. Emerson" to his friend — both noblemen and gentlemen. Yet even aristocratic England, nor republican America, can confer titles on those who are undeserving, save in name. I hesitate to claim for Carlyle the title of "Gentleman," without some allowance.

December 24

Emerson's new book of essays is stimulating reading. I read for the first time the essays entitled "Resources," "Inspiration," "Immortality," and most of the others I had heard read by him as lectures. Admirable both in thought and rhetoric. Since Milton, nothing so befitting all time.

An author who sets his reader to sounding the depths of his own thought serves him best, and teaches the true modesty of authorship. Emerson's page is suggestive, inspiring, edifying. Few if any of our modern writers are equally so; and his book may take its place with the great works in our literature.

I dipped a little into my *Tablets* after reading him, prompted by his stimulating insight to measure my page thereby, and seemed to find sentences fit to be read and remembered also. Could

I add a syllable or two to the living literature of my time, I shall not have lived in vain, and may be content.

Emerson calls and spends an hour in my study. When friends are few and Christmas gifts are rare, I may count this visit as a Christmas Eve gift, and take pleasure as well as pride in the friendship.

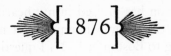

A NOTHER YEAR *of slow ripening, as of a Baldwin apple in the October sunshine. There was no Western tour in this year, but much moving about in New England. Alcott was still active in gardening, tree-planting, and that fantastic building of fences out of crooked sticks brought from the woods which so amused his contemporaries. The beauty of nature, which once he had been too absorbed in his own thoughts to see, was more dear to him as he grew older. He became aware of America's national crime in the slaughter of her forests. His love for all young and growing things now embraced trees.*

Emerson was gathering his final harvest of honors. Harris came on his now annual visit to Concord and laid plans for the School of Philosophy. May left for Europe, never to return. Alcott made acquaintance with the foundress of Christian Science. He worked at the manuscript of Table Talk, *uncertain whether to include the "Orphic Sayings" that had seemed so ridiculous to the readers of an earlier generation.*

1876

January 8

I purchased yesterday a fine illustrated copy of Wordsworth's *Poems*, London Edition. The "Ode on Immortality" is perhaps his best poem, as it is the most famous of his verses. The *Excursion* I read in my berth, crossing the Atlantic, in May, 1842. "Laodamia" Emerson has praised in my hearing more than once, and the Sonnets. I think Dr. Channing first named Wordsworth to me on my coming to Boston in 1827. I question whether a single townsman of mine had ever heard of Wordsworth at that time. David's Psalms and Watts were familiar to them through the Sunday Services. Milton, Young, Thomson and Cowper were known possibly to some of them. I remember reading them in borrowed copies found amidst books mostly unread by my neighbors. Of these, Thomson and Cowper interested me most, "The Seasons" particularly. Coleridge and Wordsworth first awakened the imagination and initiated this into the charm of noble verse. It happened that Shakespeare did not fall at once under my eye. The *Pilgrim's Progress* and *Paradise Lost* were earliest read — and the former lived as well as read, ideally.

January 17

Write to Mrs. Mary Baker Grover [1] of Lynn, thanking her for her remarkable volume entitled *Science and Health*, which I have read with profound interest. She purposes curing bodily disease by metaphysical methods, and teaches the soul's power over the body, its spirituality and immortality. Her book is an earnest and thoughtful appeal to the faith and reason of Christians, and will serve the ends of human culture by its appeals. I shall seek an interview with the author for comparing views on the transcendent themes discussed therein. In times like ours, so sunk in sensualism, one hails with joy any voice speaking an assured word for God and Immortality; and the joy is heightened the more if the words are of woman's divining. Mrs. Glover appears to have attained her revelations through deep physical [*sic*] experiences, and writes as a seeress of divine things. The popular Spiritualism

[1] Later, Mrs. Mary Baker G. Eddy. The variation between "Grover" and "Glover" is *sic*. The book had been sent to Alcott as a gift from the author. In March Alcott was asked by Mrs. Glover's assistant, D. H. Spofford, for permission to publish his commendation of *Science and Health*. This was granted, with the following characteristically mild *caveat*: "Meanwhile, Mrs. Glover, I am persuaded, will maintain the spirit and manners of a true disciple of the views which commend themselves to her faith and practice."

finds no favor from her divining spirit. I cannot vouch for the details of her teachings, but am sure of her having truths to impart deserving the attention of every well-wisher of his race.

January 20

Leave early with Miss Watson for Boston, and from thence to Lynn, to see Mrs. Grover, who responds to my letter wishing an interview.

She receives me cordially at her house, and I have an interesting visit. I find her one of the fair saints, whose attractions have drawn about her a little circle of followers which meets for fellowship at her house fortnightly, and by whose aid her book has been published. They take the name of "Christian Scientists" and find in the Christian Records the foundation of their faith, the gift of healing as practised by Christ being their central doctrine. Mrs. Glover names hers "Metaphysical Healing" — curing by sympathy with spiritual power over the mind of her patients. Drugs are wholly unused, and her cures have been many.

I find her a devoted student of the New Testament, a Christian in the truest sense, an idealist in apprehending the supremacy of mind over matter, and a faith in Spirit transcending any contemporary whom I have been fortunate to meet. I shall cultivate further acquaintance with a person of such attractions mentally and spiritually.

January 25

To Boston for deafness and dentistry. One may not be ashamed of needing a little mending at the age of seventy-six. I find myself in comfortable condition after slight repairs, and hope to last for useful services for years to come. With as few inherited ails as most of my time, and these mostly held in check by habitual temperance during my later years (never indulged inordinately) I may possibly reach my hundredth birthday, and retire with the century, (1899).

January 29

. . . Answer Mrs. Glover's note inviting me to meet herself and friends at some of their Sunday sittings at her house. I shall gladly meet them, and learn what they have for me, with docile ears and heart.

Faith, Hope, and Charity are graces too rare in modern life, and one comes within their presence with something of wonder and sweet surprise. Even if disappointed at finding one's wonder and surprise too adventurous for their novelty, his experience may be serviceable nevertheless. "Believing all things" is scriptural, at least.

February 4

Have letter from Miss Wilson of Malden, wishing me to meet her company some evening during the last week in this month.

Also from Mrs. Glover, inviting me to attend one of her Initiations.

February 7

Mr. Barry,[2] a disciple of Mrs. Glover, dines, and gives us information concerning Mrs. G.'s practice in healing. An interesting young gentleman, bearing favorable testimony to the faith and purity of the school.

I give him copies of "The Philosophemes," [3] with a number or two of *The Journal of Speculative Philosophy*. A wider acquaintance with idealism in its various phases will be serviceable to these "Metaphysical Healers" and "Christian Scientists," as they call their school.

February 9

. . . Returning, I find Emerson in the train for Concord. He tells me that he writes little or nothing now in his Journals, and does not answer his letters. I find his memory of proper names painfully oblivious, but in conversation he is charming as ever.

[2] George W. Barry, at this time one of the most enthusiastic of Mrs. Glover's followers.

[3] Oracular paragraphs of Bronson Alcott's published by W. T. Harris in his *Journal*.

February 11

Mrs. Glover writes inviting me to meet the "Christian Scientists" at her house on Wednesday evening next, for consultation and discussion. I am interested in this professed metaphysical science, and shall listen curiously to what may be shown or suggested on that occasion. A hospitable eye and open ear best becomes the scholar and thinker, especially as regards any fresh insight into humanity.

Answer Mrs. Grover's note.

I am to meet Miss Wilson's company at Malden on Tuesday evening, and Mrs. Glover's on Wednesday following.

February 16

5 P.M.: Leave for Lynn. Dr. Spofford takes me to The Falkland House, where I take tea, and meet, afterwards, Mrs. Glover's circle at her house in Broad Street.[4] The evening is passed in discussing metaphysical problems. I find her followers thoughtful and devout, without cant or egotism, students of life rather than of books, and a promising company. The slight touch of mysticism mingling with their faith renders them the more interesting, and Mrs. Glover's influence appears to be of the happiest character. Our conversation continues till near 11 o'clock. I sleep at the Falkland House.

March 20

De Quincey says he suffered during his youth under a peculiar embarrassment and penury of words when he sought to convey his thoughts adequately upon interesting subjects; and this held him for some years, though invited, from meeting Wordsworth. We know how affluent he became, and what wonderfully subtle powers of genius and expression he mastered, as shown in his writings and conversation.

A like diffidence and embarrassment I might instance, and it was not till I had passed some years in the attempt to translate

---

[4] Daniel Harrison Spofford was at this time, like George Barry, one of Mrs. Glover's most favored followers.

what pressed for utterance into the simplest phraseology that I discovered any aptitude for expression; and no one could be more surprised than I was in finding myself meeting Emerson, on terms of seeming equality, at the age of 35. I owe more to the endeavor to meet children than to any studies in logic or rhetoric. I find, moreover, that the dialect of my native district was less corrupted by foreign elements than many parts of New England.

April 18

. . . Had Whitman written in prose instead of affected poetic style, his genius would have been more readily conceded by candid critics. His freedom of treating certain subjects, particularly in his *Leaves of Grass*, offended persons of delicacy and refinement, from which cause his books have not found the reception which otherwise their especial merits would have secured. His claims to being a poet are still gravely questioned by scholars generally. I hold him in high esteem as a man, and honor him for his patriotism and humanity.

April 20

Write to Whitman enclosing ten dollars ($10), the price of his books.

August 4, 5

Resplendent days, these last, and truly Augustan. The late rains have revived the foliage, displaying the season's productiveness. Our little orchard shines with fruit, and the vines display their clusters depending from the trellis of my summer house. The mornings are delicious. Seen from my front door or study windows, the view becomes a picture gallery, the rude art blended with nature in the separate objects, my little estate being framed by the woods fringing it around, with only a vista of meadow as foreground.

Nature hastens to adopt and harmonize any piece of art . . . as if she would own at once her partnership with mind, supplying deficiencies or suppressing redundancies. My new fence, pretty at first and seemingly perfect in itself, is now supplemented with attractions of grapes at its base, and apple boughs depending picturesquely, lichens early showing how gladly things adapt themselves under the season's training to the new conditions. Even the stray leaves, if turned by accident from their chosen places, from the sun, assert at once and recover their former relation, adding new beauty to their fellows by the change. I go into my garden of a morning when my plants are in their August prime, note the picturesque geometry of the vines trailing gracefully or climbing spirally, till, losing their supports, they twine lovingly about one another, and stretch still upward in assured fellowship. The orchard, too, is glorified anew from the sunbeams glancing above the eastern hill-top, and seen from the rustic seat under the July Early.

An August morning is an illustrious invitation to the day's performance. How opulent its fullness! How perfect should be the work! Can any fail to color his composition with the tints of sunrise, approach nature's art, catch something of the glow of the morning, as if his sentences were stalk and stem of his thought, and bore their fruits in turn to whomsoever cared to pluck these from the laden branches?

August 23, 24

Opening my Diary for 1854, I find the following entry copied from notes taken at "Wayside" in 1848. Thoreau was at this time a frequent and welcome visitor.

"I asked Thoreau if it were a proof of our indifference or insufficiency that neither of us had attracted from the village some youth, some maiden — it were sufficient if but one — to our houses, and so proved our existence and right to citizenship and good fellowship. For might we not assume that such there were, who, if the doors were once opened or even ajar, would gladly avail themselves of our society and counsels? Though our towns-people had not sought our fellowship, had not opened their Lyceum but rarely to either, we on our part had not met them even on the lower planes of business where slight acquaintance were possible. Were we not the exclusives rather? Was it not the office of a good life to shine brightly and broadly around and thus attract others within its radiance? The young people at least?

" 'And yet,' I added, 'let us wait a little while and opportunities will open naturally for us, time being the best interpreter of one's character and aims.' " [5]

I do not find Thoreau's reply recorded. And now he has been withdrawn from these scenes and his townspeople many years, and before many of them had estimated his worth as a man and a philosopher.

October 5

Have a letter from Mills,[6] who writes that he is preparing for his missionary tour at the West, and wishes to speak about Emerson's early life and manners — of which I have next to nothing for him. His biographer, whoever he may be, has that interesting period to treat, and the novelty all reserved for his readers. It must be of a piece with the manhood and later days of genius like his. His extreme modesty forbids any questioning even of a friend, and I should be the last to venture questioning him, finding from earlier experiences how adroitly he evades approaches of this kind.

Though living so near, I see him seldomer than formerly, and just now only as I chance to accost him at the Post Office or in the Streets. Today I found him at the Post Office before the mail was assorted, and we walked to the Library meanwhile. On returning, as it was raining, he offered his arm and umbrella, and told me about Landor and his family, and also that his — Emerson's — Collected Poems were nearly through the press, he having a late proof in his pocket.

October 8

My wife's birthday. She closes her 76th year. Our gifts are presented in her chamber after breakfast with witty mottoes written by Louisa, an account of which will of course find place in my wife's Diary. This, with her needle, riding out, and reading, now occupies her days, the cares of housekeeping falling to Anna and Louisa.

P.M.: Louisa and I attend the interment of Miss Sophia Tho-

[5] See the entry for March 14, 1848.
[6] A Unitarian clergyman in Syracuse.

reau, who died at Bangor in Maine, and her remains are brought here and laid beside her family, — she being the last, and with more of her brother Henry's characteristics than the other brother and sister. None of the name remains with us.

Her devotion to her brother Henry was of the most affectionate kind, even to the sacredness with which she cherished his memory and his writings. The Journals, I am informed, are left by her to Henry's friend H. G. O. Blake of Worcester. He, or some one interested in Thoreau's genius, should edit selections at least from these papers. Volumes as unique and instructive may be compiled from them as those already published; and Thoreau's fame is sure to increase with years.

Emerson, who was at the grave, would have had some public service, less hurried, with opportunity for friends of Henry and his sister to have spoken of their worth.

December 4

Coleridge, first of English thinkers for me. He never wrote an unmeaning line, and every line had its note in essential being. Had I charge of the studies of theological students I should commend them to Coleridge, alike for depth and for subtlety of insight. The elements of universal faith, including all sects, are embodied in his books, and a faithful student must find in them satisfactory answers to his search for the truths revealed alike in mind and matter. Of modern teachers, he may be styled "The Divine."

I know of no modern interpreter comparable with him of the Sacred Books, and were I to name any modern mind "Master," it would be him. I could belong to the Church as this was portrayed in his thought, and cannot but wonder at the neglect which his writings receive at the hands of theologians of every shade of orthodoxy. He is a college in himself and, fairly comprehended, would render sects and schools superfluous.

December 26, 27

. . . Meet Emerson at the Post Office. He tells me that he is now preparing an article for the *North American*, which promises improvement under the new editorial management. He urges upon me the labor of putting my thoughts to paper concerning Immortality. I might have intimated that my notes would find place in *Table Talk*,[7] but literary work of mine I never mention to him, fearing to submit anything of the sort even to his hearing, so consummate is his critical judgment, and so exacting. Besides, I have the best of reasons for believing that my style and habit of thought suffer in writing. Perhaps he undervalues the latter as much as he overestimates the former in Conversation. I know he has no peer with his pen. It were too much to fancy his friend had none with his tongue.

'Tis written. Let it stand so!

[7] There is a section on "Immortality" in Alcott's *Table Talk*.

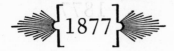

THE TREND of Alcott's thought toward an "orthodox" religious belief was accelerated in this year by the influence of his friend Dr. Joseph Cook, a Congregational minister whose "Monday Lectures" were almost as popular as the sermons of Theodore Parker had been two decades before. Cook's audiences of Boston businessmen grew accustomed to hearing Alcott spoken of as "the American Plato," but a sharp controversy arose when the lecturer cited Alcott's method of school discipline as a modern example of the Vicarious Atonement.

Alcott's third book, Table Talk, *was published in May, without the "Orphic Sayings." His summer was enlivened by the visit of an old friend, W. H. Channing, now a prominent Unitarian minister in England. There was much discussion during the summer, but with no immediate results, about the best way of publishing the manuscripts of Thoreau. In September Alcott spent several days in the region of his birth, but was called home by news of his wife's serious illness. He and Louisa and his wife left Orchard House early in November and went to live with Anna in the house once owned by the Thoreau family. There, on the twenty-fifth of November, Mrs. Alcott died.*

1877

March 6

. . . Write to Mrs. Grover, now Mrs. Eddy, of Lynn, finding I cannot conveniently meet with her class of students at Lynn tomorrow.[1]

March 8

Emerson passes the evening with me, as a rare favor. He tells that he writes nothing now, but is compiling and arranging matters selected from his Journals for future essays, Ellen assisting him. He speaks of having interesting letters in his possession addressed to him by Margaret Fuller, more brilliant and remarkable than he knew till his late readings. Shakespeare is his one scholar the world has yet produced, and another like far in the future.

April 6

. . . Certain scholars have recluse manners, and exert less influence than were wished upon the population generally. This was especially the case with Hawthorne; with Thoreau in less degree. Channing has nursed his privacy ostentatiously. Emerson has been, and is, shielded by reputation from interruption of his studies. Nor have I, while a resident, save when Superintendent of the Schools, had general intercourse with my townsfolk. May has sought a wider fellowship with the young people, while Louisa has been absent, or wishing to be known rather through her books. Sanborn has a wider acquaintance, but is far from being popular.

April 11

. . . The more facts gathered from observation of mind and matter, the greater the need of idealists to group these and generalize into systems. Theology properly absorbs and crowns the whole in one universal system.

[1] The invitation had come by telegram.

April 15

. . . Against the following passage in [Jeremy] Taylor's chapter entitled "Of Humility" [in *Of Holy Living*], I find this note of mine:

Note —
"Concord, 1848"

> "Be content that he should be employed, and thou be laid by as unprofitable; his sentence approved, thine rejected; he preferred and thou fixed in a low employment."

With Fruitlands and my Temple School lying sadly in the background at the date of this note, it is not difficult to recall the memory of that period of disappointed projects and future uncertainties.

Lowly as my employments have been since, I cannot regard myself as having been wholly profitless to myself or others, though my range has been narrow and my sentence but feebly approved. But these latter days almost fulfil the promise of my earlier, though far otherwise than I anticipated, and my ignorance rather than other infirmity is responsible for any seeming failure of schemes or of conduct. God be praised for all if I am the wiser and better for the struggle and discipline.

May 2

. . . I pass the evening with Emerson, with whom I take tea. My friend's persistent Individualism appears to mellow with years and some apparent infirmities, as should be the rule with poets and idealists. Perhaps I should find still deeper sympathy with him in thought and social intercourse were his drift of temperament less dominant and determined. — But then Emerson were not Emerson, and the fine forces of his genius had not the emphasis that tells so truly the man he is. An evening with him is a rare privilege — too rare to be sought too often, for the profit of Individualism or Personalism alike.

May 3

To Boston. Find my book[2] is in press and will be ready for the binders next week. By chance, meet Oliver Wendell Holmes,

[2] *Table Talk*, published May 19, 1877.

Dr. Hill, J. T. Fields, Dr. Bartol, and exchange views concerning the current religious movements in the city. Holmes fears that Cook's criticisms on Harvard University will prejudice the public against the reforms now adopted by the Faculty, but finds not a little to commend in the lectures, which he reads with interest. Plainly, Cook's orthodoxy is the obnoxious tenet with him, as with his other declared opponents. . . .

I call again upon Cook at his rooms, and pass a half-hour. I am surprised at finding his use of my mode of discipline in the Temple School taken up by most of the city newspapers and commented upon with doubts or approval according to the respective faiths of the writers — Unitarian and Universalists questioning, Orthodoxy approving generally. Cook tells me that he intends making still further use of it in his coming lectures.[3]

I return with Emerson, who is to read his "Rude Bridge" verses tomorrow evening at Old South — Holmes, Dr. Clark, Edward Hale, Mrs. Howe and others reading verses also. On asking him if he knew how good the verses were when first written, he, smiling, replied: "No; but Dr. Ripley did." His fame has since followed and returned home the shot then celebrated in his resounding verse.

May 13

My boys at breakfast inquire if it is not "whistle time," and the willows will wring. So after breakfast we cut sprouts from the willow tree in the garden and fashion a whistle for both and one for myself. We then serenade their grandmother in her chamber, much to her amusement.

The whistle is one of the poetic associations of boyhood, and one must attain to some skill, especially in the country, in blowing the reed. The chestnut was our favorite wood in my boyhood, from which we wrung big whistles and made merry music. These and the violin of my own manufacture were the only instruments that tempted me to try my skill, which, I fear, was at best of the scrannel and rude melody. Yet I thought my fiddle a beauty, and should be glad to trace its curves and cunning workmanship,

[3] Joseph Cook, at this time the most popular preacher in Boston, had recently likened Alcott's mode of punishment, which consisted in making the child strike him, to the Vicarious Atonement.

throughout of my boyish hands, now, in my age. But its history is lost in the distance, and the tree under which I sat at noonspells to play upon it has gone also. Only youthful feelings and faiths abide still.[4]

May 28

Louisa accompanies me to Boston and completes the purchase of the "Thoreau House" on Main Street in Concord for Anna, who purposes taking possession in July and making it her home hereafter. She pays for the same, including the garden lot, $4,500, and esteems herself fortunate in the purchase.

June 27

I am a poor solitary in a crowd, unless some official or social distinction is given me; and a public dinner is, of all festivities, to be shunned. My tastes are too individual and my wits too slow for table manners and morals. A philosophic symposium I might better become and maintain. Tomorrow's banqueting may suffice for such as I am.[5]

If not a scholar by degrees of the University, I may perhaps claim a native affinity with scholarship, and so am not wholly out of place on literary platforms and in company with University-bred scholars. I wear my ribbon in my button-hole with a certain feeling of equality with those whose badges betoken the love of letters and the graces of culture. What of egotism may steal into my pride comes more from the contrast between my Spindle Hill ambitions and the social standing, if not literary acquirements, of these later years. Honors not undeserved may be cherished with propriety and not without laudable pride.

July 1

Mr. Darwin made a series of careful observations on the early mental development of one of his sons, and is going to print them under the title of *A Biographical Sketch of an Infant.*

I have preceded the famous Evolutionist in this attempt at recording the unfolding of infant personality, having traced this

[4] A flute which is said to have belonged to Alcott is still shown at Orchard House, but nothing seems to be known about his skill in playing it.

[5] That of the Phi Beta Kappa Day at Harvard.

in my children from birth to their third year's experiences. These records are voluminous, and fall short of being accurate, as must the observations and inferences of Darwin. I shall look with hope and assurance for the publication of documents so unique and promising to give the data for a correct psychology. Studies in this connection are the hope of our time, when the relations existing between mind and matter are being sought as the foundation of an absolute philosophy.[6]

July 8

Cowley writes of his "old contemporary trees," and wishes to abide under their shadows while he lives. I too might hail mine — not indeed as contemporaneous with my senses but far more ancient, and coëval at least with the mansion they embower and ornament.[7] And moreover I might plead with the future to maintain here my residence during the remnant of years permitted to me, however shortened or prolonged these may prove. They give nobility to the mansion, and, by reflection, to the residents. How many satisfactions have these witnessed, not for us alone but for prior occupants of the estate! What sorrows we may not know, for life has been an almost uninterrupted series of family happiness and outward prosperity during the score of years of our occupancy of the spot. Under their shadows have sat select friends, how many and dear! Associations not to be forgotten haunt their forms. And how instinctively friendships cling and bind themselves about trees, as if the noblest forms of nature and of mind had a like eternal ancestry and immortal fellowship! Is it not a significant hint of the longevity of the human sentiment that plants a tree with the birth of every child into the family of man?

[6] This comment upon a newspaper clipping is one of the many proofs that Alcott was by no means an empty theorizer who took no interest in factual observation. He read eagerly all the scientific literature of a semipopular nature that he could find, and he even did some spasmodic work at what he thought the main scientific task of his day — the gathering of materials for what is now called psychology.

[7] At least one of the two great elms that shaded Orchard House in Alcott's time may really have been as old as any part of the house itself — that is, some two hundred years. This larger tree is now dead. Its stump, at six feet from the ground, is about six feet through.

July 18

. . . Sanborn brings John Burroughs the essayist, an admirer of Thoreau. A plain farmerlooking person with the grey eye telling of decision mingled with generosity.

August 13

I pass Emerson's study oftener than I should like, unwilling to interrupt or invade his privacy. This morning I call, however, and find him disengaged apparently, though he tells me that he writes nothing now, not even letters, but reads rather. Alluding to his unedited manuscripts, he says that Elliot Cabot has now access to them, and is putting them in order for final uses, printing as essays — and, I infer, though he does not say so, is to be Emerson's editor and biographer. There is material, it seems, for as many more essays as have been printed, besides his letters. And his correspondence with Carlyle is voluminous.

August 21

Write to Mrs. Eddy of Lynn, whose book on *Science and Health* is one of the hopeful signs of the time. Mrs. E. wishes to visit us and meet Mr. and Mrs. Emerson.[8]

September 14

Write to Mrs. Eddy of Lynn, declining to visit her at this time for conversation on health, etc. The good lady has wholesome views upon health and healing. A former visit of mine impressed me favorably regarding her methods, and especially her faith in spiritual as distinguished from the sorceries of current spiritualism, fast running its polluting social race into detestation.

October 8

My wife's birthday. She is 77 this day, entering upon her twelfth septenniad, which she can hardly hope to span. Bright and beautiful the morning dawns, and after breakfast Anna, Louisa, and I offer our greetings and gifts. The table is decorated with a pyramid of flowers, floral apostles, and I read Horace Smith's

[8] The proposed visit was never made. But see *Mary Baker Eddy*, by Bates and Dittemore, page 171, footnote.

"Hymn to the Flowers" as appropriate to the celebration. I present her with certain manuscript notes, with a letter — memorial tokens of our early acquaintance and plighted vows. And to crown the whole comes a letter from May, giving an account of her life and prospects in London.

November 24

My dear companion during the past fifty years is near her translation to other and tenderer companionships. Very sweet and fragrant is the memory of this life of sacrifices for the right, of good deeds, devotedness to the duties of the hour.

My days must be other, now, than when she was at my side to prompt to the instant duty, the quick sympathy with the needy and suffering; nor can I pass the remnant of my century better than by cherishing her generous counsels and following in the path of her unselfish example.

November 25

At half-past seven she passes serenely into the unseen. All day she lay in a semi-conscious state, whispering to herself the unspeakable raptures she enjoyed as a foretaste of the bliss she was soon to partake in its fullness. Her last words to me were these, as I raised her head upon her pillow that she might breathe more freely: "You make a soft pillow for me to sleep upon." And other tender words to her niece and Anna and Louisa as they watched her for the last sigh. And thus we closed her eyes.

November 28

The day is fair, and our friends assemble at the hour appointed for the last memorial services. Mr. Foot reads portions of Scripture and of the Burial Service, offers a fervent sympathetic prayer. Then Dr. Bartol gives his tribute to the character of the deceased, and Mr. Garrison follows with reminiscences of his first acquaintance with her and her saintly brother — all simply sincere and eloquent as became the speakers and the noble woman whom they eulogized. Almost every relative and friend invited were present. Mr. Emerson sat by me during the services, and Mrs. Emerson by Louisa and Anna.

December 18

Yesterday's celebration of Whittier's birthday by the contributors of the *Atlantic Monthly* partaking of a sumptuous banquet at the Brunswick Hotel, brilliant as it must have been, seems not the most befitting the plain poet whose seventieth anniversary it was designed to honor. Nor was the omission of the lady contributors, none of whom were honored with an invitation to share in the festivities and bestow their meed of admiration for the poet, a gallant act of the gentlemen who arranged the festival. Very largely have the readers of this popular *Monthly* been instructed and delighted by the charming contributions of women, some of whom have a national literary reputation, and have given a tone to the magazine abroad as at home. Nor were the poems and speeches as a whole most creditable to the poet or the occasion. The man was worthy of a manly tribute to his genius, the poet of the noblest verse of his peers — Emerson and Bryant. Some of the noblest lyrics in our literature are his. Future historians of our political conflict will point their periods with his patriotic lines. He has sung the nation's victories and defeats in numbers that will resound while the Republic stands.

It was brave in Emerson to rise and read the poet's "Ichabod," surrounded as he was by the fallen statesman's [9] worshippers. A tribute was thus publicly rendered to the merits of that lofty lyric! — And Norton's speech was admirable. [10]

[9] Webster's.

[10] When he wrote this note Alcott may not have heard of the now famous speech in which Mark Twain, at the Whittier dinner, had imagined Longfellow, Holmes, and Emerson as engaged in a drunken game of euchre in a western shanty. If he had heard of it his informant was probably Emerson, who had been interested in the speech although he did not think it remarkably humorous.

ALCOTT BORE *the loss of his wife with accustomed patience and with a perfect confidence in reunion. In spite of the ministrations of his two elder daughters, however, the rest of his life was lonely. During this year he went more frequently to Boston, and immersed himself in the talk there. At Joseph Cook's rooms in Boston, at Emerson's house in Concord, and indeed wherever he could, he held Conversations. Having now outlived the memory of his earlier heretical opinions, he spoke from many pulpits, often on the theme of "Immortality." He went about in towns and villages of his neighborhood as a "missionary" whose faith was simple and broad enough to embrace all creeds.*

The longing for human association which had always been strong in Alcott, and which was now increased, took him in May to the Anniversary Week of the reform societies, at whose annual gatherings he had not been seen for years, and subjected him there to a severe rebuke for intrusion. The same longing had led him to accept a mysterious summons from Mrs. Mary Baker G. Eddy, which he never quite understood, to a "trial for sorcery" at Salem. It increased his complacency toward reporters, autograph-hunters, miscellaneous admirers, and idly curious visitors from whom Louisa, far less socially inclined, hid herself away.

Alcott's loneliness was not lessened by the task to which he and Louisa set themselves in June — that of reading through his late wife's diary and correspondence. As Carlyle's had done on a similar occasion, the widower's heart bled at the evidence of a long struggle for the first time clearly revealed.

In March of this year Alcott's youngest daughter, May, was married in England to a Swiss named Ernest Nieriker.

In July there came from the West eight or ten old friends — among them Dr. Jones, the Illinois Platonist — for a fortnight of glorious talk. Before they left for home the Concord School of Philosophy was assured.

1878

January 22

I call at Emerson's and pass an hour. I find him confined by a severe cold, and unfitted for reading his lecture tomorrow at the Old South as advertised. He reads me a letter just received from Alexander Ireland, a friend of Carlyle's and of his, in which Carlyle's powers of conversation are said to be unimpaired at his age of 83, and his general health still vigorous. . . .

I have not allowed myself to associate mortality with my friend, but youth perennial, and hoped the fable of Tithonus might be realized in his translation. He appears to take his infirmity of memory as a sufficient excuse for solitude, and his friends are too courteous to intrude upon him often. Did he not sometimes hesitate and reach for the word, the author he wished to speak of, to his book shelves, I should not discover any abatement of his former readiness in conversation. I cannot but perceive, however, that age is doing its work upon him, and feel not a little anxious concerning his stay with us. But he has lived the century in his three score and ten, and may ascend gloriously to renew his Genius at the fountains of undying youth.

January 27

I fail to follow the reasoning of Mr. Gladden in his review of Joseph Cook's theory of atonement as given in his pamphlet entitled: "Was Bronson Alcott's School a Type of God's Moral

Government?" Neither am I sure of Mr. Cook's inferences from the instance of correction which he cites from the Record of my School. The boy's stroke on my hand had an instantaneous effect upon his feelings, touched his conscience apparently, and produced a change in his conduct afterwards. He rather than myself was punished. . . . I suffered for him that he might be touched by my taking upon myself the penalty, which he perhaps first felt he justly deserved. I deemed this the proper interpretation of the incident, and consider myself as thus illustrating the efficacy of the vicarious atonement. . . . Take this from the Christian story and you strip it of its chief power over the human heart, and have only the pagan notion of sacrifice remaining.

February 25

Accompany Mr. and Mrs. Cook to Emerson's lecture. Old South is filled, floor and galleries, with a distinguished audience; and the speaker is in spirits, reading his notes with much of his earlier animation and graceful elegance. . . . Yet I remember when even Bostonians questioned his sanity.

March 19

. . . In cultivated and principled communities there will be found a class of eminent thinkers of superior character who, though unorganized and oftentimes unknown to one another, constitute a fellowship, a free-masonry, for the promotion of the public wel-fare — men who have risen above national prejudices and know exactly when patriotism ceases to be a virtue, who are not subject to the prejudices of their inherited religion . . . to whose com-pany the high gladly condescend and the humble confidently rise.

These I define as the true lords and gentlemen of the land, and into such noble fellowship I would win my way by deserving its honors and partaking . . . of its spirit and accomplishments.

March 22

Return Thomas Taylor's translation of Jamblichus' book on the Mysteries to Emerson, and dine with him.

The old topic of Personal Immortality comes into our discus-sion, and I find my friend as persistent as formerly in his Individualism. His faith is purely ethical, and demands the certainty of facts experienced individually. His idealism hesitates and pauses, appalled at the dread facts of the Personality. True to his convictions, he modestly rests in his Individualism, and is silent concerning what lies beyond. Perhaps he may be classed as an ideal theist, with that film of pantheistic haze that hovers always about that school of thinkers. This latent pantheism has from the first characterized the New England school of Transcendentalists, and has not yet cleared itself from the clouds, most of its disciples being still touched with its indefiniteness, unable to find the certainty they seek. While it has modified favorably the materialistic tendencies of New England thinking, it has failed of planting itself upon the intuition of the Personal and Immortal. . . .

I present Mrs. Emerson with a photograph of Mr. Emerson, the best which I have seen lately taken of him. He protests against any success, and refers Mrs. Emerson to Herrick's picture given in the best editions of his poems as being almost as bad as his, and, after dinner, takes the book from his library shelves to prove his assertion. — Only one or two pictures that I have seen do him full justice: Scott's, in our Concord Library, and Rouse's, published in his second volume of poems. I am willing these should preserve his features for futurity.

March 30

By invitation of Dr. Bartol I attend Emerson's reading of his Old South Address. . . . A distinguished company is in attendance. Emerson, assisted by Miss Ellen's occasional promptings, reads to the delight of his auditors, his flashes of wit at Mrs. E.'s interferences adding a singular charm to the reading. These ragged, blotted sheets, as if they were hustled together like a pack of cards, and pasted over in parts, the leaves of different hues, the handwriting bold yet characteristic, all unpaged and oftentimes but partly filled, an impossible medley to the eye, became, by the marvelous magic of his elocution, passages of persuasion, paragraphs of power, words of wit loaded with thoughts not another of his auditors had conceived, which every one would have deemed fame to have written.

Yet the spectacle, brilliant and impressive as it was, was but a faint reflection of his earlier appearances. . . . Then he was the rhapsodist inspired and upon the tripod, uttering oracles as unexpected as they were divine to the illuminated — profane, and, it might be, demented, to others. Such beauty of thought, fitness of illustration, wealth of imagery, the poetry, the philosophy, the divinity, were as unique as they were bold and aggressive. How many old abuses, modern delusions, have his shafts of subtle irony, flashing wit, smitten away forever from the creeds of his contemporaries! How serene and unclouded the atmosphere by the uprise of this sovereign star of Genius!

Yet I am saddened by the persuasion that the oracle is soon to be dumb, and the voice that spake as none other in his time is becoming silent to human ears.

Ripe and mellow age has its accomplishments, but these must be held subordinate to temperament. The flame of Genius may flicker in its socket or blaze forth the more luminously as it is snuffed by the fingers of time. For Emerson, the former more than the latter the Fates appear to have decreed. Not a steady but a fitful flame has been his from its first kindling. The literature he leaves is of the starry lustre. It has its scintillations and its obscurities, but that it is the orbed and Olympian brightness of which he sings, none may question.

April 28

"They also serve who only stand and wait."

And waiting may be the noblest serving. The idealist may be said to stand in relation of parent to his time, and must needs wait for his young generation to come to maturity in order to appreciate his claims to authority and apply his genius to practical uses. To be left without a task, practically, is as useful a discipline as it is to be burdened with one. Leisure for thought is not less needed than opportunity for continuous labor.

My long apprenticeship in the school of leisure appears to be drawing to a close, and it is coming none too soon for one who has come to something like late ripeness of gifts for usefulness in his time. It was taken at first with not a little of restlessness, and a sense of injustice withal; but the passage of years brought recon-

cilement, and, I may add, acceptance, as it were the drill of discipline for such as myself, without which I might have proved a
waste power in my time.

May 12

. . . Mr. Eddy of Lynn comes and urges me to accompany
him home and witness a "trial for sorcery" to be held before the
Supreme Judicial Court tomorrow at Salem. A student [1] of Mrs.
Eddy's is accused of debasing his art of healing, and is prosecuted
by the patient for this abuse.

Mrs. Eddy is the author of a work entitled *Science and Health*,
in which she sets forth the principles and method of sympathetic
healing. She has a school of disciples. I have some references to
herself and work in my Diaries, having once made her a visit and
met her classes.

May 14

Accompany Mr. and Mrs. Eddy to Salem. Judge Gray, on
opening the Court, entertains the case and names Friday next for
a hearing. The young lady plaintiff is present, and has no question of the sorcery practised upon her, to the detriment of her
health and reason. [2]

May 28

To Boston. This is Anniversary Week, [3] and I may take a slight
census of the current life and thought of my contemporaries in
the movements of the time. . . .

P.M. I am at the New England Woman's Suffrage Association
sitting in Horticultural Hall, and favored with an opportunity to
speak a word of encouragement to women.

Wishing to attend the meeting called to organize a Society for
the Suppression of Vice, I leave at 4, and witness the doings at

[1] Daniel Harrison Spofford. Compare the entry for February 16, 1876.
[2] There is no further reference in the Journals to this "trial for sorcery," the
story of which may be read in *Mary Baker Eddy* by Bates and Dittemore, New
York, 1932, p. 189ff.
[3] The week, at the end of May, during which many Unitarian societies held
in Boston their annual conventions.

the Park Street Vestry. Astounding facts are narrated by Mr. Comstock, Secretary of the New York Suppression Society, and an excited sequel [4] follows his statements; but a New England Society is organized, and promises efficient service for the supression of the alarming evils that are sapping the vitals of the community.

Evening: At the Massachusetts Temperance Meeting, in Tremont Temple. I wish success may follow every effort to suppress the vice of intemperance, whether by moral or political measures. Especially do I regard as most potent and practicable the recommendation of a more chaste and salutary diet, chiefly composed of fruits and esculents, with a reasonable allowance of articles furnished by the dairy, and the common beverages. . . .

May 29

. . . Accompany young Tyndall to the Berry Street Conference of Unitarian Ministers, and hear an able discourse from Rev. Mr. Hall of Worcester, advocating a scientific study of theology. As last year, I rise to speak, but am not, as then, allowed to proceed, and am told by the Rev. Mr. Ware, in whose vestry the Conference meets, that I am not in any sense a minister and have no right to intrude my person or words upon their deliberations. He further informs me that I am not wanted, and accuses me of attempting to "put him down" by my asking the indulgence of the Conference to explain my presence there.

I am sensitive to this unexpected discourtesy, if I may not use a less respectful epithet, and leave the Conference with the sense of disappointment on finding that not a single voice is raised in apology even for my unconscious invasion of the forms of admission. It is known to many of the members that I have been admitted unchallenged to the Conference more than once, have been welcomed at Associations, and taken part in the proceedings, have preached in several of their pulpits, and was last year heard with unmistakable approbation at this very Conference. I am not accusing the Conference as a body of this discourtesy, but must hold it as unworthy of its claim to being "liberal" in holding absolute

[4] During which Anthony Comstock was called a liar by a well-informed person speaking from the floor.

silence when a word from any one might have spared me the mortification and, I add, the injustice, of this action. With not a little sympathy with its creed and aims, I am, I perceive, left to the conviction of being still deemed an outcast, an Ishmaelite.

May 30

At the Moral Education Association at Freeman's Place Chapel. Addresses are made by Mrs. Diaz, Mr. Hinckley, Dr. Dudley, and others. I have a word also, and speak for purity in heredity, spiritual and human. A little child comes near the platform while I am speaking, and I take him before me as an illustration of Christian doctrine of spiritual heredity. Of its human parentage I am ignorant till informed of its being the child of Mr. and Mrs. Hazard, of Free Love notoriety. I speak to the mother, and advise her of her errors and dangers.

2 P.M. At Mrs. Wells' lunch for gentlemen, mostly Unitarians and Free Religionists. Dr. Hedge advises my ordination for the ministry by the Unitarian association of ministers, and signified his readiness to further the rite. I prefer, if hands are laid at all, the unseen, unsectarian, should qualify me for the sacred ministry. Nor am I just now quite in the happiest mood for inviting members of the Unitarian Conference, which has questioned my claim, to give this additional sanctity. . . .

Return to Concord by late train.

June 5

I take tea with Dr. Dudley at his boardings in Worcester Square, and after tea we meet Mrs. Eddy and her class of students at Mrs. Frothingham's parlors in West Newton Street. The party consists of fifteen or more young gentlemen and ladies preparing to become healers of disease by Mrs. Eddy's theory. They call themselves "Christian Scientists," and their method the "Mental Method."

I have but an imperfect acquaintance with this theory of healing, and infer that she may have still to remove, perhaps cure, some of the nervous maladies incident to improper modes of diet and regimen, both of body and mind. There is perhaps a touch of fanaticism, though of a genial quality, interposed into her faith, which a deeper insight into the mysteries of life may ultimately remove. I judge her present gifts are rather derived from her nervous temperament, combined with the faith with which she ventures into hitherto unexplored crypts of psychology, than from any established philosophy concerning such recondite matters.

But any touch of idealism, however dashed with superstition, over-clouded with mysticism, is to be regarded as a wholesome omen in these times of shallow materialism and atheistic dogmatism, in which so many indulge.

June 10–14

I copy letters and Diaries of Mrs. Alcott.

These papers admit me, as daily intimacy hardly did, into the very soul of my companion, and my heart bleeds afresh with the memories of those days, and even long years, of cheerless anxiety and hopeless dependence. Yet here are strokes of joys intermingled, pictures of happy domesticity, and the dear children are always within her maternal embrace. And what brave bearing through these vicissitudes — eloquent appeals to those from whom sympathy and aid were due!

I copy with tearful admiration these pages, and almost repent now of my seeming incompetency, my utter inability to relieve the burdens laid upon her and my children during these years of helplessness. Nor can I, with every mitigating apology for this seeming shiftlessness, quite excuse myself for not venturing upon some impossible feat to extricate us from these straits of circumstance. I trusted too confidingly to that justice and generosity which Christian professions imply, to find these faithlessly discharged. Had I no claim for sympathy and generous support, when I had lived for the best of ends, and lost by so doing my happiest opportunity for further serving those who now voted me an outcast? Ah, me! But it is past now. And it is a sweet satisfaction that in her latter years she found in her daughters, if not in her husband, the compensations that fidelity to principles under the deepest tribulations always bring about and nobly reward. Under every privation, every wrong, and with the keen sense of injustice present, the dear family were sustained, the fair bond was maintained inviolate, and independence, a competency, honorable name, and even wide renown, was given it at last. And but for herself this could not have been won. Thrice blessed be her memory and my deserts forgotten, if such may be named with her surpassing merits!

August 8   *Waterbury, Conn.*

I read newspapers at the Bronson Library. Under the head of "Personal" I find this paragraph: —

> Miss Louisa Alcott is regarded as rather stiff and unapproachable in society. In Concord, Mass., where she lives, it is said that she "snubs" right and left, in return for the "snubs" she received when a poor working girl from those who perhaps now would fawn upon her.

Ill health, and extreme sensitiveness to all intrusion upon the sanctities of home may have given occasion for this report. As to Concord, she has never been ready to glorify its claims to pretention above other country villages, and she does not regard her popular repute with anything like pride, or overbearing its citizens. She is indeed almost indifferent to her fame.

August 8, Sunday   *Concord*

I take Sanborn to Walden and we have a bath and a splendid swim. The water is pure and agreeably cool, the sands soft, and the sun shines brilliantly on the surface. I find I have not lost my early dexterity, and move as rapidly as when on Saturdays we boys had our grand splash in the Mill ponds, playing wondrous pranks above and under the surface. Cleanliness, we read, is next to godliness, and we take ours sportively while our neighbors theirs more demurely. Let tastes be respected in this matter also — I might add "and pieties too."

October 18

I pass the forenoon with Emerson in his study. He tells me that he is busied these days with his prose writings, and has ceased to write. I show him some sheets of the *Masque of the Poets* and leave them, hoping he may oblige the publishers in contributing verses not published hitherto. He modestly says the reading public do not care for his verses, and call him "no poet."

November 25, 7 o'clock

At this hour, twelvemonth, passed my companion for fifty years here into the unseen existence. Can I doubt that she is less interested now in all that concerns the welfare of her friends she loved while with them? I seem to see her assuring smile and hospitable welcome awaiting their arrival one and all to her affectionate embrace. Let me, at least, do my work worthily meanwhile.

November 28, Thanksgiving Day

As a descendant of Puritans, I trust I am thankful for this pious parentage, and do not greatly dishonor their memories if I partake sparingly of the feast of fat things in which my neighbors indulge more bountifully.

November 29

I complete my 79th year in health, and with the reasonable promise of faculty to fulfill such engagements as I may undertake for the future.

For the month of December they stand as follows:

A Lecture at Amherst	Dec. 6
At Cambridge Divinity Hall	" 9
At Lunenberg	" 12
Young Men's Christian Association, Boston,	" 19
And, sometime during the month, at Hotel Belleview (probably)	

This moderate demand for anything of mine by lecture or conversation is almost a novelty here in New England, and is a hopeful incident in my personal history. At the West it is no novel matter. I need but pass the boundaries of the Puritan territory to speak in parlors, pulpits, and platforms whatever I have for my audiences. Possibly if I live out my century, these may be as hospitable to my words. Surely I have waited not hopelessly during the long interval since my lips were sealed, save to a few friends and small companies, chiefly of young people. And I may please myself with the belief that my methods and teachings are alike improvements on the past.

December 10

Very rainy and tempestuous.

Pass the forenoon and lunch with Longfellow, the most gentlemanly and genial of men and most popular of our poets. He has much to inquire of me concerning Emerson, and I am delighted to tell him all I may of my friends. Nor is he incurious about his visitor; while I, in turn, learn much of his pursuits and methods of work.

December 29

I suppose it would be difficult for me to account satisfactorily to a confirmed church-goer for my abstinence from public Sunday services. And the more difficult since I am occasionally known to occupy the pulpit and to preach acceptably. I think it is a matter of form, and that I can await my time without detriment to the good cause of religion, as of the churches. I judge that I am not the worse preacher for being an infrequent hearer of the Word; and the time is fast hastening for the enjoyment of both.

THE FIRST *session of the Concord School of Philosophy, meeting in the summer of this year, brought to realization a dream and a hope which had been maturing for nearly four decades. Probably no other event of Alcott's life gave him deeper satisfaction than the establishment and success of this School, so completely was it made in his own image.*

At the risk of a certain dullness, Alcott's record of the first session is given at length, because no other description of the School from his point of view is available.

The happiness caused by this success, and also by a warm reception both in the West and at Concord, was suddenly destroyed, at the end of the year, by news of the death of Alcott's youngest daughter, May.

1879

January 16

A brilliant snow storm, added to a former, clothes the fields and trees with wintry splendor. The sleigh bells jingle merrily, and winter with its romance is now here. I may say that without snow, however cold the weather, winter has not come, in fancy at least, bringing with it the lively sensation and sports of earlier days. I enjoy the cold, particularly the glow and brisk blood of

January. Then is the time for intellectual illumination, the delights of conversation, the birth of ideas. Blot out the winter weather from my calendar of experiences and my year would pale and please me far less than now. I am stimulated, brightened, beatified by its bracing agencies. A milder climate would stupify rather than stimulate and edify. I bear the cold far better than the heat, live a far brisker life, enjoy my Genius more fully in winter than in summer.

February 19

"A fellow feeling makes us wondrous kind"; so when two bright pedlar boys rang at our door today, Louisa welcomed them into my study, and, while listening to their stories of "nine in our family and only me to earn anything," which one of them told with much vivacity and graceful speech, she purchased several articles of him. The other, less gifted, seemed disappointed at his want of good luck, and so I gratified him by taking some of his trinkets. I am always pleased at the sight of a civil pedestrian calling at my door, and like to send him from it with my blessing. Lightening his parcel lightens his heart while it freights his purse a little.

The romance of my youthful adventures in this line revives, and I take part in his as if they were mine again. For though he may be bent on quite another errand from mine, he cannot well fail of becoming more of a gentleman and make a fuller acquaintance of human nature by his calling. Rude, awkward as he may be at setting forth, he returns, if not mannerly, refined, disposed to meet people, his elders at least, respectfully. A boy of genius disguised as pedlar has advantages denied to the courtier even, of learning the laws of etiquette and civility. Under that guise he is admitted to the widest range of society and on terms permitted to none other. I was perhaps too bashful and unlettered to make the best and most of my advantages while admitted into the cultivated opulent families of the Old Dominion, but returned from the kindly hospitalities shown to me a better behaved if not a wiser youth. Perhaps the predispositions inherited from my gentle mother favored and facilitated the accomplishments which I bore away from this intimacy. The recollection of those experiences now fill me with surprise, even wonder. I owe more to those as regards culture than to any school of instruction, and have sometimes fancied that my advancement in life, I may add the social victories I may have won, any literary recognition, were largely owing to these early adventures.

March 21

. . . I certainly entertain views at present more in harmony with, if not identical with Evangelical Orthodoxy, than I did at the time these Conversations [1] were conducted, and should modify, if not suppress some portions of the text were I to venture to alter this in the least to suit my present views. Forty years should have taught me something. I was then but 38 years of age, and had but entered upon my theological studies under the bias of Unitarianism — from which, if I mistake not, I am now freed.

May 12

On returning from the "Orchard" I call upon Emerson. He tells me that he has lately read a paper to the Harvard Divinity Students, but cannot recall his subject.

As lately on my leaving him, he expresses his pleasure in my good health and opportunities for useful labors, yet with a certain tragic reference to his own infirmities. This reversal of conditions is unexpected. Presumptively, he seemed likely to survive myself — and still may, notwithstanding present indications.

But a glory departs from our sky when he vanishes from the firmament.

July 15

Our School [2] opens with a full attendance. Mr. Emery takes the chair at 9 precisely. I follow with a genial welcome of our visitors to Concord and "The Orchard," giving an outline of our method of communication and the spirit of our purpose.

P.M.: Mrs. Cheney reads an interesting paper on Art in its moral relations, which is discussed by several members of the Faculty and others.

[1] *Conversations on the Gospels.*
[2] The Concord School of Philosophy.

"ORCHARD HOUSE," AND THE "CHAPEL" OF THE CONCORD SCHOOL OF PHILOSOPHY

July 16

Mrs. Cheney gives her second lecture to a good audience, and a lively discussion follows. Art is shown to be the complementing of nature by the mind of man.

P.M.: Mr. Harris lectures on the presuppositions which imply and, logically followed, conduct to the idea of Personality, and are the sum and substance of all thinking. The audience are deeply interested. Rev. Dr. Kedney, Dr. Jones, Professors Andrews and Beers,[3] with several of the students, take an eager part in questioning and discussing the subject. I confess full faith in Mr. Harris' logic but am incapable of following the steps leading to his conclusion.

Evening: At the "Orchard" with Emery, Harris, Dr. Jones, Dr. Kedney and McClure, discussing the Hegelian Idea and methods. I find my thinking is ideal, my method analogical rather than logical, and thus reaching the conclusion by concrete symbols. Accepting Personality as the Prime of things, I aim at exhibiting this alike to imagination, reason, and the conscience in its three-fold attributes as one and entire, thus speaking to the reason and faiths at once. For theological ends this method is the more significant and effective, reaching the many while the other affects but the few.[4]

July 17

I give my first Conversation.

As psychology is the key to all other knowledge, I sketch the Personality in its powers and attributes in their order of descent and return, from the pure idea to atom. I am pleased to find my "stairway" intelligible to my company, and the discussion of its method is animated and prolonged till the hour of rising. The students seem particularly interested and ready to question me. Dr. Kedney is an acquisition to our company. He shows much subtlety of thought and of metaphysical power.

[3] Professor Henry Augustin Beers, 1847–1926, of Yale College.

[4] These are the conclusions reached by W. T. Harris in the remarkably brilliant chapter on Alcott's philosophy which he contributed to Sanborn's *Memoir*.

July 18

Dr. Jones gives his first lecture. He sketches the general scope of his course: the Platonic significance of ideas, of Providence illustrating these in national events and representative minds in past eras and races of mankind. His forcible manner and novelty of thought interest and provoke eager discussion. Contrasted with the purely logical method of Mr. Harris, the idealism of his allegorical genius is refreshing to the company, and much curiosity is awakened in consequence. I am afraid, however, and sometimes question, whether the Platonic ideas are not modified essentially by the Doctor's expositions.

P.M. Mr. Harris resumes his exposition of the speculative method. His auditors listen, admire, wonder at the subtlety of his expositions and are apparently persuaded of his holding the key to the absolute truth of things, both in matter and mind. The faith he inspires is almost universal, though none, it may be, comprehend his method completely.

He draws a distinguished audience. Many of our townspeople, including Mr. and Mrs. Emerson, are present.

It is exciting to see the streets and sidewalks of our little village with the phalanx of walkers passing to and from the "Orchard" daily.

Harris calls and Blake and Russell pass the evening.

Mr. Higginson reads a critical paper on "Modern American Literature." He dates the birth of this from the Concord School: Emerson, Hawthorne, Thoreau, and Longfellow. His paper is beautifully conceived and his criticism appreciative. It gives much pleasure to the listeners, and many reminiscences of Emerson, Hawthorne and Thoreau are given by Miss Peabody, Sanborn, Higginson, and myself.

Mr. Higginson thinks the defect of the Transcendental School is the want of form, instancing Emerson's *Essays* particularly.

July 21

Dr. Jones leads in the discussion of Plato's "Apology of Socrates." He treats this as an apologue to the Dialogues, allegorically; considers Socrates representing man generally; the Athenians, the appetites and passions which put the good man to death. His novelty of interpretation excites much interest and leads to lively discussion by the more active speakers. I have my turn with the rest. Doubtless the text may be thus interpreted, and in some sense represent Plato's Ideals.

Our company receive additions daily.

3 P.M.: Harris reads a lecture on Personality. It interests his auditors deeply; is discussed till 5½ oclock.

July 22

I give my second Conversation, illustrating more fully the Heirarchy of Gifts and we have an interesting discussion following. I am happy alike in statement and illustration of the subject.

Mrs. Cheney dines with us and reads another paper at the "Orchard." She describes the Byzantine period of Art and exhibits photographic illustrations of some of the most impressive works of that period, giving anecdotes of her late tour in Italy. She interests her company.

In the evening an invited company of ladies by Louisa [*sic*] assemble in our parlors, and she explains the requirements of the new suffrage law for women.

July 23

Mrs. Cheney gives her lecture at the "Orchard," illustrating by photographs and conversation further principles of Art.

P.M. Mr. Harris lectures to a crowded company on "Immortality." As usual, his arguments are profoundly logical and abstruse, but he is heard with unbroken attention and interest. His lectures are awakening a novel interest in the subjects he treats, and his audiences increase in numbers from day to day. Such consecutive and convincing statements on themes so subtle and spiritual have seldom been treated with like clearness and conclusiveness.

July 24

I give my third Conversation, opening it by reading George Herbert's poem entitled "Man" and illustrating the incarnation of Spirit in temperamental and complexional traits. My treatment is mystic, and less intelligible than a fresher mood would have inspired. It suggested a wide range of thought and illustration and excited a spirited discussion. My method is analogical, and in striking contrast to that of Harris. Thus we address the imagination and reason respectively with less or more directness, and together express the whole round of sentiment and thought in our auditors.

P.M.: Harris again, before a crowded and eager company, many of our townspeople attending. His subject is psychological physiology, and is treated in his admirably logical method.

July 24

A Conversation at Mrs. Edward Hoar's. Our Faculty and invited students meet a select party of our village. "Education" is proposed as the theme for discourse. I open it with Plato's distribution into Gymnastics and Music, and it is considered in many aspects by several speakers: Wm. Harris, Dr. Kedney, Rev. Mr. Ward, Sanborn, and myself. We have an entertaining and instructive treatment of the subject, both in its ideal and practical aspects.

Our village is awake to the large attendance of strangers at the school and the significance of the movement.

July 25

Dr. Jones continues his interpretations of the text of the "Apologue of Socrates." His interpretations are surprisingly significant and inclusive of the spiritual and material spheres of life. He has a smaller but interested audience. Allegory is one of the most popular forms of expression, addressing the imaginative and spiritual faculties in a suggestive and alluring manner. Among our speakers, Miss Elizabeth Peabody is very ready and helpful. Dr. Jones is heard with the deepest interest by the more thoughtful students.

P.M.: Mr. Harris pursues his theme with fuller illustrations and additions.

We are having new additions to our company almost daily. Evening: An invited company at Judge French's to see the statuary of young French [5] at his new studio. His "Endymion" is a work of rare merit, and his "Head of Emerson" represents the man as he now is, touched with age yet youthful in his manly features and expression. It is the form in which we wish to perpetuate our friend.

The "Endymion" is too deeply steeped in Lethe and dreaming too delightedly to be aroused even by Love peeping over his pillow.

We now have *our* Artist.

July 26

Col. Higginson gives a lively lecture on "The Influences of Republican Institutions upon Literature," as contrasted with those of monarchical, and particularly as regards language. Upon this latter the Conversation turns, and much interest is taken in the several illustrations of the different speakers. I instance the speech of rural neighborhoods, particularly that of my native town, and acknowledge my own indebtedness to the racy dialect there spoken. Many anecdotes are told, and much enjoyed by the company.

P.M. Prof. Peirce of Harvard College [6] reads a lecture upon the Cosmogony of the Universe. His descriptions of the nebula, its motions, the meteors and sidereal phenomena, are astonishing and bewildering to the imagination. He is questioned frequently, and sheds additional light over the fields of thought discussed in his lecture. He has a crowded audience. Himself and Higginson are paid, cash, twenty dollars for their two lectures, and have thanks for the entertainment and instruction they have given.

Thus closes the second week of our School.

July 28

Dr. Jones discourses on Immortality from Plato's *Phædo*, and the subject is discussed generally. He proposes to consider it in the

[5] Daniel Chester French. His "Minute Man" had been unveiled at Concord in 1875, when he was twenty-five years old. His "Head of Emerson" is now in the Concord Free Public Library, together with his noble seated statue of Emerson.

[6] Benjamin Peirce (1809–1880), one of the most distinguished American mathematicians and astronomers of his time. Alcott's journal-entry for April 25, 1857, suggests a reason for his appearance at the Concord School.

light of Pre-existence at his next Conversation. His treatment is foreign to the Christian consciousness, and opens a new field of survey to most of his auditors.

Afternoon: Mr. Harris speaks of methods for study, perusing books methodically, and naming the masters as whetstones to the mind. He recommends Kant's Critique of Pure Reason particularly. The attendance is large. He leaves at the close of the lecture for New York, but returns to us next week.

July 29

I review my former statements, taking a more particular survey of these to familiarize my auditors to my use of terms. Much is said distinguishing Personality from Individuality, terms often used as synonymous in common speech. Dr. Jones illustrates these from the Platonic standpoint, and Dr. Kedney from the modern. The indebtedness of Christianity to Plato is also discussed.

I am gratified by the success of my statements of the descent from the Godhead into humanity and thence into matter, from person to particle, and the re-ascent from particle to person. Our discussion is spirited and suggestive.

P.M.: Mrs. Cheney reads her paper on Michael Angelo. We take our seats on the lawn and have a pleasant time looking at her photographs of some of his most remarkable works: the Moses, the Christ, Madonna and others. Suggestive remarks are made by Dr. Kedney, Emery, Miss Peabody, and myself. Such strength combined with harmony was his in a measure hardly surpassed by any artist.

July 30

We are having favorable weather for our School. Almost cloudless days, yet not oppressively hot. Our students vary their pursuits by spending days, or parts of days, on the river, or visiting Walden and other historic spots. Thus far Harris has had the larger attendance at the "Orchard" and Mrs. Cheney's readings attracted good audiences. Our rooms are generally filled on all occasions. The streets present a picturesque spectacle of a morning and afternoon when the students and visitors are going to and returning from the "Orchard." And the coaches run regularly at the convenient hours.

A.M.: Mrs. Cheney treats of Spanish Art and exhibits photographs. Her lecture is followed by comments upon these by herself and others.

P.M.: Mr. Wasson's lecture is partly read by Mr. Sanborn, his eyesight being too imperfect for his reading readily his manuscript. He treats of the prime elements in the Individual and society as constituting a community. Individuals alone do not form society. It is the reciprocity between these, and becomes personal only as this takes place. The distinction between Individualism and Personality is discussed by several persons. This distinction is radical and runs through all true thinking. It discriminates the philosopher from the man of the senses, the Personal from the phenomenal. The religious and political bodies may be classified as they accord with or diverge from the standard of ideas universal or particular.

In religion especially, any doctrine not grounded in Personality is necessarily atheistic, and in most respects pantheistic. It is only as this universal enters into and distinguishes the particular from the general, the species from genus, that a pure theism is possible.

July 31

I give my fifth Conversation.

Having heretofore treated of the ascent of the soul from particle to Personal, and discriminated its several faculties and their functions, I now trace the descent from Person into matter and mortality as preparatory to a full statement of the Incarnation and Atonement. This opens out the facts of the Soul's dualization, of sin, of guilt, remorse, of sin and its retribution.

A grave discussion follows. I am happy in maintaining the matter suggested by the subject. The origin of evil interests particularly.

P.M.: Mr. Wasson's lecture is given on the lawn, and read in part by Mr. Sanborn. He treats of the relation between the individual and the nation. A nation is composed of the whole people; individuals alone would not constitute a nation.

State rights are discussed. Miss Peabody gives an interesting account of the discussions preceding the organization of the Government — held in secret, sealed, and not disclosed for sixty years afterwards.

Dr. Kedney passes the evening with me. I present him with copies of *Table Talk, Concord Days,* and *Record of School.*

August 1

Dr. Jones' Conversation on Plato's dialectic, preparatory to his doctrine of Reminiscence, is listened to with much interest. He treats of the natural and supernatural states of the soul and illustrates his subject in modern experience. Darwinism is noticed and partially discussed.

P.M.: Mr. Wasson continues his course. The session is held out-of-doors and the discussion of the foundation of the State in Personalism, not Individualism, is lively and conclusive. He reads his own manuscript.

August 2

Mr. Davidson illustrates his lecture on Greek Antiquities by his magic lanthorn, with explanatory comments. My study and May's studio are darkened. The figures are cast upon a screen suspended between the front windows. He exhibits many views in ancient Athens, shows a map of the city, the site of its public edifices, of Plato's Academy, Aristotle's Lyceum, and interesting particulars.

Our rooms are too small to seat our visitors. Some find seats under the elms in front and discuss art matters.

The day is hot and sultry.

P.M.: Mr. Emerson reads his lecture on Memory to a crowded audience at Dr. Grant's Vestry.[7] He reads with much of his earlier eloquence, Miss Ellen prompting him occasionally. His lecture is characterised by his sententious wisdom, and sparkles with subtle insights and illustrative anecdotes. Every one is charmed and interested. Many strangers from neighboring towns and from a distance come to hear him.

[7] In the Trinitarian Congregation or "Orthodox" Church.

August 4

Jones discourses of Plato's doctrine of Reminiscence and Pre-existence. He illustrates from the fable of the Fates in the *Republic*. A brisk discussion follows; many questions are asked and further illustration is needed to satisfy some of the questioners. The doctrine is too remote from our accepted modes of thinking to be rendered intelligible at once.

Both Dr. Jones' and Harris' technics are rather too scholastic for most of their auditors, and need translating into terms more popular and plain. That is the perfect teaching which, along with the natural method of thought and of the feelings which it expresses, is both logical and analogical.

Evening: Harris speaks at the Orthodox Vestry. He has a full audience and interests as heretofore. He shows the relation of Art, Science and Religion to Philosophy or the Prime Theology. Our people are present and some of them hear him for the first time. A discussion follows in which Miss Peabody, Mr. Hazard of Rhode Island, Johnson, Harris and myself take part. Mr. and Mrs. Emerson are present. Harris has won general acceptance from all who have heard him speak, and philosophy is sure in his treatment to be a most practical and precious acquisition, one with life and the reason of things.

August 5

I discourse upon the Lapse. Reviewing my former discourses I state the three types of Souls, viz.,

1. The Integral, or Holy.
2. The Dual, or Virtuous.
3. The Demonic, or Vicious.

The discussion takes a wide range and interests deeply. As method is involved in it, the relative provinces of divination and reasoning are defined and illustrated.

Genius is a diviner and leaps to its conclusions instantly without minding the steps of its passage, enlisting all subordinate powers in its activity. I am much pleased with this discourse.

Harris gives his last lecture. He has a crowded audience and sums up the propositions of his course. He has drawn fuller audiences than the other members of the Faculty and won the confidence and respect of all who have heard him.

Evening: At Mr. Edwin Barrett's. He has lately built himself a costly residence on the spot where once "the embattled farmers stood," and his ancestor fired the resounding shot. The Concord School is invited with some of his neighbors, and I open a Conversation by reading Wordsworth's noble Ode on Immortality. An animated discussion follows in which Rev. Mr. Reynolds departs from the sentiments of the Ode and is vigorously confronted by Miss Peabody, Sanborn, and myself.

August 6

Mrs. Cheney reads papers on Art both morning and afternoon with photographic illustrations. Her afternoon paper is a full account of Albrecht Dürer, and she exhibits many copies of his chief works.

Evening: Blake reads selections from Thoreau's Journals at the Orthodox Vestry. The audience are charmed with the beauty and felicity of the sentences read. These receive added attraction by the reader's fine elocution, distinct and emphatic. He is a disciple of his author, and his enthusiasm illuminates alike his countenance and his text. The evening is a delight to the members of our School.

August 7

I discourse upon the Atonement of the Soul, treating this from the psychological standpoint and illustrating the mode of the lapsed soul's redemption and recovery. The discussion is varied and characteristic of the several speakers, Dr. Jones, Miss Peabody, Dr. Grant, Mr. Emery, Mr. Wolcott, Mr. Blake, Mr. Robinson, Mr. McClure.

Though my classes are not the largest at the successive sessions, I am gratified to find there is deep interest taken in the discussions and that no signs of weariness appear. And I receive many cordial greetings in consequence.

P.M. Wasson reads again on the Nation. He interests by his clear statements and sound principles of government.

Evening: The School assemble at Anna's, and we discuss matters connected with organization and continuance. It is to be resumed next summer under more favorable conditions, and a four weeks' session is thought the better. All members are enthusiastic about it and anticipate the happiest fortunes for it. Its success has been beyond the expectation of all.

August 8

Dr. Jones discourses on the Body, spiritual and natural. He is heard with deep interest. He shows the wealth contained in Plato's text, from which he reads a short passage only, interpreting the doctrine of body from the Platonic Ideas. We have allowed Plato's text to sleep too long. It should be read along with St. John and St. Paul.

Afternoon: Wasson reads a chapter treating of Sovereignty in the State. The subject is discussed by Sanborn, Miss Peabody, Emery and myself. Power belongs to man so long as he does not abuse the trust. Abuse of it disfranchises and exiles him from the State.

August 9

No Session of the School this forenoon. Write to my brother Chatfield, living at Oswego, N. Y. and forward Ward's notice of the Concord Summer School.

P.M.: Sanborn reads a paper on Social Science and it is briefly discussed. Mr. Walter [8] Ricketson exhibits his medallion head of Thoreau. I think it is a good likeness. He has given in its prominence the characteristic features, the nostrils and eye which are not given faithfully in former representations. The medallion is to remain in the studio for some days for further criticism.

Evening: Davidson gives a second lecture on "Greek Antiquities," illustrating with his stereopticon. His lecture is given at the Orthodox Vestry under better conditions than his former one at the "Orchard." He gives views of the Parthenon Theatre and other remains of classical fame. . . . Having been at Athens and informed himself of the present condition of that and neighboring

[8] I.e., Walton, a son of Daniel Ricketson and a citizen of Concord. His medallion of Thoreau is now owned by the Concord Free Public Library.

cities, he brings a wealth of illustration hardly surpassed by any other person.

August 10

10 A.M. I call upon Mrs. Elizabeth Thompson. She is attending our School and is the guest of the Lathrops at "Wayside." She is deeply interested in our School and purposes to have the place purchased and dedicated to philosophic culture. She will contribute a thousand dollars toward its purchase, perhaps more if more be necessary to secure it for this end. Nothing could please me more than this disposition of the "Orchard" estate. It would fulfill the dream of these later years. I have not yet relinquished the hope of returning and occupying the place so associated with the busiest and happiest years of my family life.

August 11

Dr. Jones discourses again, continuing his interpretation of the "Bodily Life," and in the afternoon Mr. Wasson reads a paper upon "Imperialism in Government." In these discussions upon Political Science Miss Peabody takes a leading part and pleads the rights of citizenship with much enthusiasm. I have words in favor of Woman Suffrage. I am gratified in the fact that my daughters are loyal to their sex and to their sainted mother, who, had she survived, would have been the first to have taken them to the polls.

August 12

I give my ninth discourse at the "Orchard," interpreting the lapses from Archangel to atom with illustrations happily spoken. We have a spirited and prolonged Conversation following. I have now justified my Genesis, Lapse, and Restoration, and now have for my part the closing exercises of the School.

After the Conversation, ride with Miss Peabody and Mrs. Thompson to Walden and see the entertainment given by the benevolent people of Boston to the poor children, 1100 of them, at the Pond. It is an interesting spectacle. We see them at their march, in the tent, and at their dinners. They are well behaved and have a memorable day.

August 13

Dr. Jones discourses in his suggestive way on the physical life and regimen. He commands attention by his strong statements and forcible rhetoric. Judge Hoar is for the first time at the "Orchard" in attendance.

P.M. Dr. Jones accompanies me to the "Wayside" and we pass an hour with Mrs. Thompson. We invite her to sit with the Faculty on Sunday next at the "Orchard House" to discuss and arrange matters for our next summer session of the School. Without the counsel of a lady our deliberations might fail of the wise arrangements.

Evening: Mrs. Cheney gives her lecture upon "French Art" at the Orthodox Vestry. It is chiefly historical and listened to with interest. There is no conversation following its delivery.

August 14

Mrs. Cheney closes her course of lectures by one upon "Contemporary Art." She speaks mostly of Art in England and particularly of David Scott's genius and works. A conversation follows. I speak of Scott's portrait of Emerson, now in our Concord Town Library, in which Emerson's characteristic gesture is given. Anecdotes are told by Miss Peabody also about Allston, and other artists. Turner's genius is also discussed.

Afternoon: Wasson reads his lecture upon "Rights." All rights are personal. Individual rights are derivative, and presuppose the Personal. Miss Peabody and myself instance the views of the children in my Temple School regarding government.

After School closes I take a charming ride with Mrs. Thompson from "Wayside" by Virginia road and Bedford street and home again. She entertains generous intentions about the "Orchard House" estate, and may purchase it herself for the foundation of our School of Philosophy and Literature.

I leave with her a copy of my book of *Tablets*, with a note.

Evening: A party at Judge Hoar's. The members of our School are mostly in attendance, and our best people also. . . .

When Judge Hoar bestows civilities upon strangers it is an assurance that he considers his company of the first respectability and social standing.

August 15

Dr. Jones closes his discourses upon "The Platonic Doctrines and Ideal." He speaks of the Regimen of Virtue and Health, giving profoundly practical instruction in regard to both. He is heard with deep interest, if not conviction, by his attentive auditors.

P.M.: Wasson lectures, treating of the conditions of "Political Liberty." Mr. Sanborn reads his papers. Robinson of Missouri takes an active part in the discussions, asserting the right of the individual voice in republican rule. Mr. Wasson would limit the suffrage and educate the community up to the intelligence imposed by guarded suffrage. I assert the necessity of general education, moral as intellectual.

August 16

10 A.M.: Dr. Bartol reads a brilliant paper upon "Education," considered in its broadest and deepest aspects and relations. He has a crowded and delighted audience. Beginning at ten oclock he holds his auditors till near twelve, and nothing remains but to dissolve into admiration and retire.

This is the first day of rain during our session.

P.M.: Mr. Wasson reads his last lecture upon the "Spirit of 1776."

Evening: Sanborn reads his lecture upon "Philanthropy and Public Charities." He instances particularly the genius and services of Dr. Samuel G. Howe, Miss Peabody adding reminiscences. The members of the School are in attendance, though many of them have left for their homes.

I address them upon the success of the School, the hospitality of our people, the social intercourse with one another, the light and inspiration which they have received, the harmony of our deliberations, and the assurance of continuing these another season.

The School closes happily.

August 22

I must conceive as well a future of action as of contemplation for myself, nor is this less inspiring to me at this age than at any former period of my life. For what were life without this but a dreaming — visionary, impassionless, resultless, listless? Enthu-

siasm implies both thought and practice, ideas and duties inter-
fused, embodied. Shall one cease to be at three score and ten, or
at four score even? With every faculty astir, ripening still, shall
he have no stake in the affairs of his time, cherish age as the time
for withdrawing into his past, striking all work for the future?
Age has promises alike for the *here* as for the *hereafter.*

August 23

. . . Call upon Emerson and find him in his study as usual.
He greets me cordially and speaks of our Summer School as a
"brave thing," successful beyond all reasonable expectation. And
so it is; but not for New England's faith and attendance chiefly,
but the believing, rather, and congregated representatives of the
West, without whose interest the School could not have been at
all. Even my neighbors looked for its failure, surprised at the
intelligence and enthusiasm that brought so many from afar. So
it may have been, as my friend says, "a brave thing" truly.

But good things come too late sometimes for those who might
enjoy them earlier, and my friend is of that number.

October 20

I begin to prepare for my Western tour, intending to leave
next Friday morning by way of Springfield and Hartford and
pass the evening Sunday in Waterbury or Wolcott. It is a less formidable matter than formerly it was to pack my trunk and sally
from home on a longer or shorter sojourn in those then strange
parts — now become almost as familiar to me as my immediate
surroundings. With friends to greet me in the chief cities I seem
at home wherever I pause for a night only.

October 23

I think it fortunate that just as I am about leaving home for
intercourse with many persons of widely differing pursuits and
creeds I may be authorized to speak concerning my friend Emerson's religious views, about which the community are more curious to learn than at any time since the Transcendental Revival,
and to assure such from his own lips that, while he stands independent of all religious bodies, he is willing to be claimed a

Christian Theist and a member of the Church Universal. Thus my statements at Andover lately do him no wrong, as some of his friends and mine have intimated in their conversations with me.

In my visit this afternoon he assures me of his acceptance of my statements at Andover, and that he purposes to withdraw his name from the use it has been put to by the friends of the *Index*.[9]

October 24

I leave at 7.50 for Hartford, *via* Springfield. At Hartford take carriage to Mr. Warner's,[10] editor of the *Hartford Courant* and author of pleasant books of travel and rural pleasures. He receives me cordially and invites me to pass the night with him and visit his neighbor, Rev. Mr. Twitchell,[11] after lunch — a witty and learned gentleman well known in literary circles by his accomplishments and humorous works. Mrs. Warner wins my regard by her personal attractions and graceful manners. Their residence is retired, embowered in ancient chestnuts and oaks, scholarly and suburban, a choice retreat for an author and editor. After lunch, Mr. Warner accompanies me to the residence of Mr. Twitchell. Find him a robust and liberal-minded minister, much esteemed for his hearty manner and catholicity of doctrine, interesting me the more by his descent from our Wolcott ancestor, John Alcock, whose daughter Deborah married Capt. Isaac Twitchell, an early settler, and who died there. Blood is significant, and tells for sympathy whether in families or races. My kinsman takes me to the Chinese Houses where I see the teachers of Chinese students preparing for usefulness on their return to China. The Principal is a native, intelligent, mannerly, and a bright boy-student shows his amiable and intelligent disposition.

The evening is passed pleasantly at Mr. Warner's with himself and lady. I may be something superstitious for an idealist, finding or imagining I find in the society of Connecticut circles a freedom from conventional formalities to which I am un-

---

[9] A journal conducted by the group, headed by O. B. Frothingham, called "The Free Religionists."

[10] Charles Dudley Warner.

[11] Rev. Joseph Twichell. One of the grand opportunities of American social history was lost when Warner decided that perhaps he had better not introduce his guest to his friend and neighbor Mark Twain.

accustomed in Massachusetts. Geographical lines may deceive one, but my nearness to my native township has unexplained attractions. . . . I remember my maternal ancestor John Bronson was an early settler in Hartford, and Hooker founded the township, my paternal ancestor George Alcock being his brother-in-law.

November 18 *Columbus, Ohio*

GUNSAULUS [12]

My young friend regards our acquaintance as a most fortunate circumstance since it has brought his book and himself into favorable notice, and his position as an independent preacher here in Columbus.

He interests me by his hearty welcome, his personal bearing, and freshness of spirit. Of Spanish descent on his father's side and Scottish on his mother's, he appears to blend the passion of the one with the metaphysical tendencies of the other in happy proportion, giving an eloquence of speech and manner at once captivating and commanding. He is plainly meant for a leader of men alike by genius and culture. Now but 24 years of age, I find him conversant with deep problems of human thought, and a religious experience that has helped to solve the mysteries of the spiritual life. He is thus furnished and prepared for doing important work in the new Christian Ministry. Bred a Methodist, he has maintained the fervor of the sect and freed himself from its dogmatism and exclusiveness. He has cleared his mind of the sectarian spirit, risen by successive steps from Unitarianism through rationalistic and pantheistic views to pure, Personal, Christian theism.

Such are my first impressions on meeting him here.

November 29 *Concord*

The Anniversary of my 80th birthday.

And, happily, I am at home and with my family and friends. Louisa returns from her city lodgings to remain with us, and the joyful news of the birth of a grandaughter [13] brings the happy mother, babe in arms, into our family circle.

[12] Frank Wakeley Gunsaulus, 1856–1921.
[13] Louisa May Nieriker, daughter of May.

Surely a gracious Providence bestows blessings profusely upon us. And may we not assure ourselves of the joy of our absent ones in our reunion, as they view us from their blessed abode? I remember that, as time measures, it is two years since the wife and mother withdrew from our vision, and left her blessing as she withdrew. Precious the memory and immortal as her being the pledge of our reunion in holier bonds of affection. Love is alike human and divine — unites in ties inseparable and immortal.

A new surprise awaits me. I am invited to meet my friends and neighbors, the members of the Fortnightly Club at Mr. Sanborn's. I am greeted as I enter the room on having reached my 80 years, with powers of body and mind unimpaired and the prospect before me of future years of service; asked, moreover, to give some sketch of my life, as a proper use of the occasion. Mr. Sanborn reads, by way of introduction, some notes of sayings of mine taken some years since, and after my sketch, which occupies the evening till a late hour, requests in the name of the Club the favor of sitting for a head of myself to our young artist, Mr. French, whose head of Emerson is pronounced an admirable likeness. At all of which I am too happy to be silent.

Was it for this honor, this assurance of friendly regard, that I ran from those profuse hospitalities of Western friends into the very hearty embraces of my friends here at home?

December 31

This morning brings us sad tidings from Paris. Mr. Emerson comes with tearful emotion and delivers a telegram announcing our dear May's departure to other scenes. She leaves her babe behind, never to know a mother's smile. What can I add, but that she has enjoyed two full years of wedded life and left the precious pledge of her affection to us? Her bright, brilliant career has closed, to open for her a wider stage and holier joys in the next existence.

Meanwhile we await in sadness full particulars of the great change. . . .

And thus the old year passes into the New.

BRONSON ALCOTT AT THE AGE OF EIGHTY

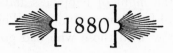

ALTHOUGH THE early months of the year were darkened by the recent death of May, Alcott worked steadily at a long narrative poem, "New Connecticut," dealing with his own boyhood. He devoted the spring to the building of a "Chapel" for the Concord School of Philosophy, and the prosperous second session of this School was the absorbing interest of the midsummer. In the early autumn May's infant daughter, Louisa May Nieriker, arrived in Concord to flood the old man's life once more with the sunshine of childhood. He set forth in October for his last tour of the West.

1880

January 31

MAY

Her temperament was elastic, susceptible. She had a lively fancy, a clear understanding. She possessed fine social qualities and her temper was imperturbable. She had a fine sense of honor and decorum. Independence was a marked trait. Her manners were positive and persistent. She held her fortunes in her hands, and failure was a word unknown in her vocabulary of effort. Her figure was graceful. She was taller than the average of her sex. When last seen by me, she was standing on the steamer's deck and waved her handkerchief till lost in the distance. Her active career has now closed in the night of happiness and fame and she has passed into a future of fuller opportunities and holier engagements. Yes, and rejoices now with those who had gone from our sight before.

February 16

. . . It is agreed that I am sufficiently orthodox to be claimed no longer by Unitarians, either of the conservative or radical type; but Emerson's faith appears to remain a debatable question still. It will be a difficult matter for any sect to classify either of us.

April 8

. . . I sometimes fancy that I am spared from confirmed mysticism, unrelieved by sober sense, in being born and nurtured amidst mountain scenery, so stimulating and unfriendly to slothful musing.[1] My hilltops were a happier aspect than the ocean, which I saw not till near twelve years old, and am not at this age familiar with water scenery, seldom taking to boating even on our Concord River flowing in sight of my chamber window. The shoreless ocean, its calm surface, has a vague significance, but one loves confines, also banks and bays; its turmoil, while majestic, deals strife in the extreme.

April 28

At the "Orchard House," preparing the premises for the erection of our Chapel. Gladly shall I see the spot dedicated to liberal learning, sound philosophy, and the theistic faith. My associations with the place are of the happiest and holiest kind. Twenty years of toil have shaped and hallowed it; and now, if it can be dedicated to high uses and ends, my labours will be consummated as I could have wished.

May 16

. . . The newspapers record the death of Jones Very of Salem, Mass. It was my fortune to have known the man while he was

---

[1] When Louisa visited Wolcott, for the first and last time, in 1872, she wrote in her Journal: "Don't wonder the boy longed to climb those hills, and see what lay beyond."

tutor in Harvard College and writing his Sonnets and Essays on Shakespeare, which were edited by Emerson, and published in 1839. Very was then the dreamy mystic of our circle of Transcendentalists, and a subject of speculation by us. He professed to be taught by the Spirit and to write under its inspiration. When his papers were submitted to Emerson for criticism the spelling was found faulty and on Emerson's pointing out the defect, he was told that this was by dictation of the Spirit also. Whether Emerson's witty reply, "that the Spirit should be a better speller," qualified the mystic's vision does not appear otherwise than that the printed volume shows no traces of illiteracy in the text.

Very often came to see me. His shadowy aspect at times gave him a ghostly air. While walking by his side, I remember, he seemed spectral, — and somehow using my feet instead of his own, keeping as near me as he could, and jostling me frequently. His voice had a certain hollowness, as if echoing mine. His whole bearing made an impression as if himself were detached from his thought and his body were another's. He ventured, withal, to warn me of falling into idolatries, while he brought a sonnet or two (since printed) for my benefit.

His temperament was delicate and nervous, disposed to visionariness and a dreamy idealism, stimulated by over-studies and the school of thought then in the ascendant. His sonnets and Shakespearean essays surpass any that have since appeared in subtlety and simplicity of execution.

June 13

I once thought classical attainment essential for the formation of a good style of writing, and despaired of attaining to anything like excellence myself. But Franklin and Bunyan disproved my views, and I took courage from their success. Perhaps my acquaintance with Emerson's excellence overshadowed my endeavour for a time, by rendering me aware of my unskillfulness. It was my settled conviction that I should not venture a sentence in print. Meanwhile, I had observed that a knowledge of many languages did not always aid the mastery of one's own, and that women without literary studies often spoke and wrote better than scholarly men.

Coleridge quotes Dr. Henry More as saying that "a man of confined education but of good parts, by constant reading of the Bible, will naturally form a more winning and commanding rhetoric than those that are learned, the intermixture of tongues and of artificial phrases debasing their style." [2]

I cannot claim any excellence in style. If there be any, it comes without any considerable classical culture.

August 14

Now that our Summer School is closed, and I am left free to reflect upon the spirit and scope of its teachings, it appears to me that the purely intellectual aspects of philosophy, as systematized by foreign masters, particularly by Plato and Hegel, have had an undue ascendancy, to the obscuring for the time, and suppression even, of the spiritual and ideal. This has given an air of secondariness to the proceedings, as if far-fetched and borrowed, which the reports [3] have again emphasized and spread abroad widely. The School is fairly open, and on this account measurably, to the shafts of ridicule launched by witty archers. I am aware, and freely concede, that speculative philosophy is mostly an uncultured field here with us, the few native cultivators having scarcely made their marks on American thought; and students naturally seek instruction from foreign sources, to the neglect of matters at home. Far-famed authorities have the precedence in consequence. Philosophy is indifferent, as such, to latitude and longitude, being its own authority, and shedding its light and warmth on all, fired with an enthusiasm for the beauty of truth pure and personal.

Hereafter we may provide more adequately for the initiating of our pupils into the vital mysteries, without some divination of which intellectual formularies are shadowy and cold. [4]

[2] This passage is underscored by Alcott in his copy of Coleridge's *Biographia Literaria*.

[3] These appeared, during the first year of the School, chiefly in the *Boston Daily Advertiser*.

[4] Although Alcott continues to admire the "dialectic" of W. T. Harris, he remains true to the intuitive and "analogical" method of Emerson and of Transcendentalism.

September 12

I read the *Life and Letters of Horace Bushnell,* lately published. Dr. Bushnell was born almost in sight of my native hilltop, and passed his childhood and youth not far from Litchfield, the spires of which were visible in the distance, over the western slopes. Born in 1802, he was but about two years younger than myself. He died in 1876. In my visits to Connecticut, when passing through Hartford, I sometimes called upon him, and once passed a memorable evening at the house of Mr. Cheney in his company.

Our interview was delightful to myself at least, comparing faiths as we did, and both surprised at finding a common agreement in our apparent differences. Positive in his convictions, he was affable, candid, giving full swing to the frankest statements, inviting the like from myself. Theologians by temperament, and he professionally, the discussion ran deep into the mysteries at once. Perhaps I glorified the Son's humanity to the overshadowing of his divinity, in his eyes, and seemed to him to be touched with pantheism — as might have been true of myself at that time. I remember that he seemed troubled at any suggestion of a possible approach of any human being to Christ's divinity, whom he regarded as the Second Person in the Godhead. I had then fathomed less satisfactorily the mystery of the Trinity than since our interview.

His later utterances approach more nearly to my present views. I find little in his life and letters to which I do not yield a hearty assent. By different ways we seem to have come to similar conclusions. His phraseology is more Biblical than becomes a layman, and, like his piety, partakes of his temperament, so unlike my own. He takes life with a certain violence, and seems pleading for a reposeful resignation, native to myself. I might add that he did not wholly shake himself free of the extreme Calvinistic theology in which he was bred. Litchfield was the seat of orthodox theology. Beecher and Bellamy [5] were dealing it forth with all their vehemence and eloquence at the time of his entrance into life

[5] The reference is to Lyman Beecher, 1775–1863. Alcott is mistaken with regard to Joseph Bellamy, who died long before Bushnell was born and who was by no means a Calvinist of the older school.

and thought. My earliest recollections of that type of preaching date from a discourse of Dr. Beecher's, delivered in the Presbyterian pulpit in my native town.

September 13

. . . Though written chiefly for my own private pleasure, and for convenience of reference to the past, my Diaries have now gathered so much of the passing history of my time and contemporaries that it has seemed to me selections might be made from the mass of manuscript for a biography of some significance.

September 19

   She Comes! [6]

Our little Louisa May Nieriker is brought safely, and looks smilingly upon us of her kindred, on this side the seas. A bright, blue-eyed babe, and motherless now. I know not whether my emotion at beholding her first eager glance partook more of surprise, of sadness, or of joy, as I recalled the accident of her birth, and prospects of her future yet all unknown to me. She is here now at last, and with her mother's kindred, to be kindly cared for during her tender infancy. Yet I were inhuman not to sympathize with the grandmother returning to her family at Baden without her grandchild.

September 23

   Now while health and spirits are given me, shall I sluggishly and selfishly seek my own ease and gratification merely? Rather let me sally forth and meet those hospitable Western people who fancy that I have something to give in return for their entertainment of my person for a few days and nights. Delightful as it were to remain at home and greet my babe's glance, pursue my thoughts and studies here with the family, I am not out of place or time in parlors, on platforms, in pulpits, the familiar intercourse which travel affords. And I enrich myself meanwhile, in taking my eyes and ears along with me.

   [6] In red ink.

October 12

Pack my trunks for my Western tour, having left things here and at the "Orchard House" in wholesome condition. The length of my absence must be determined by circumstances yet unforeseen — a month or many months, as my companies and condition shall chance to be.

Leave at 12 noon by the Fitchburg train to meet Sanborn at Gardner and from thence proceed to Northampton, and on tomorrow to Cheshire, Conn., being invited to attend the Centennial Celebration of that town.

{1881}

ON his last tour of the West Alcott spoke in thirty-seven towns and cities during a period of seven months. He was eighty-one years old; he travelled five thousand miles and often spoke three times a day, yet he felt no weariness or other ill effects. For more than half of his appearances he received nothing whatever; but his earnings, now that no one needed them, were over twelve hundred dollars.

Alcott returned to Concord in May to find his granddaughter in the first bloom of childhood and Emerson slowly fading toward death. Summer brought the joyous excitement of the School of Philosophy. In August Alcott distributed among his friends his privately printed autobiographical poem New Connecticut. Having thus completed the versified narrative of his boyhood, he proceeded to write the tale of his peddling and teaching days in verse, but did not get far. At this time, too, he began the writing of sonnets — a discipline under which, with the assistance of F. B. Sanborn, his versification rapidly improved. In September he caught his last glimpse of Walt Whitman.

1881

March 26   *Des Moines, Iowa*

. . . I have less faith in the future of Unitarianism than formerly, and suspect it has done its best work in the past. Trinitarianism appears to have the advantage of addressing the affections more warmly and directly, and as the rigor of that faith is softening, finds, particularly with the younger portion of the community, the readier acceptance.

May 15   *Concord*

I returned last evening from a seven months' tour at the West, in fair health and hopes, having met with hospitable reception in the several cities and towns which I visited. I find my daughters and grandchildren well, and as glad to welcome my return as I am.

My little maid Louisa May [1] has grown beautifully, and is a delight to my eyes. She has many of her dear mother's lively ways. I discern some of her features: the blue eyes and brown hair fine and soft. A little coy at first, she ventures into my arms today; and though she may not remember me, being only about ten months old when I left her last October, instinct is a wonderful diviner and chronicler of life. My house will be the more charming for her company and pretty prattle, for she already has mastered signs and words, runs about with agility, and is curious about things within doors and without. Her nurse, Mrs. Giles, under Louisa's instructions, has preserved her thus far from illness. A healthier child, more robust and active, none need desire. Happy for her and for us, the pleasant lines of life that she inherits and enjoys. A new trust and study she is for us all. — A house without children is a desolate and dreary mansion. Childhood and age are the complements of life and human culture.

May 21

Gratifying as it would be to see Emerson and relate my winter's adventures, I abstain, since these would pass from his mem-

---

[1] Louisa Mary Nieriker, daughter of Alcott's daughter May, who, after her mother's death, was cared for by her Aunt Louisa.

ory with the telling, and the presence of friends cannot be to him the pleasure it did [sic] in earlier days. I think myself among the privileged of his contemporaries in having known and enjoyed his company and confidence. His is a happy euthanasia, and a painless. As chance favors, I shall meet him.

May 25

This is Emerson's birthday anniversary, being seventy-eight years of age. Louisa accompanies me with little L., and a bunch of rhodoras, his favorite flower, in her hand, verses hidden within the leaves, and presents her to the poet. He takes her in his arms and carries her about, presenting her with smiling face to Ellen and Dr. and Mrs. Furness,[2] guests of his from Philadelphia. It was a pleasant surprise, apparently, and pleasant to us as well. I had a few words with him; but he does not incline voluntarily to conversation with any one, I am told. He listened to my adventures approvingly. His chief inquiry, and repeated, was, had I found any new men in those parts. I could only reply, none, in his estimation of newness.

Having enjoyed for so many of his prolific years his company, and participated in the ideas common to us, I may not dwell sadly on the reticence that has overflowed his genius during these later years of his.

June 28

Miss Lilian Whiting brings letters from the *Boston Traveller* asking the favor of reporting our Concord lectures. A bright young lady, having had some practice as a reporter. She is from the West, and shares the enthusiasm of that section about New England people and ideas.

June 29

Miss Whiting writes rather extravagantly about Concord and its people in the *Boston Traveller* of today. Our little village is

---

[2] William Henry Furness, Unitarian minister and father of the famous editor of Shakespeare, had been Alcott's friend as well as Emerson's for nearly fifty years.

not likely to suffer for want of praise, some of which might have been spared us.

July 23

My diary records little besides the daily reports of the lectures and discussions at the Orchard Chapel School. I leave at 8.50 in the morning, return at 11.50 to dinner — see callers in the afternoon, and leave again in the evening at 7. The lectures and discussions usually close at 9.50 and I am at home at 10. Thus pass the days.

Mr. Harris and Dr. Jones, this session as during the former, are favorite teachers, and draw the larger classes. They bring their authorities in thought and methods from the past schools of philosophy — the Greek and German — and are themselves masters of their themes. This wins the attention and confidence of their hearers, and this is fortunate for the reputation of the school. Dr. Kedney adds his learning and fine discriminating mind also. I am satisfied thus far with the conduct and attendance of the School.

July 27

Anna and myself are now left the sole occupants, with the servant girls, of the house. Little Louisa and her nurse, Mrs. Giles, leave this morning for New Bedford to join Louisa and the boys at Nonquitt, where they have been quartered for ten days past. I shall miss the little lady and must find some means of corresponding with her while absent. Every morning she was wont to salute me as she came trotting from her sleeping couch to my chamber, and patted my pillow, signifying this as my "bylo." She speaks prettily short sentences, and is very lovely. Her voice, heard from any apartment, draws me to her, whatever my engagement.

July 28

French sends the bust finely finished, and I accompany his assistant to the Chapel to see it set upon its bracket facing the platform, Emerson's standing on the right and mine on the left. By whose generosity the work was ordered and paid for I have not been informed. It flatters my pride as I find it accepted and placed in good company. The heads of Dr. Jones, Mrs. Thompson, Harris and Sanborn may in time be added to grace the walls.

My friends think this a good likeness. I do not. At least, I hope it is not.

August 21

I have a profound superstition about books — a faith that the book suited to my present need will be laid hold of by me instinctively, and its perusal justify my necessity. Books to which I am most indebted have found me in this wise, from *Pilgrim's Progress* to the *New Testament*. . . .

I am led to these considerations while reading this book of Carlyle's *Memoirs*, which I laid hold of thus instinctively and brought away while in the city last Friday. Sanborn has the first volume. I have just read the second. Carlyle looms grotesquely and grim before me as I close the book. A Homer he seems, and, in spite of his protest against poetry, a poet in thought. Epical, dramatic, he cannot write or think, much less discourse, in prose. Like Milton, he breaks through the current idiom of his mother tongue and borrows from all, thus constructing a style of his own, Carlylese, and inimitable. He is a mystic of the Teutonic type fallen upon times foreign to his genius and too mighty to be subordinated by his period. As a mystic of Olympian order, he had an attraction for his class, and won a share of their enthusiasm which even his later writings have not wholly drowned. I remember with what zest I first read his essays on Burns, Dr. Johnson, Goethe, Jean Paul, the *Characteristics*, and later, his *Sartor Resartus*, and am a little proud to record that my instinct, true to the laws of life, divined the secret of its authorship, hidden as this was to most of his readers at the time of its appearance. Then Emerson's acquaintance following, fortunately confirmed my impressions from my first readings.

Mine, like Emerson's, was a less muscular type of mysticism than his — meditative, rather, and free from his phlegm and melancholy; yet this reading bears out our earliest estimates of the man and of his place in life and literature. Meeting him personally as I did during my extreme individualism, even to the planting of earthly Paradises, I was a tempting butt of the giant's ridicule — a sentimentalist, as he saw me, and speechless in his presence — not for lack of faith but of adequate facility to substantiate my dream amidst his wild whirl of words. At a later period I might have justified myself, and shown how firmly I was anchored in facts and knew their worth and place.

August 23

Sanborn's notice of my *New Connecticut* comes to hand. He seems better satisfied with the poetic significance of the verses than I am, though I read these with a certain pleasure, sometimes deceived as if they were the work of another.

He alludes to Hesiod and Theocritus. The former I first read and enjoyed at Fruitlands, finding in its spirit and homely treatment something akin to my then mode of looking at life and its pursuits in general. Theocritus I first read at the "Orchard House." I was charmed with the idyllic beauty of his treatment of my themes, and while I am not conscious of being influenced in writing my Garden and other essays contained in my books *Tablets* and *Concord Days*, it was apparent enough that I was living in like relations to the landscape and myself. . . . Leigh Hunt afterwards touched the same strains, and I even came to think I too might write idyls and eclogues. Always on visiting the "Orchard House" I am touched by the spirit of the rural Muse. Virgil had less for me.

September 17

At Sanborn's, and take tea with Walt Whitman, who is passing a day here, being Sanborn's guest. Louisa is interested in Whitman, and takes tea with us.

Venerable he certainly is, while there is a certain youthfulness not less perceivable speaking forth from his ruff of beard and open-bosom collar, folded shirt-cuffs — he standing full six feet in his skirtless blue coat, supporting himself with his staff and stooping a little. He is not averse to conversation, though not inviting it, is a good listener, and appreciative of good things spoken.[3]

[3] Writing in *Specimen Days* of this occasion, Whitman says: "No doubt I seem'd very stupid to the room-full of company; but I had my own pail to milk in." He was looking at Emerson.

Very curious he seemed to learn what I might say of Emerson, Thoreau, and Margaret Fuller, whom he was disposed to honor, and gladly listened, asking for more information. I noticed a certain delicacy in his speech, as if he feared the least disparagement by his word or suggestion, and persons were to be spoken of truthfully.

We did not sympathize in the matter of Genesis. The wild man and wild apple were primitives, not degraded types. Existing civilization he deemed an improvement upon all preceding, and America the birthplace of the man that is to be.

After tea the Fortnightly Club assembled in the parlor, and the conversation was given mostly to Thoreau. Sanborn read letters addressed to Thoreau by Greeley, Margaret Fuller, Ellery Channing, and one of Thoreau's. These were interesting, and gave much pleasure to the company.

Whitman is reading the proofs of a new edition of his poems, now being printed in Boston.

With a livelier fancy and spiritualized imagination, creative instead of representative, as now, we might allow his claims to "the Bard," as he is willing to be named. I do not find that he is so fairly extricated from the flesh as to sing the noble numbers the poet loves. He is too brawny and broad to be either high or deep, and must rank with the sensuous school of thought and style. Yet, a majestic presence, and worthy of his fame.

December 1

I call at Emerson's seldomer than I would were I sure of his wish to meet his friends during these days of obliviousness. Today I carried the Book of Autographs and the Sonnets and passed an hour with him in his study, where I first met him,[4] and where so many memorable hours have been spent in his inspiring presence. Those were moments not to be equalled, hardly approached, in another's company, so pregnant with thought and the felicities of utterance. There is a pathos in his present lapse from his genius, his hesitancy for the word he would have and cannot grasp as formerly. I do not wish the shadow when the substance is so far

---

[4] Alcott's memory fails him here. The first meeting of the two men occurred at Alcott's rooms, 3 Somerset Court, Boston, in July, 1835.

withdrawn from view. It is an unexpected close of so fair a display of gifts.

December 9

The doctors recommend flesh for my little maid; and I dissent, robust and plump as she is, sprightly and graceful in every gesture. They would demonize the little saint, and dim all her beauty, for the sake of adding superfluous muscle and what they call "healthful animal life." I wish I may never cease contesting this assault upon her serenity and sweetness of soul.

1882

*T*HE LAST *volume of Alcott's Journals shows little diminu- tion in power. The handwriting is at least as firm as that of forty years before; thought and style are as clear as ever; the writ- er's interests are still growing and his feeling is still vivid and strong. During this year Alcott corresponded rather more widely than usual. He founded a "Mystic Club," chiefly for the reading of Jakob Boehme, with Sanborn and W. T. Harris, who was now a fellow-townsman. He discovered, apparently for the first time, the existence of the Theosophical Society, many of whose doctrines he had been teaching for fifty years. The best proof of his continued vitality was given by the series of poems called* Sonnets and Canzonets, *which was published in April and was well received.*

In the new library he had built at the Thoreau House out of his last year's earnings, Alcott gathered together his few but precious books, his busts of Plato and Socrates, and the half-a- hundred volumes of his Journals, expecting to round out a full century of life. Then, late in April, came the brief illness and the death of Emerson — and life was by no means so well worth liv- ing. Alcott rallied to write his beautiful monody, "Ion," which he read during the Emerson Commemoration Day of the School of Philosophy session. He gave four long and deeply thoughtful addresses at that session, and was nearly prostrated by the heat.

*Late in September he visited Wolcott for the last time, with his
only surviving sister. Upon his return, glorying in his health and
vigor, he wrote two sonnets on Immortality and finished revising
the proof of his "Ion." The last entry in his Journal was made on
the twenty-second of October. Two days later he suffered a stroke
of paralysis. He never wrote again.*

*Of Alcott's last years little is known. His first utterance after
a period in which he could not speak was the symbolic word "Up."
His mind remained clear, and he was able to attend three more
sessions of the Concord School. Louisa devoted to him all that she
could of her slight remaining strength, and made a home for him
in Louisburg Square, Boston. At last, having heard that he was
rapidly sinking, she hastened to him, and, on the way, caught cold.
Alcott died on the fourth of March, 1888, and Louisa two days
later.*

1882

January 21

. . . Evening at Emerson's. . . . It is pathetic to sit in Emerson's parlor and presence and hear his "expressive silence."

January 22

A few Churchmen have arranged for lay services at the house
of Mr. O'Brien in the Village. . . . I attend this forenoon and
take part in the responses. I remember my youthful experiences
as a lay reader at Spindle Hill School House; yet I should choose
now a less formal and more spontaneous service. Most of those
who have been bred Episcopalians remain attached to its forms
through life. My early associations abide, but I must confess my
heart is not fully in the service now.

February 2

Oscar Wilde did a graceful thing at his lecture in turning the
intended ridicule upon himself to the Harvard students, who

came to his lecture dressed in small-clothes, wigs, and other ridiculous gear. We were told they came on promise of good behavior to the Faculty; but the Faculty should have discouraged this assault upon good manners by a set of youngsters.

February 3–4

EMERSON

Oft I recall those hours so fair and free
When all the long forenoon we two did toss
From lip to lip, in lively colloquy,
Plato, Plotinus, or some schoolman's gloss,
Disporting in rapt thought and ecstasy.
Then, by the tilting rail, Millbrook we cross,
And sally through the field to Walden wave,
Plunging within the cove, or swimming o'er.
Through woodpaths wending, he, with gesture quick,
Rhymes deftly in mid-air with circling stick,
Skims the smooth pebble from the leafy shore,
Or deeper ripples raises as we lave —
Nor will his pillow press, though late at night,
Till converse with the stars his eyes invite.

March 8

Spring breezes, and the bluebird's song.

Evening, at Emerson's, at a party of our neighbors. I am so seldom abroad, save along Main Street to and from the Post Office, that salutation with most of my neighbors is the limit of association with them. It is stimulating to meet them thus socially — and where more properly than in Emerson's parlor, even though himself now is silent mostly, yet smilingly present with sympathetic greetings?

Sanborn and Harris are now taking warm and sweet places in my regard.

March 24

The evening papers announce the death of the poet Longfellow, the pride of New England and singer for all countries.

April 13

. . . Call at Emerson's and find him much pleased with the copy of Sonnets [1] which I present him with. He reads several with emphasis and delight. Leave copies also for Harris and Julian Hawthorne.

April 22

Call at Emerson's and find him confined to his bed, having exposed himself to our chilly winds without his overcoat, and threatened with pneumonia. I have not thought of him as other than well. This information gives me anxious thoughts. I see Mrs. Emerson, and am somewhat reassured by her account of him.

April 24

Emerson is quite ill, and fears are entertained that his illness may prove fatal. He doubtless prefers to leave this scene for a fairer . . . [2]

April 26

I walk this cloudless morning to Emerson's, and am admitted to his sick chamber. On being announced by Ellen, he turns his kind glance, smiling as none other, upon me, and on taking my hand he said "You are quite well?"

"Yes," I replied; "and am not used to find you in bed."

Smiling, he seemed confused, and uttered words too indistinctly to be discerned. Leaving his bedside and about going, he signified his wish to speak further with me, and, returning to his bed's head, he took my hand affectionately and said in strong but broken accents: "You have strong hold on life, and maintain it firmly," when his voice faltered and fell into indistinctness.

I came away questioning if this might not be my last interview with my long and faithful friend. Though the sun shone brightly above, the light that had illuminated our friendship so long seemed overcast, and I was soon to be left alone. My little

[1] Alcott's *Sonnets and Canzonets*, published in April.
[2] The end of the sentence is illegible.

maid smiled upon me as I reëntered my house, and stole away by her prattle and pretty ways the saddening eclipse.

Concord will be shorn of its human splendor when he withdraws behind the cloud.

April 28

Emerson passed away from us last evening at 8.30, painlessly.

At ten I call, and find Dr. Bartol has come. Miss Ellen takes us into his chamber. He lay sleeping, with but slight change of features from my last sight of him.

April 30

Attend the services at the house and church and follow the remains to their resting place in Sleepy Hollow. The concourse of attendants numbers thousands, who come to pay their sorrowing tribute to the great and good man's memory.

May 11–13

Two days of sunshine, four of showers; yet our fields begin to put on their greenery and tell that springtime is here. I fancy our friend is hardly less abroad than was his wont at this season, and can almost spy his shadow crossing the wonted places of resort. Perhaps after all our philosophizing on life with the aid of our senses, we descry friends more distinctly with closed eyes, through the vistas of memory.

No; my friend is abroad on his old tracks, as aforetime.

June 16

To Boston. I take my Emerson gift books and monody,[3] and consult Niles about publishing these in a volume — the prose to constitute Part I, the verses Part II. He thinks favorably of the matter.

Wendell Holmes takes me to his house to lunch. He hears and speaks well of my verses. I have known him but slightly. Of our elder poets only Whittier, Lowell, and himself remain to write.

[3] The essay on Emerson, once called "The Rhapsodist," and the poem "Ion," written in memory of Emerson. The former had been privately printed in 1865.

July 29

I am at the mercy of reporters.[4] My subjects, and extemporizing these, leave me open to misconception and frequent mortification. Reporters are less likely to regard what they may style a "familiar talk," as of less weight than a written lecture. I am of course read to a great disadvantage in this version of my discourses, conversational, and oftentimes making finest and subtle transitions. The sense is lost alike with the connection, and the sum is hardly more than a medley of incoherent thoughts, a jumble of sentences.

Let it pass.

August 1

. . . Our Village is livelier by this incoming of attendants at the School of Philosophy. Lodging at private houses mostly, the Barge takes them up there and returns them thither, though many prefer walking. A pretty sight it is, this passing to and from the Chapel along the sidewalks through the gate and by the winding walks inside to the stairs, the vines drooping over the doorway, and spreading along the front, almost hiding the green shades, giving a picturesqueness to the spot, and the settees under the apple trees completing the picture.

This once bank of sand glimmering in the sunshine is now clothed in shrubbery, the landscape rendered pleasing and humanized by the eye and hand of art — a fitting seat of the Muses. I might take a modest pride in the spot, and still more in the company sitting under the shade, and within the Chapel. It is almost too much to credit my eyes as I gaze upon the spectacle. Here gather now and have gathered during the last summer time, the best, the wisest persons of our time. From this humble beginning I know not what may spring and spread. Or should its present prospect fade and these walks be trodden no more by eager attendants, a creditable work will have been done on the spot for furthering good living and high thinking. The great and good things have a humble origin, and await their time, subject to

---

[4] Alcott is thinking here of the reports made in the Boston newspapers upon a discourse, very carefully prepared, just delivered before the School of Philosophy.

reverses, but succeed over their seeming failures. Philosophy knows less of the geographies than of the ideas that give place and time to all things.

August 4

I confess to less interest in the philosophic methods of German thinkers than in the more familiar English methods of treatment. With difficulty I follow even Harris in his interpretations of Hegel, Fichte, Schelling and others. I find nothing of this in Dr. Jones' methods. I fancy my method is of a subtler and more salient type than either, and implies an active and sprightly imagination inflaming the reason and divining the truths it seeks. The philosopher who finds the pure truth is also the poet, interblending imagination and reason by the alchemy of his genius.

September 17

Fair days, these. The autumnal foliage still verdant, and rain falls lately.

This season brings meditation, and thoughts of the future. With bodily ails, I might look across the stream and seek some information of the geography and way of life there; but, as Henry Thoreau said, "one world at a time" is more befitting when health and hope of yet further service here is in one's thought. To be tasked, and enjoy one's work, is the charm of this life — and, if one's instincts are trustworthy, then of the coming one. I see not why my morrow should differ from my yesterday.

September 30

To Spindle Hill. . . . I take a tramp over the fields and hills through wood-paths and roads once familiar, and revive in memory the families now widely dispersed. The landscape, save "New Connecticut," [5] is largely overgrown with timber. The homes are mostly deserted, or inhabited by strangers. The fields where I ploughed, meadows where I swung the scythe, orchards where I harvested, are grown up in sweet-fern, barren, unfenced, and all gone to ruin.

[5] The local name of a hill near Alcott's boyhood home.

October 10

John Burroughs, of Esopus, N.Y., sends by express a crate of his grapes from his vineyard on the banks of the Hudson, with a characteristic note. Burroughs was an admirer of Thoreau, and has written well about him and Emerson. His tone and temper have much in common with Thoreau's genius and treatment of nature and of life.

October 22

Mrs. John Brown, the martyr's widow, calls. She bears the marks of her self-sacrificing life and sorrows, seems observing, disinclined to speak of herself, and speaks in monosyllables when she does speak. A venerable woman, with a history unlike another. She is passing a few days with Sanborn, and returns presently to the West to her children.

Evening: Harris comes and takes me to tea at the "Orchard House." Ames is now there. We have much discussion of the Lapse. I do not succeed in showing them the place of this in my theory of the Genesis, or of the Renovation of man from the ruins of sin.[6]

[6] The last entry in Alcott's Journals.

INDEX

["I began making an alphabetical index of contents in this Diary today. This I find a work of some magnitude. The topics touched upon in these pages are various, and innumerable relations are implied."
— BRONSON ALCOTT'S JOURNALS, *June 28, 1839.*]

ADAMS, MRS. MARY, 417, 425; suggests Thoreau cairn at Walden Pond, 426; a letter from, 438.

Æschylus, and Thoreau, 214.

Agassiz, Professor Louis, referred to, xxv; described, 299–300; in Concord, 355; not ideal, 366; interrogated, 386; death and funeral of, 429, 441.

Agriculture, dignity and worth of, 407.

Alcott, the name, 447.

Alcott, Abby May, birth of, 138; disciplined, 175; begins studies, 254; as teacher, 324; her lessons in art, 361–362; sails for Europe, 405, 432; plans bust of her father, 457–458; her last trip to Europe, 463; married, 483; death of, 514; described, 515–516.

Alcott, Anna, birth of, 27; character of in childhood, 47; referred to, 175; teaches, 217; leaves home, 275, 276; engaged, 302, 308; married, 324, 326.

Alcott, Bronson, Journals his chief lifework, vii; handwriting of, vii; spelling and punctuation of, viii; his Journals, xi–xii; his motive in Journals, xiii–xiv; his earlier Journals, xiv–xv; influence of William Alcott upon, xv; reputation of, xvi; influence of, xvii; as writer, xvii–xx; and Emerson, xx–xxi; and Thoreau, xxi–xxii; wide experience of, xxii; his reading, xxii–xxiv; ideas of, xxiv–xxv; a teacher, xxv; his method in teaching, xxv–xxvi; wherein American, xxvi–xxvii; like a tree, xxvii; failure and success of, xxvii–xxviii; at Cheshire, Connecticut, 3; early religious beliefs of, 3; meets Abigail May, 4; his self-reliance, 4–5; his devotion to teaching, 6–7; his rejection of authority, 7; his rejection of majority opinion, 7; goes to Boston, 8; in love, 9–10; his religious position, 10; estimates himself, 11; his courtship, 11–12, 15–16; reviews his life, 16–17; early success of, in Boston, 18; estimates Boston preachers, 19–20; criticizes himself, 21; rejects advantageous offer, 21–22; criticizes his style in letter-writing, 24; married, 25; and Garrison, 25–26; birth of his first daughter, 27–28; begins record of daughter's life, 28; regrets lack of formal education, 29; exalts teaching, 29–30; praises Boston, 31–32; first reads Coleridge, 32; birth of his daughter Louisa, 33; reads widely, 34; dislikes Philadelphia, 35–36; reads Plato, 36; turns against English literature, 38–39; reviews his intellectual history, 39; deplores his prose style, 40; is thought impractical, 41, 43; turns Platonic, 44–45; assumes paternal duties, 46–47; prospers, 48; gives thanks for his children, 54–55; seeks society, 55–56; birth of his daughter